Social and Cultural Aspects of Language Learning in Study Abroad

Language Learning & Language Teaching (LL&LT)

The LL&LT monograph series publishes monographs, edited volumes and text books on applied and methodological issues in the field of language pedagogy. The focus of the series is on subjects such as classroom discourse and interaction; language diversity in educational settings; bilingual education; language testing and language assessment; teaching methods and teaching performance; learning trajectories in second language acquisition; and written language learning in educational settings.

For an overview of all books published in this series, please see
http://benjamins.com/catalog/lllt

Editors

Nina Spada
Ontario Institute for Studies in Education
University of Toronto

Nelleke Van Deusen-Scholl
Center for Language Study
Yale University

Volume 37

Social and Cultural Aspects of Language Learning in Study Abroad
Edited by Celeste Kinginger

Social and Cultural Aspects of Language Learning in Study Abroad

Edited by

Celeste Kinginger
Pennsylvania State University

John Benjamins Publishing Company

Amsterdam / Philadelphia

™ The paper used in this publication meets the minimum requirements of
the American National Standard for Information Sciences – Permanence
of Paper for Printed Library Materials, ANSI z39.48-1984.

Library of Congress Cataloging-in-Publication Data

Social and cultural aspects of language learning in study abroad / Edited by Celeste
Kinginger.
    p. cm. (Language Learning & Language Teaching, ISSN 1569-9471 ; v. 37)
Includes bibliographical references and index.
1. Second language acquisition. 2. Foreign study--Social aspects. 3. Language and
languages--Study and teaching--Foreign speakers. 4. Intercultural communica-
tion. 5. Language and culture. I. Kinginger, Celeste, 1959- editor of compilation.
P118.2.S623   2013
418.0071--dc23   2013012690
ISBN 978 90 272 1315 0   (Hb ; alk. paper)
ISBN 978 90 272 1316 7   (Pb ; alk. paper)
ISBN 978 90 272 7183 9   (Eb)

John Benjamins Publishing Co. · P.O. Box 36224 · 1020 ME Amsterdam · The Netherlands
John Benjamins North America · P.O. Box 27519 · Philadelphia PA 19118-0519 · USA

This book is dedicated to the memory of my beloved parents,
John Henry and Polly Langford Kinginger, who sent me
on my way to my first adventures abroad.

Table of contents

Acknowledgement

This volume was truly a collective endeavor, so my first appreciation goes to the authors, for contributing their insights and seeing the project to completion with professionalism and kindness. I would like to thank my friends, colleagues, and students in the Department of Applied Linguistics, the Department of French and Francophone Studies, and the Center for Language Acquisition for their constant support for my research. I am indebted to Nelleke van Deusen-Scholl, who invited me to propose this volume to John Benjamins, and to Nelleke, Nina Spada, and Kees Vaes for their editorial expertise and invaluable comments on the manuscript. Funding for this project was provided in part through a Title VI Language Resource Center grant to the Center for Advanced Language Proficiency Education and Research at the Pennsylvania State University from the U.S. Department of Education (CFDA 84.229A, P229A100012). However, the contents do not necessarily represent the policy of the Department of Education and one should not assume endorsement by the Federal Government.

PART I

Orientation

Introduction

Social and cultural aspects of language learning in study abroad

Celeste Kinginger
Pennsylvania State University

This chapter provides a brief survey of recent research on language learning in study abroad, explaining the rationale for the current volume. Many studies focus on outcomes, variously defined as holistic constructs, skills, or aspects of communicative competence. There are also many studies documenting the qualities of the study abroad experience from the perspective of students. Fewer in number are the studies adopting holistic approaches to language learning as a dialogic and situated affair, studies examining the subjective aspects of language development in intercultural contexts, and research offering the potential for comparative perspectives through scrutiny of less-commonly studied encounters of students and local communities abroad. Following this introductory survey, the author provides an overview of the volume.

Published in 1995, Barbara Freed's *Second Language Acquisition in a Study Abroad Context* was the first volume devoted exclusively to research on the achievements and experiences of language learners abroad. The volume illustrates the diversity of expertise that may apply to scrutiny of this complex learning environment. Freed (1995) includes studies involving measurement of language gains, studies comparing the outcomes of education abroad versus classroom learning at home in terms of fluency, communicative strategies, and proficiency, research on the acquisition of sociolinguistic capabilities, and diary studies seeking to elucidate the sources of individual variation and as well as students' own dispositions toward language learning in and outside classrooms. In his forward to the volume, Charles A. Ferguson praised the timeliness of its contributions, noting in particular that "myths" surrounding the study abroad content are pervasive, and include, for example, the view that the only way to achieve "real fluency" in an additional language is to go to a place where that language is spoken (p. xii). At the time, Ferguson argued, these myths had not given rise to systematic research, despite their strong currency among teachers and students alike. A new domain of investigation had reached the point where a book was required to summarize the knowledge base and to chart a course for future research.

Freed's volume was indeed a landmark publication inspiring research on study abroad by a new generation of applied linguists. During the interval since 1995, empirically-derived knowledge of this complex learning environment has grown and diversified as researchers continue to confront myth and reality in their scholarship. Given the wealth of new scholarly endeavor, there is now a plausible rationale for a book devoted exclusively to a subset of the research on language learning in study abroad, specifically, to research examining its social and cultural aspects. Thus, we present the current volume, initially conceived at a colloquium on The Social Turn in Study Abroad Research at the 2010 meeting of the American Association for Applied Linguistics. Our rationale rests upon three ways in which the research, the phenomenon itself, and the field of applied linguistics have evolved since 1995.

1.   Research on language learning and study abroad

To begin with the research, in Kinginger (2009) I reviewed a large number of studies focused on the language-related outcomes of study or residence abroad. These include studies assessing the development of language ability based on constructs such as fluency, proficiency, or listening comprehension, studies attempting to correlate gains in language ability with quantitative reports on students' use of time, and studies focusing on particular aspects of communicative competence, including linguistic, actional, sociocultural, strategic, and discourse competence (Celce-Murcia, Dörnyei & Thurell 1995). From this wide-ranging review, several conclusions emerged. First, overall the research presents an encouraging picture of study abroad; although the gains documented are sometimes modest, study abroad has the potential to enhance students' language ability in every domain. Secondly, study abroad appears to be particularly useful for the development of abilities related to social interaction, precisely those abilities that are least amenable to classroom instruction. To give some examples, language learners who spend time in "L2land" (Coleman 1998) broaden their repertoire of speech acts, become more aware of register and style, develop greater autonomy as conversationalists, and incorporate fluency-enhancing formulaic language into their speech. These findings alone suggest that research into the nature and developmental outcomes of social interactions in study abroad settings will be of particular interest to language educators hoping to design maximally effective curricula.

However, a third generalization about the findings of applied linguistics research in this domain offers an even stronger rationale for further inquiry into the social and cultural aspects of student sojourns abroad. One of the most common findings of studies measuring outcomes is of significant individual differences. In comparing the outcomes of Japanese language instruction for novices in the classroom at home and abroad, one contributor to the Freed volume (Huebner 1995) went so far as to suggest that study abroad *amplifies* individual differences. Why do some students return from a sojourn in L2 land with a significantly broadened second language repertoire, some do not, and some even present lower scores on a proficiency post-test than they did prior to their time away (Kinginger 2008)? Many reports of outcomes-oriented research are silent on this point, and others offer speculation about the potential role of affective or personality variables such as motivation or extraversion. As noted above, one way to explore this question is to correlate reports of student activity with measures of language development: but this strategy does not always yield easily interpretable results. For example, in attempting to understand the remarkable individual differences in post-study abroad oral proficiency scores in their research on French language learners, Magnan and Back (2007) investigated a constellation of contextual and personal variables but found only one correlation, namely the negative effect of *speaking French with other Americans*. In order to understand this phenomenon, clearly more is needed than thorough, objective accounts of student activity while abroad. The contributors to this volume would agree that we need to frame language learning as a dialogic, situated affair that unfolds in intercultural contexts and includes significant subjective dimensions.

In addition to research documenting language related outcomes, numerous qualitative studies have been devoted to achieving greater understanding of educational sojourns abroad: what students do with their time and the subjective or other meanings they ascribe to their experiences. This literature illustrates great variability in the extent to which students become engaged in local communicative settings and can in fact be reasonably classified as "language learners." Much depends on the ways in which students are received by the institutions they frequent (e.g. Churchill 2006) or by their host families (e.g. Wilkinson 1998). Sojourners abroad may be welcomed as legitimate peripheral participants (Lave & Wenger 1991) by schools and families eager to attend to their comfort and accommodate their language learning, or they may encounter indifference and occasionally, hostility (Pellegrino Aveni 2005). The students themselves may willingly approach their interlocutors, mindful of their status as newcomers, or they may withdraw from social interaction, especially if they interpret these interactions as conflictual (Kinginger 2008). Outside the home and the classroom, some students develop close ties to local communities through service work, social or religious organizations, or internships. Others escape through tourism, recoil into a sense of national superiority (Perrefort 2008), cling to social networks of co-nationals, or remain virtually "at home" via the Internet. In short, efforts to illuminate the qualities of study abroad experiences, extended in this volume, point to the sources of individual variation in learning outcomes.

Although scholarly interest in study or residence abroad has yielded a significant knowledge base, this literature nevertheless displays many limitations in scope and design. There are few longitudinal studies (cf. Alred & Byram 2002) investigating the longer-term impact of educational sojourns abroad. There is, as yet, only a handful studies accompanying the "social turn" in second language acquisition (Block 2003). Of particular relevance to this volume are limitations on the populations studied. The great majority of research has focused on the experiences of US-based undergraduate students learning the languages that have been most commonly taught in their country (French, Spanish, or German). As noted in Kinginger (2009), this emphasis may be at least partially attributed to the fact that most American study abroad participants display quite modest second language communicative ability and have little experience of border crossing, which means that, within students' careers, study abroad is interpreted as a unique opportunity to learn. Although some research on language learning in study abroad is emerging from Asian (e.g. Taguchi 2011) and European contexts (e.g. Pérez-Vidal & Juan-Garau 2011), there is a clear need for greater diversity in the sending and receiving countries represented in the literature.

2.   Contemporary study abroad

As Coleman points out (this volume) the element of time is missing from most analyses of the study abroad literature. There is an implicit assumption that experiences taking place decades ago remain comparable to those of today. Meanwhile, among the macro-level societal changes taking place since the modern American form of study abroad was initiated in the 1950s (Levenstein 2004) we may count accelerating economic globalization, the spread of global communications technologies, and the triumph of neoliberalism and accompanying consumerist ideologies (Holborow 2012). No doubt the mythic version of study abroad shared by seasoned language instructors as well as some researchers is in part based upon memories of their own successful sojourns decades ago. In this version, a sojourn abroad involved, for example, temporary separation from home-based social networks, discovery of different modes of social organization and thought, and immersion in the local language.

In developing a series of case studies of American undergraduate students in France, a project attempting to link the qualities of contemporary study abroad to its language-related outcomes (Kinginger 2008), the influence of these societal changes was highly salient. If the participants wished to learn French through engagement in French-mediated local communicative practices, they needed to foreground and struggle to maintain their identities as language learners. Immediately apparent obstacles to their participation in local activities included the lure of the American cohort, already well documented (e.g. Isabelli-García 2006; Kline 1998), but also the temptation to retain strong social ties to home-based friends and family (via the Internet but also the frequent physical presence of "helicopter parents"), the ready availability of English-medium resources, and the preference for English as *lingua mundi* among international students and in some classrooms. Several of the participants did in fact become highly engaged in local communicative activity, developing and diversifying their repertoire in French and becoming more sensitive to the intercultural dimensions of communication. However, and despite the fact that all participants claimed motivation for language learning as the study began, many of them ultimately interpreted study abroad through a consumerist lens, as a form of leisure infotainment unrelated to any investment of serious effort (Gore 2005). Others arrived unprepared to confront the image of the United States in the eyes of their French interlocutors, became involved in interactions they interpreted as conflicts, and estranged themselves from their hosts.

Clearly, study abroad in the age of Facebook is not the same phenomenon it was years ago. It is unwise to make facile assumptions about the kinds of participation available to language learners abroad or about the motives students bring to their experiences. If research on language learning in study abroad is to retain its relevance, it must attend to the social and cultural aspects of the contemporary phenomenon.

3. Epistemology and methodology in applied linguistics

Research on language learning in study abroad has always mirrored trends in the broader field of applied linguistics. Thus, in the past this research has been characterized by lack of dialogue between scholars engaged in research based on computational models of the mind and those who view the learner as a human apprentice to social practices (Kramsch 2002). On the one hand, much of this research has followed and continues to follow mainstream second language acquisition theory in its models of the learner as anonymous information processor and of the social context as information source. Within such models, study abroad is analogous to an experimental treatment and is simply assumed to provide high quality, contextualized input. On the other hand, ethnographic and other qualitative studies have the potential to illuminate findings about language-related outcomes by probing the nature of students' experiences and dispositions toward their hosts and host countries. However, these studies rarely involve documentation of those outcomes.

In the meantime, many scholars agree that the field is moving in the direction of greater epistemological and methodological diversity, and that this change can be interpreted in a positive light (Ortega 2012). In particular, alongside experimental approaches to second language acquisition there now exist several established strands of research following what Block (2003) termed the "social turn" in second language acquisition. These include: (1) language socialization research examining the transformation by which novices are simultaneously apprenticed to use language and socialized through language into the everyday practices of local communities (Ochs 2002); (2) research inspired by Vygotsky's developmental theory of the sociocultural origins of higher mental processes (Lantolf & Thorne 2006); and (3) poststructuralist approaches theorizing language as a form of symbolic capital and learners as agents of their own learning who may either accommodate or challenge the practices they encounter (Pavlenko 2002). Of these approaches, language socialization is the most visible in the study abroad research thus far (e.g. Cook 2008; DuFon 2006; Iino 2006). With the publication of this volume, we hope to illustrate the value of sociocultural and poststructuralist approaches for research on language and culture learning in study abroad contexts.

In parallel with the expansion of theoretical approaches to language learning in study abroad, contemporary scholars are working to expand the vision of language informing research. The rise of corpus-based research, enabling massively empirical descriptions based on large databases, has altered our view of the way language is organized by uncovering the significance of collocations and formulaic sequences in both speech and writing. Conversation analysis, involving close scrutiny of interactions as they unfold turn-by-turn, has drawn our attention to the crucial role, in managing interaction, of hitherto neglected aspects of language use such as vagueness and hedges. If study abroad involves access to the everyday use of languages under study, and if researchers wish to understand what students can learn, then clearly it is important to include these insights in the design and interpretation of research.

4.   Overview of the volume

This volume is intended to showcase the value of contemporary socially-oriented approaches in research on language learning in study abroad, to highlight recent attempts to refine our understanding of the living languages that students encounter and learn while abroad, and to add to the diversity of populations represented in the literature. In Chapter Two, based on considerable experience of research and advocacy for residence abroad in the UK context, James A. Coleman contributes to the framing of the volume, arguing for a more holistic and nuanced account of language learners as "whole people." When second language acquisition research reduces participants' identities to a single dimension ("language learners"), Coleman argues, they sideline many of the domains that are actually most important to students. With his taxonomy of learning outcomes and contextual variables, the author provides a framework for a broader perspective that includes personal and professional aspirations and can assist readers in assessing the comparability of studies carried out in diverse settings. With Coleman's Concentric Circles, he provides a model for description of the sociolinguistic networks that students develop while abroad. Data from an ongoing study involving European students in French West Africa illustrate the importance of valuing individual difference as an essential contribution to understanding the full picture of study abroad.

Part II of the book presents six chapters devoted to qualitative and case studies in an array of different contexts. In Chapter Three, Heather Willis Allen adopts an activity theoretical approach to the ways in which good language learners develop self-regulatory strategies, including maintenance of motivation, goal-setting, and language learning strategies. The study involved three American undergraduate students of French, and traced their activity and reflective narratives over a period of several years as they moved from the language classroom to their study abroad in France, back to the language classroom, and on to their first professional experiences. Thus, this study is one of few in the literature that includes a longitudinal dimension. The findings of the study suggest the value of narrative reflection as a tool to support students in developing self-regulation as language learners.

Chapter Four also relies on a sociocultural, activity theoretical interpretive frame to explore the development of an intercultural stance during an international field experience for US-based future teachers of English as a Second Language. The author, Elizabeth Smolcic, frames the need for a focus on the intercultural in teacher education in terms of the demographics of students and teachers in US public schools: while the student population is increasingly diverse and multilingual, teachers are predominantly White, female, and monolingual. The program under study involved a summer sojourn in rural Ecuador during which the future teachers were enjoined to explore their own cultural identities and analyze their own process of learning Spanish or Quechua in classrooms and homestay settings. The case presented here, of "Anna," illustrates how the immersion experience became a context for enhanced self-awareness, socialization into new communities of practice, and sensitivity to the needs of learners.

In Chapter Five, we move from the United States to Europe and from a preoccupation with language and culture learning strategies to a different set of priorities, namely the politics of identification with the languages students encounter while abroad. Here, Fred Dervin explores the phenomenon of *lingua franca* use (English and French) by mobile European students in Finland and France. The chapter reports on two studies: a macro-level project based on questionnaire data and examining representations of English as a lingua franca, and a case study of a Finnish student who had studied in France as an Erasmus participant for six months. On the whole, representations of "Erasmus English" (or "Globish") in the larger scale study were negative and reflected a "fetishism of the norm" that guided students' condemnation of other speakers of English as a *lingua franca* as models for language use. In the case study, however, we hear the views of a student who appreciates the advantages of speaking French with other non-natives (with the exception of Americans, with whom she spoke English); these include the ability to code-switch to English freely as well as attitudes toward linguistic performance that are relatively non-judgmental in comparison to those of native speakers.

Chapter Six is devoted to Timothy Wolcott's ethnographic study of a young American woman's experience as a participant in an "island" program in Paris. The program was designed as an introduction to Paris and to study abroad and was intended to attract undergraduate students early in their college careers. However, "Lola," the focus of the case study, along with many others, attended the program at the end of her college years, as a capstone experience after she had fulfilled the requirements for her degree. Although Lola's focus was not, at least initially, language or culture learning, Wolcott nevertheless found that the experience of living in Paris was highly significant for her. Through recent poststructuralist theories of subjectivity, Wolcott offers a fresh interpretation of American study abroad in France as a deeply personal and transcendent experience.

The experience of high school study abroad in China is the topic of Chapter Seven. Here, Tan and Kinginger examine how former participants in a summer program involving homestays with Chinese families evaluate and represent their experience. Whereas research on the home stay typically involves college-aged students who are received and interpret themselves as relatively independent adults, the high school students in this study were closely supervised both by the program and by their host families. They report numerous opportunities to become engaged in local communicative practices and to encounter both difference and similarity in their interactions with Chinese family members. Alumni of the program who have gone on to college-level study of Chinese, including further study abroad, report that the social ties established while in high school then increased their social integration in China in comparison to that of other members of their cohorts. Overall, the findings of this study point to the value of study abroad in the high school years and to the need for further investigation of this phenomenon.

Language educators interested in the design of curricula for mobile students will be particularly drawn to Chapter Eight, Jane Jackson's case study of a Hong Kong Chinese student who participated first in a year-long exchange program in Canada, and then in an elective course, *Intercultural Transitions*, desired to expand and extend learning after study abroad through guided, critical reflection. Analyzing a variety of qualitative data through a sociocultural lens, and pairing these data with quantitative scores from the Intercultural Development Index (IDI), Jackson outlines the social and personal factors that combined to influence this student's development. The chapter also illustrates the potential impact of curricular designs attending to the re-entry phase, a rare preoccupation in both teaching and research.

As noted above, study abroad appears to be most beneficial in enhancing capabilities related to social interaction, including, for example, the ability to perform speech acts, to open and close conversations, or to choose and use makers of politeness (Kinginger 2009). These abilities may be classified as aspects of pragmatic capability, often described as a composite including pragmalinguistic ability (knowledge of and ability to use the relevant forms) and sociopragmatic ability (awareness of social conventions and ability to use forms appropriately). When language teaching materials focus on the pragmalinguistic, they often do so in a cursory or incomplete manner. Sociopragmatics are often taught through simplified rules of thumb that may or may not apply in every setting. Most importantly, classroom learners rarely enjoy the opportunity to appreciate how their pragmatic performance may be interpreted as a reflection of their identity. All of these aspects combine to make of study abroad a context for the discovery of social interactive language, its meaning and use.

The four chapters in Part III of this volume illustrate a variety of methods and foci in research on the pragmatic capabilities of study abroad participants in relation to the construction of second language identities. Chapter Nine, by Maria Shardakova, reports the findings of a cross-sectional experimental study examining the extent to which American learners of Russian are able to convey desired identities through second language humor. Shardakova's approach is unique in that she is not content merely to examine learners' performance but also elicits information about the study participants' intentions. The study involved a sophisticated research design in which the identities claimed by the authors of emails with varying proficiency in Russian as a second language are compared with the identities attributed to these same authors by native speakers and other learners. The findings illustrate the many challenges issued to second language humorists, as many attempts at humor are evaluated in negative terms. More importantly, the methodology allows Shardakova to interpret her findings based on divergent cultural norms, with the American learners emphasizing personal characteristics and the native speakers of Russian invoking group solidarity.

In Chapter Ten, Noriko Iwasaki examines the performance and perception of hedging in second language Japanese. As the author argues, hedges are an interpersonally significant but often neglected aspect of second language conversational ability. Speakers of Japanese employ hedges as interactional devices for such purposes as building and maintaining rapport and managing emotion in conversation. Examining data from pre- and post-study abroad Oral Proficiency Interviews, Iwasaki demonstrates that her participants dramatically increased both their use of hedges in general and the variety of hedges they used. In addition, some students elected to use hedges that typically index a youthful identity among expert users of Japanese; these learners' speech was rated as highly sociable by a group of college aged Japanese students. Iwasaki's study therefore demonstrates that study abroad can increase students' interactional abilities.

Chapter Eleven, by Lucien Brown, considers the experience of four Anglophone learners of Korean as they used honorifics to negotiate identity in study abroad. There are two broad modes of honorifics use in Korean: *contaymal*, or "respect speech," which indexes, for example, politeness and respect for age-based hierarchy, and *panmal*, or the non-honorific language associated with in-group communication and intimate relationships. In a Discourse Completion Task all four of Brown's participants displayed strong awareness of Korean honorifics and the ability to manipulate them appropriately within an imagined context. However, Brown's data also include interviews and recordings of everyday interactions with Korean interlocutors, and here the picture becomes considerably more complex. As was the case for the learner of Japanese described by Siegal (1996), the participants encountered situations in which their status as foreigners was perceived as exempting all parties from the usual norms governing honorifics use. Case studies of each learner show a variety of responses to these encounters.

In Chapter Twelve, Julieta Fernandez proposes a corpus-based analysis of vague language use by learners of Spanish following a year abroad. As Fernandez notes, vague language, including the "general extenders" (e.g. *and stuff like that*) under study here, is generally stigmatized as imprecise but in fact carries substantial pragmatic force. For example, vague language plays a significant role in foregrounding relationships over topics in conversation and in displaying epistemic stances (i.e. the speaker's attitude toward the truth value of an utterance). Findings from an analysis of data in the Spanish Learner Language Oral Corpora show that the participants used a variety of general extenders, and that there was considerable individual variation in this use. A series of exploratory case studies of learner's motives and experiences draws parallels between the quantitative data and the nature of individual learners' study abroad experience.

A final goal of this volume is to expand the representation of student populations and languages beyond the usual focus on American undergraduates studying French, Spanish, or German. While two of the studies included examine American students of French, they do so from novel perspectives (activity theory in the case of Allen's study, and poststructuralist theories of identity in the case of Wolcott's study). The remaining papers reflect the continuing emergence of diversity in research on language learning abroad, with studies of American students learning Russian (Shardakova), American teachers learning Spanish (Smolcic), American high school students learning Chinese (Tan & Kinginger), British students learning French in Africa (Coleman), and Korean (Brown), Chinese residents of Hong Kong learning English (Jackson), and European students using French and English as *lingua francas* (Dervin).

This book offers an overview of recent efforts to update the portrayal of study abroad in the applied linguistics literature through attention to the social and cultural aspects of this phenomenon. The volume illustrates changes in the scope of theory and method, refinement of approaches to social interactive language use, and expansion in the diversity of populations and languages under scrutiny. We hope that the volume will offer useful ideas for the design of study abroad programs, insights provoking reflection on the role of study abroad in language learning, and inspiration for future research.

References

Alred, G., & Byram, M. (2002). Becoming an intercultural speaker: A longitudinal study of residence abroad. *Journal of Multilingual and Multicultural Development, 23*, 339–352.

Block, D. (2003). *The social turn in second language acquisition.* Washington, DC: Georgetown University Press.

Celce-Murcia, C., Dörnyei, Z., & Thurell, S. (1995). Communicative competence: A pedagogically motivated model with content specifications. *Issues in Applied Linguistics, 6*, 5–35.

Churchill, E. (2006). Variability in the study abroad classroom and learner competence. In M. DuFon & E. Churchill (Eds.), *Language learners in study abroad contexts* (pp. 203–227). Clevedon, UK: Multilingual Matters.

Coleman, J. (1998). Language learning and study abroad: The European perspective. *Frontiers: The Interdisciplinary Journal of Study Abroad, 4*, 167–203.

Cook, H. (2008). *Socializing identities through speech style: Learners of Japanese as a foreign language*. Clevedon, UK: Multilingual Matters.

DuFon, M. (2006). The socialization of taste during study abroad in Indonesia. In M. DuFon & E. Churchill (Eds.), *Language learners in study abroad contexts* (pp. 91–119). Clevedon, UK: Multilingual Matters.

Freed, B. (Ed.). (1995). *Second language acquisition in a study abroad context*. Amsterdam: John Benjamins.

Gore, J. (2005). *Dominant beliefs and alternative voices: Discourse, belief, and gender in American study abroad*. New York, NY: Routledge.

Holborow, M. (2012). What is neoliberalism? Discourse, ideology and the real world. In D. Block, J. Gray, & M. Holborow (Eds.), *Neoliberalism and applied linguistics* (pp. 14–32). New York, NY: Routledge.

Huebner, T. (1995). The effects of overseas language programs: Report on a case study of an intensive Japanese course. In B. Freed (Ed.), *Second language acquisition in a study abroad context* (pp. 171–193). Amsterdam: John Benjamins.

Iino, M. (2006). Norms of interaction in a Japanese homestay setting – Toward two-way flow of linguistic and cultural resources. In M. DuFon & E. Churchill (Eds.), *Language learners in study abroad contexts* (pp. 151–173). Clevedon, UK: Multilingual Matters.

Isabelli-García, C. (2006). Study abroad social networks, motivation, and atttitudes: Implications for SLA. In In M. DuFon & E. Churchill (Eds.), *Language learners in study abroad contexts* (pp. 231–258). Clevedon, UK: Multilingual Matters.

Kinginger, C. (2008). Language learning in study abroad: Case studies of Americans in France. *Modern Language Journal, 92*, Monograph.

Kinginger, C. (2009). *Language learning and study abroad: A critical reading of research*. Basingstoke, UK: Palgrave Macmillan.

Kline, R. (1998). Literacy and language learning in a study abroad context. *Frontiers: The Interdisciplinary Journal of Study Abroad, 4*, 139–165.

Kramsch, C. (Ed.). (2002). *Language acquisition and language socialization: Ecological perspectives*. London: Continuum.

Lantolf, J., & Thorne, S. (2006). *Sociocultural theory and the genesis of second language development*. New York, NY: Oxford University Press.

Lave, J., & Wenger, E. (1991). *Situated learning: Legitimate peripheral participation*. New York, NY: Cambridge University Press.

Levenstein, H. (2004). *We'll always have Paris: American tourists in France since 1930*. Chicago, IL: University of Chicago Press.

Magnan, S., & Back, M. (2007). Social interaction and linguistic gain during study abroad. *Foreign Language Annals, 40*, 43–61.

Ochs, E. (2002). Becoming a speaker of culture. In C. Kramsch (Ed.), *Language acquisition and language socialization: Ecological perspectives* (pp. 99–120). London: Continuum.

Ortega, L. (2012). Epistemological diversity and moral ends of research in instructed SLA. *Language Teaching Research, 16*, 206–226.

Pavlenko, A. (2002). Poststructuralist approaches to the study of social factors in second language learning and use. In V. Cook (Ed.), *Portraits of the L2 user* (pp. 277–302). Clevedon, UK: Multilingual Matters.

Pellegrino Aveni, V. (2005). *Study abroad and second language use: Constructing the self*. New York, NY: Cambridge University Press.

Pérez-Vidal, C., & Juan-Garau, M. (2011). The effect of context and input conditions on oral and written development: A study abroad perspective. *IRAL, 49*, 157–185.

Perrefort, M. (2008). Changer en échangeant? Mobilités et experiences langagières [Change through exchange? Mobility and language-related experiences]. In F. Dervin & M. Byram (Eds.), *Echanges et mobilités académiques: Quel bilan?* [Exchanges and academic mobility: What results?] (pp. 65–91). Paris: L'Harmattan.

Siegal, M. (1996). The role of learner subjectivity in second language sociolinguistic competency: Western women learning Japanese. *Applied Linguistics, 17*, 356–382.

Taguchi, N. (2011). The effect of proficiency and study-abroad experience on pragmatic comprehension. *Language Learning, 61*, 909–939.

Wilkinson, S. (1998). On the nature of immersion during study abroad: Some participants' perspectives. *Frontiers: The Interdisciplinary Journal of Study Abroad, 4*, 121–138.

Researching whole people and whole lives

James A. Coleman
The Open University

In tracing the author's own emerging insights into study abroad, this chapter contextualizes key aspects of the phenomenon. It queries widely accepted approaches and instruments, and asks whether, in attempting to achieve significant generalizations, we have sometimes distorted reality by narrowing our definitions and our measures, and by leaving crucial information unconsidered or even unstated. The chapter challenges the legitimacy of the expression "the study abroad context", arguing that both contextual and individual variation contribute, together with social networks, to the essential fluidity and complexity of the study abroad experience. Elements of a recent long-term study illustrate a more comprehensive perspective.

1. Introduction

Study abroad researchers sometimes dismiss high individual variation as a nuisance factor undermining the neat patterns which quantitative Second Language Acquisition research seems to require. Building on my taxonomy of learning outcomes and contextual variables (Coleman 2006a), I will argue instead that study abroad research can escape the narrow confines of cognitive SLA and see its subjects not just as language learners, but as rounded people with complex and fluid identities and relationships which frame the way they live the study abroad experience.

Study abroad remains an ill-defined research domain, embracing related but disparate experiences. Research to date disproportionately addresses certain departure zones, notably North America and Europe, although typical study abroad patterns vary considerably even between these two contexts. And since the bulk of the growing number of studies focuses on language gains, the subject is framed only as a language learner. Such an approach provides only a partial picture of study abroad participants and the impact of study abroad on their lives.

This chapter is in some respects the account of a personal quest of discovery and reflection to find out more about what we may call "study abroad." My background is not that of a conventional applied linguist: as a specialist in French Renaissance literature, I stumbled, through sheer serendipity, via co-authoring of language teaching materials, and guiding students of French, to an academic research interest in many facets of foreign language learning, what makes it happen, and the environments in which it takes place. While I have sought during my career to compensate for the absence of formal training in applied linguistics, in research methods and in pedagogy, and there are no doubt many notions which still escape me, I hope I have along the way begun to comprehend what study abroad is.

Academic research is the process by which we attempt to understand a phenomenon. The phenomenon addressed in this chapter, generally known as "study abroad", can be approached from many directions, and as an outsider I have repeatedly asked the wrong questions, or at least unconventional ones, which insiders feel no need to ask. From an administrative point of view, what can we do to make study abroad work? From an ethnographic point of view, what are its common practices and givens? From an enquirer's point of view, how have people explored it, and have they gone about it in the most appropriate and effective ways? From my current perspective as a lobbyist on behalf of modern languages, how can I persuade the UK Government that study abroad is worth supporting through policy and funding decisions, and persuade society as a whole to invest in it at a time of both globalization and economic constraint?

2.   European language proficiency survey

Fifteen years ago, in reporting a survey of over twenty thousand language students (Coleman 1996), I sought to integrate my own personal and professional insights with the statistical findings. The European Language Proficiency Survey (ELPS) used a very efficient measure of global target language proficiency, the C-Test (Coleman 1994), alongside a detailed questionnaire to profile students of French, German, Spanish and Russian in British and Irish universities, and was subsequently extended to include students of English in several continental European countries. The ELPS was guided by those who had developed the C-Test and brought genuine Second Language Acquisition (SLA) expertise to the study. The project involved a UK pre-pilot (N = 427), pilot (N = 3119) and main study (N = 18264, of whom 12477 participants were students of French, 3824 of German, 2462 of Spanish and 550 of Russian). Comparisons were drawn with students of English and other languages in Continental European universities (N = 2646).

Although a cross-sectional study, the numbers of participants allowed some generalizations to be drawn from ELPS data, notably regarding the accelerated linguistic progress during the third year of a four-year language degree, the "year abroad" spent in "L2land". I was reassured to find that all students in all institutional contexts typically acquired the L2.

> Rates of progress, however, seem to vary: rapid progress in the last two years of secondary education may not be matched during the first two years at university. Rapid gains during residence abroad seem to be followed by no gains whatever, despite tuition, during their final year.   (Coleman 1996, p. 41)

And thus "the contribution of residence abroad to the foreign language proficiency of advanced learners is greater than that of a year's tuition in the home institution" (Coleman 1996, p. 45). Longitudinal components within the study showed no language gain after return from abroad.

My principal interest, as a language teacher substantially motivated by concerns about the way languages were being taught in the UK, had been purely domestic, a fact reflected in the unconventional (and *post hoc* or *propter hoc* widely uncited) publication of the findings. However, the results shed light not only on huge and unacknowledged differences in proficiency levels between universities, but also on individual learner differences, motivation, attitudes, goals, success factors, non-specialist linguists, and transferable (including intercultural) skills.

3. Terminology

Chapter Four of *Studying Languages* (Coleman 1996) was entitled not "Study Abroad" but "Residence abroad and its impact". "Residence" not only contrasts with the standard terminology in other European languages (*Auslandsaufenthalt, séjour à l'étranger, estancia al extranjero, estadia no estrangeiro*, etc.), each of which implies a shorter and more temporary sojourn (Coleman 2001, p. 139) but also encompasses choices for the intercalary period other than formal university classes. While working on the European Language Proficiency Survey, and in particular the literature review which informed both *Studying Languages* and an overview article on language learning through student residence abroad (Coleman 1997), the North American literature I encountered had a clear (but usually inexplicit) notion that "study abroad" meant precisely that, while UK reports assumed that the norm to be investigated was working as an English Language Assistant in a foreign school. From my actual experience of the phenomenon, administering the year abroad in successive UK universities and, from 1997 to 2001, coordinating the national Residence Abroad Project (Coleman 2002), I understood that British students chose between study, assistantship and work placements.

The earliest UK study (Willis, Doble, Sankarayya & Smithers 1977) had found that a work placement enhanced both linguistic achievement and motivation. Such *stages en entreprise* accounted for 12% of UK outgoers in 1986, 22.3% in 1991/92, and 21.2% in 2009/10 (Carbonell 2011). A particular form of work placement, the language assistantship scheme, which sees language undergraduates providing native-speaker L1 input in a school in L2land, celebrated its centenary in 2005 (British Council 2005), and was for so many years the norm that some earlier UK research had not considered study or alternative types of work (Coleman 1996, pp. 59, 71). Peace Corps (e.g. Gunterman 1995) and missionary work (e.g. Rubio 2003) have also been included in study abroad research.

From a UK perspective, then, it is certainly the more inclusive "residence abroad" that should be the over-arching category, and "study abroad" a sub-category, rather than the latter being, thanks to the dominance of North American research, both an all-encompassing genus and a specific species (Coleman 2007, p. 38). The transatlantic disparities which led Barbara Freed to commission a separate European overview when she edited a special issue of *Frontiers* on language learning in a study abroad context (Freed 1998) extend also to the apparent tribal separation in the USA between study abroad researchers and administrators, and noted among others by Deardorff (2006). When, in 1997, nearly £1 million was allocated to three "year abroad" projects (including the Residence Abroad Project which I coordinated), it seemed natural to draw on both published research and the best practices embedded in the academic community (Coleman 2001, 2002; Coleman & Parker 2001). Project outcomes embraced both research and practice, a continuing UK tradition evidenced in 2010 when the University of Bath devoted a conference to "Assessment of the Year Abroad in Modern Language Degrees" (http://www.bath.ac.uk/education/research/conferences/meier/info.html). A major study of the development of criticality in arts and social science degrees (Johnston, Mitchell, Ford & Myles 2011) retains both "residence abroad" and "year abroad". A nationally funded project undertaken by the University Council of Modern Languages in 2011 refers carefully to "work or study abroad (the 'year abroad')" (UCML, 2011). For a UK observer, the phenomenon thus comprises both practical and scientific concerns, and embraces not just study but also language-teaching and other work placements.

4. Definitions

"Study abroad" or "residence abroad" is a significant but diverse phenomenon. The Organization for Economic Cooperation and Development counted 3.7 million mobile students in 2009, an increase of 77% since 2000 (OECD 2011). With consistent double-digit annual increases, student mobility is expected to double by 2020: representing currently just 2 per cent of all students, there is certainly scope for further growth. More than half of the world's mobile students are enrolled in European universities (Teichler, Ferencz & Wächter 2011).

If there exists a degree of consensus on overall totals, details are nonetheless hard to pin down, and all commentators lament the lack of precise data (e.g. Carbonell 2011; King, Findlay & Arens 2010). The primary division is between whole-program mobility and within-program mobility, also known respectively as degree mobility and credit mobility (Sussex Centre for Migration Research 2004, p. 11).

Despite the many similarities between whole-program and within-program study abroad, which includes factors such as acculturation, social networks, accommodation, integration, national academic cultures, language and culture shock, etc., applied linguists, no doubt for pragmatic reasons, tend to limit their research either to incoming students or to outgoing within-program students. Even here, there is substantial diversity. The US and Europe represent the bulk of study abroad research (Kinginger 2009, pp. 7–8, citing Block 2007), but whereas in the U.S.A. 1.5% of eligible students undertake study abroad each year, mostly for 6 to 8 weeks, with only 0.05% of eligible students spending a whole academic year abroad, the Erasmus exchange program alone involves 0.85% of eligible European students each year, with a typical stay of at least one semester; a similar number of "free movers" undertake study abroad independently.

Definitions of "study abroad" vary depending on the particular research context, and the professional identity and disciplinary background of the researcher, for "study abroad", being such a substantial social and educational phenomenon, not unexpectedly retains the attention not just of linguists, but equally of academics concerned with higher education policy, economics, psychology, social identity, gender studies, human geography and many more (see for example the chapters in Dervin 2011).

Kinginger (2009, p. 29) refers to study abroad as a "sub-field of applied linguistics." But if we ask, "Which sub-field?," we encounter uncertainty. At the 2010 conference of the American Association for Applied Linguistics (AAAL), where the symposium which gave the impetus to the present volume was held, language-related "study abroad" papers appeared under no fewer than seven headings – RWL, LCS, BIH, LLC, SLA, DIS, and SOC – and interculture-related study abroad papers also under LID and TEC,[1] in other words more than half of the available strands or sub-fields.

---

1. RWL Reading, writing, and literacy; LCS Language, culture, socialization, and pragmatics; BIH Bilingual, immersion, heritage, and language minority education; LLC Language and learner characteristics; SLA Second language acquisition, language acquisition, and attrition; DIS Analysis of discourse and interaction; SOC Sociolinguistics; LID Language and ideology; TEC Language and technology.

Definitions usually emphasise the educational context, for example:

> extended L2land residence as an integral component of a university degree programme involving one or more foreign languages.   (Coleman 1997, p. 1)

> a temporary sojourn of pre-defined duration, undertaken for educational purposes.   (Kinginger 2009, p. 11)

Collentine and Freed (2004, p. 156) adopt a more restrictive definition to include both in-class and out-of-class language learning:

> [in] the study abroad (SA) context… a hybrid communicative-learning context. Students attend formal classes and thus employ the L2 in learning contexts

while a European study looks more broadly:

> students who enroll in university courses, participate in work placements or simply undertake language courses abroad.
> (Orr, Schnitzer & Frackmann 2008, p. 130)

Additional European definitions reviewed by Carbonell (2011, p. 7) include "any form of international mobility which takes place within a student's programme of study in higher education" (Sussex Centre for Migration Research 2004, p. 11), and "crossing country borders for the purpose of or in the context of tertiary education" (Richters & Teichler 2006, p. 78).

For present purposes, I propose to define "study abroad" as simply undertaking all or part of university education abroad. It must be borne in mind, however, that the lack of consensus on the precise dimensions of the phenomenon means low comparability across studies, and constitutes an obstacle to generalization.

5.   The matrix

Study abroad is a multi-dimensional phenomenon, which I initially tried to visualize as a multi-dimensional space populated by disparate studies. By identifying a matrix of relevant coordinates, and ideally locating them within some form of Linnaean taxonomy, it should be feasible to locate the findings of each individual study within the space. It soon became apparent that just one corner was so far densely filled – US students on foreign-language study abroad, who in fact represent just 3% of mobile students.

Locating coordinates requires defining dimensions, and in successive attempts at painting the big picture I enumerated separate features of the learning *context* (Coleman 2006a, 2007, 2009) together with variables concerning language gain pre- during- and post-sojourn (Coleman 2007, p. 46). The most recent iteration of the matrix (Coleman 2009, p. 183, see Appendix 1) listed twenty contextual variables, but the table, comprising over a hundred cells, is rendered virtually unusable by the smallness of the font. In an attempt to acknowledge the very different nature of the variables, I abandoned "taxonomy" and "matrix" to borrow from Herring (2007) the term "faceted classification". A librarian's term since expanded to assist data retrieval in complex domains, a faceted classification lists, in an unordered, non-hierarchical, open-ended way, facets which have been shown, independently or in combination, to condition variation in at least one study. Categories are heterogeneous but each can include a range of values or a null value. The resulting list is an aggregation rather than a powerful and coherent theoretical definition, and in study abroad, as in all real life, the sum of the parts is greater than their individual contribution, so a truly valid analysis would need to take account of the interactions among discrete facets, as well as the particular context.

The faceted classification of study abroad included

- Within-program or whole-program
- Learning objectives and outcomes
- Age
- Program at home university
- Home country and L1
- Previous language learning/pre-departure proficiency
- Preparation, institutional support, debriefing, follow-up, assessment
- Type of group (if any)
- Host country and L2
    - institutional L2
    - societal L2(s)
- Accommodation type, shared with...
- Host university courses (if any)
    - language courses
    - non-language courses
    - courses taught by...

Because one of the few constants across definitions is the educational setting, one key to classification would clearly be the learning objectives or learning outcomes. Defining and measuring outcomes was already a principal feature of the Study Abroad Evaluation Project involving the American Junior Year Abroad, European Joint Study Programme (predecessor of Erasmus) and German and Swedish programs in 1983–86 (e.g. Carlson, Burn, Useem & Yachimowicz 1990; Opper, Teichler & Carlson 1990). An alphabetical list of over-arching categories, derived originally from the Government-funded UK Residence Abroad Project (Coleman & Parker 2001), comprises

- – Academic
- – Cultural
- – Intercultural
- – Linguistic
- – Personal
- – Professional

The categories are expanded in Coleman (2007, pp. 40–41). Similar lists have been developed in the USA, for example by Engle and Engle (2003) and Bolen (2008), and Huebner (1998) reviews not only goals but also relevant research approaches. Although more than ten years have elapsed since the six alphabetical categories were defined, they have proven remarkably robust, and there seems no reason to revise them as a convenient classification which embraces all research studies and all pedagogical approaches. Learning objectives or outcomes offer a broad perspective. Through students' academic activities, study abroad research relates to studies of higher education policies, practices and the economics of a global market. As future workers, often in international careers, the study abroad period may be crucial in developing learners' employability and professional skills. Cultural and intercultural insights can parallel accelerated personal development, leading to enhanced self-esteem and capability to operate effectively in new linguistic and cultural contexts.

But there are serious objections. Firstly, the study abroad experience never has just one single outcome or objective. Secondly, objectives – what you hope to gain – are unlikely to correspond exactly to outcomes – the changes which actually take place. Thirdly, the narrowly educational objectives and outcomes will not map neatly on to learners' *personal* objectives, which will include fun, tourism and novelty, or *personal* outcomes which include aspects of identity.

A mixed method study (N = 2325) conducted by the Residence Abroad Project (Coleman 2003) found, for example, that personal concerns tended to outweigh issues of linguistic or academic progress, cultural or work-related insights. And googling "Erasmus Orgasmus" or a look at the lively thirdyearabroad.com website will soon convince that to define sojourners principally as "learners", let alone the even narrower "language learners", is to restrict the perspective to a single lens, which can only result in distortion. Linguists, who focus principally on study abroad as a language learning activity, although more recently they have broadened their concerns to embrace identity and social network issues, need to acknowledge that for educational researchers, as indeed for students themselves, the foreign language is just one aspect of a complex phenomenon with multiple outcomes.

A wider issue with Coleman's faceted classification concerns the fact that a taxonomy of *contexts* fails to capture three other crucial elements of study abroad research. The first is variation across individual studies (research method, number of participants, measures and scales used). The second is individual variation within each study (see next paragraph below), which is virtually the only constant finding of study abroad research. The third is the societal or political objectives and outcomes which underpin all study abroad schemes, even those run for commercial reasons; this dimension emerges clearly from statements of aims, for example of Erasmus at ⟨http://ec.europa.eu/education/lifelong-learning-programme/doc80_en.htm⟩ or UNESCO at ⟨http://www.unesco.org/education/studyingabroad/what_is/mobility_wche.shtml⟩. In announcing its Erasmus for All program, the European Commission (2011a) asserted that evaluations show "significant systemic impact, far beyond the benefits to individual participants", in the form of international higher education cooperation, curriculum development and transparency, while its *Draft conclusions on language competences to enhance mobility* (European Commission 2011b) reiterate the link between student mobility and the grandest political ambitions, which include a mobile workforce, understanding between peoples, a competitive economy, social cohesion, intercultural dialogue, and a dynamic labor market. Joseph Nye, who coined the term "soft power," sees international academic·exchanges as promoting US values and interests (2005).

Dörnyei (2005, p. 2) neatly encompasses the issue of individual variation: "Many researchers find individual differences detrimental to social sciences and this also applies to the domain of educational studies." Yet individual trajectories are in fact the essence of recent study abroad research, in which the focus has shifted from quantitative to qualitative, from product to process, from a search for generalizability to a recognition of complexity and variation. The recent literature offers many in-depth studies of individual trajectories, among them Murphy-Lejeune (2002), de Federico de la Rúa (2003), Papatsiba (2003), Ehrenreich (2004), Pellegrino Aveni (2005), Isabelli-Garcia (2006), Dervin (2008), Jackson (2008), and Kinginger (2008). Despite varying theoretical perspectives, they share a focus on social networks and identity, and several other concepts:

- A rejection of essentialized notions of "culture"
- Awareness of the continuing risk of essentializing "context"
- An acceptance that contexts, like culture, identity, agency, beliefs and motivation are fluid, dynamic, situated, and constantly reconstructed through interaction
- An attempt to capture the whole context (lifewide learning) and the whole individual, not just the "language learner", but the cognitive, affective, physical and social being
- Complementarity of cognitive and sociocultural approaches

6.   Rethinking the research paradigm

Why are we still so far from capturing the reality of the study abroad phenomenon? "A review of study abroad research literature shows general inconsistencies and inconclusiveness on certain issues, particularly on study abroad outcomes and their factors", asserts Wang (2010, p. 50). If forty years of research have brought so few certainties, is there perhaps something wrong with the definitions, underpinning theory and/or research design?

"That researchers and practitioners in the study abroad field continue to ask these basic questions, and strive to organize and classify studying abroad in ways that are systematically observable, shows that there is little consensus still on how to best define studying abroad and how to best study its effects", concludes McKeown (2009, p. 106).

It is not hard to reiterate the deficiencies of some linguistic studies: unvalidated proficiency measures; ceiling effects; tests too blunt to reveal subtle changes in sociolinguistic or advanced morpho-syntactic competence; reliance on mechanical measures of what can be straightforwardly quantified, i.e. classroom skills such as syntax, fluency and vocabulary rather than advanced pragmatics or prosody; self-reporting; the varying (and at times unreported) extent of formal language classes while abroad; the fuzzy definition of proficiency levels ("intermediate", "at least two semesters"); the absence of delayed post-testing and long-term follow-up.

Language learning through study abroad relies on the expectation that massive exposure to the L2 will lead to L2 acquisition, exposure both in interactions with native and expert speakers of the L2 and non-interactive input from the L2 environment. But any overview of research findings shows the process is fallible: "the SA students had many opportunities to engage in a diverse array of extracurricular Spanish language activities, but not all students took advantage of them" (Segalowitz & Freed 2004, p. 191).

Individual variability of course comprises a number of cognitive, affective, and biographical variables, each of which can itself can be infinitely sub-divided, and each of which is fluid and context-dependent. Affect, for example, includes language anxiety, which varies from one individual to another, from classroom to naturalistic use, from task to task, and from moment to moment.

A second step must be to recognize the heterogeneity of the study abroad environment occasioned by the factors listed in the taxonomy. Charitably, one can interpret references to "*the* study abroad context" (singular with definite article) as accidental slips, although in such cases as Pellegrino Aveni's (2005) book, Schauer's (2009) book and (2007) article, or Davidson's use of the phrase twice in introducing a journal special issue (2010a, p. 3) and eight times in his own article (2010b, p. 7), the phrase appears deliberate.

A principal concern with virtually all study abroad research is the matter of time, or more precisely of historical date as a contextual feature. Until recently, the dimension of time has not been adequately considered in study abroad research, especially in literature reviews. Within the scientific or positivist paradigm of experimental research which so much applied linguistics research seeks to ape, the date at which a study is conducted has little bearing. It is simply one element of the bibliographical reference. Planets, genes, carcinomas or *drosophila melanogaster* will behave the same in 2008 as in 1998. Not so with humans in a social context. The question of developing communication technologies (Coleman & Chafer 2010) is just one aspect of the rapidly and profoundly changing social context of study abroad, albeit one with considerable impact on social networks and identities, and with profound implications for the degree of immersion and engagement with the target language community which study abroad can offer to the facebook-ing, skyping, tweeting students of today.

Kinginger (2009, pp. 25–26) reminds us too that successive fashions in theory and related research methods have not been static, describing the story of study abroad research as "one of increasing emphasis on particularity (van Lier 2005) in which efforts to arrive at generalizations raise more questions than they answer."

The experimental paradigm is time-limited, and research funding constraints have meant that far too few studies have sought to explore the long-term impact of the always challenging and often life-changing experience of study abroad. Humans are the longest lived of all primates, and the impact of significant life events is not restricted to the immediate aftermath, or even a post-test delayed by a few months. A list of studies of the long-term impact of study abroad (e.g. Akande & Slawson 2000; Alred & Byram 2002, 2006; Dwyer 2004; Opper et al. 1990; Parey & Waldinger 2007; Teichler 1997) is woefully short. Do we not need more studies which address both lifewide and lifelong outcomes?

One problem which can be traced to the scientific method is that of comparative studies, in which the "treatment" (study abroad experience) of an experimental (SA) group is contrasted with that of a control group (AH for At Home or IM for domestic immersion). This is a form of misrepresentation. Not only can the study not be double-blind as the Cochrane protocol requires, but participants cannot be randomized, and SA groups are typically wealthier, whiter, more female, and better educated than non-SA groups in both the USA and Europe. And while recognizing that, by some valid and reliable measures, motivation towards language learning of SA and AH groups can be equal (Allen & Herron 2003; Allen, this volume), to equate their overall motivation seems illogical: some do and some don't. Do virgins and promiscuous students have the same motivation towards sex? Segalowitz and Freed themselves acknowledge the non-identity of SA and AH groups as regards attitudes and strategies, albeit in a footnote (2004, p. 196).

My attempts at a study abroad taxonomy were triggered partly by dissatisfaction with those studies which ignore the wider dimensions and conflate research from very divergent contexts, a process to which even the most eminent researchers can be susceptible. For example, Dufon and Churchill (2006) equate Collentine's (2004) study with that of Howard (2001), while DeKeyser (2007) lists together two studies showing increased fluency by objective measures following study abroad, namely Segalowitz and Freed (2004) and Towell, Hawkins and Bazergui (1996). But how informative is it to compare near-beginners (2 semesters of Spanish) on their first educational trip abroad with near-native speakers on their nth visit to L2land after up to nine years of specialist language study? Are the same processes at work, and can conclusions legitimately be generalized across dissimilar groups?

Looking at the contextual variables and the individual variables separately underplays the complexity of what is happening. One significant theoretical attempt to combine individual differences and environmental features is Cynthia White's learner-context interface (White 1999), which places at the center of language learning "the individual learner's capacity to construct an effective interface with target language sources in the learning environment" (White 2003, p. 86).

But both individual and context are unstable, so a still more promising approach, which supersedes any taxonomy or faceted classification, must be the environmental approach of van Lier (2003), Bronfenbrenner's nested ecosystems (1993) or that of complex dynamic systems (Larsen-Freeman & Cameron 2008), already applied to questions such as language learner motivation (Sade 2011). Larsen-Freeman (e.g. 2011) sets out twelve principles of complex dynamic systems, which Mercer (2011) summarizes thus:

> Complexity theory [...] replaces cause-and-effect, linear models with organic, complex, holistic models [...], in which the emergent properties of the system as a whole represent more than merely the sum of its parts. [...] In a complex system, context or environment is seen as an integral part of the system rather than as an external variable. [...] Everything within the system is considered to be in a constant state of flux which can lead to changes in the system as a whole and to the ways in which the components of the system interact with each other. (p. 337)

The generic objectivity of study abroad research reports has too often erased the most significant elements of the sojourn. Ask any applied linguist confidentially, in the corner of a bar, about their own time abroad as a student, and the emphasis will never be on enhanced TL lexis and mean length of utterance, but rather on romance, on discovery of self and others, on people and places. As study abroad research moves from a simplistic and inadequate model of causality and controllable (in)dependent variables – which has unsurprisingly produced contradictory findings – to a recognition that each variable interacts with every other variable, both singly and in combination, to create individual trajectories in which both person and context are in constant interaction and flux, we need to focus on individuals and their trajectories, identifying patterns but not adopting a determinist perspective. Before exemplifying such an approach, we consider the crucial factor of study abroad social networks.

7. Social circles

Students on study abroad are not, as some research might suggest, isolated entities whose body is no more than a means of transport for taking the acquisitive brain from interaction to interaction. Not only are the cognitive and affective processes of the brain inseparable from each other, but both are intricately interwoven within each intellectual, sensual, physical and social individual.

As Kramsch has often underlined, SLA researchers have tended to pay "more attention to the processes of acquisition than to the flesh-and-blood individuals who are doing the learning" and have divided learners' "minds, bodies and social behaviors into separate domains of inquiry and studied how language intersects with each of them" (Kramsch 2009, p. 2).

The nature and extent of interactions with native and expert L2 speakers has been a key focus of research within both cognitive and socio-cultural paradigms, and there is wide recognition that the social networks a student establishes, maintains and develops while abroad are crucial to learning outcomes, since they can determine access to linguistic and cultural input, and the quantity, nature and functional coverage of target language interactions. The issue of social isolation or integration has long informed debate about choices between studentship, assistantship and other work placement (e.g. Doble & Griffiths 1985, p. 203; Wilson & Everett 1989, p. 72; Byram & Alred 1993, p. 30), and in study abroad research has been linked with Schumann's model of acculturation, "the social and psychological integration of the learner with the target language group" (Schumann 1986, p. 379). Both group and individual acculturation have predominantly been studied in the context of migration (see e.g. overview in Berry 2005) and of temporary sojourners (e.g. Ward & Kennedy 1999), but studies of the psychology of acculturation have themselves been criticized for adopting a positivist, quantitative approach rather than a multi-method, multidisciplinary approach (Chirkov 2009).

Researchers and practitioners have also long recognized that socializing with co-nationals is both a natural response to the challenges of a sojourn in an unfamiliar cultural and linguistic setting, and a potential obstacle to achieving the immersion which is necessary for the learning objectives to be attained (e.g. Teichler 1991).

de Federico de la Rúa (2003, 2008) links the thinking behind the Erasmus program to Allport's (1954) "contact hypothesis", whereby interaction between members of different social groups should foster understanding and solidarity. But she points out that incoming Erasmus students have more to gain from interactions than do locals (unless the latter are linguistically motivated), and that the expected outcomes are frequently not realized – a frequent finding (e.g. most recently for the UK in Brown & Richards 2012). While virtual networks with family and friends at home may meet some practical and psychological needs, incoming Erasmus students, in order to counter isolation, also quickly establish local networks. These comprise the "three types of friendship ties" which de Federico de la Rúa labels local people, compatriots or fellow countrymen, and people from other countries. She traces graphically (2008, p. 97) the growth of networks, in which multinational groups predominate – one of many features of Erasmus life captured by the romanticized film *L'auberge espagnole* (Cédric Klapisch 2002) which, incidentally, should be compulsory viewing for study abroad researchers. But de Federico de la Rúa does note that, over time, friendships with local people increase:

> Once the immediate needs were satisfied with same nationality or Erasmus friends, students seem to have been more and more able to access locals in a slower rhythm of friendship renewal, and the security provided by sharing familiar norms and the same mother tongue may have become less important (2008, p. 101).

I have proposed the idea of three concentric circles to help us better understand the dynamic socialization patterns (social networks and language contact) of students during study abroad (Figure 1). This concentric circles model of study abroad social networks is more concerned with the dynamic nature of friendship groups and less concerned with the intensity of friendships than Dunbar's well-known Circles of Acquaintanceship (Dunbar 2010), which, within his evolutionary-psychology view of social networks, moves outwards from intimates through good friends and friends to acquaintances, all within the 150 individuals who comprise the maximum number for an effective human social network. My concentric circles concern the social groups within which friends are made. There is nothing new in identifying three overlapping study abroad social networks: Bochner, McLeod and Lin (1977, p. 277) already discuss (albeit in a different order, and ignoring any longitudinal changes) "a conational network whose function is to express the culture of origin", "a network with host nationals, whose function is the instrumental facilitation of academic and professional aspirations" and "a multi-national network whose main function is recreational". But social models have arguably been under-emphasized in quantitative investigations.

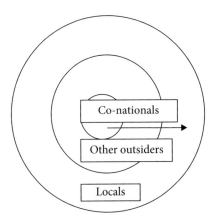

Figure 1. Coleman's concentric circles representation of study abroad social networks

The model – it is not a theory – emerges from extensive reading of those study abroad reports which cover socialization and friendships, as well as from the Senegal study described below. The progression from social networks comprising co-nationals, through wider contact with other out-group members (often other foreign students), towards the L2-speaking local community is not universal, automatic or uni-directional, but given motivation, time and effort, alternatively labeled agency, initiative or proactivity, movement tends to be centrifugal.

The model ignores individual and contextual variation, and over-simplifies reality. National cultures composed of like-minded and like-spoken individuals are mythical (Kramsch 1995). Study abroad socialization may develop or fossilize. And other patterns exist: for example, pre-existing social networks involving co-nationals have been shown, along with rankings and international openness, to influence the choices made by Chinese students as to where to study abroad (Ding & Li 2012).

However, the concentric circles model may provide a helpful and not untypical way of conceiving socialization and acculturation patterns during study abroad – not least within a pre-departure preparation program, or to inform individual and institutional strategies for optimizing study abroad outcomes. For researchers, social networks are a major influence on the variability of the study abroad experience. And <u>COL</u>eman's Concentric Circles at least has the merit of a mnemonic acrostic, relating to <u>C</u>o-nationals, <u>O</u>ther <u>O</u>utsiders and <u>L</u>ocals.

Those with institutional responsibility for student mobility have long recognized the tendency for students on an international campus to clot together in homoglossic and/or culturally similar groups, and have sometimes taken deliberate action such as "mix and mingle" events to counter such ghettoization (e.g. Wilkinson 2012, p. 20). It is standard practice to provide advice on the effort required to make native-speaker contacts, advice on loci of socialization (e.g. student restaurants rather than bars) and some strategies building on home activities (e.g. choir, hobby, sport, church – my greatest achievement was finding a suitable spot for an international-level synchronized swimmer) in order to get to know L2landers, a process which is nearly always easier outside university premises and away from clusters of other foreign students. Such advice could be regarded, together with homestays, work placements, or language partners as an attempt to short-circuit the natural process, to jump directly from the inner to the outer circle.

Homestays, as the literature shows, interact with other factors and achieve mixed success, mostly allowing access to only a very narrow segment of the outer circle (Hoffman-Hicks 2000; Jackson 2008; Magnan & Back 2007; Rivers 1998; Wilkinson 1998). Language partners may be identified by the host university; home institutions also often recommend (subject to security precautions) putting up a small ad to find an L2lander seeking conversation in the outgoer's L1. These and other routes may lead via contact with one L2lander to new social groupings. Sexual partners (cf. de Federico de la Rúa 2003, p. 99) probably provide the ideal short-cut to the outer circle: this is one finding of the Senegal data, but, in general, study abroad research has eschewed engaging with what nonetheless seems to be a widespread acculturation strategy.

The concentric circles model, first expounded at the 2010 Bath conference mentioned above, and alluded to in Coleman and Chafer (2011, p. 73), has already found some echoes (e.g. Bray, Gill & Randall 2011, p. 269), but is too recent to have been explored much in research terms, although Meier and Daniels (2011, p. 20) "found that the concentric circle model and social capital theory allowed the analysis of the interview data [...] and the categorization of the different relationships that students formed on their year abroad."

8.   The languages of the concentric circles

The concentric circles model also has implications for language socialization, use and learning. The inner circle, unless an agreement is in force to use the L2, will use the L1: part of the function of the co-national community is to relieve the stress and effort of extensive target language use. The outer circle will use one or sometimes more L2s (French and Wolof in the case of Senegal). The middle circle will use a Lingua Franca or code-switch among Lingua Francas, but the principal choices will be the L2 and/or English. The internationalization of higher education is already leading to domain loss for languages other than English thanks to English-medium instruction within the classroom and lecture theatre (Coleman 2006b): this Englishization is reflected in out-of-classroom middle-circle interactions.

9. Whole people and whole lives: The Senegal study

The Senegal study of graduates who, during a degree in French at a British university, undertook a work placement and sometimes university study in Dakar, the capital of the West African country, constitutes an attempt to broaden study abroad research to embrace whole people and whole lives. The Senegal study has adopted both quantitative and qualitative data elicitation methods, and addresses the same issues as in all study abroad, albeit in sharper focus because of the heightened contrasts between L1land and L2land.

A questionnaire comprising closed and open items was emailed from summer 2009 to all those who had participated in the program, directed by Tony Chafer at the University of Portsmouth, UK, since its inception in 1985. Forty-seven individuals (36F, 11M) returned the questionnaire (82.5% response rate), as did three former language assistants (2F, 1M). Quantitative data were complemented by over 29,000 words of open commentary. Five in-depth telephone interviews have so far been conducted, with others scheduled if external funding is forthcoming. The participants opted for the Senegal placement, and the research relies on self-report, with the range of graduation years (from 1988 to 2010) lending more or less reflective distance and adding more or less intervening experiences to the memories of the sojourn in Senegal. Interviewees, even more than questionnaire respondents, will perform constructed identities during recall, and perhaps especially when remembering experiences which have shaped their subsequent lives. Nonetheless, a comparison of questionnaires and interviews conducted a year or more later shows consistent and coherent accounts, incorporating both objective events and subjective interpretations, but little evidence of rehearsed narratives.

In reporting (an early analysis was published as Coleman & Chafer 2011), all quotations are unchanged, and all names pseudonyms. The findings reflect both changing contexts, including electronic communication mentioned earlier (Coleman & Chafer 2010) and the long-term impact on individuals' lives.

Space precludes detailed analysis here, but the shifting patterns of accommodation exemplify the variability of a complex dynamic system: most (28) shared with other foreigners, 10 began with homestay, but by the end, 8 were in homestay, 2 in a residence, 2 in their own apartment, and 4 sharing with locals. The choice of where to live often chimed with other aspects, including friendship patterns and language use.

French is an official language in Senegal, but Wolof the most widely spoken vernacular: 45% of Senegalese are Wolof native speakers, especially in Dakar and the North. Items based on the Language Contact Profile (Freed, Dewey, Segalowitz & Halter 2004) and additional items on Wolof elicited that participants used French seven days a week, for a median of four hours a day, partly thanks to their work and the unavailability of any other Lingua Franca. Both participants and home-university staff believe that resulting proficiency gains in French were greater than for students who had spent an Erasmus sojourn in France. The vast majority learnt some useful words and phrases in Wolof, and one in twelve achieved a good basic level. In general, greater progress in Wolof was linked not only to a longer stay, but also to greater social integration, moderation of outsider status, less hassle and "bumstering" (locals begging or trying to sell small items or services to Europeans), and other adaptations such as adopting local dress and public transport.

All study abroad is a gendered experience, since socially constructed gender roles change with the social, geographical, socio-economic and chronological context. In Senegal, gender interacted with ethnicity and the visibility of Europeans in sub-Saharan Africa. The UK women learnt to deal with sexual approaches and spontaneous offers of marriage; some took to wearing wedding rings and referring to non-existent husbands. Probably more difficult were the obstacles to social communication posed by gender in an Islamic society: "the girls were all kept locked away by their husbands and the guys would not understand the concept of 'friendship' and would want to marry me after a few hours", said Diane. Both men and women recognized that the former had more opportunities for turning acquaintances into friends, and were initially accorded more respect in work contexts. The fact that both males and females reported more gender-related incidents by the end of their stay may suggest that the experiences of both sexes led to a clearer understanding by sojourners of the cultural enaction of gender.

The Islamic context led all the respondents bar two already well-travelled men to reflect on religion, often for the first time. Noting (cf. Polanyi 1995) that while any faith was acceptable to local Senegalese, atheism was inconceivable, respondents reacted sometimes with respect to a pervasive and family-friendly religion, sometimes with hostility to a force of social and psychological control linked (through the *talibés*, boys forced to beg for the benefit of their *Marabout* or Islamic teacher) to systemic child abuse.

Half the graduates had experienced initial homesickness, but for some it abated or evaporated completely while for others it worsened: the individual variation could sometimes be related to ongoing contacts with home through visits, absent partners, telephone and online communication. As the concentric circles model illustrates, initially most socialized with fellow-Brits, but as other locals and non-locals typically became more important, Brits became much less so. Most made both non-local and Senegalese friends, including at least one close friend. A majority were, at the date of the questionnaire, still in touch with friends made in Dakar.

Intimate friendships were also made, although nearly half had left a partner in the UK (not all relationships lasted). One in four students (12 respondents, 2M, 10F) found non-local partners, one in five (9 respondents, 1M, 8F) Senegalese partners, and of the three language assistants one (M) a non-local partner, and one (F) a Senegalese partner. The fact that 21 of 45 who answered this question (5M, 16F) formed a new intimate relationship during their stay abroad seems likely to have influenced the linguistic, cultural, intercultural and attitudinal outcomes of the sojourn. If seen less as an indexical characteristic and more as a language learning strategy, sex perhaps deserves more attention in study abroad research.

As the UK belatedly follows North America in conceiving university study more as an investment than as an education, graduate employability is not only a *Leitmotiv* of EU language policy (e.g. European Commission 2011b) but also a key trump card in seeking to persuade Government that a student year abroad deserves support. A 2001 Residence Abroad Project questionnaire study of 1117 UK former participants in the year abroad, graduating between 1959 and 1999 (Coleman 2011), showed the importance of experiential learning abroad for subsequent employability. The same items in the Senegal study drew confirmation that the skills gained during the year abroad had been a factor in landing both first and subsequent jobs for a majority of respondents, a significant factor for up to half, and the determining factor for more than one in ten. Equally significant is the impact that the stay in Africa had on the nature of subsequent careers. All respondents without exception viewed their semester(s) abroad as a good investment, virtually all found the skills learned valuable in their employment, and more than three-quarters were in a job requiring cultural mediation. Full analysis and publication of results must await completion of the interviews, but eight out of ten viewed the stay abroad as a turning point in their lives, and the experience demonstrably had a huge impact on their subsequent trajectory in educational, geographical, personal and professional terms.

10.   Conclusion

Academic researchers are whole people too. They know that quantitative studies can be quicker and neater to conduct than qualitative or mixed-method studies, and that a reputation is more often made through theoretical innovation than reiterated empirical investigation. A career orientation quickly settles the choice between off-the-shelf quantitative tools and fuller, more qualitative investigation of the complex dynamic system which is the study abroad experience for language learners; between what is easiest and what might be most valuable. Theories come and go, i + 1 is replaced by ZPD, and the justification for particular research instruments and methods evolves too. But the data remain, and the evolving phenomenon which they seek to capture. All data contribute to describing and understanding study abroad – but whoever boosted their citations and built an academic career with mere data?

Nor can researchers today shut themselves in a cupboard labeled "SLA" and disregard the social context of their research, which is itself embedded in the complex dynamic system which is higher education funding. In introducing "impact," both economic and societal, as a criterion in compulsory national research assessment for the Research Excellence Framework 2014, the UK Funding Councils remind us that our research addresses a wider agenda than that of academic specialists. And in a world where academic mobility is both a political and an economic reality, applied research can make a real difference. The recent position statement *Valuing the Year Abroad* (British Academy & University Council of Modern Languages 2012) thus contributed to a campaign whose outcome was a capping of student fees for study abroad and the payment of fee compensation to home universities in England.

Nor must we forget that for participants, language gains are just one aspect of study abroad:

> Learning mobility – meaning transnational mobility for the purpose of acquiring new knowledge, skills and competences – is one of the important ways in which citizens can strengthen their employability, enhance their intercultural awareness, creativity and personal development, as well as participate actively in society.
>
> (European Commission 2011b, p. 6)

Understanding the study abroad phenomenon requires researchers to take into account the whole person and the whole context. "If structural and cognitive factors can be shown to account for no more than half of the documented variation in learning outcomes in the Study Abroad context", asserts Davidson (2010a, p. 4), "other individual and social variables, some of them unknown, are assumed to account for the balance."

"There can be no sensible generalizations from a variety of individual experience", argue Byram and Alred (1993, p. 59), though within a complex dynamic system we can conceive of the sum of unique study abroad experiences as sharing typical common features. As linguists and researchers, we do well to recall that study abroad language gain is embedded in real life, and that identity does not stop evolving on return from study abroad. Ema Ushioda's call with regard to motivation research applies equally well here:

A focus on real persons, rather than on learners as theoretical abstractions; a focus on the agency of the individual person as a thinking, feeling human being, with an identity, a personality, a unique history and background, a person with goals, motives and intentions; a focus on the interaction between this self-reflective intentional agent, and the fluid and complex system of social relations, activities, and multiple micro- and macro-contexts in which the person is embedded, moves, and is inherently part of.   (Ushioda 2009, p. 220)

References

Akande, Y., & Slawson, C. (2000). A case study of 50 years of study abroad alumni. *International Educator, 9(3)*, 12–16.

Allen, H.W., & Herron, C. (2003). A mixed-methodology investigation of the linguistic and affective outcomes of summer study abroad. *Foreign Language Annals, 36*, 370–385.

Allport, G.W. (1954). *The nature of prejudice*. Reading, UK: Addison-Wesley.

Alred, G., & Byram, M. (2002). Becoming an intercultural mediator: A longitudinal study of residence abroad. *Journal of Multilingual & Multicultural Development, 23*, 339–352.

Alred, G., & Byram, M. (2006). British students in France: 10 years on. In M. Byram & A. Feng (Eds.). *Living and studying abroad: Research and practice* (pp. 210–231). Clevedon, UK: Multilingual Matters.

Berry, J.W. (2005). Acculturation: Living successfully in two cultures. *International Journal of Intercultural Relations, 29*, 697–712.

Block, D. (2007). *Second language identities*. London: Continuum.

Bochner, S., McLeod, B.M., & Lin, A. (1977). Friendship patterns of overseas students: A functional model. *International Journal of Psychology, 12*, 277–294.

Bolen, M.C. (Ed.). (2008). *Guide to outcomes assessment in education abroad*. Carlisle, PA: Forum on Education Abroad.

Bray, M., Gill, H., & Randall, L. (2011). French Studies and employability at home and abroad: general reflections on a case study. In P. Lane & M. Worton (Eds.), *French Studies in and for the twenty-first century* (pp. 262–271). Liverpool: Liverpool University Press.

British Academy & University Council of Modern Languages (2012). *Valuing the year abroad. The importance of the year abroad as part of a degree programme for UK students*. London: British Academy/UCML. Retrieved from ⟨http://www.britac.ac.uk/⟩.

British Council (2005). *Breaking the barriers. 100 years of the Language Assistants Programme, 1905–2005*. London: British Council/Department for Education and Skills.

Bronfenbrenner, U. (1993). The ecology of cognitive development: research models and fugitive findings. In R.H. Wozniak & K.W. Fischer (Eds.), *Development in context: Acting and thinking in specific environments* (pp. 3–44). Hillsdale, NJ: Lawrence Erlbaum Associates.

Brown, L., & Richards, S. (2012). The British host: just how welcoming are we? *Journal of Further and Higher Education, 36*, 57–79.

Byram, M., & Alred, G. (1993), *Paid to be English. A book for English assistants and their advisers in France*. Durham, UK: University of Durham School of Education.

Carbonell, J.A. (2011). *Growing numbers in UK student mobility (from 2005–06 to 2009–10)*. London: Kingston University.

Carlson, J., Burn, B.B., Useem, J., & Yachimowicz, D. (Eds.). (1990). *Study abroad: The experience of American undergraduates.* New York, NY: Praeger.

Chirkov, V. (2009). Critical psychology of acculturation: What do we study and how do we study it, when we investigate acculturation? *International Journal of Intercultural Relations, 33,* 94–105.

Coleman, J.A. (1994). Profiling the advanced learner: The C-Test in British further and higher education. In R. Grotjahn (Ed.), *Der C-Test: Theoretische Grundlagen und praktische Anwendungen* [The C-Test: Theoretical foundations and practical applications] (Vol. 2) (pp. 217–237). Bochum: Brockmeyer.

Coleman, J.A. (1996). *Studying languages: A survey of British and European students. The proficiency, background, attitudes and motivations of students of foreign languages in the United Kingdom and Europe.* London: Centre for Information on Language Teaching and Research.

Coleman, J.A. (1997). Residence abroad within language study. *Language Teaching, 30,* 1–20.

Coleman, J.A. (2001). Residence abroad and university language learning. In H. Pürschel & U. Raatz (Eds.), *Tests and translation. Papers in memory of Christine Klein-Braley* (pp. 137–168). Bochum: AKS-Verlag.

Coleman, J.A. (2002). Translating research into disseminated good practice: The case of student residence abroad. In R. Macdonald & J. Wisdom (Eds.), *Academic and educational development: Research, evaluation and changing practice in higher education* (pp. 88–98). London: Kogan Page.

Coleman, J.A. (2003). Student voices on residence abroad. Proceedings of Setting the Agenda: Languages, Linguistics and Area Studies in Higher Education (UMIST, June 2002). Retrieved from ⟨http://www.llas.ac.uk/resources/paper/1259⟩.

Coleman, J.A. (2006a, June). Study abroad research: a new global overview, Paper delivered at the annual meeting of the American Association for Applied Linguistics/Association Canadienne de Linguistique Appliquée, Montreal.

Coleman, J.A. (2006b). English-medium teaching in European higher education, *Language Teaching, 39,* 1–14.

Coleman, J.A. (2007). A new framework for study abroad research. In C. Way, G. Soriano, D. Limon, & C. Amador (Eds.), *Enhancing the Erasmus experience: Papers on student mobility* (pp. 37–46). Granada: Atrio.

Coleman, J.A. (2009). Study abroad and SLA: Defining goals and variables. In K. Kleppin & A. Berndt (Eds.), *Sprachlehrforschung: Theorie und Empirie, Festschrift für Rüdiger Grotjahn,* (pp. 181–196). Frankfurt: Peter Lang.

Coleman, J.A. (2011). Study/work abroad and employability. Retrieved from ⟨http://www.ucml.ac.uk/sites/default/files/shapingthefuture/102/20%20-%20jim%20coleman%20inter%20resource%20template_0.pdf⟩.

Coleman, J.A., & Chafer, T. (2010). Study abroad and the Internet: Physical and virtual context in an era of expanding telecommunications. *Frontiers: The Interdisciplinary Journal of Study Abroad, 19,* 151–167.

Coleman, J.A., & Chafer, T. (2011). The experience and long-term impact of study abroad by Europeans in an African context. In F. Dervin (Ed.), *Analysing the consequences of academic mobility* (pp. 67–94). Newcastle upon Tyne: Cambridge Scholars.

Coleman, J.A., & Parker, L. (2001). Preparing for residence abroad: Staff development implications. In J. Klapper (Ed.) *Teaching languages in higher education: Issues in training and continuing professional development* (pp. 134–162). London: CILT.

Collentine, J. (2004). The effects of learning contexts on morphosyntactic and lexical development. *Studies in Second Language Acquisition, 26,* 227–248.

Collentine, J., & Freed, B.F. (2004). Learning context and its effects on second language acquisition. *Studies in Second Language Acquisition, 26,* 153–171.

Davidson, D.E. (2010a). Guest editor's message. *Foreign Language Annals, 43,* 3–5.

Davidson, D.E. (2010b). Study abroad: when, how, and with what results: New data from the Russian Front. *Foreign Language Annals, 43,* 6–26.

de Federico de la Rúa, A. (2003). *Réseaux d'identification à l'Europe. Amitiés et identités d'étudiants européens* [Networks of identification with Europe : The friendships and identities of European students]. Unpublished Ph.D. thesis, Université des Sciences et Technologies de Lille/Universidad Pública de Navarra.

de Federico de la Rúa, A. (2008). How do Erasmus students make friends? In S. Ehrenreich, G. Woodman, & M. Perrefort (Eds.), *Auslandaufenthalte in Schule und Studium: Bestandaufnahmen aus Forschung und Praxis* [Study abroad in school and higher education: Taking stock from research and practice] (pp. 89–103). Münster: Waxmann.

Deardorff, D.K. (2006). Identification and assessment of intercultural competence as a student outcome of internationalization. *Journal of Studies in International Education, 10,* 241–266.

DeKeyser, R. (2007). Study abroad as foreign language practice. In R. DeKeyser (Ed.), *Practicing in a second language: Perspectives from applied linguistics and cognitive psychology* (pp. 208–226). New York, NY: Cambridge University Press.

Dervin, F. (2008). *Métamorphoses identitaires en situation de mobilité* [Identity metamorphoses in situations of mobility]. Turku: Turku Yliopisto.

Dervin, F. (Ed.). (2011). *Analysing the consequences of academic mobility and migration.* Newcastle upon Tyne: Cambridge Scholars.

Ding, L., & Li, H. (2012). Social networks and study abroad — The case of Chinese visiting students in the US. *China Economic Review, 23,* 580–589.

Doble, G., & Griffiths, B. (Eds.). (1985). *Oral skills in the modern languages degree.* London: CILT.

Dörnyei, Z. (2005). *The psychology of the language learner.* Mahwah, NJ: Lawrence Erlbaum Associates.

Dufon, M.A., & Churchill, E. (Eds.). (2006). *Language learners in study abroad contexts.* Clevedon, UK: Multilingual Matters.

Dunbar, R. (2010). *How many friends does one person need? Dunbar's number and other evolutionary quirks.* London: Faber & Faber.

Dwyer, M. (2004). Charting the impact of studying abroad. *International Educator, 13*(1), 14–17.

Ehrenreich, S. (2004). *Auslandsaufenthalt und Fremdsprachenlehrerbildung* [Study abroad and foreign language teacher education]. Munich: Langenscheidt (Münchener Arbeiten zur Fremdsprachen-Forschung, Band 10).

Engle, L., & Engle, J. (2003). Study abroad levels: towards a classification of program types. *Frontiers: The Interdisciplinary Journal of Study Abroad, 10,* 1–20.

European Commission (2011a). *Erasmus for all: The EU programme for education, training, youth and sport.* Retrieved from ⟨http://ec.europa.eu/education/erasmus-for-all/doc/com_en.pdf⟩.

European Commission (2011b). *Note 16744/11* (Draft conclusions on language competences to enhance mobility, November 2011). Retrieved from ⟨http://register.consilium.europa.eu/pdf/en/11/st16/st16744.en11.pdf⟩.

Freed, B.F. (Ed.). (1998). *Language learning in a study abroad context.* Special Issue of *Frontiers: The Interdisciplinary Journal of Study Abroad.*

Freed, B.F., Dewey, D.P., Segalowitz, N., & Halter, R. (2004). The Language Contact Profile. *Studies in Second Language Acquisition, 26,* 349–356.

Gunterman, G. (1995). The Peace Corps experience: Language learning in training and in the field. In B.F. Freed (Ed.), *Second language acquisition in a study abroad context* (pp. 149–170). Amsterdam: John Benjamins.

Herring, S. (2007), A faceted classification scheme for computer-mediated discourse. *Language@internet, 4.* Retrieved from ⟨http://www.languageatinternet.de/articles/2007/761⟩.

Hoffman-Hicks, S. (2000). *The longitudinal development of French foreign language pragmatic competence: evidence from study abroad.* Unpublished Ph.D. thesis, Indiana University, Bloomington.

Howard, M. (2001). The effects of study abroad on the L2 learner's structural skills: Evidence from advanced learners of French. *EUROSLA Yearbook, 1,* 123–141.

Huebner, T. (1998). Methodological considerations in data collection for language learning in a study abroad context. *Frontiers: The Interdisciplinary Journal of Study Abroad, 4,* 1–30.

Isabelli-García, C. (2006), Study abroad social networks, motivation and attitudes: Implications for second language acquisition. In M. Dufon & E. Churchill (Eds.), *Language learners in study abroad contexts* (pp. 231–258). Clevedon: Multilingual Matters.

Jackson, J. (2008). *Language, identity, and study abroad: Sociocultural perspectives.* London: Equinox.

Johnston, B., Mitchell, R., Ford, P., & Myles, F. (2011). *Developing student criticality in higher education.* London: Continuum.

King, R., Findlay, A., & Ahrens, J. (2010). *International student mobility literature review.* Bristol: HEFCE/British Council.

Kinginger, C. (2008). *Language learning in study abroad: Case studies of Americans in France.* Modern Language Journal, 92, Monograph.

Kinginger, C. (2009). *Language learning and study abroad: A critical reading of research.* Basingstoke: Palgrave Macmillan.

Klapisch, C. (Director) (2002). *L'auberge espagnole* [film]. France/Spain: BAC Films, Ce Qui Me Meut, France 2 Cinéma, Mate Producciones S.A., Studio Canal, Via Digital.

Kramsch, C. (1995, April). The privilege of the non-native speaker. Paper presented at the meeting of the Teachers of English to Speakers of Other Languages, Long Beach, California.

Kramsch, C. (2009). *The multilingual subject.* Oxford: Oxford University Press.

Larsen-Freeman, D. (2011). Complex, dynamic systems: A new transdisciplinary theme for applied linguistics? *Language Teaching, 45,* 202–214.

Larsen-Freeman, D., & Cameron, L. (2008). *Complex systems and applied linguistics.* Oxford: Oxford University Press.

McKeown, J. (2009). *The first time effect. The impact of study abroad on college student intellectual development.* New York, NY: State University of New York Press.

Magnan, S., & Back, M. (2007). Social interaction and linguistic gain during study abroad. *Foreign Language Annals, 40,* 43–61.

Meier, G., & Daniels, H. (2011). 'Just not being able to make friends': social interaction during the year abroad in modern foreign language degrees. *Research Papers in Education* iFirst article. Retrieved from ⟨http://dx.doi.org/10.1080/02671552.2011.629734⟩.

Mercer, S. (2011). Understanding learner agency as a complex dynamic system. *System, 39,* 427–436.

Murphy-Lejeune, E. (2002), *Student mobility and narrative in Europe: The new strangers.* London: Routledge.

Nye, J. (2005). *Soft power and higher education.* Forum for the Future of Higher Education. Retrieved from ⟨http://net.educause.edu/ir/library/pdf/FFP0502S.pdf⟩.

OECD. (2011), *Education at a glance 2011: OECD indicators.* OECD Publishing. Retrieved from ⟨http://dx.doi.org/10.1787/eag-2011-en⟩.

Opper, S., Teichler, U., & Carlson, J. (1990). *Impact of study abroad programmes on students and graduates.* London: Jessica Kingsley.

Orr, D., Schnitzer, K., & Frackmann, E. (2008). *Social and economic conditions of student life in Europe.* Bielefeld: Bertelsmann Verlag.

Papatsiba, V. (2003), *Des étudiants européens "Erasmus" et l'aventure de l'altérité* [On European "Erasmus" students and the adventure of otherness]. Bern: Peter Lang.

Parey, M., & Waldinger, F. (2007). *Studying abroad and the effect on international labor market mobility: Evidence from the introduction of ERASMUS.* London: Centre for the Economics of Education, LSE.

Pellegrino Aveni, V. (2005). *Study abroad and second language use. Constructing the self.* Cambridge: Cambridge University Press.

Polanyi, L. (1995). Language learning and living abroad: Stories from the field. In B.F. Freed (Ed.), *Second language acquisition in a study abroad context* (pp. 271–292). Amsterdam: John Benjamins.

Richters, E., & Teichler, U. (2006). Student mobility data: current methodological issues and future prospects. In M. Kelo, U. Teichler, & B. Wächter, (Eds.), *EURODATA: Student mobility in European higher education* (pp. 78–95). Bonn: Lemmens.

Rivers, W.P. (1998). Is being there enough? The effects of homestay placements on language gain during study abroad. *Foreign Language Annals, 31,* 492–500.

Rubio, F. (2003). Structure and complexity of oral narratives in Advanced-Level Spanish: A comparison of three learning backgrounds. *Foreign Language Annals, 36,* 546–554.

Sade, L.A. (2011). Emerging selves, language learning and motivation through the lens of chaos. In G. Murray, X. Gao, & T. Lamb (Eds.), *Identity, motivation and autonomy in language learning* (pp. 42–56). Bristol: Multilingual Matters.

Schauer, G.A. (2007). Finding the right words in the study abroad context: The development of German learners' use of external modifiers in English. *Intercultural Pragmatics, 4,* 193–220.

Schauer, G.A. (2009). *Interlanguage pragmatic development: The study abroad context.* London: Continuum.

Schumann, J.H. (1986). Research on the Acculturation Model for second language acquisition. *Journal of Multilingual and Multicultural Development, 7,* 379–392.

Segalowitz, N., & Freed, B. (2004). Context, contact, and cognition in oral fluency acquisition: Learning Spanish in at home and study abroad contexts. *Studies in Second Language Acquisition, 26,* 173–199.

Sussex Centre for Migration Research (2004). *International student mobility.* Bristol: HEFCE. Retrieved from ⟨http://www.hefce.ac.uk/pubs/hefce/2004/04_30/⟩.

Teichler, U. (1991). *Experences of ERASMUS students. Select findings of the 1988/89 survey.* Kassel: Gesamthochschule Kassel.

Teichler, U. (1997). *The ERASMUS Experience. Major findings of the ERASMUS Evaluation Research.* Luxembourg: Office for Official Publications of the European Communities.

Teichler, U., Ferencz, I., & Wächter, B. (Eds.). (2011). *Mapping mobility in European higher education. A study produced for the Directorate General for Education and Culture (DG EAC) of the European Commission.* Brussels: European Commission.

Towell, R., Hawkins, R., & Bazergui, N. (1996). The development of fluency in advanced learners of French. *Applied Linguistics, 17*, 84–119.

University Council of Modern Languages (2011). *Study/Work abroad and employability.* Retrieved from ⟨http://www.ucml.ac.uk/sites/default/files/shapingthefuture/102/20%20 -%20jim%20coleman%20inter%20resource%20template_0.pdf⟩.

Ushioda, E. (2009). A person-in-context relational view of emergent motivation, self and identity. In Z. Dörnyei & E. Ushioda (Eds.), *Motivation, language identity and the L2 self* (pp. 215–228). Bristol: Multilingual Matters.

van Lier, L. (2003). A table of two computer classrooms: The ecology of project-based language learning. In J. Leather & J. van Dam (Eds.), *Ecology of Language Acquisition* (pp. 49–63). Dordrecht: Kluwer.

van Lier, L. (2005). Case study. In E. Hinkel (Ed.), *Handbook of research in language teaching and learning* (pp.195–208). Mahwah, NJ: Lawrence Erlbaum Associates.

Wang, C. (2010). Toward a second language socialization perspective: Issues in study abroad research. *Foreign Language Annals, 43*, 50–63.

Ward, C., & Kennedy, A. (1999). The measurement of sociocultural adaptation. *International Journal of Intercultural Relations, 23*, 659–677.

White, C.J. (1999). Expectations and emergent beliefs of self-instructed language learners. *System, 27*, 443–457.

White, C.J. (2003). *Language learning in distance education.* Cambridge: Cambridge University Press.

Wilkinson, R. (2012). English-medium instruction at a Dutch university: Challenges and pitfalls. In A. Doiz, D. Lasagabaster, & J. M. Sierra (Eds.), *English-medium instruction at university worldwide: Challenges and ways forward.* Bristol: Multilingual Matters.

Wilkinson, S. (1998). On the nature of immersion during study abroad: some participants' perspectives. *Frontiers: The Interdisciplinary Journal of Study Abroad, 4*, 121–138.

Willis, F.M., Doble, G., Sankarayya, U., & Smithers, A. (1977). *Residence abroad and the student of modern languages: A preliminary survey.* Bradford: University of Bradford, Modern Languages Centre.

Wilson, J.C., & Everett, W.E. (1989). *An invitation to the study of French.* Oxford: Blackwell.

Appendix 1. Twenty parameters for study abroad research (Coleman, 2009: 183).

	Parameter or category	Parameter settings (or variables within the category)					
1	Academic context	Within-program(me)			Whole-program(me)		
2	Learning outcomes	Academic	Cultural	Intercultural	Linguistic	Personal	Professional
3	Age	Secondary education (teenagers)		Higher education (young adults)		Adults (all ages)	
4	Program(me) at home institution	Specialist language degree	Other specialism or modular degree		Postgraduate		Teacher training
5	Previous language learning	Continuum from very little to ten years or more					
6	Proficiency prior to departure	Continuum from beginner through elementary, intermediate, advanced; CEFR A1 to C1					
7	Preparation	Integrated to previous study for a year or more	Program(me)		Briefing(s)	None	
8	Duration	Two to six weeks	Below one semester	One semester (including summer semester)	One year or two semesters	Full degree program(me)	
9	Outgoing/incoming group	Large and coherent		Small, informal		Individual	
10	L1	X shared by all participants		Mixed but predominantly X		Mixed	
11	L2	English in L1-English host country		English in non-L1-English host country	Other international lingua franca	Other language	
12	Accommodation	Homestay	University residence with other foreign students	University residence (integrated)		School (for assistants)	Individually arranged
13	Accommodation shared by	Only locals		Only other L1-speakers		Other L1-speakers but in a local family	Other foreigners

(Continued)

Appendix 1. Twenty parameters for study abroad research (Coleman, 2009: 183). (Continued)

	Parameter or category	Parameter settings (or variables within the category)				
14	Program(me) of non-language courses followed	For the group alone	For foreigners only	Principally for locals (options selected by home institution)	Principally for locals but options selected by student	None
15	Program(me) of language courses followed	For the group alone	For foreigners only	For both locals and foreigners (e.g. translation)	None	
16	Program(me) taught by	Home institution staff	Host institution staff		Mixture	
17	Program(me) taught in	L2	Lingua franca (usually English)		Mixture	
18	Professional content	Work placement	Teaching / assistantship	Volunteering	None	
19	Institutional support	Bilateral	International office	Home institution only (island model)		None ('free mover', 'spontaneous mobility')
20	Assessment	By home institution	By host institution	By host but 'interpreted'		

PART II

Qualitative and case studies

Self-regulatory strategies of foreign language learners

From the classroom to study abroad and beyond

Heather Willis Allen
University of Wisconsin

Motivation plays an important role in foreign language (FL) learning outcomes, academic performance, and student persistence in language study. Success depends not only on learners possessing motivation from within; they must also see themselves as agents of processes shaping their motivation. Taking an activity theory perspective, this study traces the development of self-regulatory strategies (Dörnyei 2001), i.e *motivation maintenance strategies*, *goal-setting strategies*, and *language-learning strategies* of three U.S. college students of French over several years, including a six-week sojourn in France. Findings point to the value of reflective narrative data as a tool to support FL learners' self regulation and to the need for new forms of motivational scaffolding to assist students both in and out of the classroom.

1. Introduction

Motivation plays an important role in foreign language (FL) learning outcomes, academic performance, and student persistence. However, its precise influence on FL learners' study abroad (SA) experiences is far from evident. For example, although it might be assumed that students who participate in SA are the most motivated of learners, research has shown in certain cases that prior to sojourns overseas, SA participants have language-learning motivation levels comparable to those of to non-SA peers (Allen & Herron 2003; Hernandez 2010).[1] In addition, research has yet to determine whether motivational factors predict language use or linguistic gain during SA, with some studies (Hernandez 2010; Isabelli-García

---

1. As one reviewer pointed out, such research on the motivational tendencies of FL learners planning to participate in SA versus FL learner peers who do not study abroad is limited and has relied for the most part on survey instruments inspired by the Gardnerian notion of integrative motivation. Thus, comparison of other motivational components for SA versus non-SA participants remains largely unexplored.

2006; Yashima, Zenuk-Nishide & Shimizu 2004) supporting this claim and others (Freed 1990; Martinsen 2010) contesting it. Thus, students' unwillingness to use the FL or their lack of success in doing so during SA may not be attributable to motivational deficiencies alone.

Another question is whether SA enhances students' ongoing motivation to learn or use a FL, and, once again, existing research is inconclusive. For instance, whereas Ingram (2005) and Lewis and Niesenbaum (2005) concluded that even a short-term SA program can enhance students' motivation to continue FL study or travel abroad, Allen and Herron (2003) found no change in students' motivation or attitudes related to FL study or the host culture after short-term SA. Qualitative and mixed-methods studies (e.g. Allen 2010b; DeKeyser 2010; Kinginger 2004; Wilkinson 1998) in particular have revealed the role of cognitive, cultural, and social factors in mediating SA participants' motivation and language use during SA. Great variability exists in students' motivational trajectories following SA, even for students within the same SA cohort with similar initial linguistic proficiency. Findings from these studies support a view of motivation as a *dynamic* element based on factors both internal to individual learners, such as self-regulatory strategies and linguistic knowledge, and external to learners, such as learners' social networks in the host community. As Ushioda (2008) explained, "[G]ood language learning is never simply in the hands of the motivated learner … Good language learning and motivation are in this sense socially constructed or constrained, rather than simply influenced, positively or negatively, by the social context" (p. 25).

Regrettably, empirical studies embracing this view of language-learning motivation are "surprisingly few in number" (Ushioda 2008, p. 29) as are studies of the ways in which FL learners develop motivational self-regulation skills (Van Lier 2008). Further, as Ushioda claimed, "Good language learners have much to teach us about motivation" (p. 29). This statement is particularly relevant for SA research, as there is much to learn about how good language learners navigate the transitions from the home classroom to SA and back again and how their motivational trajectories evolve during these transitions.

The current study addresses these gaps in existing research and explores how three "good language learners" developed motivational self-regulation strategies during and after SA. Two research questions were addressed:

1. What motivational self-regulation strategies did the participants display during SA in relation to their stated language-learning goals?
2. Were the participants able to maintain their language-learning motivation following SA and, if so, what ongoing self-regulation strategies did they use?

Because research shows that motivation tends to drop off as the cognitive burden of learning increases (Bernaus, Moore & Avezedo 2007; Williams 2004), this study examines the cases of three FL learners with long histories of language study and advanced proficiency levels. In this regard, participants were unique insomuch that, until SA, they sustained their language-learning motivation over an average of seven years, opting to persist despite having met their university's language requirement through high-school level credit. In the following section, a brief history of language-learning motivation research is provided along with an explanation of this study's theoretical perspective.

2. Background

Despite a general consensus that motivation is a critical element in FL study, researchers disagree as to what motivation is, what factors affect it, and how motivational processes function (Ushioda 2008). From the late 1950s until the 1990s, a social psychological perspective on language-learning motivation was dominant and concentrated on two orientations – an *integrative* one, or identification with and willingness to adopt behavioral features of another linguistic community, and an *instrumental* one, with emphasis on the practical value of language learning (Gardner 1985). However, beginning in the 1990s, criticisms of this perspective emerged. For example, Dörnyei (2001) pointed out an increasing gap between the prevailing social psychological view and theories of motivation from education and psychology, calling for increased convergence of these approaches. Researchers involved in this shift highlighted two elements not given full consideration in previous research: students' own perceptions of their abilities, performances, and possibilities, and the language-learning context (Mills, Pajares & Herron 2007; Ushioda 2008).

   In relation to the first element, researchers began focusing on how FL students' engagement in learning is shaped by their patterns of thinking, drawing on attribution theory, personality trait psychology, self-determination theory, and social cognitive theory (Dörnyei 2003, 2009b). For example, numerous researchers have investigated *intrinsic* (i.e. learning something as an end in itself) and *extrinsic* (i.e. learning something as a means to something else) motivations. According to Ushioda (2008), both motivations are valuable, but the critical factor lies in whether they are internalized and self-determined or externally imposed and regulated by others. Another strand of research, seeking to reinterpret the concept of integrative motivation, has investigated the notions of the *ideal L2 self*, i.e. one's imagined ideal language self image, and the *ought-to L2 self*, i.e. the envisioned attributes that learners imagine they should possess to meet expectations and avoid possible negative consequences (Dörnyei 2009b).

   The concept of *self-regulation*, or the processes by which learners activate and sustain cognition, behavior, and motivation, was relatively absent from language-learning research until the late 1990s and remains poorly represented (Ushioda 2008). Of the three types of self-regulatory strategies identified by Dörnyei (2001), *motivation maintenance, goal setting,* and *language-learning strategies,* only the last has received significant attention (Mills, Pajares & Herron 2007). Yet, as researchers in educational psychology have shifted their interest toward self-regulation over the past decade, language-learning researchers began exploring related constructs including *perceived competence, willingness to communicate,* and *self-efficacy.* The common thread among these constructs is the notion that learners need more than motivation from within, they must also see themselves as agents of the processes shaping their motivation to avoid falling into patterns of negative thinking and self-perceptions with detrimental consequences (Ushioda 2008).

Concerning the second element, the role of the learning context in mediating motivation, its current place in language-learning research reflects a broader trend of applied linguists' recent interest in the interrelationships among language learners, the language of study or use, the immediate learning environment, and the broader sociocultural context (Dörnyei 2009a). In reviewing research on individual differences and FL learning, Dörnyei (2005) named as the most significant emerging theme the situated nature of learner characteristics and dynamic conceptualizations "in which [individual difference] factors enter into some interaction with the situational parameters rather than cutting across tasks and environments" (p. 218). Yet, despite this recognition of the dynamic, socially mediated nature of motivation, the challenge of finding an integrated theoretical framework adequate to investigate learners' internal psychological and linguistic processes as well as contextual forces shaping motivation remains. Dörnyei (2001) called this a central issue:

> Meeting this challenge requires more than simply adding a few situational factors to existing theories … it necessitates the *combination* of the individualistic and the societal perspectives. We need to introduce sufficiently dynamic concepts that can bridge the gap between the two perspectives, while simultaneously doing both aspects justice (p. 16).

This study attempted to account for both perspectives by adopting a sociocultural perspective. In the following section, this orientation is described.

3. A sociocultural theoretical perspective on self-regulation and language-learning motivation

Vygotskian cultural-historical psychology (Vygotsky 1978), often called sociocultural theory in language-learning research, is a theory of mind "that recognizes the central role that social relationships and culturally constructed artifacts play in organizing uniquely human forms of thinking" (Lantolf 2004, pp. 30–31). *Mediation* is an essential concept in sociocultural theory, meaning that humans' relationships to the world are established using physical and psychological tools, with language as the primary tool for directing and controlling behavior and relating to the world (Lantolf & Appel 1994). *Learning*, from this perspective, is first other-regulated by a more competent interlocutor (e.g. a parent or teacher) with the goal that the learner will eventually appropriate regulatory means and assume an agentic role in learning, leading to the capacity for independent problem solving, i.e. self-regulation (Lantolf 2000). However, as Newman (2003) pointed out, a permanent progression from other- to self-regulation does not occur; rather, occasions will arise when the self-regulated learner will take the initiative to seek out other-regulation, or the assistance of more knowledgeable others.

The role of affect, including motivation, in cognition and learning was little explored in Vygotsky's empirical research, and the motivational dimension of sociocultural theory remains relatively under-theorized, as researchers have concentrated more on cognitive aspects of the theory (Wertsch 1985; Ushioda 2007). Nonetheless, the interrelatedness of affect and cognition was clearly posited in the following statements by Vygotsky in *Thought and Language*:

> Thought is not begotten by thought; it is engendered by motivation, i.e. by our desires and needs, our interests and emotions. Behind every thought there is an affective-volitional tendency, which holds the answer to the last 'why' in the analysis of thinking. A true and full understanding of another's thought is possible only when we understand its affective-volitional basis.   (1986, p. 252)

In addition to affirming the role of affective processes in generating cognition, Vygotsky further specified that affective processes were not static but "nomadic," meaning that they change over time as they interact with other internal and external processes (1987, p. 334).

A more complete conceptualization of motivation was developed in *activity theory* (Engeström 1999; Leont'ev, 1981), which unifies various concepts from sociocultural theory and explicitly focuses on the motivational dimension of human activities. Activity theory holds that human activities are motivated by specific biological or culturally constructed *needs*. A need becomes a *motive* once directed at an *object* (the activity's focus or orientation), giving direction to the activity (Engeström 1999). Motives, or the cultural-psychological-institutional impetus guiding activity toward an object, are considered inherently unstable and gain or lose power depending on the conditions, content, and course of activity (Lompscher 1999). Activities are instantiated concretely as goal-oriented actions, and *goals*, in contrast with motives, have clear start and end points and relate to specific actions (Engeström 1999). Thus, goals have a regulatory function in activity and, like motives, are unstable as they are modified, postponed and even abandoned (Lantolf 2000).

From an activity theory perspective, *motivation* results from the alignment of a motive and goal with a sense of participation in a new *community of practice* and is contingent on the learner positing his or her own goals for learning (Lave & Wenger 1991; Markova 1990). This conception of how motivational factors interrelate foregrounds learner *agency*, which links motivation to action, and is viewed as a co-constructed phenomenon, constantly renegotiated with those around the individual in the learning environment (Lantolf & Pavlenko 2001). Kim (2007), who explored the development of English-learning motivation for Korean immigrants to Canada, explained: "For example, if tension exists between an L2 learner and her L2 community, such as a homestay family or an ESL class, her motive to learn the L2 may not be transformed into a motivation" (p. 39). Supporting this statement, past SA research taking an activity theory perspective has demonstrated that participants' language-learning motivation is mediated by their beliefs about language learning, struggles in adapting to classroom learning abroad, and challenges in accessing social networks abroad (Allen 2010a, 2010b; Douglass 2007; Kinginger 2004, 2008).

Several concepts from sociocultural and activity theories were explored in the current study of the self-regulation strategies and motivational trajectories of three FL learners during and after SA. Those concepts included *self-regulation* in relation to *motives* and *goals*, learner *agency*, learner participation in a *community of practice*, and language-learning *motivation*. The following section describes the design of the study.

4.   Study design

4.1   Participants and their SA program

Three undergraduate students participated in this study – Adam, Rebecca, and Taylor (all pseudonyms) – selected from a larger group of participants in a six-week SA program in Summer 2006 (see Table 1). At the study's onset, the participants were in their third year of study at a public U.S. university in a Mid-Atlantic state; all were U.S. citizens who spoke English as their first language. Further, each had a long history of French study and intended to major in French. Their cumulative grade point averages ranged from 3.3 to 3.7 out of 4.0 points, meaning that all had a strong academic record. During the term before SA, the participants were enrolled in third-year French courses such as Advanced Written French and

Introduction to French Civilization. Each had limited international travel experience, having traveled to just one country outside the U.S., although Adam had spent five weeks in France the summer prior to SA. A final commonality shared by the participants was that all stated that they had voluntary contact with French prior to SA, distinguishing them from many of their SA peers.

Table 1. Participant profiles

Pseudonym/ Gender	Age	Academic Level	GPA	Field(s) of Specialization	French Study
Adam/M	20	Junior	3.7	French, Political Science	4 years, high school 1.5 years, college
Rebecca/F	19	Junior	3.3	French, Psychology	2 years, middle school 4 years, high school 2 years, college
Taylor/M	20	Junior	3.3	French, Psychology	1 year, middle school 4 years, high school 2 years, college

The SA program in Nantes, France, was organized by the participants' home university, and students were taught by a U.S. faculty member and two native-speaking university professors of French based in Nantes. Advanced students in the program, including the study participants, completed three courses abroad – French Art History, Advanced French Culture and Conversation, and Creative Writing in French. Per program rules, students were obliged to use French to communicate during class, attend weekly cultural activities organized by the program assistant, and spend free time in the academic facility. Thus, immersion in the French language was a key element of the SA program although no explicit effort was made to teach motivational self-regulation strategies to students in their academic courses or co-curricular cultural activities. Students lived with French homestay families (one U.S. student per family) who provided a private bedroom and daily meals. Among the participants, Adam lived with a married couple and their 16-year old son, Rebecca lived with an unmarried couple and their three adolescent children (ages 12, 17, and 18), and Taylor lived with a married couple and their 19-year old daughter.

4.2   Data collection and analysis

Data from multiple sources were collected to gain a sense of the participants' self-regulatory strategies and motivational trajectories during and after SA and to understand the meanings of their actions from their own perspective. Because past SA research has shown that narratives enable a focus on personal aspects of language learning, blogs were the primary data source, serving as a means to follow the development of the participants' language-learning motivation over time. As part of their writing course, students completed ten blog entries that were assessed by the instructor only for task completion, composing them in English or French or a mix of both languages.[2] Among this study's participants, Adam blogged mostly in French and Rebecca and Taylor mixed both languages (i.e. one entry in English, the next in French). Blog prompts related to French learning and use outside the classroom, how linguistic motivations evolved, and how linguistic goals were pursued during SA. In addition, three semi-structured interviews conducted in English, recorded, and transcribed verbatim took place a month before SA, during SA's final week, and three years after SA.

Secondary data sources included questionnaires administered before SA and during the program's final week. The pre-SA questionnaire was comprised of a Language-Learning History and Language Contact Profile adapted from Allen and Herron (2003). The post-SA questionnaire contained the Language Contact Profile and 18 SA Impact questions in response to which participants indicated how SA had influenced their FL and cultural learning and their level of satisfaction with their learning. Other secondary data were learner narratives from program application essays and e-mail correspondence between the researcher and participants over a period of four years, beginning in the summer of the SA program, wherein participants provided updated accounts of their current studies or employment and ongoing contact with French.

In relation to this study's data analysis, themes from blogs, interviews, program application essays, and email correspondence related to the research questions and theoretical perspective framing the study were identified using inductive techniques and coded using a qualitative software program. After initial coding categories were established, these were clustered into broader categories containing multiple subcategories. This process was recursive and led to multiple codings.

Several strategies were used for verification of emergent analysis. Data were collected over a four-year period including the six-week SA program wherein the researcher, serving as program director, interacted with participants several times weekly, allowing establishment of trust. Multiple data types were used to establish a confluence of evidence, and, conversely, the researcher searched for negative case evidence by looking for disconfirming data. Member checks took

---

2. Blog data that appears in this chapter are cited exactly as participants posted them, meaning punctuation, capitalization, and spelling have not been changed.

place as participants re-read and commented on blogs and interview transcripts, offering corrections or commentary. Even so, readers of this study should note that data analysis was based on participants' *representations* of their experiences rather than on observations or measurements of behaviors or learning outcomes. Transferability of this study's implications should therefore be interpreted by readers themselves, as the study's findings may not be generalizable to other student populations, settings, and program types.

5.   Findings

In the following pages, findings regarding the participants' self-regulatory strategies (Research Question 1) and their motivational trajectories (Research Question 2) are summarized. Blog data appears exactly as written by participants with researcher translations provided for postings originally written in French.

5.1   Adam

5.1.1   *Pre-study abroad*

The semester before SA, Adam described his motives for learning French as attaining fluency and "pursu[ing] a career in foreign service [requiring] me to not only communicate with the French people but to better *understand* them" (SA application essay). Given these interests, Adam also took college courses in other languages, eventually earning a certificate in Russian and East European Studies to complement his French and Political Science majors. He described his ongoing passion for French in a pre-SA interview as follows: "[A]ll throughout high school I loved French… I always liked the idea of being able to use different languages and travel … I dreamed of working in France after high school or university."

During the summer after Adam's freshman year in college, his father arranged an internship for him in a French affiliate of his own company. Adam called his one-month stay in Valence, a southern French town, "very hard," as he did full-time factory work and lived with a French family who spoke little English. Although he enjoyed spending time with the family's 20-year old son in particular, he found interactions with French youth frustrating given their speech was "fast and colloquial and I didn't understand too much of it … I'd just listen to them speak" (pre-SA interview).

Instead of leading to linguistic demotivation, Adam's struggle to participate in conversations in France drove him to enroll in SA in Summer 2006, where, as he explained in a pre-SA interview, he planned to pursue goals to "greatly improve my speaking ability," "have [French people] understand me," and "communicate with someone my age." Further, he expressed a strong belief in the value of immersion for FL learning, stating:

> [I]f you are forced to speak French constantly, then eventually you don't really have any choice but to think in French. When I was there last summer, sometimes I'd be lying in bed and if I had a thought in English, I couldn't help it, it would be translated to French.   (4/14/2006)

Consistent with those experiences, Adam sought out French contact in the U.S., including occasional conversations with friends from his French classes, occasional letter exchanges with the family from Valence, and "practice translating my thoughts or daily speech into French" (pre-SA questionnaire). In this regard, he employed various language-learning strategies, demonstrating a sense of participation in a French community of practice that went beyond the requirements of his French coursework.

5.1.2   *Study abroad*

Once in France, Adam wrote about challenges to pursuing his linguistic goals and strategies that he was using:

> Je dois surmonter mes tendances timides … la partie plus difficile … c'est le point ou je casse la conversation courante pour ajouter mes idees … Mais *ces situations de disconfort sont vraiment le moyen d'amelioration et je crois qu'ils aident mes abilites.* Hier soir pendant diner, *j'aurais ete parfaitment content* de seulement manger mon diner en silence, boire de l'eau, puis lire mon roman dehors. *Mais,* sans etant brusque, j'ai interrompte les conversations pour extriquer une clarification ou d'ajouter mes idees.

> [I have to overcome my shy tendencies … the most difficult part … is the point when I interrupt the flow of conversation to add my ideas … But *these uncomfortable situations are really the means of improvement and I believe they help my abilities.* Last night during dinner, *I would have been perfectly content* to just eat my dinner in silence, drink water, then read my novel outside. *But,* without being rude, I interrupted the conversations to [ask for] a clarification or to add my ideas.]   (Blog, SA Week 2, 5/30/2006, my emphases)

Adam's comments above illustrate how he used blogging as a means of motivation maintenance, as he reinforced for himself that "uncomfortable situations" were a "means of improvement" that "help [his] abilities." Further, he recalled the sorts of actions that he carried out, i.e. asking for clarifications and adding his own ideas, as means of pursuing his linguistic goals.

By Adam's second week in France, he began to feel that being part of a SA cohort was constraining his linguistic progress, writing that it was hard to learn French in France through talking with other Americans. He was dismayed that

"L'annee derniere, j'ai commence a penser en francais apres y etre une semaine. Ici, ce proces est plus lent parce que je ne suis pas oblige de m'integrer avec les francais TOUT LE TEMP. [Last year, I started to think in French after being there a week. Here, this process is slower because I'm not required to integrate into the French community ALL THE TIME.]

By the midpoint of SA, Adam called himself satisfied with his linguistic progress, describing specific actions that he carried out in relation to his linguistic goals:

> [C]'est facile a dit rien, de rester seul et silent, mais *pour avancer il exige un effort* ... Au marche Talensac, j'ai approche les marchardes pour faire de la conversation. J'ai achete un poir pour que j'ai pu parler avec la vendeuse au sujet de leur ferme. Donc c'est le vouloir que je apprends surtout ...

> [It's easy to say nothing, to stay alone and silent, but *to progress it necessitates effort* ... At the Talensac market, I approached the sellers to make conversation. I bought a pear so that I could talk with the salesgirl about their farm. So it's the willingness that I'm learning above all ...]   (Blog 6/5/2006, my emphasis)

Despite his continued use of productive self-regulatory strategies, Adam did experience some linguistic demotivation, as illustrated by a Week Four blog entry on his "paresse" [laziness] and "mon attitude, qui devient pire, il apparatrait" [my attitude, which is worsening, it would appear.] On the one hand, he stated that "il n'y a pas de situations dans lesquelles je me sent mal a l'aise ... sauf parler avec les jeunes, je pense que n'ai pas besoin d'assistance en France" [there aren't any situations in which I feel uneasy.... except for talking with young people, I think that I don't need help in France.] However, his focus on language development was waning due to two factors: lack of interest in his classes, particularly the art history course, for which he had received poor grades that week, and an inability to socialize as much as he wanted with his host family's 16-year old son given their age difference. The latter was exacerbated by his frustration with the SA cohort, which Adam described as "aggravant" [aggravating] due to group dynamics that he stated "me rapport du lycee" [remind me of high school.]

During his final weekend of SA, Adam regained some of his linguistic motivation by traveling to see his former host family in Valence. In his blog, he described the visit:

> I was very comfortable. I remember last year, there was a constant dread of misunderstanding because EVERYTHING was harder to do ... But when I went out with [the teenage son] and his friends, I found myself following conversations and understanding questions much better. I could do more than just reply and nod my head ... and that's the key right there, just knowing what people are saying to you, then you can, if you try, communicate any idea you have.   (6/26/2006)

He further outlined specific strategies that he learned to use during SA that made him feel comfortable interacting with French people his age, including slowing down rather than "imitating the french by speaking way too fast," relaxing rather than "scrambl[ing] the idea," and "trying not to just translate american into french." In addition, in service encounters, he claimed that his "outil de survivance" [survival tool] had been to use simple, short phrases instead of formal, long ones that he had previously learned. Upon reflection, he realized that in English, no one would utter phrases such as "Where is found the market?" or "Is it so that you work every day?" so he avoided using such convoluted sentences in French.

In an interview at SA's end, Adam called his biggest accomplishments communicating with his host family, being capable of understanding "30 to 40 percent" of what their 16-year old son said, and "g[etting] along with the people I met last year" in France. According to a post-SA email, he called interactions with his host family "90% of my agent for improvement." He indicated in his post-SA questionnaire that his oral French had been impacted "to some degree" by SA and his listening comprehension "to a high degree." He also called himself "satisfied" with his overall French development and realization of personal linguistic goals.

5.1.3   Post-study abroad

In the year after SA, Adam completed courses required for the French major. He enrolled in a course on the history of the French language during his first semester back on campus and found it uninspiring, as it did not help "improve [his] communication skills at all." However, the following semester, while taking a French writing course and a seminar on post-colonial francophone film, he reported a boost in his linguistic motivation. This, he explained in a later interview, was due to the following:

> [M]y courses started to overlap in French and Russian that dealt with film and political science dealing with the European Union and the past century ... the way things have gone. And my French developed a lot ... my knowledge of French skyrocketed. I like writing and I tend to learn a lot as a writer.   (12/16/2009)

During Adam's final undergraduate year, despite being enrolled in two French literature courses to complete his major, he did not sustain his motivation to delve further into French studies, and he turned his attention more to Russian and East European studies. That interest was sustained as he learned of an opportunity to teach English as a second language (ESL) in Vladimir, Russia, which he eventually secured, and spent a year there from 2008 to 2009, serving as an ESL instructor of students ranging from early adolescents to retirees.

Teaching in Russia was of particular interest for Adam given that, as he wrote in a 2009 email, he was concerned that he could "lose" his Russian more quickly than French as he had studied it for just three years. He also wrote "the bug had bit me … *this indescribable, corporeal need* to go to Russia and see it, feel it, and live it" (my emphasis). These comments suggest that at that time, Adam's motive related to Russian was stronger than his ongoing motive to use French, and, it was instantiated through a valuable opportunity to "see it, feel it, and live it" in Vladimir. That said, Adam did travel to France for a week in December 2008 to visit the family in Valence and meet two former SA peers who were teaching English in France.

The following year, facing a difficult job market at home and desiring to combine "us[ing] my language skills, writing, and teaching," Adam served as a volunteer ESL/American Civics instructor for new immigrants to the U.S. while also holding two part-time jobs "to try to get onto my own two feet." He continued to exchange emails with the family in Valence and regularly watched movies and read in French "to use it and keep it alive." As this study ended, he moved to Washington, D.C., and found a position as a financial manager at an international development company, where he capitalizes on his Russian and, to a lesser degree, his French in his everyday work.

5.2   Rebecca

5.2.1   *Pre-study abroad*

After six years of French in middle and high school, Rebecca initially decided to continue college-level coursework for no apparent reason than her long history of studying the language. However, a clearer sense of her language-learning motive emerged in her pre-SA interview, as she explained that a week spent in Haiti as a volunteer just before college made her think, "[I]f I know French, then maybe I can teach it [in Haiti] one day." She further stated in her SA application essay "[O]ne of my main ideas is to teach." To do so, she was considering graduate study of French literature or foreign language education.

Rebecca's choice to participate in SA related to her perceived inability to use French confidently in oral interactions in class. As she explained in her pre-SA interview, "I always talk myself out of it, because maybe it will be wrong." In her view, SA would facilitate two linguistic goals: becoming "fluent" (which she defined as understanding and holding conversations at a higher level and having a "higher vocabulary") and gaining confidence in her spoken French. However, as her comments below illustrate, she seemed to believe that the SA environment itself rather than her own participation in a French community of practice abroad was the key element to realizing her goals:

> [B]eing in an atmosphere that is all French all the time, that will obviously happen … if I'm in France, then I know obviously I can do it … then I can come back and still be able to do it and still know that I can.
>
> (Interview 4/12/2006, my emphasis).

This belief may have been due to the fact that, among the participants, Rebecca had the least reported contact with French outside her coursework. According to her pre-SA questionnaire, she "rarely" read in French, "rarely" spoke in French with high school friends who had studied the language, and "occasionally" listened to French music.

5.2.2   Study abroad

Once in France, Rebecca quickly realized that simply being in an immersion environment would not transform her French capabilities. In her first blog, she used terms to describe her interactions with her host family including "pas si relaxe" [not so relaxed] and "un peu stressant" [a little stressful] and seemed particularly concerned about her limited contact with the three adolescent-age children, writing, "Les enfants dans ma famille ne parlent pas beaucoup avec moi … pour la plupart les enfants ne sont pas tres a l'aise avec moi encore … je pense que *ca va venir avec du temps*" (my emphasis) [The children in my family do not talk much with me … for the most part the children are not very comfortable with me yet … I think *that will come with time.*] But the next week Rebecca reflected about two days spent in Lille with the family, during which she found herself on the periphery of conversation at a Mother's Day lunch:

> I sat there and just ate, and listened, and pretty much said nothing. It was a bit of a reunion for everyone … so *they didn't put in effort to talk to me, nor did I put in effort to ask questions or respond* … I spent a lovely 3.5 hour meal essentially as silent Rebecca … I just haven't gotten to the comfort level yet where I can just randomly add to the conversation. I think *I think about what I'm going to say too much, and then I end up saying nothing.*   (Blog 5/29/2006, my emphases)

This last comment echoes Rebecca's prior remarks about her hesitancy to participate in classroom conversations; in France, despite a goal to converse more fluently in French, her actions were identical to her reported behavior in French classes at home. She may have begun to see that it took more than "an atmosphere that is all French all the time" to fulfill her linguistic goals. Further, she may have started to comprehend that the "comfort level" that she was seeking would not simply "come with time."

A turning point came at the end of Rebecca's second week in France, when her blog captured the role of her own agency in pursuing her linguistic goals:

> I got home and felt awkward because some of the family seemed to be working on something in the kitchen … but *it seemed as though I was interrupting. So I went to my room frustrated* until dinner … Dinner was fine and I helped clean up and all, *then it felt awkward again and so I felt defeated* and was heading back up to my room. *I decided I needed to be downstairs*, so I brought postcards to write and

my book to read and sat at the kitchen table hoping that could encourage some interaction ... *That ended up being a GREAT idea.* [Marie] came and brought her book and we both sat there reading. Then after we both ended at a certain point, it allowed for conversation ... *that was a huge help in my attitude.*

(5/31/2006, my emphases)

This entry demonstrates how a situation moved from being potentially demotivating (e.g. "I felt defeated") to motivating (e.g. "that was a huge help in my attitude") given Rebecca's initiative and the receptiveness of her homestay mother to interacting at the kitchen table.

In the following weeks, Rebecca's blog detailed a number of self-regulatory strategies related to her linguistic goals. These included volunteering to help with family housework as a means of interacting (Weeks Three and Five), listening to and noting how the family communicated among themselves (Week Three), asking her host family members questions related to words and expressions that she did not understand (Weeks Three and Four), and reading free weekly papers in French to expand her vocabulary (Week Three). Her blog also made several explicit references to discussions with peers (Adam and another advanced student) about linguistic and cultural challenges of SA. For Rebecca, these discussions among a small circle of friends "qui partagent mes objectifs" [who share my goals] was an important means of "work[ing] for what we want here," i.e. maximizing French use.

At SA's end, Rebecca reflected on the evolution of her initial linguistic goals, writing in her final blog, "[O]nce you're here, you realize there's more to it than just learning vocabulary and being around the language ... I decided that [through] learning how the French people actually use their language in their daily lives." In other words, through participation in a new community of practice, i.e. living with a French family, Rebecca's goals shifted from mastering vocabulary and not "saying something wrong" to understanding how language is used in specific ways in particular contexts and imitating those linguistic practices herself. In her post-SA questionnaire, she stated that her oral French was impacted "to a high degree" by SA and her comprehension "to a very high degree." Further, she felt that her "confidence in general with using the language" was much enhanced, another pre-SA goal. Overall, she called herself "satisfied" with her French development abroad and accomplishment of her own goals.

5.2.3 Post-study abroad

In the year after SA, Rebecca completed four courses toward her French major and explained by email that she "definitely ha[d] a higher comfort level in using my French" in class. In this way, she achieved what she set out to do through participating in SA. During that year, she also completed coursework in African history, music, and literature, eventually completing a certificate in African Studies. Further, she returned to Haiti in Summer 2007 as a volunteer, an experience that, as she explained in a 2009 interview, she "got a lot more out of" in comparison to her previous trip there, as her ease with French now facilitated "building more relationships with the kids."

Whereas Rebecca previously considered channeling her interests in French, Haiti, and Africa into graduate-level study in French literature, after enrolling in an M.A. course in Francophone literature in Fall 2007, she decided against this option. However, she continued to have significant contact with French during the 2007–2008 academic year as a tutor for Elementary French Online students, meeting with several students each week for one-on-one conversation. As she explained by email in 2008, this too allowed her to get "a lot more comfortable with conversational French," a further mention of one of her initial linguistic goals.

In Summer 2008, Rebecca joined the Peace Corps and began teaching English at a high school in the village of Kankalabe, in Guinea, West Africa, a region of the world she had ranked highest among possible destinations due to its "French colonial background." In a 2009 interview, she traced her interest in the Peace Corps back to high school, when someone had come to talk to her French class about it, but she assumed the opportunity would "never really materialize." According to Rebecca, her French was useful in Kankalabe, as it allowed her to be trained in Pular, the local language, earlier than non-French speaking U.S. peers. Proficiency in French also facilitated friendships with Guineans who had some schooling in that language: this was critical for Rebecca since no one in the village spoke English. Thus, although she was, at this study's start, motivated to continue studying French to teach it someday, as circumstances shifted, Rebecca did become a teacher, but of English, with French playing a different role than previously anticipated.

At this study's end, Rebecca used French to correspond frequently with Guinean friends and returned Peace Corps volunteers. In her words, using French was a way to avoid "forget[ting] everything about Guinea" and the experience that she shared there with other volunteers. Having been forced to return early from Guinea due to political instability in late 2009, Rebecca went to work with a division of the Catholic Church in the United States focused on educating children about the developing world. This work involves regular visits to Haiti.

5.3   Taylor

5.3.1   *Pre-study abroad*

Based on a long history of French study dating back to middle school, Taylor attributed his devotion to the language to an "amazing" high school teacher who "could have made me love anything, and it just happened to be French," according to his pre-SA interview. His ongoing motive for continuing French in college was either to join an international company that involved "using French to communicate with [its] foreign branches" or to pursue graduate work in French literature. Although undecided, he felt certain that he would "take a year off" after college given that he would graduate in three rather than the customary four years.

Taylor's primary reason for going abroad, according to his pre-SA questionnaire, was "to further advance [his] fluency" in French. He outlined three linguistic goals for his sojourn in a pre-SA interview: achieving a better accent, gaining confidence in conversing with native French speakers, and developing more fluidity in his oral speech. As he described it,

> I have a big inferiority complex ... I can speak really well with people I know aren't going to catch my errors [but] when someone I know speaks better, I get really caught up ... I know that they know I'm making a mistake and that makes it stressful.   (Interview 4/12/2006)

Taylor's comments demonstrate awareness of how his affective responses to interactions in French were mediated by the identity of his interlocutors. However, he did not seem to believe that once abroad, this dynamic would impact his capacity to achieve his linguistic goals, as he stated in his pre-SA interview, "I just guess everyone expects their language to improve when they go abroad *mostly just because you're living with French people* ... I'm just hoping that everything improves *just from being around it all of the time*" (my emphases). Thus, the role of Taylor's own intentions was minimized in his conception of how linguistic development would emerge abroad.

Prior to SA, Taylor reported a moderate amount of contact with French outside his coursework according to his questionnaire responses. This included "occasionally" speaking with his classmates outside of shared courses, "occasionally" reading online journalism, "rarely" instant messaging with friend in another U.S. city, and "rarely" listening to French music.

5.3.2   *Study abroad*

Taylor's transition to SA, particularly in relation to his host family, was challenging. Unbeknownst to him at the time, his host mother's own mother was gravely ill, eventually dying two weeks after his arrival, so both she and her husband had little time to spend with Taylor. In addition, Taylor remarked in his blog that he was already "absolument fatigué avec les attitudes des étudiants Americans" [completely tired of the other American students' attitudes]. Thus, the program began with his initial expectations for French contact with both his peers and his host family going largely unmet. However, one motivating element for Taylor was time spent with his 19-year old host sister and her friends, because they taught him a variety of idiomatic expressions in French used by people their age.

An ongoing theme in Taylor's blog over the six-week program was the constraint of being part of an American SA cohort. On the one hand, he viewed the varied linguistic levels among the 26 students (including some with as little as two semesters of French) as a limitation for the most experienced students. Further, as he explained in a Week Four blog, "English time became progressively more prevalent" during whole-group activities, so students more motivated to use French were held back. On the other hand, as he described in a Week Five blog, Taylor felt strongly that it was wrong to join the "in-group," i.e. the most fluent of his peers, as he "refuse[d] to ruin someone else's experience because they are annoying, needy, [or] unskilled in French." These issues, in combination with his host family's attention being diverted, presented obstacles to Taylor's integration into a community of practice abroad.

Despite these motivational challenges, little by little, Taylor began to perceive linguistic progress. In Week Three, he wrote in his blog, "I am definitely more comfortable conversing with strangers in French, which is something that used to make me very nervous." However, he was also gaining a new sense of the complexity of achieving "fluency" in French, and in the same blog posting he stated, "France has somewhat tempered my desire to continue French past undergrad. It has made me feel inferior in my linguistic ability." Nonetheless, he persisted in communicating with host family members, reporting in a blog posting at Week Three's end that he had started watching French television with his host sister and discussing linguistic and cultural elements during their viewing time. In addition, he mentioned new self-regulatory strategies related to his linguistic goals in Week Three and Four blogs. As he explained, "Je vais essayer de parler plus lente et plus claire" [I am going to try to speak slower and more clearly] in service encounters and "I also listen a lot more than I speak … because I find that I learn more that way." Regarding the latter strategy, he realized that he had to adapt his native language habits, i.e. "I spoke a lot and listened little," to better fit his new context.

During his final week of SA, Taylor assessed how his linguistic goals and perceptions of his French abilities had shifted during his time in France, writing in his blog:

> My linguistic goals completely changed … When I came here, I wanted to work on not sounding like a foreigner; I realized however that such a feat would take years to accomplish … I still do try to improve my fluidity. However *now it is more of trying to improve as to not slow down the conversation, as opposed to working on speeding up … I realize now how vague the idea of "improving my accent" is; instead, I aim more now to improve my pronunciation …* As for confidence,

I think it will always be a struggle. Yes, now I can speak with my host family without fear; I can go to a patisserie without breaking a sweat … Confidence has many echelons; I've reached one, but *I realize there are more than I ever imagined.*
(Blog 6/26/2006)

These comments demonstrate that the shift in conditions of language learning from the U.S. classroom to SA brought about a related change in Taylor's linguistic goals. Further, his consciousness was raised in relation to the notion that linguistic confidence is not absolute but associated with specific contexts of language use. In his post-SA questionnaire, Taylor stated that he thought his oral French and comprehension abilities had been impacted "to a high degree" by SA. In addition, he called himself "satisfied" with his overall language development and "extremely satisfied" with accomplishment of his linguistic goals.

5.3.3   *Post-study abroad*
In the year following SA, Taylor completed two final French courses required for his French major on his home campus. In a Fall 2006 email, he explained that his ease with using French had been much enhanced in comparison with his pre-SA capabilities: "I can sit in class and understand everything … I never have to sit and contemplate how exactly to say what I want to say, I don't really have to look up words while I'm reading." Based on these successful experiences, he applied and was accepted to his university's M.A. program in French literature for the next school year.

To his surprise, graduate studies in French were nothing like his undergraduate studies, despite the fact that he had stayed in the same institution and the same department. As he described it,

> [T]here seems to be this line between graduate study and undergraduate study that your language is supposed to magically improve, your critical reasoning is supposed to magically improve, your reading is supposed to magically improve, but no one tells you why or how … it was really hard to go from sort of this your papers were your thoughts and it was OK to make errors to now it was unacceptable to make French errors and it can't be your thoughts, it has to be somebody else's thoughts.   (Interview 12/15/2009)

Thus, once again, Taylor found his conditions of learning shifting, this time unexpectedly. Hence, he adjusted his strategies as he had done while abroad. This time, he explained that he had to "accept that [he] was the bottom of the pile now" and reach out to others for assistance. For example, he asked native speakers in his M.A. program to help him work on his French as well as edit his term papers. These examples demonstrate how, in a Vygotskian sense, Taylor took the initiative to seek out other-regulation in situations where he felt that he could not independently and completely regulate his language use.

Following a challenging first year of graduate school, Taylor decided to serve as the exchange student from his department to a university in Tours, France, where his responsibilities included teaching 20 hours of English per week to French college students. Although he claimed that he spent a great deal of his free time outside work with Anglophone colleagues while in France, he also stated this he was much more intentional in his language-learning strategies during this second stay abroad. For instance, he described reading signs and analyzing the gender of words and noticing new vocabulary and then "working back in things that I had learned into a conversation ... intentionally us[ing] it again." As he explained in an email from late 2009, he now realized that maximizing language learning abroad was not just a matter of being there: "[I]immersion learning is not like water. You immerse yourself in water, you get soaked. Immerse yourself in French, and you only soak up as much as you choose to."

At this study's end, Taylor completed the final year of his French M.A. and spent a few months contemplating his future direction. He found work at the headquarters of a U.S. textbook publishing company as an editorial assistant specializing in French and German college instructional materials. He reads and watches movies on occasion in French.

6. Discussion

This study provides a detailed account of motivational self-regulation strategies evidenced by three "good learners" of French during and after SA. The findings illustrate the participants' dynamic motivational trajectories as the conditions of their language learning and use shifted over several years. In this section, I will synthesize and interpret the findings, drawing on key notions from sociocultural and activity theories, and relating these findings to instructional implications for the collegiate FL curriculum.

Regarding the first research question, each participant evidenced motivational self-regulation strategies during SA related to his or her initial linguistic goals. Among the three types of strategies identified by Dörnyei (2001), *language-learning strategies* were by far the most frequently reported. These included: speaking more slowly rather than more quickly to improve comprehensibility, concentrating on clear pronunciation rather than on developing a native-like accent, using simple phrases rather than convoluted ones, listening well rather than talking a lot during conversations, avoiding translation from English to French, engaging in household tasks and sharing down time with hosts to encourage interaction, asking hosts questions about linguistic matters and observing how they interact with each another, and reading for pleasure to improve vocabulary.

A notable finding related to the language-learning strategies seen in the data was that all but one strategy related to *oral* interactions. In effect, an obvious degree of similarity existed in the three participants' initial linguistic goals, which all linked in some way to spoken French (e.g. the desire to improve comprehensibility, fluency, fluidity, or accent) or gaining confidence in interacting with more competent or native-speaking interlocutors. None of the participants posited initial goals related to achieving advanced literacy in French, and mentions of reading or writing beyond the SA classroom were scant in the participants' accounts of experiences abroad.

Motivation-maintenance strategies were evidenced in two participants' blogs (Adam and Rebecca) but were far fewer than language-learning strategies. For both students, articulating their experiences as a language learner through blogging seemed to serve as a useful tool for maintaining motivation and identifying specific actions carried out in pursuit of linguistic goals. For example, Adam stated, "[T]hese uncomfortable situations are really the means of improvement and I believe they help my abilities," and Rebecca wrote, "That ended up being a GREAT idea … that was a huge help to my attitude." In both cases, blogging appeared to facilitate the learners' stepping back from a specific interaction, interpreting it through language in light of their own intentions, and relating it to their ongoing goals.

Another interesting finding was that for one participant, Rebecca, verbalizing linguistic and cultural struggles abroad within a group of like-minded peers seemed to serve as a means of maintaining or enhancing her motivation. However, for Adam and Taylor, the American SA cohort was viewed as a limitation for both linguistic development and motivation maintenance. This dichotomous perception among the participants, i.e. that SA peers were perceived as a constraint to learning by two students and an affordance by another, echoes earlier findings from Allen (2010a), who reported that within Adam, Rebecca, and Taylor's larger SA cohort, just 44 percent viewed peers as an affordance for linguistic development.

The third type of motivational self-regulation strategy, *goal setting*, was relatively absent in participants' data in comparison to the two other types of strategies. Whereas each participant identified initial linguistic goals via the pre-SA questionnaire and elaborated on them in an interview, it was not the case that broad initial goals (e.g. "greatly improve my speaking ability") were translated into more concrete sub-goals over the six-week SA program. On the other hand, some shifts were evident in how participants articulated linguistic goals before SA to how they described them at SA's end. This was particularly true for Rebecca and

Taylor, who seemed to move from an idea of language that focused on normative notions of correctness and sounding like a native to a preoccupation with understanding specific uses of language in particular contexts. All in all, goal specificity and the establishment of concrete, short-term linguistic goals did not emerge to any significant degree in data collected during SA.

Regarding the second research question, taking a short-term perspective, the three participants' language-learning motivation appeared to be maintained if not enhanced by SA in the semesters immediately following the program. Based on their self-regulatory strategies discussed above, it would seem appropriate to infer that, to varying degrees, by SA's end, each participant posited himself or herself as an active agent of learning, seeing his or her own intentions and actions as critical components to the realization of linguistic goals. Further, all three participants expressed satisfaction with their linguistic development and accomplishment of linguistic goals during SA. In addition, despite struggles to adjust to the norms of interactions within their French host family, by SA's end, each viewed those interactions as a valuable affordance for meeting their linguistic goals.

To state that this study's participants viewed themselves as agentic learners may, in a sense, seem unsurprising given their long histories of French study prior to SA. However, for two participants (Rebecca and Taylor), this was not apparent at the study's start, as they made statements such as "[B]eing in an atmosphere that is all French all the time, [linguistic development] will obviously happen" and "I'm just hoping that everything improves just from being around it all of the time." In both cases, these students appeared to realize *during* SA that learning does not emerge organically from the learning context but depends in great part on agentic behavior and efforts to observe and integrate into one's community of practice abroad. In Taylor's case, this insight was reflected during his subsequent stay in France, when he reported being more intentional in his language-learning strategies. The example of Rebecca and Taylor stands in contrast to findings reported in Allen (2010b) wherein a participant from their SA cohort did not experience such an agentic shift and suffered tremendous demotivation, resulting in her abandoning French study shortly after SA. It may be the case, as the example of this study's participants suggest, that a first sojourn abroad (either with a SA cohort or independently as was the case for Adam) has the *potential* to bring about a critical awareness of the role of agency in one's language learning.

It is more difficult to answer definitively the question of whether this study's participants sustained their language-learning motivation over the long term. On the one hand, none are holding positions today consistent with the future plans that they described at the study's start, and neither of the two participants who considered specializing in French as an academic career did so. Further, all three participants indicated some sense of disappointment or frustration with at least one aspect of their post-SA French coursework, and it is questionable whether their university's advanced undergraduate French curriculum helped to sustain their motivation, given that two participants (Adam and Rebecca) pursued new certificate programs after SA rather than taking additional, non-required courses in French. Clearly, Taylor experienced significant demotivation as he navigated the transition from undergraduate to graduate studies in French. On the other hand, all three participants currently hold jobs in which French and other FLs play a critical role, whether in translation of documents from French and Russian to English (Adam), development missions to Haiti (Rebecca), or editorial work with French and German textbooks (Taylor). In this regard, the professional choices of this study's participants reflect both their own ongoing engagement with using FLs and the varied meaningful avenues beyond academia open to advanced FL learners in the 21st century.

6.1   Instructional implications

A number of pedagogical implications related to the collegiate FL curriculum can be drawn from this study's findings. Many FL students begin their sojourns abroad lacking strategies to negotiate encounters with speakers who do not scaffold and sustain interactions according to classroom discourse norms (Lafford 2004; Cohen & Shively 2007). Further, in the traditional FL classroom, goals are typically imposed on learners by teachers (Ushioda 2003), whereas in contexts with drastically changed learning conditions like SA, learners struggle to relate their reasons for FL learning to the pursuit of concrete linguistic goals and to maintain their motivation. In other words, the conditions and activities of classroom FL study may not promote self-regulated learning or the development of motivational self-regulation strategies. This study's findings suggest this is the case even for "good language learners" with long histories of FL study.

Thus, the collegiate FL curriculum should place emphasis at all levels not only on linguistic development and the development of analytical abilities related to literary-cultural content but also on the development of students' motivational self-regulation skills. But how might such emphasis be instantiated? Several ideas are outlined below in relation to the three types of self-regulatory strategies identified by Dörnyei (2001).

1. *Motivation maintenance*: Reflecting in writing on one's struggles and accomplishments as a FL learner and user can be a valuable means of motivational maintenance, and a tool such as blogging can be used in traditional FL learning contexts or SA. Such an activity should be dialogic, with a more-experienced interlocutor providing feedback and assistance, when

needed, in helping learners articulate strategies for enhancing motivation. Another practice that can facilitate motivation maintenance is portfolio assessment, which can help learners develop agency by offering choices regarding what is and is not assessed and taking stock of linguistic development over time.

2. *Goal-setting*: Even "good language learners" are challenged to articulate specific linguistic goals and establish concrete sub-goals. Although goal setting can be accomplished through an activity like blogging, it can also be incorporated in FL courses, either as a required oral or written component of a specific assignment (e.g. What were your goals for this recording? Were you able to accomplish them? If not, what obstacles did you face?) or as a beginning (e.g. Linguistic Autobiography) or end-of-semester activity (e.g. What did you set out to accomplish this term and was this achieved? What will your linguistic goals be in the future? Why?). As with motivation-maintenance activities, students should be provided opportunities for discussion and reformulation of goal statements, and goal setting should be a recurrent element of the curriculum rather than a haphazard occurrence.

3. *Language-learning strategies*: Learners experience challenges in linking linguistic goals with means of achieving those goals. For this reason, the FL curriculum should offer learners guidance in language-learning strategies appropriate to specific levels and courses. As an example, lower-division courses might have an orientation on maximizing oral participation in class and finding useful tools for completing homework. A more advanced course in cultural studies might incorporate strategies for conducting research in the FL using appropriate tools or for making a persuasive argument in a debate. In relation to SA, Kinginger (2008) recommended "an orientation to language learning, including information on the nature of language and on the use of strategic approaches to learning, might [help] students to better apprehend the nature of the task they [set] for themselves" (p. 110). Such an orientation can go far in preparing future SA participants for the challenges awaiting them, and a guide such as *Maximizing Study Abroad* (Paige, Cohen, Kappler, Chi & Lassegard 2002) can be a helpful tool to structure those sessions.

In conclusion, as Ushioda (2008) pointed out, "[R]esearch insights from learners themselves in a variety of learning contexts are much needed to substantiate and inform our theorizing, particularly in relation to the socially situated growth and regulation of motivation" (p. 29). This study contributes a fresh perspective on how FL learners come to use self-regulatory strategies and on specific ways in which collegiate FL curriculum may better assist learners in developing those strategies. In the end, the dispositions and strategies related to FL learning that our students develop and use at home and abroad depend greatly on how we construct the conditions of learning in our classrooms.

References

Allen, H.W. (2010a). Interactive contact during study abroad as linguistic affordance: Myth or reality? *Frontiers: The Interdisciplinary Journal of Study Abroad, 19,* 1–26.

Allen, H.W. (2010b). Language-learning motivation in short-term study abroad. *Foreign Language Annals, 43,* 27–49.

Allen, H.W., & Herron, C.A. (2003). A mixed methodology investigation of the linguistic and affective outcomes of summer study abroad. *Foreign Language Annals, 36,* 370–384.

Bernaus, M. Moore, E., & Azevedo, A.C. (2007). Affective factors influencing plurilingual acquisition of Catalan in a Catalan-Spanish bilingual context. *Modern Language Journal, 91,* 235–246.

Cohen, A.D., & Shively, R.L. (2007). Acquisition of requests and apologies in Spanish and French: Impact of study abroad and strategy-building intervention. *The Modern Language Journal, 91,* 189–212.

DeKeyser, R. (2010). Monitoring processes in Spanish as a second language during a study abroad program. *Foreign Language Annals, 43,* 80–92.

Dörnyei, Z. (2009a). Individual differences: Interplay of learner characteristics and learner environment. *Language Learning, 59,* 230–248.

Dörnyei, Z. (2009b). The L2 motivational self system. In Z. Dörnyei & E. Ushioda (Eds.), *Motivation, language identity, and the L2 self* (pp. 9–42). Bristol, UK: Multilingual Matters.

Dörnyei, Z. (2005). *The psychology of the language learner: Individual differences in second language acquisition.* Mahwah, NJ: Lawrence Erlbaum Associates.

Dörnyei, Z. (2003). *Attitudes, orientations, and motivations in language learning: Advances in theory, research, and applications.* Malden, MA: Blackwell.

Dörnyei, Z. (2001). *Teaching and researching motivation.* Harlow, England: Longman.

Douglass K. (2007). From the learner's perspective: A case study on motives and study abroad. In S. Wilkinson (Ed.), *AAUSC issues in language program direction: Insights from study abroad for language programs* (pp. 116–132). Boston, MA: Heinle.

Engeström, Y. (1999). Activity theory and individual and social transformation. In Y. Engeström, R. Miettinen & R.-M. Punamäki (Eds.), *Perspectives on activity theory* (pp. 19–38). New York, NY: Cambridge University Press.

Freed, B.F. (1990). Language learning in a study abroad context: The effects of interactive and non-interactive out-of-class contact on grammatical achievement and oral proficiency. In J. Alatis (Ed.), *Linguistic, language teaching and language acquisition: The interdependence of theory, practice and research* (pp. 459–477). Washington D.C.: Georgetown UP.

Gardner, R.C. (1985). *Social psychology and second language learning: The role of attitudes and motivation.* London: Edward Arnold.

Hernandez, T.A. (2010). Promoting speaking proficiency through motivation and interaction:The study abroad and classroom learning contexts. *Foreign Language Annals, 43,* 650–670.

Ingram, M. (2005). Recasting the foreign language requirement through study abroad: A cultural immersion program in Avignon. *Foreign Language Annals, 38,* 211–222.

Isabelli-García, C. (2006). Study abroad social networks, motivation and attitudes: Implications for second language acquisition. In E. Churchill & M. DuFon (Eds.), *Language learners in study abroad contexts* (pp. 231–258). Clevedon, UK: Multilingual Matters.

Kim, T.-Y. (2007). Second language learning motivation from an activity theory perspective: Longitudinal case studies of Korean ESL students and recent immigrants in Toronto. Unpublished doctoral dissertation, University of Toronto.

Kinginger, C. (2008). *Language learning in study abroad: Case studies of Americans in France.* Modern Language Journal, 92, Monograph.

Kinginger, C. (2004). Alice doesn't live here anymore: Foreign language learning and identity reconstruction. In A. Pavlenko & A. Blackledge (Eds.), *Negotiation of identities in multilingual contexts* (pp. 219–242). Clevedon,UK: Multilingual Matters.

Lafford, B. (2004). The effect of context of learning on the use of communication strategies by learners of Spanish as a second language. *Studies in Second Language Acquisition, 26,* 201–226.

Lantolf, J.P. (Ed.). (2000). *Sociocultural theory and second language learning.* Oxford: Oxford University Press.

Lantolf, J.P. (2004). Sociocultural theory and second language and foreign language learning: An overview of sociocultural theory. In K. Van Esch & O. St. John (Eds.), *New insights into foreign language learning and teaching* (pp. 13–34). Frankfurt: Peter Lang.

Lantolf, J.P., & Appel, G. (1994). Theoretical framework: An introduction to Vygotskian approaches to second language research. In J.P. Lantolf & G. Appel (Eds.), *Vygotskian approaches to second language acquisition* (pp. 1–28). Norwood, NJ: Ablex.

Lantolf, J.P., & Pavlenko, A. (2001). (S)econd (L)anguage (A)ctivity theory: Understanding second language learners as people. In M. Breen (Ed.), *Learner contributions to language learning: New directions in research* (pp. 141–158). London: Longman.

Lave. J., & Wenger, E. (1991). *Situated learning: Legitimate peripheral participation.* New York: Cambridge University Press.

Leont'ev, A.N. (1981). *Problems of the development of the mind.* Moscow: Progress.

Lewis, T.L., & Niesenbaum, R.A. (2005). Extending the stay: Using community-based research and service learning to enhance short-term study abroad. *Journal of Studies in International Education, 9,* 251–264.

Lompscher, J. (1999). Motivation and activity. *European Journal of Psychology of Education, 14,* 11–22.

Markova, A.K. (1990). Ways of investigating motivation for learning in school children. *Soviet Psychology, 28*(6), 21–42.

Martinsen, R.A. (2010). Short-term study abroad: Predicting changes in oral skills. *Foreign Language Annals, 43,* 504–530.

Mills, N., Pajares, F., & Herron, C. (2007). Self-efficacy of college intermediate French students: Relation to achievement and motivation. *Language Learning, 57,* 417–442.

Newman, R. (2003). What do I need to do to succeed when I don't know what I'm doing? In A.Wigfield & J. Eccles (Eds.), *Development of achievement motivation* (pp. 285–303). San Diego: Academic Press.

Paige, R.M., Cohen, A.D., Kappler, B., Chi, J.C., & Lassegard, J.P. (2002). *Maximizing study abroad: A students' guide to strategies for language and culture learning and use.* Minneapolis, MN: Center for Advanced Research on Language Acquisition, University of Minnesota.

Ushioda, E. (2008). Motivation and good language learners. In C. Griffiths (Ed.), *Lessons from good language learners* (pp. 19–34). Cambridge: Cambridge University Press.

Ushioda, E. (2007). Motivation, autonomy and sociocultural theory. In D. Little, J. Ridley & E. Ushioda (Eds.), *Learner autonomy in the foreign language classroom: Teacher, learner, curriculum and assessment* (pp. 5–24). Dublin: Authentik.

Ushioda, E. (2003). Motivation as a socially mediated process. In D. Little, J. Ridley & E. Ushioda (Eds.), *Learner autonomy in the foreign language classroom: Learner, teacher, curriculum and assessment* (pp. 90–103). Dublin: Authentik.

van Lier, L. (2008). Agency in the classroom. In J.P. Lantolf & M.E. Poehner (Eds.), *Sociocultural theory and the teaching of second languages* (pp. 163–186). London: Equinox.

Vygotsky, L.S. (1987). Thought and word. In R.W. Riber & A.S. Carton (Eds.), *The collected works of L. S. Vygotsky*, Volume 1 (pp. 243 – 288). New York, NY: Plenum.

Vygotsky, L.S. (1986). *Thought and language.* Cambridge, MA: The MIT Press.

Vygotsky, L.S. (1978). *Mind in society: The development of higher psychological processes.* Cambridge, MA: Harvard University Press.

Wertsch, J.V. (1985). *Vygotsky and the social formation of mind.* Cambridge, MA: Harvard University Press.

Wilkinson, S. (1998). Study abroad from the participants' perspectives: A challenge to common beliefs. *Foreign Language Annals, 31,* 23–39.

Williams, M. (2004). Motivation in foreign language learning. In M. Baynham, A. Deignan & G. White (Eds.), *Applied linguistics at the Interface* (pp. 167–180). London: British Association for Applied Linguistics.

Yashima, T., Zenuk-Nishide, L., & Shimizu, K. (2004). The influences of attitudes and affect on willingness to communicate and second language communication. *Language Learning, 54,* 119–152.

"Opening up to the world"?

Developing interculturality in an international field experience for ESL teachers

Elizabeth Smolcic

Pennsylvania State University

This chapter reports on a study exploring the developing intercultural awareness of novice ESL teachers as they become border crossers in an English as a Second Language (ESL) teacher preparation program. In addition to learning about instruction of English Language Learners (ELLs), the study abroad experience encouraged teachers to explore their own cultural identities, to develop conceptual understanding of culture and interculturality, to analyze their own L2 learning process in classroom and homestay settings, and to uncover the macro-social relationships underlying processes of global human migration. Analysis of ethnographic data uncovered how immersion promotes enhanced self-awareness, frequently bringing about dissonance which in turn leads to transformations in personal identities, changing goals for the future, and a means of gradual socialization into new communities of practice.

1. Introduction

The history of the United States is a story of immigration; converging ethnicities and languages coexisting with assertions of racial, cultural and linguistic identity. In today's world, immigration is once again a dynamic social force, challenging our school systems with the greatest number of immigrants in the nation's history (Capps et al. 2005; Suárez-Orozco, Suárez-Orozco & Todorova 2008). More than ever before, students in public schools are culturally and racially diverse, and often bi- or multilingual. Meanwhile, teacher candidates are predominantly White, female and monolingual and often bring little experience of cultural or linguistic diversity to the activity of teaching (Frankenberg 2006; Sleeter 2001; Taylor & Sobel 2001, p. 488). The demographics point to a growing disparity in life experience, background and values between teachers and their students. Today, a central challenge facing teacher education is to help teacher-learners enrich a monolingual and first culture life experience and encourage their movement towards interculturality.

This chapter investigates the developing intercultural awareness of novice ESL teachers as they became border-crossers in a Teaching English as a Second Language (TESL) certificate program which included an international field teaching and culture/language learning experience abroad. A primary focus of activity of the international field experience was to guide teachers in exploration of their own cultural identities, to develop conceptual understanding of culture and interculturality, to analyze their L2 learning processes, and to uncover the macro-social relationships that underlie global human migration. This chapter presents a case study of one of the teachers, referred to here as Anna, as she participated in the TESL certificate program over a seven-month period and continuing three months afterwards as she moved back into her home context. Anna came to the program with some intercultural experiences and was an experienced public school educator (French and emotional support aide). Anna's case offers a window into the complexities of a short-term intercultural learning experience for teachers, revealing many of the affordances and constraints common to other participants in the study. The case study addresses the following questions: How does the mediation involved in the experience of an international immersion teacher education experience influence the unfolding of intercultural learning? What particular conditions of possibility or particular constraints might the immersion experience create for intercultural learning? How does what a participant brings to the experience (her goals, motives, past experience with second language and culture learning) affect what she takes out of the experience?

2.   Theoretical commitments: A (Re)unification of language and culture

There is great interest in 'teaching culture' as a part of the second language learning project. However, language and culture still frequently occupy separate spaces in second language curricula, study abroad programs and the minds of teachers, learners and researchers. Additionally, in the broader field of teacher education, a concern for effective teaching of diverse learners has focused attention on how culture can be a barrier to improved teacher performance. Teachers tend to see the world from their own racial, linguistic and cultural location and may be unaware of the multiplicity of 'languacultural' realities their students bring to the classroom (Scahill 1993). In a globalized world, teacher education should help teacher-learners to reflect critically on their own cultural stance and develop an awareness of how human difference may be used by people in power to rationalize inequities and maintain their position of dominance in society (May 1999; Merryfield 2000).

This study and the teacher preparation program it investigated assert a commitment to promoting the reunification of language and culture (Block 2003; Johnson 2006, 2009; Kinginger 2009; Lantolf 2006; Lantolf & Johnson 2007). An early articulation of this intellectual stance is Agar's (1994) notion of *languaculture* which seeks to move beyond the dichotomy of language *versus* culture originating in the thinking of the early 20th century linguist, de Saussure. In de Saussure's (1959) efforts to make linguistics an objective science (for which he is celebrated as a founder of modern linguistics) he drew a firm distinction between *language* and *speech*, the former being a pure, clean inventory of the symbols that make up language (the focus of interest for linguistic study) and the latter (speech) as the messy actualization of language in everyday life. According to Agar (1994) and others (Risager 2006, 2007), de Saussure drew a line around language and left culture out. The term, languaculture, is a move towards reunification.

This teacher education program assumed that teachers who teach English as a Second Language will benefit, both professionally and personally, from their own forays into other cultures, analysis of symbolic cultural representations, and efforts at second language learning. The need to insert a multicultural/lingual ideology into the mainstream activity of our schools and individual life stories of teachers is critical to a successful academic experience for the diverse spectrum of learners in our schools and to promote healthy relationships in an increasingly interdependent world.

2.1   A sociocultural view of teacher learning

Vygotskian-inspired sociocultural theory asserts that cognitive development (or learning) is a socially mediated activity. Thus, the way in which our consciousness develops depends on the specific social activities in which we engage, and the symbolic and physical artifacts with which we interact (Vygotsky 1978; Johnson 2006, 2009). According to a sociocultural view of learning, cognitive development is transformational and is not simply a transfer of knowledge; it is a dialogic process of change to the self and to the activity. Teacher learning builds on prior knowledge of the self and beliefs about the world, both of which are historically and socially situated. Recent views of teacher development characterize learning as lifelong and socially embedded, emerging from a process of reshaping existing knowledge and beliefs and not simply the application of new theories and methods (Sleeter 1999; Johnson & Golombek 2011).

Meanwhile, research in the field of applied linguistics and second language teaching mirrors this shift in perspective. Freeman (2007) claims that Firth & Wagner's (1997) groundbreaking article calling for a "reconceptualization" of the field of second language acquisition, "redescribed the territory, or spaces, in which instructed language learning was seen to take place. Spaces that had been seen as largely internal to the learner; and therefore private, they argued, could be seen as interactional and thus publicly accessible to both study and intervention" (p. 895). Investigations into language learning moved away from a fixed concern with individual learners and internal mental activity towards language in interaction and language linked to relations of power (Kinginger 2008, 2009). As Lantolf and Pavlenko (2001) have insightfully stated, second language learning "…is about much more than the acquisition of language forms: it is about developing, or failing to develop, new ways of mediating ourselves and our relationships to others and to ourselves" (p. 145).

Johnson argues that "a sociocultural perspective changes the way we think about what constitutes professional development" (2009, p. 5). Teacher learning is pushed outside of university classrooms, workshops and seminars and towards on-going reflective inquiry of teaching practices and student learning as teachers are engaged in the socialization process that occurs in classrooms, schools and wider professional communities (2009, p. 6). Models of inquiry-based professional development (Cochran-Smith & Lytle 1993, 1999, 2001; Weinbaum et al. 2004) are designed to support teachers' concept development, create alternative structural arrangements to sustain dialogic mediation between and among teachers and teacher educators, and provide assisted performance as teachers work though issues that emerge as important in their classroom teaching (Johnson 2009, p. 6).

2.2 A "third space" for intercultural learning

One of the strategies advocated in the literature to prepare teachers for cultural diversity is field experience that puts teacher-learners in direct contact with others of different cultural, linguistic, racial or ethnic backgrounds (Pence & Macgillivrary 2008; Villegas & Lucas 2002; Willard-Holt 2001; Zeichner & Hoeft 1996). Teacher educators seem to agree that coursework and academic analysis alone are insufficient to bring about the affective and cognitive changes needed to develop intercultural competence (Finney & Orr 1995; Zeichner & Hoeft 1996). Byram (1997, p. 70), calling the process decentreing, believes that learners need to move outside of their own cultural frame in order to achieve the complex psychological change involved in intercultural learning. To decentre requires that learners problematize their culture's representation of the world, taking an outsider's view of their own culture, which they had before known only as an insider. Thus, their cognitive schemata are modified to take into account new representations that either extend their understanding or challenge their established views of the world. A student moving towards interculturality begins to see the role that their own culture (or race, language background, or social standing) plays in their interactions with others both in and outside of their own cultural community. Therefore, decentreing involves personal development that is deeper than attitudinal shift and involves some sort of re-interpretation of the self or transformation of social identities.

Similarly, Bennett (1993) in his developmental model of intercultural learning sees true intercultural sensitivity as the ability to step away from one's own cultural background and identify the cultural values and reasoning behind beliefs, actions and behaviors of the other. This notion he names, constructive marginality (Bennett 1998, p. 29); it is a parallel concept to the component skill of interpreting and relating in Byram's model. In contrast to earlier models of intercultural learning, learners are no longer required to take on the target culture, replacing their own values and behaviors, but rather enter a metaphorical space of hybridity and multiplicity of cultural identity. It is important to point out that many scholars have put forth strong criticisms against a reified vision of culture (Dervin 2007; Kramsch 2011; Kumaravadivelu 2008, May 1999). Scholars concerned with theorizing identity now more frequently see identity as multiple and ever-changing. Similarly, cultures are not seen as unified and static, but liquid, dynamic and internally diverse. Thus, we can recognize that we are all intercultural to some extent because we manage plurality on a continual basis.

In specific application to second language learning contexts, Kramsch (1993, p. 234) has theorized the concept of "third place or third culture" as the site of struggle for recognition and legitimating of meanings in which people of different cultures meet and where ideas and cultures merge or collide and re-emerge. In a similar way, Agar (1994, p. 100) uses the term "rich points" to describe the spaces where contradictions or uncertainties occur when different languacultures come together. Risager (2006, 2007) expands the concept of languaculture to include three dimensions: (1) the semantic & pragmatic, (2) the poetic and (3) the identity dimension. She also emphasizes that languaculture is both structurally constrained as well as socially and personally variable. Languaculture is the bridge between language structure and the personal idiolect which arises out of personal experience (Risager 2007, p. 172). In more recent work, Kramsch (2011) asserts that the concept of culture today is seen less as a world of national cultures and historical traditions and more through actual, imagined and virtual discourse worlds in which we interact to make meaning of our life experiences and share that meaning with others. In her words,

> The self that is engaged in intercultural communication is a symbolic self that is constituted by symbolic systems like language as well as by systems of thought and their symbolic power. This symbolic self is the most sacred part of our personal and social identity; it demands for its well-being careful positioning, delicate facework, and the ability to frame and re-frame events.   (Kramsch 2011, p. 1)

Likewise, a group of Australian scholars (Lo Bianco, Liddicoat & Crozet 1999) posit a "third space" as a metaphorical meeting place of different worldviews. They claim that an intercultural encounter entails finding an intermediary space between cultural frames, and in this act, the learner in an interaction is an experiencer, and not just an observer of difference. While all of these theoretical notions apply, very little empirical work has investigated how this intercultural *third space* might be experienced by an individual learner. The following analysis attempts to do that by describing the experience of Anna as she moves into and out of a *third space*.

2.3   Activity theory

The study set out to uncover the historical, contextual and social factors that impinge upon the processes of second language and culture learning. Activity theory, an outgrowth of Vygotskian sociocultural theory, first articulated by Leont'ev (1978, 1981) and more recently developed by others (Engeström 1987, 1999; Lantolf & Thorne 2006; Thorne 2004) was adopted as a theoretical framework to orient the analysis.

Lantolf & Johnson cite Vygotsky's (1986) key argument, (later examined by activity theorists), that cognitive development occurs when tension or conflict arise between the individual (or group) and the world of other individuals within social and intellectual activity (2007, p. 890). An activity system analysis focuses on what people (*subjects*) actually do, the *objects* that motivate their activity, the *tools* they use, the various *communities* within which they interact, the *rules* that delimit their actions and the *division of labor* that patterns the human interactions. All of the former are resources that mediate the relationship between human *subjects* and the *objects* of their actions (Roth & Tobin 2004). These resources, or *means of mediation*, are seen to be in constant flux, partly due to the system's continual reorganization in response to contradictions (Engeström 1999, p. 3). Contradictions in activity theoretical terms are not inherently bad, but are the driving force for change and development. Learning can be seen as a resolution to tensions that arise due to changes in the conceptual, social and material conditions in everyday life; these changes then, create new contradictions, which we can again see as opportunities for development (Lantolf & Thorne 2006). In activity theoretical terms, however, contradictions are historically accumulated inner conflicts; they are not surface expressions of problems or conflicts, but are inherent to the activity system itself (Roth & Lee 2007, p. 203). Additionally, they have to become conscious or visible in order to act as forces for change. Therefore, from the perspective of the individual *subject*, an important step to working towards change is to be able to locate and identify contradictions (or in sociocultural terms, *externalize*) and then remove or resolve them.

A central premise of activity theory, that development involves contradiction, disequilibrium and transformation, plays out clearly in the immersion situation of this project. Both direct personal interaction with cultural and linguistic others and the dissonance resulting from immersion in a foreign setting are pivotal embodied experiences that lead to inner conflict, transformation and development. The data illustrate how student learning during an immersion experience is crucially dependent on an individual's past history, dispositions and motives for learning and the *mediational means* (i.e. the symbolic and material tools for learning as well as the individuals of the activity system) that are present in the learning situation (Smolcic 2011).

3. The study

The ESL certificate program was a seven-month long (spring and summer session) program offered by a liberal arts college, "Woods College" (all names used in this chapter are pseudonyms) in the northeastern U.S. The international immersion experience, which took place between the courses offered on campus, occurred during a three and half-week summer session in a small city and university in the Andean highlands of Ecuador. The teacher education program was designed around two learning activities that were thought critical to successful preparation of ESL teachers: (1) a mentored teaching practicum with English learners in a classroom setting, and (2) informal (out of classroom) exposure to and structured learning of a second language and culture. A teaching practicum with Ecuadorian children and a homestay with an Ecuadorian family during the experience abroad provided the situation in which to enact these learning activities. Before the immersion experience, two courses were completed on campus; the first an overview of the systematic workings of the English language, and the second, an exploration of culture in English language teaching. Reflective practices about oneself as well as the learner's developing teaching practice are integrated into each course and the group is taught explicitly about the conceptualization and processes of reflection. A linguistic autobiography (to uncover language attitudes, history, and previous L2 learning experience) and a visual metaphor project (to express teacher identity) are two examples of the reflective activities completed before departure.

In sum, the certificate program took up three primary learning objectives for teacher learners: (1) to build cultural sensitivity, develop interculturality and geopolitical awareness of an immigrant-sending nation; (2) to apply teaching strategies that are responsive to culturally and linguistically diverse students, and; (3) to reflect on and enrich teaching practices effective for instructing ELLs. The immersion program included the following learning activities:

1. a mentored teaching practicum with Ecuadorian English language learners
2. classroom instruction on ESL teaching pedagogy and second language learning theory
3. daily life with a local host family
4. ethnographic investigation into local cultures
5. informal talks by community members on Ecuadorian history, economics, the indigenous political movement, music, and ecology/sustainability
6. second language (Spanish or Quichua) classroom learning
7. visits to local Ecuadorian schools
8. weekend excursions to distinct cultural and ecological regions of Ecuador for a broader perspective on the country and its peoples
9. daily group "check-in" sessions to discuss cultural "rich points," misunderstandings and share the breadth of experience with individual host families

Program participants self-select to participate in this particular educational experience and the focal cohort included ten in-service and pre-service teacher-learners representing a broad range of ages (20–62), teaching experience, and background. Four individuals were selected as focal participants because they represented the diversity of age and experience of the group. The researcher was a participant-observer, acting as one of the program instructors and program coordinator.

3.1   Data collection & analysis

The empirical data upon which the following discussion is based constitute one segment of a larger study that explored the learning experience of the group of teachers as they became border-crossers in a multicultural/lingual learning situation. The data included semi-structured interviews, journal entries, written reflective papers, researcher field notes and post-observation conferences during the practice teaching experience. Data were collected and analyzed from three chronological phases of the program: (1) before departure for Ecuador, (2) during the experience abroad, and (3) up to 6 months after program completion. This longitudinal view offered a valuable perspective on intercultural learning as a process developing over time. The data were analyzed according to a grounded analysis, using the constant comparative methodology outlined in Glaser & Strauss (1967). In a second pass through the data, an activity theoretical analysis allowed the researcher to uncover relationships between elements of the learning situation and patterns of interaction that were significant for individual learners as well for the learning system as a collective whole.

4.   The findings: Anna's experience in the activity system

In the following section, I offer excerpts from the data to illustrate Anna's experience of intercultural learning within the TESL program. Due to space limitations, learning that is specific to the process of teaching and interacting with ELLs is not addressed here. While we cannot use a single participant's experience to make broad generalizations about learning that takes place during study abroad, we can look to a detailed analysis of individual experience to offer important insights into the conditions that facilitate (or alternatively, impede) learning in a short-term study abroad experience.

4.1   A descriptive profile

When the TESL certificate program began, Anna was a 59 year old public school teacher with 20 years of experience. She had taught French, was certified in both special education and social studies, and currently worked as a "therapeutic" aide with children who had been identified by the schools as exhibiting behavioral problems. Anna grew up in a bilingual community in Quebec, Canada and learned French as a child. She moved to the U.S as an adolescent. Before working in the public schools, she taught French at a private boarding school. She had studied German formally and had begun to study Spanish independently in preparation for the study abroad portion of the TESL program in Ecuador. In the past, she had traveled abroad to several countries for short-term study and recreation and had a strong interest in languages and cultures. While Anna considered herself neither bilingual, nor bicultural, and had lived and worked in a rural and monolingual English-speaking environment over the past 30 years, her life experiences were a foundation upon which movement towards intercultural learning might be built. Thus, this focal case study illustrates the potential impact of a short-term immersion experience on individuals who are receptive to change and intercultural experience.

4.2   Anna's learning about diversity: A conceptual mapping

Activity theory offers an analytical framework in which the particularities of Anna's experience may be revealed, and the interrelationships among actors and artifacts (*mediational means*) within the system made visible. Appendix 1 offers a conceptual map of Anna's learning, according to the activity system framework.

Anna was dissatisfied in her current job and viewed the TESL program as a way to explore new professional possibilities. As she began the program she commented, "I am working on a new future here." Thus, Anna was oriented towards change; she was hopeful that the learning experiences of the program would move her along a new career path. The *object* of the activity system for Anna was her desire for change in her life. The *community* that lent direction (or at times offered sources of conflict) and shaped her experience in the TESL program included her Ecuadorian host family, the Ecuadorian English language learners, her mentor-teacher, and her co-teacher in the teaching practicum. Various *rules* were significant to Anna's experience, but perhaps the most important to her learning was a program expectation that she reflect in writing on her language and cultural learning and development as a developing ESL teacher. Anna initially struggled with how to be reflective in her journal writing task, but in the end, it became clear that the externalization of her thoughts and experiences was a key *mediational means* for learning. The *division of labor* demonstrates how power was distributed throughout the learning system. An example is the requirement that teacher-learners collaborate in co-teaching English language classes in their practice teaching experience. Anna's relationship with her co-teacher became a source of conflict and in time, a source of awareness about herself as a teacher and individual. Among other factors, some key *mediational means* were her host family's language and cultural scaffolding and the articles and theoretical knowledge offered in the program courses.

Below I fill in the conceptual map displayed in Appendix 1 with narrative detail to give a nuanced understanding of Anna's learning process throughout the seven-month program, including her perspective looking back several months after the program's completion. What is most interesting (and deserving of greater research attention) are not the details of Anna's personal experience in themselves, but the affordances and constraints of this situated experience that interacted as Anna moved forward in her learning about diversity. Three primary themes emerged from the data that elucidate Anna's learning about culture and language learning (1) the importance of the personal socio-history that Anna brought to the experience abroad (or her *subject* position); (2) the opportunity for personal interactions with the "other" (a *mediational means* made available through the activities of the study abroad experience); (3) the creation of a "third space" and the dissonance of interaction in different and unknown *languacultures* (another *mediational means*).

4.3   Socio-historical resources: What Anna brought to the experience

In our first pre-departure interview, Anna told various anecdotes of her past interactions with people of cultural difference, including incidents from a trip to Panama, a language study program in France, her childhood growing up in Quebec, and a best friend early in her marriage who was Austrian. Over the years, she and her husband had hosted over 30 exchange students in their home. The time in Ecuador would clearly not be Anna's first experience interacting with cultural others. She anticipated the experience with excitement and saw it as a longer, more intense cultural exploration than her previous interactions in other cultures.

> The idea that I'll be living with a family and I've done that before and it's always been an absolutely wonderful experience. But I've always either had an interpreter or known the language. This time will be different and it'll be an extended time…So, I'm expecting that it will be a really positive experience (pre-interview, p. 7).

Anna was motivated to learn Spanish and spent an hour each day studying it on her own before departure. She remarked, "I don't want to be totally illiterate when I get there. I want to be able to communicate with my family. Plus, I really love Spanish….the music of the language" (pre-interview, p. 20).

Ecuador lies on the equator and Otavalo, a small city in the Andean highlands where the program unfolds, is situated at approximately 10,000 feet above sea level. Several volcanoes reaching to 15,000 feet soar above the town and are significant elements of the visual landscape. At the street level, indigenous Otavalans wear colorful and distinctive traditional dress and barter for their art and handicrafts in one of the largest open-air markets in South America. A stay in Otavalo brings with it a constant (and delicious) visual reminder that one is not at home. Anna clearly enjoyed the obvious cultural and sensory environmental differences of her surroundings in Otavalo. As Anna told me about an upcoming visit to an indigenous community, she said,

> INTERVIEWER: *uh-huh. And so this town [Otavalo] feels different from a town at home? In what ways?*
> Yeah. Oh my gosh! There's this guy that walks his goats down the street every day. One day I got lost coming home and there was an um indigenous person sitting in the middle of, you know, it's like an empty lot, with her sheep…. and then the cows were grazing in the strip right beside the Pan-American Highway. **I mean, that to me, is just like totally foreign.** No matter where I – where you go in the States, you don't see that. **But I love it. I just love it!**
> (during interview 1, p. 11)

Anna's response to the new cultural context was consistently positive, evidenced by the frequent and highly positive evaluative terms that she used to describe what she observed. She saw learning about culture as an adventure and related several anecdotes where she had fun as an "outsider" in a new culture. Anna expressed the freedom of being a sojourner within another culture in which she did not feel constrained by home cultural norms.

An example took place early in her stay with the host family in Ecuador:

> I was really noticing everybody at the table today and – at my house [in Pennsylvania] we have all these rules. I'm trying to teach my husband good table manners (chuckle), because that-that was what I grew up with in Canada; you had to be perfect all the time, uh, with your manners and your speech, and he never was. And so, you know, it's like, your napkin has to be on your lap…And you don't put your elbows on the table, and yada, yada, yada; and so everybody's grabbing Coke and-
>
> INTERVIEWER: *Here?*
>
> Yeah. -at the table and the-… everything's informal, and it was so much fun! You know, I just didn't have to think about my manners….
>
> INTERVIEWER: *Uh-huh. So you- you're allowed to be more comfortable, 'cause you know those rules, you don't even have to think about?*
>
> Right, they're out the window.   (during immersion, p. 38)

Anna's intercultural learning during this immersion program was predicated on her past experiences with other cultures and her positive orientation towards and enjoyment of difference. In several recent studies of intercultural learning in study abroad contexts, previous experience with otherness is observed to be a powerful predictor of the degree to which study abroad participants profit from cultural exposure (Byram & Alred 2002; Ehrenreich 2006; Murphy-Lejeune 2002). Byram and Alred (2002), drawing on Doyé (1992) and Berger and Luckmann (1966), argued for a process of "tertiary socialization" to explain what happens when learners are confronted by a target language/culture whose norms or concepts may be incompatible with those acquired in primary (familial, childhood socialization) and secondary socialization (subsequent socializing within other segments of the society) (p. 341). Byram and Alred (2002) hypothesize that when tertiary socialization takes place it is not one set of beliefs and schemata that are replaced by others, but that new beliefs and schemata are held side by side with existing ones (p. 343). Byram and Alred (2002) offer some evidence that individuals who had some degree of tertiary socialization before going abroad had increased gains in intercultural learning as compared to those with little previous experience with otherness. Anna had undergone a process of tertiary socialization early on as an adolescent. As she acted within the program and made sense of the experience afterwards, Anna had cognitive schemata and positive attitudinal resources available to further her process of intercultural learning. This process did not happen automatically, however, the immersion experience itself and the mediational structures of the program played critical roles, as detailed in following sections.

4.4   Cultural noticing

Activity theory acknowledges that the relation between any two elements of a field of activity (i.e. subject, object, artifacts, rules, community and division of labor) is mediated by a third element of the system. Of particular value to Anna' s learning are the *rules* of conduct that structure the field, for example, expectations that the participants will interact with host family members and critical reflections on those interactions. Cultural exploration is assumed to be a continuous activity through-out participants' time in Ecuador. Participants are explicitly taught ethnographic techniques for gathering cultural information and are asked to use the host family context as a place for cultural learning. A process of looking outwards and then inwards, interviewing a cultural other and then, contrasting and comparing cultures was adapted from Schmidt (1998) for this purpose. (For application of this process to teacher learning see Assaf and Dooley (2006)). Thus, the role of the teacher-learner in Ecuador is mediated by *rules* which support particular peda-gogical approaches; here an emphasis on direct experiential learning of the target culture relying on host culture informants (the host family, Ecuadorian students, Ecuadorian staff) and guided critical reflection. The purpose is to enlarge the sub-jective positions of teacher-learners and therefore, gradually over time, broaden the range of concrete actions available to teachers as they interact with English lan-guage learners in classrooms.

Growing up in a bicultural community in Quebec may have created a height-ened sensitivity toward other cultures for Anna. She drew frequent comparisons between the culture she was immersed in, her home culture and other cultures she had experienced in her past. In one of the pre-departure courses, the group was introduced to a framework for understanding specific aspects of intercultural encounters (D.I.C.E – Description, Interpretation, Checking, Evaluation) (Ryffel 1997) and Anna attempted to use the process to understand the values/history that underlie certain cultural practices that she observed enacted by the Ecuadorian people around her. She expressed curiosity about many aspects of her host family's life and explored issues such as gender roles in the family, the degree to which the family valued education, the family's participation in religious events, and how race and class intersected with social privilege in the Otavalan community. Her cultural explorations seem to involve both observing and asking direct questions to the host mother or other cultural informants. When I asked her how she would describe her host family, she said:

> Highly educated. Um, very intelligent and very, very close. Very close. They're always together, they're always hugging and kissing each other. Even the empleada [housekeeper] came in at the end of dinner when the soccer game was on and was sitting and hugging one of the family members. Although she did eat in the kitchen.

INTERVIEWER: *Uh-huh. There's a place, huh?*
Yeah. But she seems to be more family than a lot of empleadas [housekeepers]
might be.   (immersion interview 1, p. 4)

Anna interrogated the familial role of a live-in housekeeper in a middle/upper
class Latin American family. In our pre-departure interview, when telling me
about her previous visit to Panama, the same topic came up:

> And, of course the family, being a middle-class family, still sent their kids to a
> private school and still had a – what's the name in Spanish for maid? And they
> actually sort of adopted her as a member of the family, but in the books that I've
> been reading it says that's how it is. And yet, you know, you're [the maid] never
> equal with them.   (pre-interview, p. 12)

In both of these excerpts, Anna considered class as an element in interpersonal
relationships within Latin American cultures, however, she tended to describes
the cultural groups in an essentialist national culture way. In her first visit to
Panama, she also deferred to the "expert" knowledge of what books say about the
Panamanian culture.

The relationship Anna built with the Ecuadorian host family was an emotional
anchor for her throughout the immersion experience. The importance of the interaction with the host family cannot be understated. In a few weeks time, it is hard
to imagine Anna getting equivalent exposure to the host culture in any other manner. She enjoyed daily observation of family life, was very willing to ask questions
(despite her limited L2 proficiency) and invested in developing personal relationships with family. The family responded in kind. Anna perceived the host family as
warm, caring and genuinely interested in making her comfortable, and she in turn,
was very willing to be flexible to fit into the rhythm of their home life. She said:

> It's obvious that they really like me to be here and that they want to make sure that
> I'm happy being here.   (immersion interview 1, p. 4)

> **We're friends. Friends. I mean I'm not gonna be as close as family at all, but uh,
> they're accepting of me and I'm accepting of them.** And it's like, whatever they
> want me to do, I'll do (chuckle). But they're very-It's like, when I said I was going
> tomorrow, that was fine with them.   (immersion interview 1, p. 5)

She offered evidence of their caring by explaining special things that they did and
how they went out of their way to care for her when she was sick at home. When I
asked her about the event, experience, person or thing that had made the biggest
impression on her so far during the first two weeks, she said:

> No, that one's easy. It's been the conversations with Laura [host mother].
> INTERVIEWER: uh-huh, and why?

Um, because she is so warm and friendly and so giving of herself and so accepting;
and it just-and I'm learning so much Spanish from her

(immersion interview 1, p. 37)

4.5   Direct and personal interactions with the other

Anna's bicultural history growing up in Quebec and on-going experience of cultural "otherness" with exchange students had made culture a visible thread of the fabric of her life which she continued to investigate while in Ecuador. Anna was determined to complete the program and highly motivated to learn from it. For Anna the *object* of the activity system was clear and held firmly in her mind. Building on her previous language learning experiences and sojourns in other cultures, she demonstrated a high degree of intentional exploration of the target language and cultures. This is expressed clearly in a culminating paper she wrote after returning to the US.

> Being immersed in an Ecuadorian family, and choosing to spend a lot of time with the family, has given me a good beginning of an understanding of Latin American culture. **I devoured the culture lectures. In Ecuador, I began to understand the acculturation process and I picked up Spanish more quickly than I ever thought possible. I worked hard at observing, interpreting and clarifying everything I found around me, particularly in my family. I even checked to see how my family differed from other families.**   (post-reflection paper, p. 23)

In a post-program reflection paper, she stated the importance of the direct experiences she had with cultural others and the relationships she developed with individuals during the brief time period in Ecuador.

> **Because of the culture lectures, living with a family, and having Maria and Luis [local program staff] as consultants I was able to learn about Ecuadorian culture (and get a feel for Latin American culture). I <u>felt</u> the closeness of a Latin[o] extended family. I feel privileged to be so accepted and so much a part of the family.** I was part of family enthusiasm (dozens of roses brought home from work, 7-year old Daniela going to the shore for a week with a friend, fireworks to celebrate the Virgin, Laura's brother returning home from Germany with gifts for the whole family, Elena returning from Ibarra with a new car.) I was part of family sorrows and family difficulties....   (post-reflection paper, p. 23)

4.6   Scaffolding for second language learning

> **From my own experience, I learned how vital language is. To understand a culture, it is necessary to communicate with the people – to ask questions, to build relationships, to understand the values, to learn rituals.**

(post-reflection paper, p. 21)

Anna's host family was a critical aspect of her cultural exploration and source of emotional support during the program. The family also actively scaffolded her language learning. The family had previous experience hosting international students and perhaps had developed particular strategies to support communication with L2 speakers. The following example illustrates how Anna's host family mediated her Spanish learning. During the first week of the program, I asked her how Spanish was going and she replied:

> …nobody's laughing at me when I practice and the-I know my grammar's not right. And it's like it doesn't matter, as long as I communicate, that's what's important. And at the beginning, I understood about half of what Laura [host mom] would tell me and I'm finding now that, when she and I are talking – she slows down – and you know, I'll question a certain word, she'll find another way to say it. And I'm understanding 95% of what she says.
>
> (immersion interview 1, p. 18)

> …fortunately, I had a host mother and a host family that was really willing to work with me and refused to allow me to talk English unless it was like a crisis kind of situation which almost never happened. We had one crisis I couldn't- she couldn't tell me how to-she needed my dirty clothes that day and I couldn't understand her so we got someone to translate and that took care of that and after that it was either drawing pictures or she just made me talk.
>
> (post-immersion interview 1, p. 4)

Thus, it is clear that the host mom's circumlocution, slowing down of speech and willingness to negotiate meaning were aspects of the daily life within the host family that pushed along Anna's developing L2 proficiency. In this immersion situation, the authenticity of the communication, or the exchange of meanings between Anna and her host mom was a key factor in Anna's second language learning. In a final paper, she summarizes:

> In my host family, there was comprehensible input and I attended to the conversation completely giving myself up to the experience. With the input alone, I would have learned very little. It was the conversation – the authentic conversation – that gave me a chance to practice my Spanish, correct myself, learn new words and phrases (scaffolding), and talk to my host mother about interesting concepts such as the construction of the Panama Canal, Ecuadorian fruits and vegetables, soups, farming, flower farms, recipe sharing and so on. We were not only talking in Spanish, we were exchanging information.
>
> (post-reflection paper, p. 15)

4.7   Tension & discomfort within the "third space"

Juxtaposed to these expressions of comfort with her host family, Anna acutely felt the discomfort of being within a new cultural framework. In a journal entry, Anna wrote of an evening shortly after arrival to Otavalo when her host mother failed to appear at the agreed-upon time at the university.

> Today I felt like I was lost in a place where I had no language, no sense of place, no protection…. **I felt abandoned. I was frightened.** Where was my host mother? Was she on Ecuadorian time? Was there a miscommunication? Did she just forget about me? Questions in my mind…what should I do? Everyone walking past is going to steal my backpack. Should I wait? Should I try to find my way? Should I call? ….**Here I am 59 years old, unable to navigate my way home. I felt so dependent, but with no one to depend on. …I felt like a child lost in a maze…** such relief to see Elena and Negrito. And it really wasn't so bad after all – I had the wrong street! (immersion journal entry, p. 9)

Anna seemed aware that her fears were not rational, but the absence of cultural cues left her feeling lost, out of control and dependent. Additionally, there was stress resulting from the combined fatigue of interacting in an L2 in which she had only beginning ability and the pressures of an intensive educational program.

> I'm also tired--tired of speaking Spanish, tired of no time alone, exhausted at the end of a 10 hour work day preceded and followed by long conversations in Spanish which are incomprehensible. My style has always been flight. The **feelings of being overwhelmed make me want to escape** – to go home to the safety of husband, pets, computers. So now I have to fight. I have to fight the feelings of being overwhelmed, of homesickness, make myself happy (self-talk) and keep going, one reflection at a time, until each task is done! (immersion journal entry, p. 23)

Incidents in which Anna felt lost or anxious within the new cultural environment were related as bounded experiences with distinct beginnings and endings. The anxiety related to having to act without cultural cues did not permeate her experience in Ecuador, and the incidents in which she expressed anxiety are not particularly long in duration. Significantly, these low points seemed to be offset by her determination to learn the language and culture, the strong relationship Anna developed with her host mother and the general caring and welcoming environment she enjoyed within the host family.

In contrast, the conflict that developed between Anna and her practice teaching partner, Carrie, was an ongoing theme throughout the program. In the post-program interview, when I asked Anna about some worst moments, she cited this relationship, "dealing with Carrie that would be the number one worst thing." (p. 12)

While both Anna and Carrie lived in similar, neighboring communities, they were of different generations (Anna was 59 and Carrie was 21) and of different socio-economic backgrounds. Interestingly, Anna's discomfort with Carrie was rooted in value differences. In parallel with her interactions with local Ecuadorians, we can view Anna's interactions with her teaching partner as an intercultural encounter and learning experience. As co-teachers, they worked closely together both in planning and in delivering lessons to the Ecuadorian English learners. During the immersion program, when I asked Anna about any new awareness about herself, she said:

> I've done a whole lot of that kind of investigative thinking into my own-own self. **But the one thing that I had never realized before was after the first teaching class…and I realized I want control.** I don't like to share anything. I want to be in charge.   (immersion interview p. 52)

Near the end of the program, Anna decided that a lot of the discomfort around her relationship with Carrie had to do with Carrie displaying personality traits that recalled Anna's mother with whom Anna had experienced a lot of conflict during her life. In this excerpt her past comes alive in her present experience. In describing an incident involving Carrie that occurred on the last day of the program Anna "names" Carrie as her mother.

> ….that not only bothered me just because of what she did because the girls [their Ecuadorian students] went running to her while I just walked inside…that is my mother – that is the way my mother behaves, has behaved all my whole life [*sort of attention getting*] attention getting, um, not sensitive to other people, um you know she's 45 minutes late, it's too bad, everybody has to wait for her, I mean that's been her whole life…it wasn't just Carrie that was bothering me, **it was all those buttons that were being pushed from my past** and you know…. **I was unable to be who I am because she was being my mother!**   (post- interview 1, p. 14)

And later in another journal entry, she related what she had learned from this new personal awareness. There is evidence that the process of working intimately with her co-teacher put Anna in a position to acknowledge Carrie as different, then accept, and to some degree, appreciate the value differences that were uncovered in that individual. I propose that Anna's close and continuous interaction with an "other," in this case another program participant from the same region where Anna resides, seemed to bring about contradiction and conflict. Journaling and discussing details of the practice teaching situation with a teaching mentor, and subsequently, writing about and discussing the experience with the researcher, led to an eventual acknowledgement of her co-teacher's differences. The key factors are direct experience plus guided reflection. The collaborative activity of the teaching practice compelled the two individuals to share ideas, develop teaching materials and plans, and enact them as a team. The guided reflection encouraged Anna to consider the reasons for the conflicts that arose and relate them to her own personal experience and previous life experience. The collaborative teaching activity created dissonance, but also allowed Anna to resolve and make sense of that dissonance which led to a greater awareness about working with people of difference.

> The success of our class was not my success: it was our success, so I don't have total ownership of it. Again – loss of control. **But, I learned more than teaching ESL. I learned to work with someone whom I didn't particularly like. And I found some really good qualities I didn't expect to find.** Ceding control allowed ideas to flow and change. Together, our class was better than it would have been individually. We have discovered that we can work together, so I won't have to "walk on eggs" at the beginning of our next meeting.   (immersion journal, p. 21)

> Working with her forced me to at least acknowledge her, and you know, see more to her than I had seen before but, um there's, **she just a totally different person from me um I guess her values are not the same as mine at all?**
> (post-interview 1, p. 13)

5. Conclusion

An immersion program in another linguistic and cultural context can provide a different range of experiences than can traditional university courses. In this immersion experience for teachers, the activity system offered multiple opportunities for direct personal experience with the other, and secondly, the *mediational means* to conceptualize and analyze the processes of languacultural learning. Ongoing and guided reflection both in writing and orally with experienced cultural facilitators were critical mediators of the intercultural learning process for Anna.

The cultural and linguistic immersion experience itself was a source of dissonance and a third space that opened up opportunities for Anna to look at herself in ways that she might not have done in her home context. However, the lived experience of languaculture could easily have been experienced and not internalized, or have had no effect on the way Anna thinks about herself and about L2 learning. It seems that the *mediational means* which were critical to Anna's process of development around language and culture learning had to do with both what she brought to the learning situation and the pedagogical activities that guided her to reflect on what she was experiencing. These reflective interventions included writing about the experience in a dialogue journal with her instructors, discussing what she was experiencing in the host family with other students in a systematic and structured manner, and the ongoing interviews with the researcher after the program's conclusion which encouraged a revisiting of the experience months later.

In both personal and professional ways, Anna's experiences in the program seemed to change her views of herself. The duration of this immersion situation

(3.5 weeks) is quite brief: any claims to enduring transformation of self and pro-fessional abilities must be taken up cautiously. That said, in our final interview, Anna spoke directly to a sense of accomplishment and building of self-confidence through participation in the activity system of the program.

> **It just really shoved my self-esteem way up like I feel like you know I can do anything** and so I just turned 60 last weekend and…it's like you know I still have a whole life to live out there. I don't feel like I'm old. I don't feel like I need to retire. **I just feel like I've discovered so much about me and about learning and about culture that I can just build on all of that.** (post-interview # 2, p. 3)

5.1   Implications for teacher education

Because personal identity is tied up with second language and culture learning, we might expect that learners will experience some type of re-negotiation of identity as part of the process. (See Smolcic 2011 for another case study that explores iden-tity shifts in an immersion situation.) Consequently, teacher-learners need both conceptual models to understand culture and language learning *and* exposure to lived experience of languaculture in order for these processes to play out. The pre-departure course on culture and language is a critical space in which learn-ers are encouraged to articulate the values and practices of the cultures that have influenced their primary socialization as well as the ongoing development of their cultural identities. In sum, from a pedagogical point of view, two types of learn-ing, conceptual (theoretical) and experiential, should be components of a pre-departure preparation that strives to move teachers along in their journey towards interculturality. In the case of this program, it includes two three-credit courses which explore culture and language and their role in personal development as well as teaching and learning interactions.

By the program's end, Anna is clearly aware that the *object* of the activity sys-tem and her personal motives (her *object*) for cultural learning coincide. There is also evidence that she related her immersion experience to the situation of English language learners in the US context.

> …our trip to Ecuador was designed to be an understanding of and immersion into a new culture. **For me, culture turned personal…In Ecuador, I was trying to accomplish tasks using their set of rules. And I didn't know all the rules.** There were cultural rituals with deep meaning, and I didn't understand the deep meaning behind everything I saw. But I asked! **For ELL's in the US, the same issues would exist. They are trying to fit into a culture which they do not understand and which they may or may not be trying to absorb…..As an ELL teacher, I will encourage them to discuss their own cultures while also helping them to understand US culture.** (post-reflection paper, p. 20)

Anna understood that the cultural practices of Ecuadorians around her were rooted in deep cultural values. Moreover, Anna was able to transfer her personal experience of immersion in another culture to empathize with the experience of ELLs in the U.S. and expressed an intention to explore the process with future learners.

In line with assumptions of Vygotskian-inspired sociocultural and activity theory, an activity system analysis should lead to practical, programmatic innovations and change. As a result of this analysis, the notion that language and culture are interwoven (languaculture) has come more clearly into focus and has motivated increased attention to the homestay situation and guided reflection by the instructors in talking about the culture and language learning that may take place in that situation. Since the program already involved individualized teacher coaching by experienced ESL mentor teachers as part of the teaching practice, we were able to include analysis of cultural experiences as part of the dialogue between mentors and teacher-learners. Program participants now meet weekly during the immersion experience to debrief with a cultural advisor (an experienced facilitator to push participants to deeper explorations of their experience). The program is also exploring how to incorporate a follow-up course in the semester after students return to campus to guide them to look back and continue their reflections and discussion about intercultural learning.

This project attempted to address how teacher education practices can move teacher-learners towards interculturality, an important challenge for teacher education in light of significant increases in culturally and linguistically diverse students in today's classrooms. The study used an activity theory analysis and assumptions from sociocultural theory to highlight the meditational means within an international immersion situation that brought about intercultural learning. At the same time, however, this project has several limitations. First, intercultural learning is a lifelong endeavor that involves self-reflection, learning about culture general topics and direct intercultural experiences. While intercultural learning was a primary learning goal of the ESL certificate program, learning objectives related to instructional practices for ELLs are also of tremendous import and within a seven-month program time is greatly limited. Second, in terms of the research effort, because the participants were not followed back into classrooms after the certificate program was completed, we cannot know how shifts in the teacher-learners' cultural awareness may translate into specific teaching practices that will benefit culturally and linguistically diverse students.

The data demonstrate how the specific characteristics of a short-term immersion situation interact with one's individual motives, past history and personal capabilities and can open up possibilities for moving (perhaps, temporarily) into a third space. Anna was unique among participants in the clarity of her motives for this program and the richness of cultural (and lifetime) experience that she brought to the learning activity. Other participants with different personal histories, and perhaps distinct motives for participation will move along differing trajectories of learning. While the actual immersion experience is very brief, we can clearly see that Anna's interactions within the activity system moved her towards more complex understandings of culture and language learning as well as empathy for the English learners she will encounter in her own classrooms.

References

Agar, M. (1994). *Language shock: Understanding the culture of conversation.* New York, NY: William Morrow.

Assaf, L.C., & Dooley, C.M. (2006). "Everything they were giving us created tension": Creating and managing tension in a graduate-level multicultural course focuses on literacy methods. *Multicultural Education, 14*, 42–50.

Bennett, M.J. (1993). Towards ethnorelativism: A developmental model of intercultural sensitivity. In R.M. Paige (Ed.), *Education for the intercultural experience* (pp. 21–71). Yarmouth, ME: Intercultural Press.

Bennett, M.J. (1998). Intercultural communication: A current perspective. In M.J. Bennett (Ed.), *Basic concepts of intercultural communication* (pp. 1–34). Yarmouth, ME: Intercultural Press.

Berger, P., & Luckmann, T. (1966). *The social construction of reality.* Harmondsworth: Penguin.

Block, D. (2003). *The social turn in second language acquisition.* Washington, DC: Georgetown University Press.

Byram, M. (1997). *Teaching and assessing intercultural communicative competence.* Clevedon, UK: Multilingual Matters.

Byram, M., & Alred, G. (2002). Becoming an intercultural mediator: A longitudinal study of residence abroad. *Journal of Multilingual & Multicultural Development, 23*, 339–352.

Capps, R., Fix, M.E., Murray, M., Ost, J., Passel, J.S., & Hernandez, S.H. (2005). *The New Demography of America's Schools Immigration and the No Child Left Behind Act.* Retrieved from ⟨http://www.urban.org/url.cfm?ID=311230⟩.

Cochran-Smith, M., & Lytle, S.L. (1993). *Inside/outside: Teacher research and knowledge.* New York, NY: Teachers College Press.

Cochran-Smith, M., & Lytle, S.L. (1999). The teacher research movement: A decade later. *Educational Researcher, 28*, 15–25.

Cochran-Smith, M., & Lytle, S.L. (2001). *Beyond certainty: Taking an inquiry stance on practice.* New York, NY: Teachers College Press.

Dervin, F. (2007, June). *Dissociation and "complex" interculturality.* Paper presented at the NordicBaltic conference of the World Federation of Language Teacher Associations (FIPLV), Riga.

Doyé, P. (1992). Fremdsprachenunterricht als Beitrag zu tertiärer Sozialisation [Foreign language teaching as a contribution to tertiary socialization]. In D. Buttjes, W. Butzkamm & F. Klippel (Eds.), *Neue brennpunkte des englischunterrichts* [New foci in the teaching of English] (pp. 280–295). Frankfurt: Peter Lang.

Ehrenreich, S. (2006). The assistant experience in retrospect and its educational and professional significance in teachers' biographies. In M.F. Bryam, A. (Ed.), *Living and studying abroad: Research and practice* (pp. 186–209). Clevedon: Multilingual Matters.

Engeström, Y. (1987). *Learning by expanding: An activity theoretical approach to developmental research*. Helsinki: Orienta-Konsultit.

Engeström, Y. (1999). Activity theory and individual and social transformation. In Y. Engeström, R. Miettinen, & R. Punamaki (Eds.), *Perspectives on activity theory* (pp. 19–38). Cambridge: Cambridge University Press.

Finney, S., & Orr, J. (1995). "I've really learned a lot, but...": Cross-cultural understanding and teacher education in a racist society. *Journal of Teacher Education, 46*, 327–333.

Firth, A., & Wagner, J. (1997). On discourse, communication, and (some) fundamental concepts in SLA research. *Modern Language Journal, 81*, 285–300.

Frankenberg, E. (2006). *The segregation of American teachers*. Cambridge, MA: The Civil Rights Project at Harvard University.

Freeman, D. (2007). Research "fitting" practice: Firth and Wagner, classroom language teaching, and language teacher education. *The Modern Language Journal, 91* (Focus Issue), 893–906.

Glaser, B.G., & Strauss, A.L. (1967). *The discovery of grounded theory: Strategies for qualitative research*. Berlin: Aldine de Gruyter.

Johnson, K.E. (2006). The sociocultural turn and its challenges for second language teacher education. *TESOL Quarterly, 40*, 235–257.

Johnson, K.E. (2009). *Second language teacher education: A sociocultural perspective*. New York, NY: Routledge.

Johnson, K.E., & Golombek, P.R. (Eds.). (2011). *Research on second language teacher education: A sociocultural perspective on professional development*. New York, NY: Routledge.

Kinginger, C. (2008). Language learning in study abroad: Case studies of Americans in France. *The Modern Language Journal, 92*, 1–124.

Kinginger, C. (2009). *Language learning & study abroad: A critical reading of research*. London: Palgrave Macmillan.

Kramsch, C. (1993). *Context and culture in language teaching*. Oxford: Oxford University Press.

Kramsch, C. (2011). The symbolic dimensions of the intercultural. *Language Teaching, 44*, 354–367.

Kumaravadivelu, B. (2008). *Cultural globalization and language education*. New Haven, CN: Yale University Press.

Lantolf, J. (2006). Re(de)fining language proficiency in light of the concept of 'languaculture'. In H. Byrnes (Ed.), *Advanced language learning: The contribution of Halliday and Vygotsky* (pp. 72–91). London: Continuum.

Lantolf, J., & Johnson, K.E. (2007). Extending Firth & Wagner's (1997) ontological perspective to L2 classroom praxis and teacher education. *The Modern Language Journal, 91* (Focus Issue), 877–892.

Lantolf, J., & Pavlenko, A. (2001). (S)econd (L)anguage (A)ctivity theory: Understanding second language learners as people. In M. Breen (Ed.), *Learner contributions to language learning: New directions in research* (pp. 141–158). London: Longman.

Lantolf, J., & Thorne, S. (2006). *Sociocultural theory and the genesis of second language development*. Oxford: Oxford University Press.

Leont'ev, A.N. (1978). *Activity, consciousness and personality*. Englewood Cliffs, NJ: Prentice Hall.

Leont'ev, A.N. (1981). *Problems of the development of mind*. Moscow: Progress Press.

Lo Bianco, J., Liddicoat, A.J., & Crozet, C. (Eds). (1999). *Striving for the Third Place: Intercultural competence through language education*. Melbourne: Language Australia.

Martin, L.M.W. (1993). Understanding teacher change from a Vygotskian Perspective. In P. Kahaney, A.M. Perry & J. Janagelo (Eds.), *Theoretical and critical perspectives on teacher change* (pp. 71–90). Norwood, NJ: Ablex.

May, S. (1999). Critical multiculturalism and cultural difference: Avoiding essentialism. In S. May (Ed.), *Critical multiculturalism: Rethinking multicultural and antiracist education* (pp. 12–45). London, UK: Falmer Press.

Merryfield, M.M. (2000). Why aren't teachers being prepared to teach for diversity, equity, and global interconnectedness? A study of lived experiences in the making of multicultural and global educators. *Teaching & Teacher Education, 16*, 429–443.

Murphy-Lejeune, E. (2002). *Student mobility and narrative in Europe: The new strangers*. London: Routledge & Kegan Paul.

Pence, H.M., & Macgillivrary, I.K. (2008). The impact of an international field experience on preservice teachers. *Teaching & Teacher Education, 24*, 14–25.

Risager, K. (2006). *Language and culture: Global flows and local complexity*. Clevedon, UK: Multilingual Matters.

Risager, K. (2007). *Language & culture pedagogy: From national to a transnational paradigm*. Clevedon, UK: Multilingual Matters.

Roth, W.-M., & Lee, Y.-J. (2007). "Vygotsky's neglected legacy": Cultural-Historical Activity Theory. *Review of Educational Research, 77*, 186–232.

Roth, W.-M., & Tobin, K. (2004). Coteaching: From praxis to theory. *Teachers and Teaching: Theory and Practice, 10*, 161–179.

Ryffel, C. (1997). D.I.C.E.: Many sides to what we "see". In A.E. Fantini (Ed.), *New ways in teaching culture* (pp. 203–205). Alexandria, VA: TESOL.

de Saussure, F. (1959). *Course in general linguistics*. San Francisco, CA: Jossey-Bass.

Scahill, J.H. (1993). *Meaning-construction and habitus*. Paper presented at the Annual Meeting of the Philosophy of Education Society. Retrieved from ⟨http://www.ed.uiuc.edu/EPS/PES-Yearbook/1993.html⟩.

Schmidt, P.R. (1998). The ABC's of cultural understanding & communication. *Equity & Excellence in Education, 31*(2), 28–38.

Sleeter, C.E. (1999). Toward wisdom through conversation across epistemologies. In J.D. Rath & A.C. McAninch (Eds.), *What counts as knowledge in teacher education?* (pp. 1–27). Stamford, CT: Ablex.

Sleeter, C.E. (2001). Preparing teachers for culturally diverse schools: Research and the overwhelming presence of whiteness. *Journal of Teacher Education, 52*, 94–106.

Smolcic, E. (2011). Becoming a culturally responsive teacher: Personal transformation and shifting identities during an immersion experience abroad. In K.E. Johnson & P.R. Golombek (Eds.), *Research on second language teacher education* (pp. 15–30). New York, NY: Routledge.

Suarez-Orozco, C., Suarez-Orozco, M.M. & Todorova, I. (2008). *Learning a new land: Immigrant students in American society*. Cambridge, MA: Yale University Press.

Taylor, S.V., & Sobel, D.M. (2001). Addressing the discontinuity of students' and teachers' diversity: A preliminary study of perservice teachers' beliefs and perceived skills. *Teaching and Teacher Education, 17*, 487–503.

Thorne, S. (2004). Cultural historical activity theory and the object of innovation. In K. van Esch & O. St. John (Eds.), *New insights into foreign language learning and teaching* (pp. 51–70). Frankfurt: Peter Lang.

Villegas, A.M., & Lucas, T. (2002). Preparing culturally responsive teachers: Re-thinking the Curriculum. *Journal of Teacher Education, 53*, 20–32.

Vygotsky, L.S. (1978). *Mind in society: The development of higher psychological processes.* Cambridge, MA: Harvard University Press.

Vygotsky, L.S. (1986). *Thought and language.* Cambridge, MA: The MIT Press.

Weinbaum, A., Allen, D., Blythe, T., Simon, K., Sieidel, S., & Rubin, C. (2004). *Teaching as inquiry: Asking hard questions to improve practice and student achievement.* New York, NY: Teachers College Press.

Willard-Holt, C. (2001). The impact of a short-term international experience for pre-service teachers. *Teaching & Teacher Education, 17,* 505–517.

Zeichner, K., & Hoeft, K. (1996). Teacher socialization for cultural diversity. In J. Sikula, T.J. Buttery & E. Guyton (Eds.), *Handbook of research on teacher education* (2nd ed.) (pp. 525–547). New York, NY: Simon & Schuster.

Appendix 1

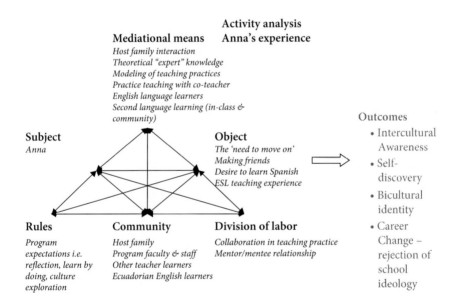

Politics of identification in the use of lingua francas in student mobility to Finland and France

Fred Dervin

University of Helsinki

This chapter examines the mobility of students to Finland and France. I am interested in the perceptions of the use of lingua francas in these contexts. The students have to speak languages of which they are not always "native speakers" and finding a common ground often results in using a lingua franca. In the chapter, English and French are the main lingua francas used by the students. Even though the cases of Finland and France are different in relation to the number of speakers of their languages (6 million people live in Finland compared to 70 million in France), the results show that similar attitudes and opinions seem to be shared by students who have spent time in these countries.

1. Introduction

This chapter addresses language and identity in student mobility by exploring the use of English and French as Lingua Francas (LFs hereafter) in the daily life of mobile students in Finland and France. English as Lingua Franca (ELF hereafter) has an expanding significance in the field of applied linguistics (Firth 2009; House 2002; Mauranen, Hynninen & Ranta 2010; Seidlhofer 2004; etc.), which has been established officially by the yearly organization of the International Conference of English as a Lingua Franca (Helsinki, Southampton, Vienna, Hong Kong and Istanbul) and the release of two large international corpora (the Vienna-Oxford International Corpus of English, VOICE, and the Corpus of English as a Lingua Franca in Academic Settings, ELFA). Research on French as a Lingua Franca (FLF hereafter), on the other hand, is in its embryonic state (see also; Dervin 2009; Dervin & Vlad 2010; Johansson & Dervin 2010; Yun & Demaizière 2008).

Though there are many studies on identity and language (e.g. Llamas & Watt 2009; Pavlenko & Blackledge 2004; Polyani 1995; Norton 2000), research on LFs has only begun to tackle the theme of identity, having worked mostly on the effectiveness of ELF use (e.g. in academia), language policy and planning, and the description of language forms and functions (e.g. Mauranen & Ranta 2009).

If we consider the context of European academic mobility, the studies on the use of LFs are also limited to these topics (see also Behrent 2007 for FLF; Cogo 2008; Kalocsai 2009 for ELF; Shaw, Caudery & Petersen 2009).

The few studies on identity and LF use are related to the context of formal language learning and teaching (e.g. Baker 2009; Firth 2009; Jenkins 2007; Prodromou 2009). Dervin (2009) and Virkkula and Nikula (2010) are, to my knowledge, the only researchers to have worked on these issues in the context of student mobility. For Virkkula and Nikula (2011, p. 256), who have examined the use of ELF by Finnish trainees abroad, "this is perhaps because ELF has been perceived as serving very practical purposes of information transfer rather than featuring strongly in identity construction." But this perception does not do justice to the *identity game* in the use of LFs: whenever two individuals interact, there cannot be but *identification* (Abdallah-Pretceille 2006; Brubaker & Cooper 2000), be it in a 1st, 2nd, or nth foreign language or in a LF. In this chapter, I follow the anthropologist Ewing's proposal that:

> in all cultures people can be observed to project multiple, inconsistent self-representations that are context-dependent and may shift rapidly. At any particular moment a person usually experiences his or her articulated self as a symbolic, timeless whole, but this self may quickly be displaced by another, quite different 'self', which is based on a different definition of the situation.
>
> (1990: 251)

Her words summarize well the poststructuralist, postmodern or constructionist understandings of identity whose principles I try to apply here. Inspired by Bauman's insights into identity, which he divides into "solid"-modernist and "liquid"-postmodern (2004), identity is understood in this chapter as acts of co-construction which take place between *complex* individuals, who *do* identity together in an ongoing transformative process in specific contexts of interaction – for better or for worse, in a non-free floating manner (cf. Dervin 2008b; Kramsch 2011; Piller 2000; see also Wolcott's chapter in this volume).

2.   Representations of lingua francas in study abroad

My understanding of representations in this chapter is derived from social psychology and, amongst others, the work of Jovchelovitch (2006, p. 11) who states: "the reality of the human world is in its entirety made of representation: in fact there is no sense of reality for our human world without the work of representation". This is why when one works on, for example, a language (LFs here), one cannot claim to find a *reality*, a single *entity* summarizing identity at work because what people say about languages cannot but be the result of representations, of "the interrelations between self, other and the object-world" (Jovchelovitch 2006, p. 11).

The concept of lingua franca, though it has stabilized recently, is sometimes used interchangeably with other expressions such as *interalloglot language* (Behrent 2007), *vehicular language, international language, artificial language* and even *langue de traîte* ("trade language") (Renaud 2001; for a discussion of these terms, see Dervin 2010). In this chapter, I concentrate on the use of *invisible,* supranational and intercultural LFs (Dervin 2009), in opposition to official, political and traditional lingua francas (Calvet 1985; Renaud 2001; Wright 2007). Lingua Francas are thus understood here as *unofficial contact languages,* which speakers do not share as a first language but as a 2nd, 3rd, 4th... language. Speakers can be geographically from near or far. In addition, LFs can be spoken in any sort of space: the countries of origins, the destination country, over the Internet (e.g. via social media), etc. Let us note also that the question of LFs is often related to the classical issue of the native/non-native speaker and has allowed further questioning of this dichotomy in applied linguistics (Berns 2009; Dervin 2009; Knapp & Meierkord 2002; Mauranen & Ranta 2009; Seidlhofer 2001, 2005). Research on representations and the *doxa* (commonsense) attached to LF use started to emerge in English-medium research in the early 2000s, especially for ELF (Jenkins 2007). These studies emphasize negative perceptions and attitudes towards ELF, especially because of its hybrid and unstable nature: it is often characterized by language *mélange* (or mixing) and non-standard use. Results also show that ELF speakers have a strong preference for native speakers of the language (Jenkins 2007). Most studies have examined the context of formal language learning and teaching by surveying teachers and learners. Professional, personal and casual contexts are rarely at the center of studies on representations of LFs.

While English as a Lingua Franca has been studied from many different perspectives, French as a Lingua Franca still needs to be explored. To my knowledge, Behrent (2007) is the only researcher, besides myself, who has carried out systematic work on speakers of FLF, especially in the context of academic mobility. Based on a corpus of interviews and recorded daily situations at the *Cité Universitaire Internationale* in Paris France, what the researcher has to say about their use of FLF can be summarized as follows – note that these elements can be generalized in a way to any LF user:

– FLF not being a 1st language, the students' language skills are rather heterogeneous, which means that even though they are non-native speakers, there is still potential hierarchy between them;
– recourse to other languages in FLF is common: *code-switching* or *mixing* are often present in FLF interaction.

In terms of representations:

-   the students know that they do not know;
-   they may or may not have a need or wish to improve language skills;
-   many students have suspicions towards FLF speakers in terms of skills and they often use "discursive technology tools" such as grammar books, dictionaries, etc. (Paveau 2006) to "check errors";
-   as a consequence Behrent identifies a clear sense of "fetishism of the norm" (Fenoglio 1996) in the students' discourse.

Behrent has concentrated on describing the forms and use of French as a Lingua Franca but has not really looked into the issue of identity. Just like ELF, its use is potentially very interesting for the study of self-images and identification. Pellegrino Aveni (2005, p. 6), who has worked extensively on identity and language use in study abroad tells us that: "language plays a fundamental role in the development, manipulation and expression of the self." When we think of LF use this has some interesting consequences as when people interact in a LF, they are, in a way, in-between languages, cultures, spaces, etc. For instance when we think of FLF, what are its cultural boundaries? France? (Official) French speaking countries? The same can be said about ELF or any other foreign language for that matter. It is easy to see how this can lead to extremely unstable identification and how mechanisms of creating the self can be enhanced, diminished but also threatened or protected. Thus, in this chapter we examine: how do mobile students present and construct themselves as LF users? What does the study reveal about their attitudes towards LFs in student mobility?

3.   Researching identification

In the early 2000s, inspired by socioconstructivism, Piller (2000, p. 21) suggested a change in the way scholars analyze intercultural communication, which she defines as follows:

> Just as research on language and gender has moved away from a focus on difference ("women's language vs. men's language") to an interest in the social construction of a gendered identity (…), I am suggesting that a social construction approach would also offer new insights in the field of intercultural communication. Instead of asking how Germans and Americans, for instance, use different communication styles, it might be much more useful to ask how cultural and national identity is 'done,' i.e. how it is constructed in ongoing interactions.

The term *identification* translates this process-oriented understanding of identity. Bauman's liquid identity is also synonymous with identification. Though it is often misunderstood as a "free-floating" element, it is not: there are many restrictions imposed on identity in interaction, as the sociologist asserts (2004). The concept of identification has also been suggested to clarify the anti-essentialist approach to identity that was put forward in research a decades or more ago (Brubaker & Cooper 2000). In order to study identification and at the same time representations, the methods used are: content analysis of documents (questionnaires, interviews, observation-participation), matched-guise technique, folk linguistics, and the like. But these methods can be extremely unsatisfactory if they fail to reflect the fact that discourse is unstable and contextual and that therefore identity is also in a mode of perpetual co-construction. Of course this does not mean that identity is "free-floating" (Brubaker & Cooper 2000, p. 11) and that people can do what they want when they identify, i.e. project an image of the self which will be accepted and simply co-created by others the way people want it to be. For Bauman (2004, p. 15), identity is "invented rather than discovered."

The following analysis is based on two different types of data. First, I use answers from a questionnaire distributed anonymously to exchange students in Finland via the Internet (N = 250). These data inform a *macro-level* study of identification in ELF, as I am interested here in a general approach to the theme and to make general representations emerge. As such, questionnaires have often been critiqued as a valid way of collecting data (Gray 2009, Chapter 3). They are used here not in an exhaustive or statistically oriented manner but to study some representations and thus *politics of identification* (Abdallah-Pretceille 2003) in relation to LFs in study abroad. In other words, I am not interested in uncovering the "truth" about the students and LF use (the data are anonymized) but in discourses of identification, which cannot but be constructed. The second analytical section derives from an interview with a Finnish student who was on an exchange programme in France. This second type of data will afford a *micro-level* analysis of identification. Just as Denzin (2009: 255) suggests, "theory (will) emerge out of data", and this will include a clarification of processes involved in the emergence of identification (solid and liquid identity) in study abroad.

4.   A macro approach to the politics of identification in the use of ELF

4.1   Representations of Spoken English

A few words about the Finnish context of study abroad are needed here to clarify some of the elements from the questionnaire presented below.

The data were collected from Erasmus students, a specific type of mobile student in Europe. Based on my previous studies (Dervin 2008a; Dervin 2008b, 2011) and those of other scholars' (Ballatore 2010; Murphy-Lejeune 2002; Tsoukalis 2008), it seems that the experiences of Erasmus students in Finland are not exceptional but resemble what most mobile students experience in other European countries: the students find it difficult to meet the locals (i.e. Finns) as they are often in segregated positions in Finnish society (they have their own district in student villages, Finnish institutions create special courses in English for the students, etc.). As a result, students form special "cocoon communities" (Dervin & Korpela 2012: introduction) with other foreign students and become weary of being "parked" together and disappointed at not living a "Finnish life". I have explained elsewhere the imagined realities conveyed in these arguments (Dervin 2008b). Within this specific context, the students are often led to use English as a Lingua Franca with each other. They also use their own first language – depending of course on the presence or absence of co-nationals. For many students, learning English, or improving their English, is actually one of key rationales for study in Finland. In fact if we look at the statistics provided by Finnish institutions, it is clear that the majority of exchange students are non-native speakers of English: e.g. in 2007 there were 1,241 students from Germany, 1,020 from France, 815 from Spain and 500 from Poland versus 235 from the UK, 36 from Ireland and 246 from the USA.

Finland has become a popular destination for Erasmus and international students, especially thanks to its excellent results in most international educational rankings (Sahlberg 2011). The vast majority wishes to experience the much celebrated Finland "miracle" (Niemi, Toom & Kallioniemi 2012). Of course other reasons are also cited, such as experiencing the "exotic North", learning and practicing an easily understandable English (compared to the Englishes spoken for example in the UK), and tourism, as Finland is situated between Scandinavia, Russia, the Baltic countries and Lapland. When asked why they chose Finland as their destination, many exchange students mention learning Finnish culture (Dervin 2008b). This goal is very problematic and obviously can rarely be met not only because encounters with Finns are extremely rare, but also because there is no such thing as an anthropological Finnish culture in a hyperindividualised world (Hermans 2001).

In the questionnaires, the students were asked what sort of English they felt they spoke in Finland. The question was formulated in such a way that the plurality of Englishes was emphasized. It is interesting to note that one student reacted strongly to it by answering: "*What sorts of English are there? Strange question!*", showing his belief in the unity and homogeneity of the English language.

Amongst the types of English which were described by the participants, I found what I call Solid Englishes, or forms of canonical – yet imagined – English attached to a specific space (without making any social, regional, foreign distinctions):[1]

(1)   British English mostly. I did Cambridge Certificate I spent one year in Britain so i speak british English Native speaker-level with a strong British accent

(2)   I'm speaking American-English coz I was in the US during high school

For these participants, having had physical, relational or institutional experiences in these countries authorized them to define their English as solid (i.e. "strong" in (1)).

Contrary to the Englishes described above, altered versions of the language are also mentioned by the participants. These are often represented as deteriorated, less good and less valuable than the Solid Englishes described above. They also often mark an identity metamorphosis for the speakers as they start to speak such devalued forms of English. Internationalized English is often described in negative terms; its characteristics are *mélange*/mixing but also incorrectness:

International broken English
(3)   easy for everyone to understand easy structures and words being used with some systematic mistakes my pronunciation isn't really good and I do not know many words

Erasmus English
(4)   we have even joke – that we have Erasmus English – English with many mistakes I call it Erasmus English:) In my opinion it's limited to a certain amount of words (as there's not much native speakers to improve your vocabulary while speaking) It can be poor English sometimes Erasmus English, with my German accent, without getting better, the same vocabularies, grammer is not correct

European English
(5)   It contains a lot of mistakes, especially in grammar and the usage of some kinds of words and phrases, e.g. sayings which one directly translated from the respective language Globish which is defined as a simplified English spoken in the international community

Hybridity appears to define their English, and as the anthropologist Pieterse (2004) asserts, even though hybridity is natural, it can be very unpopular. The

---

1.   All the excerpts are verbatim and have not been corrected.

use of evaluative words and phrases such as *easy, limited to a certain number of words, a lot of mistakes, systematic mistakes, bad pronunciation...* confirms a rather negative view of these forms of English. The absence of native speakers in Finland is also noted by one student as a negative influence on the state of the mobile students' English.

It is clear in what follows that English as a Lingua Franca also means having to become an Other. The following quotes give the impression that ELF alters the students' identity. English is:

Slower
(6)   I need to speak slow to be in synch with Finns

Basic
(7)   I use fewer idioms and simpler grammatical constructions

(8)   I try to use unambiguous international English

It has become Finnish
(9)   My English sounds Finnish now adapted to the Finnish pronunciation

All these comments are interesting as they seem to suggest that the students are becoming – for the majority – Finnish in their English even though they keep claiming that they have no contacts with Finns. Again here the idea that their English is a less prestigious version of canonical English is palpable in the use of such words as *fewer* and *simpler*.

English use is even described as having deteriorated by some students, especially because of the negative influence of the others:

(10)   My English got a bit worse since most other people exchange students aren't native speakers and therefore make quite a lot of mistakes which you eventually get used to and adopt I used to speak good English until I landed in Finland I have to slow down and speak in a way that people understand that means no grammar, just broken words

(11)   When I talked to other exchange students I did recognize how my English became worse, because I adjusted to their style of speaking luckily I had the chance to speak with native speakers

(12)   English that I speak is quite familiar coz I speak to people who are not native speakers I speak not a good English because I usually speak with foreigners not very good because the problem is that there are too less native speaker so if you are not sure about grammar or words you can't really ask someone and therefore continue to speak wrong English

The native speaker plays a central role in defining the deficiency linked to ELF. S/he is presented in the second quote as a savior ("luckily I had a chance to speak to native speakers"). In these narratives clear indications of the transformations can be found in the use of certain words, especially verbs (adjust/adapt/used to/ got worse). For most students, it seems evident that they are conscious of these issues and they express clearly the strategies they use to try to avoid what could be labeled as contamination – or becoming like the other speakers:

(13)   Correcting in my head the mistakes I hear others make – so that I do not acquire them because you get used to the bad Erasmus English. And also you have to be aware that Finns have an accent and you shouldn't get it.

In a few cases, the students' discourses show that they position their use of English in a dichotomous manner, rendering the usual dichotomy of the native/non-native speaker more complex. Through these continua, the students demonstrate that they are aware of the transformative nature of ELF (though in a rather neo-essentializing way: identity is reduced to two aspects only):

(14)   Informal/formal (depending on with whom I speak)

(15)   Common English (discos)/special English (at university)

(16)   Slang form (with friends)/medical English (at university)

(17)   Instrumental English/communication English (shops vs. friends)

(18)   Proper English (at university, essays)/simple English (friends/flatmates)

The proposed dichotomies are context-bound (e.g. as formal and informal contexts). We can see that the informal is reserved for a far less developed kind of English (simple, communication English). The compartmentalization of English taking place here is also described in less general terms but in relation to specific interlocutors:

(19)   I have to use simple English to speak for instance with Spanish friends on the other side I can try to be more complicated speaking with native English speakers.

A few descriptions indicate hybrid/mixed versions of languages (usually the students' 1st language and other languages), genres, etc.:

(20)   Lithuanian-English/Chinglish/Polish-English, Itanglish…

(21)   a funny but helpful mix of 'MTV-slang'-like English polished up with scientific vocabulary

(22)   I speak multilanguage English… why? Because of different accent that depends on who i am speaking to and also because we sometimes add some words in many other languages. It's not a strict English (esp. About the grammar) it is a kind of slang-globalvillage-language

It is interesting to note that these are the two only excerpts that do not contain negative assessment of ELF.

As a whole, representations of ELF in the questionnaire appear to be quite negative. Most participants seem to be aware of what they report as the damaging impact of ELF use on their own skills, and on its hybrid aspect. This confirms results from previous studies on English as a Lingua franca from language education (Baumgarten & House 2010; Jenkins 2007). What emerges also from this macro analysis is the fact that the students seem to be aware of the fact that ELF means having to adapt to speakers – and thus identify differently. Many of these comments are based on ethnocentrism or linguocentrism.

4.2   The others' English

When the students describe their own English, they cannot avoid mentioning others' language skills as we have already seen in the previous section. One item on the questionnaire was specifically about this point. Most of the received comments resemble differentialist categories which have been proposed, for example, by the interculturalist Hofstede, sharply criticized for having classified the world into clear-cut cultural spheres (McSweeney 2002). Of course we need to bear in mind that asking this question led the students to position themselves toward other users of English, and thus skews the results. Yet the following comments give a potentially good indication of how English as Lingua Franca is used to identify others (and thus the self).

Finns are usually assessed positively. The use of adjectives speaks for itself (excellent, exceptional, good):

(23)   Finns speak English good but they are too shy to accept it

(24)   As far as Finns go, I find that generally their English is exceptional I think that Finnish people speak excellent English but their problem is that they do not believe in their skills

(25)   easier to understand than native speaker

Two of the above respondents use a somewhat auto/hetero-stereotypical explanation for Finns' lack of "belief in their skills" – reducing 5 million people's identity to these words. Sometimes, the "locals" are also described as being slow speakers (see above):

(26)   in general I think Finns have a better English than most foreigners concerning the pronunciation and vocabulary

(27)   Finns speak slow in general so they speak English slow also

A few students even propose rankings of Finnish speakers of English, which shifts the previous categories and renders them more complex:

(28)   on the scale of 10: the academics have grade 8–9 (with some exceptions – it could be either 10 or lower), those in the public institutions have grade 5, those in shops have grade 5. Those who are selling sausages, or strawberries in the summer – they do not need English I would say that younger generations spek it better than the older ones. I do not know if the ones who sound 'less Finnish'(=have more intonation and not that monotonous and using more the article) are simply more talented or if they watched more TV:)

When they talk about the other exchange students, the respondents also create categories, which reflects perceived Englishes and levels of English. Two students assert that:

(29)   Spanish people: mostly bad english; portugese people: very good english, Italians: bad english; Czek Republic: generally good English; polish people: quite good; Netherlands: very good English; Germans: in the most cases good English, but very often the awful German accent

(30)   That depends on the home country of these people. I have the feeling that people from the Netherlands, Belgium and from germany have better language skills than, let's say, people from Southern Europe or Africa.

The words are simple and do speak for themselves again (e.g. "good," "bad") in the proposed gradation and thus hierarchy – rather than e.g. variation – between ELF speakers. This differentialist approach to others' English is tantamount to the way cultures are compared and evaluated as Phillips (2010) has demonstrated.

People from the participants' country (France and Italy here) are also often assessed negatively:

(31)   As I am French, I am one of the worse English speaker here... As you must know it, French people have so many issues with foreign languages so in a way I have some linguistic complexes

(32)   hehehe other people knows English better than italians, for sure! But this is a problem of our school that only in the last year introduced English also in the primary school.

Maybe unsurprisingly, discourses on ELF reflect a categorization of the world which has been noted in other fields in the human and social sciences, e.g. in relation to cultures. Based on these data, it is impossible to define how much of what the students write to answer the questionnaire is based on reality (i.e. their own experience) or on *doxic* discourses, i.e. generic discourses developed within groups of Erasmus participants.

4.3 Speaking English as a Lingua Franca with people from one's own country?

In Europe – but also elsewhere – many students complain about the fact that there are too many representatives of their own country in exchange student communities and that this has many consequences for their language use (Tsoukalis 2008). The participants were asked if they use ELF with people from their own country. Their answers are quite revealing of the attitudes and representations that the students hold toward LFs.

4.4 Refusal of sameness

The questionnaire data confirm the negative attitudes and representations exposed in the previous section. The choice of adjectives to describe speaking English with people from the same country is interesting in this sense: *too artificial, useless, bizarre,* etc. On the other hand when they write about using a common first language, the situation then becomes *more comfortable, more precise, easier.* Often the students assert that their compatriots' language skills are too limited to allow interaction in ELF. It is fascinating to see that this sort of discourse seems to be shared by people regardless of their country of origins. The only time when it appears acceptable to use ELF is when there are speakers of other languages around them:

(33)   when there are some non-Korean around, we only speak English because we think that speaking Korean in front of people who can not understand it is impolite.

The negative attitude toward using ELF with compatriots appears to be generalized but at least in two cases, the respondents show that, in their cases, the question is irrelevant. That is the case of one student from Namibia and another from Spain, whose home context urges them to be more plurilingual:

(34)   we have about 7 different languages spoken in my home country and some of the namibians I met here do not speak my language, so we speak English

(35)   yes I speak english with some Spanish students, because I am from barcelona and I speak catalan, not Spanish, and with them I prefer speak english because it is not very easy for me speak spanish fluently and in this way I will improve my english

European Nation-States were built upon the idea of linguistic *unicity* (Bauman 2004), i.e. citizens should share the same language and not cultivate their local dialects. Most of them have thus one official language only. Even if the idea of multilingualism is taking on greater significance in this context, especially through the work of the European Union, the norm in terms of national interaction is based on one language and the use of LFs seems not to be accepted or acceptable amongst co-nationals. This is, in a way, a blow to the current omnipresent discourse on the uncontested value of multilingualism promoted by both the EU and member countries.

4.5   Disappointment with Finnish

For most students, it is clear that the use of ELF is a positive thing as it allows them to interact with others, as they do not know Finnish or Swedish, the two official languages in Finland. These two languages are taught to Erasmus students but they rarely reach a higher level than "Survival Finnish/Swedish" (as these courses are named at Finnish universities).

(36)   It feels comfortable Finland does not force me to use Finnish at all I can go everywhere with my English and this is very good it is simply natural to speak English here

Yet some students note the paradoxical situation and the impact it has on their identity:

(37)   I am pretty happy. However I should reduce speaking English and put effort to start speaking some Finnish

(38)   good and guilty at the same time I should be speaking Finnish since I am also a resident of Finland

The use of the modal "I should" shows that there is an external force (him/herself? Finland? His friends and family back home? EU discourses on student mobility?) pressuring the student to consider learning Finnish. Some students use adjectives such as "guilty", "ashamed", "ignorant", "sad" and "impolite" to talk about the situation, as if by not learning the language, part of their identity does not correspond to what is expected of them.

(39)   I feel a bit guilty I feel as though i should spaak their language

(40)   I feel a bit ashamed that i have not committed myself to learning the Finnish language more. I really feel like an ignorant foreigner...

(41)   would rather try to speak Finnish as I feel it's rude not to comfortable but rude (when speaking to Finns) because I do not know much Finnish

Phipps (2007, p. 119) reminds us that, while abroad, people face an important issue as far as learning the local language is concerned: "*our own status as good guests is up for grabs* (...)". Yet all the students in the questionnaire who wished to present a positive face to the locals by speaking their language report being rebuked and answered back in English.

The linguistic context in Finland has an influence on the students' language use. As minority languages in Europe, Finnish and Swedish are not learned extensively. The only alternative for students visiting the country is to use ELF. We have seen in this macro-outlook on ELF in Erasmus mobility that ELF is double-sided: on the one hand, it allows the students to communicate with each other and the locals but, on the other, it limits the learning of the local languages, constrains encounters with the locals and in some cases, transforms the students' English language skills "for the worse."

5. A case study: French as a Lingua Franca in study abroad

Moving on in our examination of identification and representations of LFs, I would now like to look at an interview with a Finnish university student of French who had studied in Paris as an Erasmus student for 6 months. France is usually the main target country for students of French; very few choose Canada or Switzerland for their stays abroad. This section represents a *micro-level approach* to LF. The student had been a student of mine during her study time at Turku University in Finland so we shared many ideas on issues of interculturality and language, which probably had an impact on the data reported below. As always, it is difficult to identify the boundaries between discourses in what she has to say about her experience (Linell 2009).

5.1   A few words about the method

The suggested method for examining identification in relation to LF use here takes into account the writings of such authors as Abdallah-Pretceille (2003), Holliday (2010) and Nynäs and Illman (2006) on diversity and intercultural communication. All these scholars examine the intercultural from a constructionist, intersubjective and contextualized perspective (see Jackson in this volume). The concepts of positioning and repositioning are central in the approach and will serve the purpose of identifying the gaps and fluctuation in identification (Hermans 2001) and of detecting instability/diversities of identities in seemingly stable and homogeneous self-images. The method is based on the central idea of "self-others interdependence" (Markova, Linell, Grossen & Salazar Orvig 2007, p. 1), which can be reformulated as "self-images = self-other-images" in the sense that there is no self without the other/others, thus no voice without other voices and no sense-making without other sense-makers (Linell 2009, p. 36).

The concept of voice is essential here. Any discourse is intersected by many and varied voices which construct what is being said and at the same time, construct identification. These voices constitute strategies (see Dervin 2008b; Tannen 1989), which allow speakers to negotiate, build up and work on their identities during interaction. Voices can be internal (I as a lecturer, I as a neighbor, I as a father...) and/or external, that is, they "refer to people and objects in the environment that are (...) relevant from the perspective of one or more internal positions" (Hermans 2001, p. 252). Interaction between these voices takes place within conversations: internal positions interact between themselves (*I said to myself*), internal and external positions interact (*I told Matt*), and so do external positions between themselves (*Paul said to Henry...*). What these voices are made to say and how, contributes to constructing identification.

5.2   Ideal-type of the pro-FLF user

The student under scrutiny is very interesting for our purpose as she represents one of the few students that I have interviewed who is a pro-FLF user. Generally speaking, attitudes towards FLF appear to be as negative as what has been reported on ELF in the previous section. Her position might be first explained by the fact that the student seems to be as very much socially-oriented vs. linguistically-oriented as is shown in the first excerpt:

(42)   *Je suis d'accord qu'il faut parler avec les Français ou les natifs ou les*
        francophones pour apprendre plus mais c'est pas seulement le côté
        d'apprentissage pour moi c'est important que dans une conversation je me
        sens bien moi[2]
        (I agree that we need to speak to the French or native speakers or
        Francophones in order to learn but it is not just the learning aspect of it
        that is important to me, I also have to feel like myself in a conversation)

She describes her social networks during her stay in Paris as being composed mostly of other exchange students, with whom she shared FLF. She also had a few French acquaintances (with whom she used French), American friends (with whom she used English and possibly some French) and a few Finns (with whom she spoke Finnish and some French).

5.3   Deficiency in French – competence in FLF?

During the interview, the student co-constructs with the interviewer a consistent self-image in relation to French. This image appears as principally deficient and she often compares her French Self to others' (natives/non-natives) and to

---

2.   The interview was in French. My transcription is orthographic. S = student; I = Interviewer.

her own English self – her competences in English are excellent – to justify her negative perception of her own skills. In the following abstracts she describes her French:

(43)   I: *Y a des différences entre votre français et celui des francophones natifs?*
       S: *Oui bien sûr y en a*
       I: *Quel aspects?*
       S: *Bon ben je parle pas très bien français ça c'est une différence* (laughter)
       (I: Are there differences between your French and native French speakers'?
       S: yes of course there are
       I: Which aspects?
       S: Well I do not speak French very well that is a difference (laughter))

(44)   S: *(...) quant à moi je parle pas si bien le français (...)*
       (S: (...) I do not speak so good French (...))

(45)   S: *Tous mes amis ont parlé français mieux que moi*
       (S: All my friends spoke better French than me)

Two main voices appear in these excerpts: the self and others ("all my friends," which contains an extreme case formulation; Pomerantz 1996), allowing her to describe and emphasize her identity as a deficient speaker (through the constant use of negations and comparatives) and the fact that she cannot reach an ideal self in the language, which is, in a sense, represented by her friends.

5.4   Deficiency expressed through others

The interviewee often shows that she feels insecure and that the French fail to validate her as a competent user of their language. The latter are represented as very powerful.

(46)   *Parce que j'ai pas si peur que avec les natifs bien sûr j'ai l'impression que les Français pensent que moi je suis idiot parce que je peux pas parler la langue si bien et avec des non natifs ils comprennent que c'est pas facile*
       (Because I fear the natives of course I feel that the French think that I am an idiot because I can't speak the language so well while with non-natives they understand that it isn't easy)

In this excerpt three main voices can be identified: the Self, "the French" and FLF users. It is through the imaginary figure of the "French" that the student's Self is diminished and presented as deficient. The "French" are also made to evaluate her in a negative light through a represented discourse: "*les Français pensent que je suis idiot*" ("the French think that I am stupid"). The voices of other imaginary and generalized figures (FLF users) are used to empathize with her. The choice of the verbs to qualify what the French and other non-native speakers do to her is relevant as to the support or boost she gets from both groups in terms of identification: understanding (FLF users: *ils comprennent*/they understand) vs. judgment (native speakers: *ils pensent que*/they think that) (on students as agents of processes shaping their motivation, see Willis Allen's chapter in this volume).

In the next excerpt, the student uses the same voices to confirm the importance of non-native speakers for her:

(47)   *Il y a une grande différence à mon avis franchement en France pour moi c'était un soulagement de parler avec les non natifs en français parce que avec les natifs c'est vous savez très lourd et parce qu'ils connaissent très bien la langue et c'est vite et tout ça et avec les non natifs c'est plus facile et moi je peux parler plus ouvertement*
(I believe that there is a big difference in France I felt relieved to speak to non-natives because with the natives it is quite intense because they know the language very well and they speak fast and all that and with non-natives it is easier and I feel I can speak more freely)

FLF users represent relief and ease for the student. She can be "herself" with them and especially be in control of what is occurring and being constructed in interaction. FLF also represents an opportunity for her Self (positive identification) to emerge in French. When she talks about the native speakers, many subjective markers are used; *très lourd* (very intense), *c'est vite* (its fast), *soulagement* (relief) to express the notion that these interlocutors forbid her from projecting a desired self-image, that of a legitimate speaker of French.

5.5   Strong identification with FLF users

During the interview it appears clearly that the student has a preference for the use of FLF. What she has to say about the "natives" gives the impression that she is leading a common battle with other non-natives. She even goes as far as to use two war-related metaphors: "*on était tous comment on pourrait dire en guerre une bataille*" (we were all… how shall I put it?… at war, battling). Through the use of the impersonal pronoun *on* in French (which can be translated here as the generic first person plural), she constructs an imagined collectivity, that of non native speakers, who together with her become comrades in arms. This seems to give her Self a positive boost.

Furthermore, in this "battle" and identity game, English is presented as an important crutch:

(48)   I: *Entre non natifs, on ose se corriger?*
S: *Oui voilà et on peut ajouter des mots en anglais et ça passe aussi avec des Français s'ils peuvent parler anglais bien sûr mais pour moi c'était*

impratiquant si quelqu'un ne comprend pas un mot d'anglais et je vais
rajouter un verbe comme RUN quoi?
(I: Do non-native speakers correct each other?
S: yes and we (*on*) can add words in English and it can work with the
French if they speak English of course but for me it was impractical if
someone does not understand a word of English and I would add a word
like RUN what?)

Four different voices are put on the scene to construct her discourse: *on* (FLF
users/exchange students), some French people, somebody (*quelqu'un*) as well as
particular French native who participate in the enacted dialogue. The pronoun *on*
underlines again the importance of the English crutch which helps her (because
it is "practical"), makes her feel confident and is shown to boost her Self. On the
other hand, the voice of the French is enacted through a represented dialogue:
"*RUN quoi?*" (RUN what?). This French voice represents again an element which
threatens her face and does not allow her to be a fully accepted speaker of French.
The possibility of using English means that she can feel more confident when
interacting in French.

5.6   Compartmentalized in-groups

In her interview, the student presents several groups, as we noted earlier. Each
group seems to have a different impact on her Self. In this excerpt, she talks about
the use of FLF with her American friends:

(49)   *À Paris moi j'ai parlé français avec les autres Erasmus ou les autres*
        étrangers presque toujours mais y a une exception c'était les Américains
        en fait parce qu'on était moi et cinq Américains et moi et dans cette
        situation ce serait un peu bizarre si on parlait toujours français parce que
        moi je parle beaucoup meilleur anglais que français et pour eux c'est la
        langue maternelle
        (In Paris I spoke French with other Erasmus students or other foreigners
        nearly always but there was an exception the Americans, in fact because
        there were five Americans and myself and in that situation it would be a bit
        bizarre if we spoke French because I speak better English than French and it
        is their mother tongue)

Two different voices are used here: the Americans, who impose the use of English
on her and lead her to position her English self ("*dans cette situation ce serait un*
peu bizarre", in that situation it would be a bit bizarre); the Self, which is presented
as stronger when it expresses itself in English. The use of English is presented as
normal and positive in this context.

As to her Finnish contacts, her discourse is different:

(50)   *et bien sûr avec les Finlandais Finlandaises je parlais finnois à mon avis c'est*
        assez prétentieux si on parle en anglais ou en français avec les autres qui parlent
        finnois (…) Oui oui parce qu'on a quand même une langue commune et a mon
        avis c'est c'est assez nul d'utiliser une autre langue (…) mais bien sur si on a des
        autres qui parlent pas anglais ou finnois on va parler français ou anglais
        (and of course with Finns I speak Finnish in my opinion it is quite
        pretentious to speak English or French with those who speak Finnish (…)
        yes yes because we share the same language and in my opinion it's uncool
        to use another language (…) but of course if there are people who do not
        speak Finnish or English we'll speak French or English)

Three voices are presented: Finns (her Finnish Self) through the use of *on* to
describe another constructed collectivity; her FLF and ELF selves with Finns,
which she qualifies negatively (as a "fake" Self: *prétentieux, nul*). She also mentions
the fact that when other foreigners are present, it is fine to use a French self with
Finns (see also the results of the first section). All in all, different nationalities seem
to be attached to different attitudes toward LFs and thus to different identification.
The compartmentalization of language speakers is practiced by the student during
the interview.

5.7 FLF vs. ELF

For the student, and as has been shown earlier, FLF and ELF differ in terms of
representations. For Pellegrino-Aveni (2005: 55): "Learners' sense of Self in social
interactions is inextricably linked with the language they use." This is very true for
the Finnish student:

(51)   (…) *pendant l'automne quand je rencontre des Polonais ou des Russes surtout*
        ça et je parle anglais entre nous je crois que j'ai beaucoup des stéréotypes
        des … que je pense bien que je sais que c'est pas vrai je pense qu'ils sont plus
        stupides ou je sais pas quoi parce qu'ils ont un accent de l'est
        ((…) during the autumn when I met especially Poles or Russians and
        I spoke English with them I think that I have many stereotypes about…
        that even though I know it isn't true I think that they are stupid or
        something because they have an accent from the East)

This episode is narrated through different voices: the Self, which differentiates
itself from the Russian and Polish exchange students, but also interestingly repli-
cates the negative evaluation that she presented earlier as what the French thought
of her (stupid). She is well aware of this attitude and stereotypes (modalities: *je
crois que, je sais que…* I think that, I know that…).

The student also expresses her awareness of the fact that the language one speaks impacts on identification and that different skills in different languages will modify the image that one has of people. She recounts the following:

(52)   *mais en français parce que les gens que j'ai rencontrés une Tchèque au moins et un Macédonien ils ont parlé un français très bon et ils étaient tous les deux intelligents et gentils tout ça*
(but in French because the people I met someone from the Czech Republic at least and a Macedonian they spoke very good French and they were both of them clever and nice and all)

In this excerpt, the voices of two FLF speakers from Eastern Europe are used to show this change of attitudes. She had the impression that they were "stupid" when they spoke English but when they speak French, they sound "intelligent." In becoming aware of this, the comparison with her own double identity (competent in English, deficient in French) may have comforted her in the idea that she can be both "stupid" and "intelligent" depending on the language she speaks. French as a Lingua Franca seems to have changed her attitudes towards some national or linguistico-ethnic categories and decreased her willingness to accept and revoice common stereotypes.

6.   Conclusion

This chapter addressed two questions: how do mobile students present and construct themselves as LF users in Europe? What does the study reveal about their attitudes towards LFs and individuals? The central concept of identification, especially in its representational and political aspect, was the main emphasis of my analysis.

Returning now to Ewing's comments at the opening of this chapter: "I argue that in all cultures people can be observed to project multiple, inconsistent self-representations that are context-dependent and may shift rapidly" (1990: 251). Did we find some examples of rapidly changing and multiple self-representations in the answers?

For the questionnaires, it is indeed hard to say: a macro-level approach to identity through questionnaires tends to be static (it was not always possible to check if the students were consistent in they way they talked about ELF). Yet there is an indication that ELF modifies the way students identify with others – and thus their self-images.

As far as the interview is concerned, the pro-FLF use student appears to be consistent in her opinions about the self and the use of FLF. Her self-images and what she has to say about others are quite stable for French/FLF. Her feelings of security and insecurity are associated with the same groups (natives/non-natives). We noticed that one group may hold different attitudes toward languages, lingua francas, identities and self-images.

But such images are always unstable – even if they appear otherwise in discourse. Once again, according to Ewing (1990, p. 251): "the person will often be unaware of these shifts and inconsistencies and may experience wholeness and continuity despite their presence." As such the Finnish student's representations of FLF are positive but this does not mean that she has a positive attitude towards LFs in general, for example when she speaks about ELF, she clearly compartmentalizes speakers (e.g. Russians or Poles) but modifies her attitudes when she talks about similar people speaking FLF.

There were similarities and differences in the way ELF and FLF were portrayed as is reflected in the following Table 1:

Table 1. Comparison of data set

Characteristics	ELF	FLF (+ ELF)
Similarities	– Fetishism of the norm – The students know that they do not know – The students mix languages – The students reject speaking ELF to their co-nationals	– Fetishism of the norm (for English too) – The student knows that she does not know – The student allows herself to use some English when she speaks FLF – The student rejects speaking FLF/ELF with co-nationals
Differences	– The students are aware that they use different types of English (multiple identities) – The students assess ELF and qualify it in an often negative light – The students are suspicious towards ELF users and fear becoming like them	– The student says she is deficient in French but is not really aware of her multiple identities in French – The student is not judgmental towards FLF – The student is critical of French speakers; she forms a common in-group with FLF users – The student is aware of the fact that the use of languages can trigger certain representations

All these elements could be invoked in language education to raise some awareness, question commonsense notions about LFs and help future mobile students to move beyond them. Teaching about the use of LFs before, during and after student mobility might actually help students to learn to question fixed categories and to reconsider stability in identification, to challenge their representations of Self and others and thus to lead them to greater understanding and empathy for others as well as to use less judgmental evaluations of their own capabilities.

As educators (and researchers), we need to help students to avoid reinforcing fixed categories such as language, culture and identity (see Coleman in this volume). As was reported in this chapter, many mobile students feel disappointed after their stay abroad, having only been able to interact with non-native speakers and using LFs. The benefits of the awareness raising proposed here would be to make these students realize and understand that these situations are not as "negative" or "useless" as they believe them to be. Linking up language and intercultural education, especially in its postmodern form which emphasizes "liquid identity" (see the above section on researching identification), might also be a good way of helping mobile students to look at intercultural encounters from a different and less solid, less national perspective. Working on hybridity and *mélange* in language, culture and identity could also help mobile students to be less disappointed at the end of their stays. Very little research is available on this type of preparation for study abroad, since many courses are based on solid approaches to language and culture. Such systematic (action) research is needed more than ever to boost student mobility and make it an even more fruitful experience.

References

Abdallah-Pretceille, M. (2003). *Former et eduquer en contexte hétérogène. Pour un humanisme du divers* [Education in heterogeneous contexts: Towards a humanism of diversity]. Paris: Economica.

Abdallah-Pretceille, M. (2006). *Métamorphoses de l'identité* [Metamorphoses of identity]. Paris: Economica.

Baker, A. (2009). The cultures of English as a Lingua franca. *TESOL Quarterly, 43*, 567–592.

Ballatore, M. (2010). *Erasmus et la mobilité des jeunes Européens* [Erasmus and the mobility of young Europeans]. Paris: PUF.

Bauman, Z. (2004). *Identity*. Cambridge: Polity.

Baumgarten, N. & House, J. (2010). I think and I do not know in English as Lingua Franca and native English discourse. *Journal of Pragmatics, 42*, 1184–1200.

Behrent, S. (2007). *La Communication alloglotte* [Communication in a non-local language]. Paris: L'Harmattan.

Berns, M. (2009). English as lingua franca and English in Europe. *World Englishes, 28*, 192–199.

Brubaker, R. & Cooper, F. (2000). Beyond "identity." *Theory and Society, 29*, 1–47.

Calvet, L.-J. (1985). *Les langues véhiculaires* [Vehicular languages]. Paris: PUF.

Cogo, A. (2008). English as a lingua franca: Form follows function. *English Today, 95*, 41–44.

Denzin, N. (2009). *The research act: A theoretical introduction to sociological Methods*. New York: Transaction publisher.

Dervin, F. (2008a). Le Français Lingua Franca: un idéal de la communication interculturelle inexploré? [French as a Lingua Franca: An unexplored ideal for intercultural communication?] *Synergies Europe, 3*, 139–154.

Dervin, F. (2008b). *Métamorphoses identitaires en situation de mobilité* [Metamorphoses of identity in situations of mobility]. Turku: Humanoria.

Dervin, F. (2009). Impediments to engulfment into Finnish society: Exchange students' representations on their experiences in Finland. *Research on Finnish Society, 2*, 19–27.

Dervin, F. (Ed.). (2010). *Lingua Francas.* Paris: L'Harmattan.

Dervin, F. (2011). A plea for change in research on intercultural discourses: A 'liquid' approach to the study of the acculturation of Chinese students. *Journal of Multicultural Discourses, 6* (1), 37–52.

Dervin, F. & Korpela, M. (Eds.). (2012). *Cocoon communities.* Newcastle upon Tyne: Cambridtge Scholars.

Dervin, F. & Vlad, M. (2010). Pour une cyberanthropologie de la communication interculturelle – Analyse d'interactions en ligne entre étudiants finlandais et roumains [Toward a cyberanthropology of intercultural communication: Analysis of online intercations among Finnish and Rumanian students]. *Alsic, 13.* Retrieved from ⟨http://alsic.revues.org/index1399.html⟩.

Ewing, K.P. (1990). The Illusion of wholeness: Culture, self, and the experience of inconsistency. *Ethos, 18,* 251–278.

Fenoglio, I. 1996. Conscience linguistique [Linguistic awareness]. In H. Goebl, P.H. Nelde, & W. Wolfgang (Eds.), *Kontaktlinguistik. Ein internationales Handbuch Zeitgenössischer Forschung* [Contact linguistics. An international handbook of contemporary research.] (pp. 675–684). Berlin: de Gruyter.

Firth, A. (2009). The Lingua Franca factor. *Intercultural Pragmatics, 6,* 147–166.

Gray, E.D. (2009). *Doing research in the real world.* London: Sage.

Hermans, H.J.M. (2001). The dialogical self: Toward a theory of personal and cultural positioning. *Culture & Psychology, 7,* 243–281.

Holliday, A. (2010). *Intercultural communication and ideology.* London: Sage.

House, J. (2002). Developing pragmatic competence in English as a Lingua Franca. In K. Knapp & C. Meierkord (Eds.), *Lingua Franca communication* (pp. 245–267). Frankfurt: Peter Lang.

Jenkins, J. (2007). *English as a Lingua Franca: Attitudes and identity.* Oxford: Oxford University Press.

Johansson, M. & Dervin, F. (2010). Cercles francophones et français lingua franca: Pour une francophonie liquide [Francophone circles and French as a Lingua Franca: Toward a liquid Francophonie]. *International Journal of Francophone Studies, 12,* 385–404.

Jovchelovitch, S. (2006). *Knowledge in context.* London: Routledge.

Kalocsai, K. (2009). Erasmus exchange students. A behind-the-scenes view into an ELF community of practice. *Apples – Journal of Applied Linguistics Series, 3* (1), 25–49.

Knapp, K. & Meierkord, C. (Eds.). 2002. *Lingua Franca communication.* Frankfurt: Peter Lang.

Kramsch, C. (2011). The symbolic dimensions of the intercultural. *Language Teaching, 44,* 354–367.

Linell, P. (2009). *Rethinking language, mind, and world dialogically.* Charlotte, NC: Information Age Publishing.

Llamas, C. & Watt, D. (Eds.). (2009). *Language and identities.* Edinburgh: Edinburgh University Press.

Marková, I., Linell, P., Grossen, M. & Salazar Orvig, A. (2007). *Dialogue in focus groups: Exploring socially shared knowledge.* London: Equinox.

Mauranen, A., Hynninen, N. & Ranta, E. (2010). English as an academic lingua franca: The ELFA project. *English for Specific Purposes, 29*, 183–190.

Mauranen, A. & Ranta, E. (Eds.). (2009). *English as a Lingua Franca. Studies and findings.* Newcastle upon Tyne: Cambridge Scholars.

McSweeney, B. (2002). Hofstede's model of national cultural differences and their consequences. *Human Relations, 55*, 89–117.

Murphy-Lejeune, E. (2002). *L'étudiant Européen Voyageur, un nouvel Etranger* [The travelling European student: The new strangers]. Paris: Didier.

Niemi, H., Toom, A. & Kallioniemi, A. (Eds.). (2012). *Miracle of education. The principles and practices of teaching and learning in Finnish schools.* London: Sense Publishers.

Norton, B. (2000). *Identity and language learning: Gender, ethnicity and educational change.* Harlow, UK: Longman Pearson Education.

Nynäs, P. & Illman, R. (2006). *Kultur, människa, möte: Ett humanistiskt perspektiv* [Culture, people, encounters: A humanistic approach]. Stockholm: Studentliteratur.

Paveau, M.-A. (2006). *Les prédiscours* [Prediscourses]. Paris: Presses de la Sorbonne Nouvelle.

Pavlenko, A. & Blackledge, A. (2004). *Negotiation of identities in multilingual contexts.* Clevedon, UK: Multilingual Matters.

Pellegrino Aveni, V. (2005). *Study abroad and second language use.* Cambridge: Cambridge University Press.

Phillips, A. (2010). *Gender and culture.* Cambridge: Polity.

Phipps, A. (2007). *Learning the arts of linguistic survival. Languaging, tourism, life.* Clevedon, UK: Channel View.

Pieterse, N.J. (2004). *Globalization and culture: Global mélange.* Lanham, MD: Rowman and Littlefield.

Piller, I. (2000). Language choice in bilingual, cross-cultural interpersonal communication. *Linguistik Online, 5*(1). Retrieved from ⟨http://www.linguistik-online.com/1_00/index.html⟩.

Polanyi, L. (1995). Language learning and living abroad: Stories from the field. In B.F. Freed (Ed.). *Second language acquisition in a study abroad context* (pp. 271–291). Amsterdam: John Benjamins.

Pomerantz, A. (1996). Extreme case formulations: A way of legitimizing claims. *Human studies, 9*, 219–229.

Prodromou, L. (2009). English as a lingua franca: A corpus-based analysis. *Applied Linguistics, 29*, 521–524.

Renaud, P. (2001). De la véhicularité [On vehicularity]. In K. Boucher (Ed.). *Le Français et ses usages à l'écrit et à l'oral: Dans le sillage de S. Lafage* [The use of French in speaking and writing: Following the influence of S. Lafarge]. (pp. 49–72). Paris: Presses de la Sorbonne nouvelle.

Sahlberg, P. (2011). *Finnish lessons: What can the world learn from educational change in Finland?* New York: Teachers College Press.

Seidlhofer, B. (2001). Closing a conceptual gap: the case for a description of English as a lingua franca. *International Journal of Applied Linguistics, 11*, 133–158.

Seidlhofer, B. (2004). Research perspectives on teaching English as a Lingua Franca. *Annual Review of Applied Linguistics, 24*, 209–239.

Seidlhofer, B. (2005). English as a lingua franca. *ELF Journal, 59*, 339–340.

Shaw, P., Caudery, T. & Petersen, M. (2009). Students on exchange in Scandinavia: Motivation, interaction, ELF development. In A. Mauranen & E. Ranta (Eds.), *English as a Lingua Franca: Studies and findings* (pp. 178–199). Newcastle upon Tyne: Cambridge Scholars.

Tannen, D. (1989). *Talking voices*. Cambridge: Cambridge University Press.

Tsoukalis, I. (2008). The double life of Erasmus students. In M. Byram & F. Dervin. (Eds.), *Students, staff and academic mobility in higher education* (pp. 131–152). Newcastle upon Tyne: Cambridge Scholars.

Virkkula, T. & Nikula, T. (2010). Identity construction in ELF contexts: A case study of Finnish engineering students working in Germany. *International Journal of Applied Linguistics, 20*, 251–273.

Wright, S. (2007). French as lingua franca. *Annual Review of Applied Linguistics, 26*, 35–60.

Yun, H. & Demaizière, F. (2008). Interactions à distance synchrones entre apprenants de FLE. Le clavardage au service du français académique [Synchronous interactions among learners of French as a Foreign Language: Chatting to learn academic French]. *Cahiers de l'Acedle, 5*, 255–276.

An American in Paris

Myth, desire, and subjectivity in one student's account of study abroad in France

Timothy Wolcott
University of San Francisco

As "island" study abroad programs (Goodwin & Nacht 1988) increase in popularity, critics suggest that the student participants are merely cocooning themselves in an insulated community wherein they recreate American cultural practices and identities. That is, these students see their term abroad as ultimately about themselves, and this self-obsession is deemed proof of an intransigent American habitus (Bourdieu 1984). In this chapter, I examine how an American undergraduate accounts for her experiences in an island program in Paris. While at first this student's testimony seems to confirm the dire predictions outlined above, in the end I draw on post-structuralist theories of *subjectivity* (Kramsch 2009) to demonstrate that this student's deeply personal *subject positionings* transcend any ostensibly American identities.

1.   Introduction

In this chapter, I will provide a case study of an American undergraduate, Lola,[1] who spent a semester studying abroad in Paris in a non-immersion program designed and run by her home university. This program was originally designed to provide first and second year undergraduates with an international education experience early on in their degree progress, with the hope that these students would be inclined to include a more defined international component (via foreign language and/or area studies majors/minors, additional study abroad, etc.) in their academic majors later on in their studies. Designed as an introduction rather than a capstone, this program provides an intentionally insulated or *island* experience (Goodwin & Nacht 1988; Woolf 2007), with the all the non-language courses instructed in English by either American instructors or French faculty

---

1.   A pseudonym.

who had agreed to conform to the prescriptions of the academic culture of the American host university (i.e. syllabus, weekly reading assignments, regular assessments throughout the semester, teaching assistants with separate sections, etc.). However, the program never succeeded in attracting its target demographic; even during its first year, the vast majority of participants were third or fourth year students for whom the convenience and accessibility of the program were of primary importance.

Given this mismatch between the program goals and those of its participants, one might question if the students who choose this program are capable of developing either the communicative competence applied linguists describe or the intercultural competence international educators suggest (Williams 2005) as the desired outcome of study abroad. Moreover, one might also wonder if these students are using study abroad primarily to validate and reinforce their status as members of a "cosmopolitan elite" (Skeggs 2004) who view study abroad in Paris as an opportunity for a 21st century Grand Tour, i.e. a type of edutainment whose educational outcomes matter much less than the symbolic capital that one accrues by participating in such a conspicuously costly yet practically superfluous educational experience.

Indeed, in the early stages of my data analysis, it seemed to me that Lola and the three other focal students in the study represented exactly the kind of self-obsessed, interculturally indifferent American undergraduates critiqued by applied linguists and international educators alike (Citron 2002; Engle & Engle 2002; Feinberg 2002; Kinginger 2008; Ogden 2007). During our first in-country interview (see below), Lola indicated that she had not come to Paris with the primary goal of improving her French. In fact, she admitted to having arrived with few or no concrete learning goals tied specifically to the study abroad program itself. Studying abroad in Paris, for her, was neither about language learning nor any specific academic coursework; instead, it was about learning about French culture firsthand, with culture generally understood in a hierarchical and collective sense (Risager 2006) as a blend of French high culture and an essentialized and romanticized notion of the French way of life (cf. Kramsch (1991, p. 218) on those who see culture as "food, fairs, and folklore").

In fact, Lola and the other focal students had selected this particular program for its logistical accessibility and the degree of freedom it allowed its participants to explore France on their own terms without the academic exigencies typical of their home universities (see interview excerpts below). They could spend a semester in Paris, take unchallenging classes in English, live on their own in an American dormitory, and decide for themselves how to occupy their extensive free time. All in all, this seemed like an American study abroad worst-case scenario: unmotivated and unchallenged undergraduates living in an insulated community with only the most stereotypical understanding of French culture. Admittedly, my initial assessment of these students' motivations for spending a semester living and studying in Paris was very much line with what Gore (2005) identifies as a "dominant discourse" about American study abroad; namely, that undergraduates study abroad "not to gain purposeful knowledge so much as to gain social standing and enjoy private pleasure" (p. 32).

However, as the study progressed, I found that my focal students described their study abroad experiences in ways that suggested that – despite the diminished focus on language learning by them and the program itself – their experiences abroad impacted them in relatively profound and deeply personal ways. For these students, studying abroad in France triggered something of an identity crisis wherein the need to set themselves apart from familial and peer identity pressures often elicited an emotionally – laden urge to re-imagine themselves in a manner of their own choosing. Some researchers have dismissed this as the unfortunate consequence of the shift in American study abroad away from intensive language learning and toward a coming of age model (Levin 2001) that merely reinforces American undergraduates' inclination to resist the more challenging aspects of "negotiating difference" in immersion settings (Kinginger 2009, p. 216, 2010; Papastergiadis 2000).

However, it is important to note that even in more recent, qualitative, identity-focused investigations of study abroad, researchers have maintained a fairly narrow focus on language learning as the primary purpose of a term abroad. As a result, these studies typically presented student testimonies centered on more personal, life-historical elements as evidence of an urge to cling to the familiar, i.e. of a fundamental failure on the part of the student to break with an American worldview. Moreover, despite their call for an expanded and diversified conceptualization of learners' identities as multiple, changing, and potentially contradictory, these scholars still retained a fundamentally *structuralist* understanding of (social) identity as correlated with recognizable communities into which learners have been differentially socialized across the lifespan. Furthermore, the nature of the differences that learners were seen as more or less successfully negotiating remained, for the most part, fairly essentialized according to a "linguistics of community" (Pratt 1987, p. 56) in which one-(national)-language is mapped onto one-(national)-culture. To be sure, as their testimonies often demonstrated in rich detail, the salience of these "imagined communities" (Anderson 1983, p. 6) was often interactively accomplished by the learners themselves in their retrospective and *in situ* descriptions of their study abroad experiences (Dolby 2004; Kinginger 2004, 2008, 2010; Pellegrino Aveni 1998, 2005; Wilkinson 1998, 2002).

In the present study, however, I adopted a more poststructuralist orientation to identity. This view conceptualizes identity – understood as *subjectivity* (Weedon

1987; Kramsch 2009) – as an interactive achievement of *subject positioning* in which individual agency and subjective (emotional, affective, and imagined) meanings are understood as operating in tension with more objective constraints. I did this for two main reasons. First, my participants did not, for the most part, focus on language learning experiences; instead, they saw study abroad as a primarily cultural activity, with culture understood as both something that nations have and as something that individuals can cultivate through a re-imagining and re-alignment of one's personal priorities, lifestyle choices, and autobiographical self-understanding (Risager 2006). Second, given my participants' lack of linguistic proficiency and their enduring withdrawal from interactions with French native speakers, their ways of speaking about their experiences abroad tended to focus quite squarely on *themselves*, i.e. their inherently subjective perspectives on the impact of their term abroad. While a structuralist orientation to these data would have led me to dismiss these personal accounts and ruminations as "too trivial to bother with" (Rampton 2006, p. 23), a poststructuralist perspective afforded a consideration of these students' accounts as offering insights into the more subjective dimensions of "when individuals move across geographical and psychological borders, immersing themselves in new sociocultural environments... find[ing] that their sense of identity is destabilized and...enter[ing] a period of struggle to reach a balance" (Block 2007, p. 864).

However, as the ensuing case study and discussion will demonstrate, a poststructuralist view of identity as subjectivity does not suggest that individuals are free to adopt any identity they wish, nor does it claim that an individual's attempt to re-imagine him/herself is a purely risk-free and unencumbered self-construction. That is, post-structuralist does not mean anti-structuralist (McNamara 2010); rather, a poststructuralist approach merely emphasizes the ways in which human beings more or less successfully negotiate the tension between invention and convention in concrete discursive practices through which they attempt to reconcile "the uncertainty of feeling a part and feeling apart" (Block 2007, p. 864). Moreover, given the role of imagination in this process, these self-constructions draw heavily on stereotypes, "myths", "desire" (Kramsch 2009, p. 10, 14), and other essentializations that are clearly embedded within a symbolic order that these individuals perceive as assigning, *from without*, varying degrees of symbolic capital (Bourdieu 1991) or "purchase" (Rampton 2006, p. 24) to subject positions that seem to originate *from within*.

In the end, then, what I intend to argue is that Lola's account of her experiences studying abroad in Paris, while decidedly self-centered, provides a glimpse into dimensions of identity-work that are typically excluded from consideration in the existing SLA research on study abroad, but, if included, could help researchers and program designers better understand the range of symbolic resources that learners draw on as they attempt to reconcile their study abroad experiences with the totality of their life experiences as "whole people" with "whole lives" (Coleman 2010, this volume). In particular, this case study (and the larger project of four case studies (Wolcott 2010) from which it is drawn) sought to address the following questions:

1. How do these students' accounts elucidate how study abroad fits into their particular experiences as learners and as people?
2. Are there any disparities between the institutionally stated goals of study abroad and the actual goals, experiences, and evaluations of these participants? If so, is there merely a mismatch to be overcome, or are there other factors at work that need to be addressed?
3. Which conceptualizations of identity best account for these students' representations of their experiences studying abroad?

2.   Research design

2.1   Participant selection and program details

All of my focal students were undergraduates participating in the same American public university's study abroad program in Paris during the fall semester of 2006. Other than the French language courses, which were taught primarily in French, all classes were conducted in English by American and French faculty and graduate students. Eligible students were required to have no less than one, but no more than three, semesters of college level French. As such, most students in this program were functioning at around the beginner to advanced beginner level. So, while language study was an integral part of this study abroad program, it was not a French language program *per se*, and none of the incoming students were French majors or minors.

In this regard, however, the program is in line with the curriculum design of the vast majority of American study abroad programs. According to the Institute for International Education (2010), 95.5% of American students who studied abroad did so for one semester or less. Moreover, this student population, in being primarily social science majors, represents the majority (33%) of students who studied abroad through this statewide system between the 2000 and 2005 academic years (UOEAP, SM&C Research, 2005). Therefore, in this research project, while I may not have had access to students involved in more language-intensive programs, I was able to report on the experiences of a highly representative sample of American undergraduates pursuing study abroad.

Of course, Lola and the other self-selected students in the larger study represent a convenience sample insofar as I could not ensure a representative sample of the broader population of students. However, since participation was strictly voluntary, I could accept only those students who elected to participate. Moreover, while it is impossible to generalize from a single case study, my interactions with the rest of the program participants through my work as a researcher, residence advisor, and assistant instructor suggest that Lola and the other focal students shared many of the same goals and attitudes as the majority of their peers.

2.2   The "island" study abroad program

My research site represents an increasingly popular and, by some accounts, quintessentially American (Coleman 2000) form of study abroad – the *island* or *enclave* model. Following distinctions originally developed by Goodwin and Nacht (1988), in "enclave" or "island" study abroad programs, unlike traditional immersion models, "the home institution sets up a special program, sometimes termed pejoratively an 'enclave,' using predominantly local staff and reflecting only to a very limited extent the curriculum and teaching methods of the host country" (p. 42). The historical archetype for such "overseas campuses" is the "self-contained teaching and living centers operated for decades by Stanford University across Western Europe" where the informal motto is allegedly "no hassle, no language" (p. 42).

However, as my participants repeatedly mentioned while discussing their reasons for choosing this program, such island programs do offer some considerable bureaucratic and academic benefits. For example, unlike students taking courses at French universities and other non-American organizations, a student at this program can be sure of the transferability and the quality of their courses taken abroad. While many immersion students in France must petition to have some or all of their courses count toward their degree requirements, these students can resolve all these weighty issues before ever leaving their home campus. Although one may argue that such winnowing of Franco-American academic cultural differences precludes a valuable source of intercultural negotiation (cf. Vande Berg 2007), programs like this exist precisely to offer a more controlled academic and intercultural environment.

Designed for beginner through advanced beginner students of French, this program is geared toward the American-style academic study of selected aspects of French and European history, society, and culture. The implicit assumption seems to be that students without advanced language skills are better served by the scaffolding of American academic culture in which rigorous intellectual investigation compensates for the loss of the cultural authenticity experienced (with its attendant problems) in more immersion-style programs. In fact, some international educators argue that it is exactly this kind of student-centered intervention that is required to maximize the educational gains of the average American study abroader (Woolf 2007; Vande Berg 2007).

2.3 Data collection procedures

For this project, I primarily employed the ethnographic methods of participant observation (field notes) and participant interviews (audio taped, during and post-program, and transcribed verbatim; see Appendix 1 for transcription notation). In these semi-structured interviews (Smith 1995), I used some pre-scripted prompts, yet I allowed and encouraged the informants to chart their own narrative course within the thematic boundaries of my question set. As an ethnographer, I was interested in gleaning an *emic* (i.e. participant-relevant [Pike 1967]) perspective on the experience of study abroad in France. To this end, while I came to the study with some fundamental questions, I also remained open to the topics and concerns that my informants found most relevant to my lines of inquiry. Although I still used my interview scripts as topic guidelines, the interviews were very informal and I rarely posed any of my pre-scripted questions directly; my topic control was more subtle, with the topics seemingly just coming up in the course of the conversation, and my only obvious recourse to the script typically occurred toward the very end of the interview when I wanted to verify that we had covered all the topics I had intended to discuss. Still, I understand that even this most open-ended interview technique is embedded within an asymmetrical power relation that must be considered in any analysis of its speech data (Briggs 1986; see Wolcott 2010 for a full discussion).

All interviews in Paris took place in my apartment in the dormitory. Lola was interviewed twice, once in early November and once in early December. I also conducted one follow-up interview during the spring semester following her return to her home campus, and I interviewed the founding director of the study abroad program in person at his home campus in the United States (Smith interview, 09/25/08).

In the first stage of analysis, transcripts were coded for narratives and recurring themes. These themes were later expanded as the complete transcripts were taken into account. The emergent analysis was verified through a triangulation with field notes, program materials, and member checks with focal students.

2.4 Analytical foci and the relation between language and identity

With some minor exceptions, the bulk of the interview excerpts analyzed below were drawn from the in-country interviews. The reasons for this decision are both methodological and analytical. First of all, while the follow-up interviews varied widely according to the time, place, and medium of communication, all of the interviews in Paris were face-to-face, took place in one location, and occurred roughly within the same month. Second, in the early stages of data analysis, the salience of the deeply personal consequences of these students' sojourns eclipsed any consideration of the more academic outcomes of their term abroad. As a result, I shifted my attention to their *in situ* accounts in order to focus on their more immediate reactions and interpretations. Finally, while I did discover some interesting shifts in the ways in which some of these respondents evaluated and narrated their study abroad experiences post-sojourn, this was not the case for all participants, thus eliminating the prospect of any analyses across case studies.

In what follows, I focus on how the form and content of Lola's interview accounts provide textual evidence of more deeply personal processes of meaning making. Issues of context – from the situational to the cultural – are largely excluded in favor of close linguistic and intertextual analyses (Fairclough 1992). I recognize that this kind of close textual or *content analysis* is increasingly viewed with suspicion by discourse analysts and narrative theorists (Atkinson 1997; Atkinson & Silverman 1997; Pavlenko 2007; cf. Freeman 1999). However, the symbolic complexities of these accounts led me first to consider these comments in relative isolation from the more interactional and conventional constraints that impinged upon their production. That is, while in the larger study (Wolcott 2010) I eventually turn my attention to the ways in which the students' accounts represent interactively-negotiated *acts of identity*, i.e. active efforts at identifying with recognizable social groups/personae, I first examine the degree of idiosyncratic creativity displayed as these social agents negotiate, play with, idealize, and *mythify* (Barthes 1957; Kramsch 2009) such ready-made identities. Moreover, this kind of "poetic construction of selfhood" (Freeman 1999, p. 99) is central to my discussion of the utility of the post-structuralist notion of subjectivity (Kramsch 2009; see Discussion below) for re-conceptualizing the educational products and processes of a term abroad.

3.   Case study: Lola

Lola was a 21 year-old fifth year senior interdisciplinary studies major working on a self-constructed degree drawing on anthropology, linguistics, and psychology. Given her advanced stage in the degree progress, Lola had already satisfied all of her course requirements for her major. That is, none of the courses Lola was taking in Paris counted directly toward her degree. As a result, Lola deliberately enrolled in the fewest number of courses allowed by the program requirement. For Lola, the semester in Paris was, academically speaking, more or less irrelevant: "It's *just* for fun, it's all for personal enjoyment" (Interview 1). However, Lola had done a considerable amount of research prior to choosing this particular program: in addition to attending information meetings held by study abroad staff, she also contacted former student participants from two of the Paris programs offered by her home university system. She credited the conversation she had with one of these students for helping her make her final decision:

> L: (…) so, but then I researched programs in France and they had two in Paris for liberal arts you know you didn't have to be any particular major, so I um, I got a list of emails from the office for both programs, you because I was comparing which one to do, and um, I talked to a few kids and I said you know why did you do X and why do you think it might have been better than Y, and then same with (…) kids who had done the Y program, and I pretty much only got one re, one or two responses from the Y program, but one of the people who responded was like 'if you want to meet up and talk about it'
>
> T: uh huh
>
> L: 'I'd be happy to talk to you about it,' and she kind of, um, con::vinced me, not that it was better, but I just agreed with her that it would work better for me because X you have to do a *homestay:*, it's over in the 7th, like by the Eiffel Tower, which like would have been fine, it's a nice part of town, but it's just, I didn't really know much about the Bastille neighborhood, in particular, but I knew a lot about the geography of Paris, and um, it's just a really *posh* neighborhood you know, you have to do a homestay so you can't live in like in the dorms   (Interview 1)

For Lola (and her peer), it seems, the chief criteria for selecting a study abroad program in Paris were the desirability of its arrondissement and the degree of freedom its living arrangements afforded. Indeed, in this excerpt, Lola emphasizes her control over her study abroad experience – like a well-informed consumer, she knows what she wants ("I knew a lot about the geography of Paris") and is merely selecting the product that will "work better for [her]". She is the agent of her own study abroad destiny who is "not convinced" but who "agrees" that this program is right for her. In keeping with this desire to remain in control of her study abroad experience, Lola eschews the program that requires a homestay housing arrangement.

Personally, I was surprised by her aversion to homestays; in my own experience doing a Junior Year Abroad in France in the mid 1990s, my host family played a vital role in my language learning and acculturation, and I was shocked to hear a student speak of expressly avoiding what I saw as an invariably enriching living arrangement (cf. Wilkinson 1998, 2002). When I pressed her on this topic, Lola's response both continued along the familiar lines of neighborhood shopping and opened up a hitherto unknown aspect of her biography:

> T: Why didn't you want a homestay?
>
> L: Um (.1) because I have, family friends in Paris, my mom lived here for ten years on and off in the seventies, I was staying with them, it was, you know if I would've done a homestay I could've done it with someone I *knew* already, I didn't *need* like a French family to teach me French, I felt, I didn't want to take the risk of being in a crappy place with um, people who weren't nice or who didn't work for me
>
> T: Did you hear that from some of the people you talked to? Who'd done homestays?
>
> L: Um, well, I just, I had actually heard goo-, positive stories from people who did homestays, but at the same time they were like, it's always hit or miss, you know, and coming here and seeing the people who have homestays, some of them are the 2nd and in Montparnasse and right by here, or in like, Place de la République, but um, some of them are in like the suburbs and in the 16th, I just didn't want (.1) in B I never lived in the dorms I always lived off campus, (…) pretty far away from campus, and I uh, I didn't want to be far away from, so, I wanted to have the experience of being right down the street from school, walking distance to school, just not have to like take the metro to school everyday, not have to have anybody that I have to *come home* to, not have anybody to *answer* to really, I'm just a very, *very* independent person in general, and I thought that uh (.1) I just thought I don't need to meet a French family to, to know France, I already have so, so many connections.   (Interview 1)

So, on the one hand, Lola didn't want the demands of a homestay to impinge upon her autonomous exploration of Paris on her own terms. For Lola, a host family, like the study abroad program itself, had to "work for [her]". On the other hand, Lola's reasons for this housing choice went beyond merely wishing to do what she pleased in Paris and delve into more personal and biographical issues: Lola was conceived in Paris, but her mother separated from her French father immediately afterwards, moved back to the United States for Lola's birth, and Lola grew up with almost no contact with her Parisian father.

However, as she explained, her mother's contacts in Paris represented a local network for her that she felt was a more than adequate substitute for the dubious potential of a homestay. That is, unlike a host family who may have imposed itself on her autonomy ("anybody that I have to *come home* to […] to *answer* to"), her Parisian contacts were ostensibly risk-free and optional, i.e. under her control. So it seems that, for Lola, selecting this particular study abroad program was merely a risk-free means to her pre-determined ends of personal enjoyment and deepening her already substantial knowledge of Paris.

However, Lola's goals for her term abroad extended far beyond consuming Paris according to her own itinerary. Indeed, while it may seem at odds with her decisions to enroll in an English-language program and live in an all-American dormitory, Lola had come to Paris to "be French" (Interview 1). Moreover, Lola's decision to study abroad in Paris was in fact a much more risky endeavor than the previous excerpts suggest. Haunted by dreams of her absent French father, Lola had come to Paris to reconcile herself with a French ancestry that she has spent most of her life actively ignoring:

> T: Yeah (1.5) ok, so::::: um, ok, so the first question's pretty straightforward, why did you decide to study abroad in France?
>
> L: Ok, I always knew I wanted to study abroad
>
> T: Uh huh
>
> L: Part of the college thing, um, so I was taking Italian at community college, I took Italian for a year, and I thought I wanted to study in Florence cuz that's where everybody goes, um, I had come to Paris when I was nine, and didn't really like it, my dad's French and we never had a relationship, he always lived in Paris, so like um, I was really against it a lot, like for most of my life, like didn't want to come to Paris didn't want to learn French or anything, um, and then when I was 18, um I was studying Italian, I started having all these like *weird dreams* about my *dad* like showing up and being like 'Don't want to see you!' so I was like damn I need to like (.2) deal with this (.1) situation you know and just go see him, and get it out of the way you know, if I want these dreams to go away (.1).   (Interview 1)

Clearly, studying abroad in Paris held a far greater significance – and presented far more considerable risks – for Lola than her previous comments suggest. However, over the course of our interviews, Lola rarely raised the subject of her father in direct terms. When she did, however, a theme emerges: while she might not have been able to fully reconcile with her French father, this did not preclude the possibility of re-connecting to her French roots on her own:

> T: Did you stay, so wait, does your dad live in Paris?
>
> L: He does live in Paris
>
> T: Ok, and you said that part of your motivation was to see him?
>
> L:Um
>
> T: But you didn't stay with him?
>
> L: No, it was just like, um (.2) I, if had ever said "mom, I want to go to Paris" it would have been "well, you have to see your father"
>
> T: uh huh
>
> L: So in 2004 I saw him, and it was the same old, like no, no good vibes, no connection really, just like when I was little, just the same, it wasn't any different, so 2005 I was like well I *don't* want to see him and you know I can go and *not* see him, and my mom was kinda freaked out, like "well, you know, what's gonna

happen," but it was fine, I didn't see him, maybe he knew I was here, I just didn't, I didn't see him, um (.1) and then (.1) I started taking French only, I researched like which *program*, I knew there, there are tons of programs in Paris that you can do, (Interview 1)

That is, she could have Paris *on her own terms*, whether or not her father – or her *mother* – was a part of the situation. Indeed, Lola not only distanced herself from her father's hold on her relationship to her French inheritance, but she also rejected her mother's attitude toward Lola's nascent francophilia as inherently self-serving:

T: How many times have you been to France?

L: I had been when I was nine and then in 2004 and 2005, I just=

=T: (unintelligible)=

=L: Yeah, I didn't like it, I didn't get anything out of it, after 2004 though I was like I *can't stay away*, I need to go back as soon as possible, I just *love* Europe, I *love* travelling, I *love, love love* Paris

T:] But you said your mom lived in France but you didn't grow up with French in the house because your father, who was French, was living in France? =

=L: Yeah he was living in Paris yeah (.1) and if *she* had tried to speak French to me I would have been like *shut up* I don't want to hear it I don't want anything to do with France and French (.1) um (.3) but then I came and I was like *oh my god* I'm a part of this *great amazing* (.2) thing, that's so big and wonderful and that so many people have loved=

=[T: Would you consider your mom a francophile, though?

L: Yeah, absolutely, she con, she ((laughs)) I uh, she considers herself a francophile.

T: So did you grow up with her sort of saying, you know

[L: (high pitch) "Oh France is so wonderful, Paris is so amazing, it's so much fun to live there" but now that *I* want to live here she's like "well, you'll get sick of it, just like I did," just cause she wants me to be closer to her but um (.2)=
(Interview 1)

Clearly, Lola was intent on deciding for herself how to embrace her French identity. While this may suggest a fundamental conflict for her to resolve, in the majority of her comments about her experiences in Paris, Lola made no mention of any difficulties or struggle. On the contrary, during our interviews she described the French people, culture, and language in only the most glowing terms. However, the issues of ancestry and inheritance permeate many of Lola's comments about her experiences in Paris. In the absence of getting in touch with her French-ness through her French father, Lola emphasized her capacity to personally activate her French genetic endowment. For example, although she had only taken one undergraduate French course prior to her term in Paris, Lola felt that the language was coming naturally to her due to her "genetics":

> I just waited until the semester before to take French (.1) and I got a really great recommendation from my French (one) teacher who I just *adored*, L.M. (.1) so I took it with her last spring and was just *so good*, it was like I did better (.1) *maybe* it was the Italian that helped, but I felt that French came more natural *naturally* to me than even Italian (.1) whereas it's supposed to be one of the harder languages to learn because of the pronunciation, the rules about how you pronounce words and everything but um (.1) it *wasn't* an issue for me at *all* (...) But yeah I probably get it from her [her mother] (.1) and from being French just by genetics but (.1) when I was here in 2005 and 2004 I kinda felt like (.1) knowing the Italian (.1) and um, listening a lot to people speaking French that I *had it* already in my brain and maybe because of genetics but I *had it* already in my brain and like I just needed to kinda *tap into it* like if I just took a class and learned the rules and learned the words (.2) that it would like *come very naturally* and it *totally did.* (Interview 1)

However, despite her assumption that her proficiency would emerge organically due to her genetic endowment, Lola actually worked quite hard in her French classes. In fact, half way through the semester she requested to test into a higher-level French course as she felt that she had progressed beyond the level she had been assigned during the initial placement exams. Indeed, in my own experiences as chaperone during the initial weeks of the program, I had been impressed by Lola's dogged determination to learn French. During a mandatory field trip to the Père Lachaise cemetery, which was conducted in English, she regularly asked the tour guide to repeat any biographical or geographical names uttered in French, much to the annoyance of the guide and the snickering of her peers (Field Notes, 08/23/06). Furthermore, Lola's emerging proficiency – both linguistically and pragmatically – became a point of pride for her in contradistinction to her mother's dysfluencies and intercultural gaffes when she visited Lola in Paris:

> L: [...] so what happened at the restaurant was, the people let her use the phone, we were leaving, I wanted to eat somewhere else, she, takes, like a two euro coin and like holds it up in the air and is like *merci! merci monsieur!* Like showing him like I-am-going-to-leave-you-tip-because-you-were-nice-to-me, I was like, and she like *slams it down* on the bar, so as we were leaving I was like mom, you know, when you tip in France tipping in France is a very, you know *discreet thing*, you just leave it on the table, they'll find it, they'll appreciate it, you know, you don't have to show them, you know, you can say thank you very much for letting you use the phone, as if she like, it's *just so American* and like *obnoxious*, and, we go into Galerie Lafayette and she's like, and, she's like yelling at the top of her voice, I'm like [quietly] sh:::, but even that, that would upset me if someone was like sh! all the time you know=

=T: uh huh=

=L: but there's no, way to be po-, like, I'll try not to lose my temper but, either way, or like when I correc-, she lived in Saint Germain des Pres like in five different apartments, like during the seventies, yet we get in the cab and she like um, oui, she's like on va à Saint Germain *du Prés*, and I'm like mom it's *des prés*, and she's like *don't correct me alright! Don't correct me! You make me feel horrible, like don't* correct me, I'm like but mom, first of all you lived there, and second, it changes the meaning, it's Saint Germain *of the fields,* it's plural, like you can't go around saying *du pres* it changes the meaning of what you're saying, she's like *don't correct me or I'm gon-, I'm leaving, or I won't see you,* yeah! I'm like but *you speak French! I shouldn't have to correct you!* Just a whole

[T: ((laughs)) bunch of situations like that, it's been *awful*=   (Interview 2)

So, between her absent French father and her bumbling American mother, Lola saw no chance for a reliable familial role model for her emerging French identity. Instead, Lola sought authenticity in the streets of Paris. She was particularly enchanted by French children, as they seemed to offer her a glimpse into the life she *could have had* if her parents had stayed together in France:

L: […] one day I was walking back from the Petit Palais which is the museum I'm doing for my paper in Art (.1) and um (.1) which was *gorgeous* I fell in love with it when I went in that's why I decided to do it (.1) and I was walking across the street and it was a *beautiful* day and I looked over at the Invalides and I was like *ah* (.1) *Paris* you know (unintelligible in French) *so:* beautiful and then I go back to the metro and right outside the metro there were these little puddles from where it was raining (.1) and these *little* kids are going around on their tricycles and like going through the puddles and making this kind of *spiral* design with the water (.1) around the puddles I was like (.1) [higher pitch] *that is SO beautfiul* (.1) French children, I don't I'm not a big kids (.1) little kids person but (.2) French children, that makes me really happy they're *so:: cu::te* and then they speak their with their little French voices and the little kids who play ball in the courtyard and they're all speaking French I'm just like (.2) they're French is so *good* you know ((laughs))

[305] T: ((laughs)) totally=

L: I just, I don't know, part of me wishes (.1) cause we were *supposed* to come, to live in Paris I was supposed to be raised French (.1) and it like changed all at the last minute, my mom and my dad split up when I was like two weeks old, but she had bought an *apartment* and had it all *furnished* and ready to go, and we were all supposed to come back to France (.1) and then they split up, and we stayed in California but I would have *been* like (.4) I would have been a French person like going to bilingual school, you know, so it's kind of like=

=TW: How old were you when this happened?=

=L: I was like just a day, I was like just born [sips water] I was a new-born when they split up but I found out *later*, like she told me later on, 'you know you were supposed to, we were supposed to live in *France*,' and I was like 'oh great' but now I'm like *WHOA* what if *I* had been a *French person!* (.2) and I'm kinda happy that I, that I've had English as my first language just cause it's such an advantage (.2) um, internationally, and you know, just makes everything a lot easier (.1) um (.2) and also I can still *be French*, I can still take advantage of everything, that it has to offer, and=

=T: What do you mean by that?

L: Well I'm going to get my citizenship

T: Or you are? You can?

L: Yeah (.2) yeah I just have to do it, I just have to go to the consulate and get the papers from my dad.   (Interview 1)

Clearly, Lola's connection to Paris – however imaginary – motivated her beyond checking off tourist attractions on a to-do list; she elected to actively seek French citizenship and make plans to live some version of the French life her life circumstances denied her as a child. Moreover, this feeling of connection engendered a level of fascination with the city and its inhabitants that seemed to transcend the detached observations of the typical "tourist gaze" (Urry 2002, p. 1). The most striking example of this is a story that Lola repeated across all three interviews about the day she "started crying in the Tuileries" (Interview 3). The following is the version of the story she provided during our first interview in Paris:

T: Did you have, like, can you tell me about like, when you first got here, like any kind of especially memorable kind of experiences you had, you know in Paris?

L: Sometimes I would find myself in places were it would just be *so:::* (.1) *beautiful*, not the scenery, but I'll give you one example (.4) I was in the (.1) I was meeting my mom's friend one day in the Tuileries (.2) (or at the) Tuileries station and I walked into the park while I was waiting for her (.1) and I was sitting on the (.1) fountain and they you know the kids that go around with their um (.1) the sticks to push the boats in when they come to the edge (.2) and it was just *so::* beautiful I like started *crying* I was like [higher pitch] "this is the most beautiful place on earth!" cause it was just=

=T: What was it about it that was so beautiful?=

=L: Just the *people* it's not even like the fact that the Tuileries is so beautiful it's the *people IN the city* it's the (.1) the city's *gorgeous* obviously and the people can be *dicks* but you know in the way they treat if you know, if you don't (.1) my thing is you have to know these like (.2) you have to follow their rules if you want them to be nice to you (.1) they have very *high* standards for politeness but if *you* don't follow the rules *they* won't follow the rules back so if you don't say (higher pitch) "excusez-moi monsieur" you know if you go up to someone and say (higher pitch) "excusez-moi de vous deranger" they're like what can I do for you, you know? ((laughs))   (Interview 1)

In this narrative, Lola offers a perspective on her experience that maintains a tension between touristic objectification and deeply personal and aesthetic epiphany. On the one hand, the Parisian children are presented as nameless and eternal objects of her privileged scrutiny, akin to actors/reenactors in a staged tourist attraction or amusement park ("they you know the kids that go around with their um (.1) the sticks to push the boats in when they come to the edge"). On the other hand, Lola is so deeply touched by the beauty of the situation that she is moved to tears in public. Moreover, she consciously links her aesthetic response to a more rational – if rather essentialized – understanding of French cultural codes of conduct ("you have to follow their rules if you want them to be nice to you (.1) they have very *high* standards for politeness but if *you* don't follow the rules *they* won't follow the rules back"). While Lola's insights may very well amount to a kind of "descriptive romanticism" (Nussbaum 1997, p. 124), it seems that she is also demonstrating exactly the sort of myths and desires that Kramsch (2009) argues are typical of eager beginner language learners (see Discussion below). As extreme outsiders, these beginner learners relate to the linguistic and cultural forms (i.e. the sounds and surfaces) in much more personal, emotional, and aesthetic ways.

For Lola, who yearned to see what her life would have been like as a French child, the actual Parisian children she encountered become condensed symbols of an idealized *French Childhood-ness* she can now only imagine as an American English monolingual adult. The actual biographic details of who these children really were is not of primary importance for Lola; instead, they function as signifiers to be emptied of their historical specificity and re-filled with Lola's a-historical myth of pure, quintessential French Childhood-ness. That is, these French children act as signifiers for the French childhood Lola did not, or rather, *could not* have due to her biological parents' inability to sustain their relationship in France ("I was supposed to be raised French"). As such, these children signify an imagined past that exists not historically but *symbolically* (Kramsch 2009; Kramsch & Whiteside 2008); therefore, Lola draws on their objective reality, i.e. their forms, only in order to imbue them with a deeply subjective symbolic content.

Interestingly, the temporal structure of her narrative further reinforces this mythic timelessness. First of all, by embedding the children's actions within the past progressive action of Lola's "waiting," they are framed within an elongated and suspended moment of non-action within the overall minimal narrative sequence (Labov 1972) of Lola's simple past tense actions ("I walked into the park"/ "I like started *crying*"). Furthermore, the children's own actions are presented in the simple present tense, thereby casting their actions as habitual, perhaps perpetual (e.g. "the kids that go around" versus "the kids that went around" or "the kids that were going around"). The overall effect of this temporal structuring of events removes the children's actions from an historic, verifiable event with specific children on a specific day and time and imbues their activity with a timeless quality (i.e. "the kids that are *always* going around") that further reinforces their mythic status in Lola's account.

Closely related to the notion of myth is "desire" (Kramsch 2009, p. 14). Desire drives language learning and cultural adaptation – it is the learner's deep motivation to identify with another linguistic and cultural reality. It is undeniable that desire was a driving force in Lola's attachment to Paris. During our discussion about the feasibility of her returning to live and work in Paris after graduation, Lola explicitly equated the city with a *lover*:

> I feel *so at home* here and so comfortable and really I do not miss California at all (.1) uh, I just miss my dog, if I could bring my dog I feel like my life would be *complete* like (.1) I don't even *care* that like I don't have a *boyfriend* and like (.1) I'm *happy* that I don't have a boyfriend to *miss* but (.1) like, eh, just *being here*, I'm *fine* being single, I'm, it's like this *great* feeling of *independence* and like, *Paris* as my *lover*, you know, I just *love* living here so much I don't need anything else (.1) I just need some, I just need something do, I need some money to earn ((laughs)) you know and I need my dog and I just want to be here   (Interview 1)

Seen in this light, and in light of the deeply personal significance of her time spent studying abroad in Paris, Lola's self-centeredness and her exaggerated, highly affective appraisals of France and the French take on added meaning. Yes, she was trying to have Paris on her own terms, but she did not simply remain within a privileged and cocooned vantage point from which she alone could decide how her time abroad would impact her. Not altogether unlike a student in full linguistic and cultural immersion, Lola began to understand that France offered a way of life that could not be replicated in English and/or in the United States. Of course, her appraisals remained largely on the surface of things, but this overflowing enthusiasm can perhaps be seen as positive early indicator of Lola's potential for eventually becoming, in her words, "a part of this *great amazing* (.2) thing, that's so big and wonderful and that so many people have loved" (Interview 1).

3.1 Post script

In the end, Lola chose not to pursue French citizenship as her efforts to contact her father were complicated by his financial and health problems. She did return to Paris during the summer after graduation as part of a month long trip across several countries in western and eastern Europe that culminated with Lola spending two months studying Spanish in Spain. Following that, Lola briefly returned to the United States before deciding to move to New Zealand then Australia, where she still lives at the time of this writing.

4.   Discussion

As the preceding case study suggests, Lola interpreted her experiences studying abroad in Paris in highly personal ways. However, in the bulk of the recent applied linguistics research on study abroad, these individual differences have been typically understood within a "linguistics of community" (Pratt 1987, p. 56) that posits such idiosyncrasies as undermining students' ability to accommodate to native speaker communities. In this view, students' tendency to see study abroad as mainly about themselves is a symptom of a dysfunctional inclination to cling to the familiar and underscores their incapacity to break with an American view of the world and to see the Other on its own terms (Citron 2002; Kinginger 2008, 2010; Ogden 2007). Similarly, international educators have become increasingly skeptical of the current state of American study abroad in terms of its potential for getting American undergraduates to notice the cultural specificity of their own worldview (Engle & Engle 2002; Feinberg 2002).

While I agree with many of these critiques, my findings in this study led me to consider the deeply personal orientations of my participants from a more post-structuralist perspective that sees these subjective interpretations of experience as both inevitable and fundamentally "recuperable" within the study abroad curriculum (Wolcott 2010, p. 104). Furthermore, the kinds of continuities these students' actively maintained, though undeniably leading them to fail to engage with their environment in more systematic and durable ways, also highlight a hitherto hidden dimension of study abroad that I see as a universal component of international education in general and language learning in particular. Finally, though the mismatches evidenced by these testimonies are in many ways the product of inter-cultural breakdowns – i.e. the transfer of an American cultural perspective/identity into a French cultural context – the more personal and biographical conflicts triggered by studying abroad in Paris attest to subject positionings that exceed or at least blur the boundaries of structurally-defined identities.

In what follows, I will begin by addressing the more common, i.e. cultural, interpretive frames and discourses that Lola brings to bear on her experience abroad. From there, I will segue into a discussion of the more subjective dimensions of Lola's accounts, with particular attention paid to the symbolic negotiations of self *vis-à-vis* the more idealized and imagined subject positions mentioned in the preceding analyses.

As mentioned in the introduction, all of my focal students considered study abroad as an opportunity to learn about French "culture." However, for them, culture was understood primarily as a commodity more or less equally available given sufficient proximity to its source, i.e. France. By spending a semester in Paris, these students had come in search of a cultural authenticity unavailable at a distance, i.e. in the United States. Of course, this perspective elides intensive language- and culture-learning as a necessary prerequisite for "cultivation" and smacks of a "cosmopolitan elitism" (Skeggs 2004) one would assume is antithetical to a study abroad intended to help students "negotiate difference" (Kinginger 2010, p. 216) in ways that trigger a critical reflection on one's position in a global network of social, cultural, political, and economic systems or "flows" (Blommaert 2005; Hannerz 1992). However, these students' understanding of culture also represents a widely held, non-specialist conceptualization with wide circulation in American public and private discourse. Indeed, as Risager (2006) argues, this blending of individual and collective notions of hierarchical culture is representative of modern democratic views of the individual in society:

> In general, one can say that by virtue of the interplay between the individual and the collective meaning of the concept of culture is an epochal concept which to a particular extent characterizes modern society. It thematises the possibility for individuals to be able to cultivate themselves and to become members of the cultivated classes no matter what their origins, without innate privileges. (p. 36)

As such, Lola's description of this program as less about language learning and more about culture can be seen as the animation (Goffman 1981) of a discourse with extensive purchase; that is, by speaking of study abroad in this way, she was foregrounding what she considered to be largely normative beliefs about the purposes and products of international education (Hoffa 2002). Of course, it is exactly these kind of commonsense or folk beliefs (Miller & Ginsberg 1995) that a well-designed study abroad program can anticipate and counteract. However, as I mentioned in the introduction, this program was specifically created as a cushioned international education teaser for first and second year students and had yet to curricularly respond to the participant demographic it actually attracted (Smith interview). As a result, while Lola's fixation on high-culture-as-commodity clearly compromised her inclination to step outside of American cultural perspectives, it is equally clear that her orientation was shaped as much by collective pressures as by some kind of willful self-absorption and/or snobbery.

Moreover, as the preceding analysis illustrates, in the course of her term abroad, the commonality of this American folk perspective on culture did not in fact yield a uniformity of meanings ascribed to her experiences. On the contrary, while she ostensibly approached her term abroad aiming at accruing collectively recognized forms of cultural capital, she has relatively little to say about these intended outcomes. Instead, Lola focuses on the unintended consequences of her term abroad, namely the deeply personal and often troubling subjective reactions triggered by living in Paris. Admittedly, most of these reactions involve a large degree of stereotypification and romanticization – a distanced musing on the biographical significance of her experience embedded within emotional and aesthetic meanings that reference the Other in only the most superficial manner. However, if seen through the lens of more recent work on subjectivity in language learning (Kramsch 2006, 2009), these musings take on new meaning.

As Kramsch argues (2006, 2009), learning a new language and being confronted with new cultural meanings engages the learner in processes of meaning-making that are rarely limited to the objective realm of linguistic and cultural norms. On the contrary, beginner learners in particular often respond to the forms and surfaces of the language and its speakers in ways that are highly idiosyncratic and imagined. As in the fundamental tension between a word's collectively-determined meaning (de Saussure's *langue* [1972]) and the individual speaker's highly personal relationship with both the form of the word and his/her memories tied to that word across the lifespan, the second language learner often resists and resignifies a word's denotation in deeply personal ways. This tension, Kramsch argues, persists at the margins of individual meaning-making, even as the learner increasingly conforms to the norms of the speech community.

For example, while one may begin learning French because it sounds "sexy" or "fancy," this seminal orientation to French sounds and its speakers may persist throughout even the most advanced stages of proficiency. Moreover, while this may be rarely admitted, this symbolic motivation for learning the language may very well account for the learner's ability to endure the innumerable shocks and reality checks encountered as the he/she confronts the diverse – and often sobering – realities of the life of the language. Indeed, it is this tension between the meaning of the language in the individual's life and its life independent of the learner, i.e. across history and actual contexts of communication, that Kramsch sees as at the very core of the language learning project. Through analyses of language learning memoirs of bi-/multi-linguals, Kramsch (2009) points out how these individuals interpret and account for their experiences in ways that draw on both the real and the unreal, the objective and the subjective, the historical and the "mythic" (Barthes 1972/1957, p. 109) in order to reconcile themselves with a life in and between two or more languages.

It is perhaps questionable to compare Lola's account of English-dominant study abroad with the symbolic negotiations of advanced bilinguals. However, as I mentioned above, Kramsch argues that these symbolic struggles are not the exclusive domain of the advanced learner; on the contrary, it is in the very early stages of language learning when these more subjective orientations to the language and its speakers are most salient. Moreover, as the above case study illustrates, often these participants are intimately connected – however symbolically or literally – to multiple languages and linguistic and cultural identities. Finally, how they make sense of this orientation, i.e. how they account for their experiences abroad in relation to the totality of their life experience, is a highly subjective affair, and one that is vehiculated by myth and desire (Kramsch 2006, 2009).

As I mentioned above, Kramsch sees the beginner language learner as less concerned and/or aware of the objective and denotative realities of a language and its speakers. Instead, the novice language learner orients him/herself more to the sounds and surfaces of things. These emotional, aesthetic resonances with the foreign language forms Kramsch calls "myths":

> Myth, then, is a use of symbolic forms (verbal or visual) that is not primarily meant to refer or inform, but to act upon listeners' or readers' sensibilities and influence their perceptions. [...] It is a way of using language less for its objective truth value than for the subjective beliefs and emotions that it expresses, elicits, and performs. [...] Because it condenses a variety of historically contingent meanings into one timeless symbol, myth often functions as a 'condensation symbol' [...] Because myth is anchored in an imagined reality that does not operate in chronological, historical time, it has been called 'a-historical' (Barthes 1972/1957).   (Kramsch 2009: 11–12)

For example, Lola's descriptions of the French are grounded not in the real-time objective realities of the actual French people she encountered during her time in Paris; instead, Lola's descriptions of the French children in the Tuileries are rooted in an atemporal nowhere of imagined and idealized essences. Moreover, what she wanted to get from these mythologized French children is not their language or their culture, objectively speaking, but rather an idealized subject position within her own biographically understood self-identity. In Lola's case, she yearned for a means to symbolically reconcile the French childhood denied her by her parents' separation with her adult life as an American native speaker of English. Since this reconciliation was impossible in the objective realities of her life experience, Lola constructed a myth of French childhood-ness, an essence that was purely symbolic and thus attainable – a means of achieving a subjective plenitude, or fullness, in a biography fundamentally disjointed by objective circumstances outside of her control.

From the perspective of most structuralist research on identity in applied linguistics, Lola's subject positionings via these myths would be seen as nothing more than stereotyped and romanticized views of native speakers, i.e. as impediments to understanding the French on their own terms. However, if seen from the perspective of recent scholarship on the "multilingual subject" (Kramsch 2009), Lola's predicament underscores her effort to retain symbolic control over her subjectivity:

> Subjectivity...is our conscious or unconscious sense of self as mediated through symbolic forms. It is the symbolic meaning we give to ourselves, to our perceptions, reactions, and thoughts that orients our relationship to others.   (Kramsch 2009, p. 18)

As in other post-structuralist correctives to the reductionism of the category of "student" or "learner" (Firth & Wagner 1997; Norton-Pierce 1997; Lantolf & Pavlenko 2001; Kinginger 2008), Kramsch argues for considering language learners' efforts at identification (Bucholtz & Hall 2004) as a process of meaning-making that draws on symbolic resources that transcend the immediate space and time of any given moment of linguistic performance. This approach considers the more deeply personal ways in which people position themselves *to* and *through* the symbolic resources at their disposal. Moreover, this view of meaning-making is less concerned with the kinds of motivation that drive face-to-face interaction on the interpersonal plane of existence; instead, Kramsch argues for a more serious consideration of the highly subjective desires that undergird a subject's ongoing negotiation of symbolic equilibrium or "self-fulfillment". Kramsch (2006) writes:

> This need for identification with others, with their language, their way of speaking is so strong that Kristeva gave it the name 'desire' (Kristeva 1980). Desire in language is the basic drive toward self-fulfillment. It touches the core of who we are. Anyone who has spent some time learning a foreign language while studying or working abroad knows the thrills and frustrations of desire.   (2006b: 101)

As in myth, a subject's desire is loosely grounded in the objective realities of lived experience. One may "fall in love" with French or a French speaker in the early stages of learning the language, but the desire that drives one's learning is ultimately an inwardly generated and generative motivation that exceeds and endures beyond "lost loves." In Lola's case, for example, her love for all things French, though obliquely related to the lost love of her French father, was equally self-generated through her mythification of French children and Paris itself ("Paris as my lover"). However, desire is not only a force of attraction, a drive to bring things together. Self-fulfillment can also be achieved through symbolic processes of distinction and differentiation.

For example, while at first Lola's distancing from her French father seems to stand in stark contrast to her belief in the possibility of activating her French genetic endowment, in fact resistance and confidence are but two sides of the same coin of desire (Kramsch 2009, 2006). Like the second language learner who actively resists accommodating to native speaker norms, e.g. who deliberately retains an English accent while speaking French, Lola's acceptance of her monolingual English self underscores her "desire to preserve what is [hers]" (Kramsch 2009, p. 15). Although desire is at the core of the basic drive toward self-fulfillment, this drive is often a fundamentally defensive orientation toward perceived "threat[s] to [one's] integrity as [a] subject." That is, desire accounts for the more personal, i.e. subjective, dimensions of identification, and sheds light on how this "positive or negative identification with the Other" (Kramsch 2009, pp. 14–15; Kristeva 1980) is dialogically accomplished by a subject positioning that is fundamentally *inter-subjective*. In Lola's comments, for example, she was negotiating a subject position both within the context of the research interview and within the textual worlds she created in her autobiographic accounts.

Overall, while this case study fits neither the traditional SLA focus on intensive language learning nor international educators' view of intercultural communication, perhaps this discussion of the more subjective dimensions of an American undergraduate's account of study abroad heeds the call for a more holistic conceptualization of the study abroader in an applied linguistics research that Coleman says should consider "whole people and whole lives" (2010, this volume). Perhaps by understanding how students like Lola make sense of their term abroad, and how they account for its impacts, program designers can consider ways of getting students to discuss and interrogate these evolving understandings more systematically within the program itself (see Wolcott 2010 for curricular suggestions). That is, while I support Kinginger's (2008, 2010) call for developing programmatic means of foregrounding language learner identity, I do so provided the assumption isn't to disregard or suppress the subjectivity of the whole person. As I hope my case study demonstrates, it is important not to see this subjective dimension only as a distraction and/or a narcissistic distortion of the reality of the L2 speech community – something to be anticipated, pointed out, then curtailed, reigned in, in order to allow the real business of SLA to occur.

Looking at the subjective responses of students abroad can elucidate their desire to "cling to the familiar" (Kramsch 2009, p. 15) by avoiding contact with native speakers and retreating to the company of their peers and/or the "electronic umbilical cord" (Kinginger 2010, p. 223) of online interaction. However, it can also account for the unrelenting drive of some learners to learn a language at all costs, to persist through all the shocks and reality checks that can be disheartening for even the most committed learner. Students' desire to learn a language is often rooted in, and fundamentally depends on, deeply personal motives – emotional, aesthetic resonances with the language, its literature, or the history and cultures (however romanticized) of its speakers. Studying abroad in France in English is not altogether unlike the early stages of language learning, when the shapes and sounds of all these new signs, whose conventional meanings are still outside one's grasp, allow one to personalize their meaning, to dream and idealize – even to essentialize – for one is (temporarily) free to imbue them with any essence one wishes.

References

Anderson, B. (1983). *Imagined communities.* London: Verso.

Atkinson, P. (1997). Narrative turn or blind alley? *Qualitative Health Research, 7*, 325–344.

Atkinson, P., & Silverman, D. (1997). Kundera's immortality: The interview society and the invention of the self. *Qualitative Inquiry, 3*, 304–322.

Barthes, R. (1972 [1957]). *Mythologies.* New York, NY: Farrar, Straus & Giroux.

Block, D. (2007). The rise of identity in SLA research, post Firth and Wagner (1997). *The Modern Language Journal, 91*, 863–876.

Blommaert, J. (2005). *Discourse: A critical introduction.* Cambridge: Cambridge University Press.

Bourdieu, P. (1984). *Distinction: A social critique of the judgment of taste.* Cambridge, MA: Harvard University Press.

Bourdieu, P. (1991). *Language and symbolic power.* Cambridge, MA: Harvard University Press.

Briggs, C. (1986). *Learning how to ask: A sociolinguistic appraisal of the role of the interview in social science research.* Cambridge: Cambridge University Press.

Bucholtz, M., & Hall, K. (2004). Language and social identity. In A. Duranti (Ed.), *A companion to linguistic anthropology* (pp. 363–394). Oxford: Blackwell.

Citron, J.L. (2002). U.S. students abroad: Host culture integration or third culture formation? In W. Grünzweig & N. Rinehart (Eds.) *Rockin' in Red Square: Critical approaches to international education in the age of cyberculture* (pp. 41–56). Münster: LIT.

Coleman, J.A. (2000). Mobility with quality: Spreading best practice in student residence abroad. *European Language Council Informational Bulletin, 6*, 8–12.

Coleman, J.A. (2010, March). Researching whole people and whole lives. Paper presented at the 2010. Annual Conference of the American Association for Applied Linguistics (AAAL), Atlanta, GA.

Dolby, N. (2004). Encountering an American self: Study abroad and national identity. *Comparative Education Review, 48*, 150–173.

Engle, J., & Engle, L. (2002). Neither international nor educative: Study abroad in the time of globalization. In W. Grünzweig & N. Rinehart (Eds.), *Rockin' in Red Square: Critical approaches to international education in the age of cyberculture* (pp. 25–39). Münster: LIT.

Fairclough, N. (1992). *Discourse and social change.* Cambridge: Polity Press.

Feinberg, B. (2002). What students don't learn abroad. *Chronicle of Higher Education.* 3 May 2002. Retrieved from ⟨http://chronicle.com/prm/weekly/v48/134/34b02001.htm⟩.

Firth, A. & Wagner, J. (1997). On discourse, communication and (some) fundamental concepts in SLA research. *Modern Language Journal, 81*, 285–300.

Freeman, M. (1999). Culture, narrative, and the poetic construction of selfhood. *Journal of Constructivist Psychology, 12*, 99–116.

Goffman, E. (1981). *Forms of talk.* Philadelphia, PA: University of Pennsylvania Press.

Goodwin, C., & Nacht, M. (1988). *Abroad and beyond: Patterns in American overseas expansion.* Cambridge: Cambridge University Press.

Gore, J.E. (2005). *Dominant beliefs and alternative voices: Discourse, belief, and gender in American study abroad.* New York, NY: Routledge.

Hannerz, U. (1992). *Cultural complexity: Studies in the social organization of meaning.* New York, NY: Columbia University Press.

Hoffa, W.W. (2002). Learning about the future world: International education and the demise of the nation state. In W. Grünzweig & N. Rinehart (Eds.) *Rockin' in red square: Critical approaches to international education in the age of cyberculture* (pp. 57–72). Münster: LIT.

Institute of International Education (2010). *Open doors 2010.* New York, NY: IIE.

Kinginger, C. (2004). Alice doesn't live here anymore: Foreign language learning and identity reconstruction. In A. Blackledge & A. Pavlenko (Eds.), *Negotiation of identities in multilingual contexts* (pp. 219–243). Clevedon, UK: Multilingual Matters.

Kinginger, C. (2008). *Language learning in study abroad: Case studies of Americans in France.* Modern Language Journal, *92*, Monograph. Oxford: Blackwell.

Kinginger, C. (2009). *Language learning and study abroad: A critical reading of research.* New York, NY: Palgrave/Macmillan.

Kinginger, C. (2010). American students abroad: Negotiation of difference? *Language Teaching, 43*, 216–227.

Kramsch, C. (1991). Culture in language learning: A view from the United States. In De Bot, K., R.B. Ginsberg & C. Kramsch (Eds.), *Foreign language research in cross-cultural perspective* (pp. 217–240). Amsterdam: John Benjamins.

Kramsch, C. (2006). The multilingual subject. *International Journal of Applied Linguistics, 16*, 97–109.

Kramsch, C. (2009). *The multilingual subject.* Oxford: Oxford University Press.

Kramsch, C., & Whiteside, A. (2008). Language ecology in multilingual settings: towards a theory of symbolic competence. *Applied Linguistics, 29*, 645–671.

Kristeva, J. (1980). *Desire in language: A semiotic approach to literature and art.* New York, NY: Columbia University Press.

Labov, W. (1972). *Language in the inner city: Studies in the Black English Vernacular.* Philadelphia: University of Pennsylvania Press.

Lantolf, J.P., & Pavlenko, A. (2001). (S)econd (l)anguage (a)ctivity theory: Understanding second language learners as people. In M.P. Breen (Ed.), *Learner contributions to language learning: New directions in research* (pp. 141–158). London: Longman.

Levin, D.M. (2001). *Language learners' sociocultural interaction in a study abroad context.* Unpublished doctoral dissertation, Indiana University, Bloomington.

McNamara, T. (2010, March). Language divided: Derrida and the shibboleth. Paper presented at the Annual Conference of the American Association for Applied Linguistics (AAAL), Atlanta, GA.

Miller, L., & Ginsburg, R.B. (1995). Folklinguistic theories of language learning. In B. Freed (Ed.), *Second language learning in a study abroad context* (pp. 293–315). Amsterdam: John Benjamins.

Norton-Pierce, B. (1997). Language, identity, and the ownership of English. *TESOL Quarterly, 31*, 409–429.

Nussbaum, M. (1997). *Cultivating humanity: A classical defense of reform in liberal education.* Cambridge, MA: Harvard University Press.

Ogden, A. (2007). The view from the veranda: Understanding today's colonial student. *Frontiers: The Interdisciplinary Journal of Study Abroad, 15*, 35–55.

Papastergiadis, N. (2000). *The turbulence of migration.* Cambridge: Polity Press.

Pavlenko, A. (2007). Autobiographical narratives as data in applied linguistics. *Applied Linguistics, 28*, 163–188.

Pellegrino Aveni, V.A. (1998). Student perspectives on language learning in a study abroad context. *Frontiers: The Interdisciplinary Journal of Study Abroad, 4*, 91–120.

Pellegrino Aveni, V.A. (2005). *Study abroad and second language use: Constructing the self.* Cambridge: Cambridge University Press.

Pike, K.L. (1967 [1954]). *Language in relation to a unified theory of the structure of human behavior.* The Hague: Mouten.

Pratt, M.L. (1987). Linguistic utopias. In N. Fabb, D. Attridge, A. Durant, C. MacCabe (Eds.), *The linguistics of writing: Arguments between language and literature* (pp. 48–66). Manchester, UK: Manchester University Press.

Rampton, B. (2006). *Language in late modernity: Interaction in an urban school.* Cambridge: Cambridge University Press.

Risager, K. (2006). *Language and culture: Global flows and local complexity.* Clevedon: Multilingual Matters.

Ross, J. (2007). Students abroad: Escaping the American bubble. World Hum Retrieved from ⟨http://www.worldhum.com/travelblog/item students_abroad_escaping_the_american_bubble_39071105/⟩.

de Saussure, F. (1972). *Course in general linguistics.* Chicago, IL: Open Court.

Skeggs, B. (2004). *Class, self, culture.* London: Routledge.

Smith, J.A. (1995). Semi-structured interviewing and qualitative analysis. In J. Smith, R. Harré, & L. von Langenhove (Eds.), *Rethinking methods in psychology* (pp. 9–26). Newbury Park, CA: Sage.

Universitywide Office of the Education Abroad Program (OEAP), Station Management & Control (SM&C) Research. (2005). UCEAP participation by field of study, 2000/2001–2004/2005.

Urry, J. (2002 [1990]). *The tourist gaze: Leisure and travel in contemporary societies.* London: Sage.

Vande Berg, M. (2007). Intervening in the learning of U.S. students abroad. *Journal of Studies in International Education, 11*, 392–400.

Weedon, C. (1987). *Feminist practice and post-structuralist theory.* Oxford: Blackwell.

Wilkinson, S. (1998). On the nature of immersion during study abroad: Some participants' perspectives. *Frontiers: The Interdisciplinary Journal of Study Abroad, 4*, 121–138.

Wilkinson, S. (2002). The omnipresent classroom during summer study abroad: Students in conversation with their French hosts. *Modern Language Journal, 86*, 157–173.

Williams, T.R. (2005). Exploring the impact of study abroad on students' intercultural communication skills: Adaptability and sensitivity. *Journal of Studies in International Education, 9*, 356–371.

Wolcott, T. (2010). *Americans in Paris: A discourse analysis of student accounts of study abroad.* Unpublished doctoral dissertation, University of California, Berkeley.

Woolf, M. (2007). Impossible things before breakfast: Myths in education abroad. *Journal of Studies in International Education, 11*, 496–509.

Appendix

Transcription Conventions

,	=	quick pause, less than .1 sec
(.1)	=	pause in tenths of sec
italics	=	added stress, slight increase volume
CAPS	=	high volume utterance
(word)	=	best guess at unclear utterance
(unintelligible)	=	unintelligible utterance
so:::::	=	elongated vowel sound

Exploring the potential of high school homestays as a context for local engagement and negotiation of difference

Americans in China

Dali Tan & Celeste Kinginger

Northern Virginia Community College / Pennsylvania State University

This chapter examines the experiences of American high school students participating in a summer study and home stay program in China. Drawing on a corpus of qualitative interviews with high school participants and college-aged alumni, the authors examine how these students represent the extent to which their experience involved active engagement in communicative settings, including the negotiation of difference. The participants report having enjoyed many opportunities to become involved in routine family interactions while also encountering challenges to their common-sense understandings and values. The findings thus suggest that high school home stays may be quite different from those of the older students typically portrayed in the research literature on study abroad.

1. Introduction

Research on the qualities of language learning experiences abroad normally focuses on the sojourns of college – age students learning the languages that have historically been the most commonly studied. The experiences of students at the secondary level are infrequently documented, as are those of students learning Chinese. Some research in European contexts (Perrefort 2008) suggests that the home-stay experience of high school students abroad can be quite different from that of the older students whose stories are told in the professional literature. Younger students may be positioned to take distinct advantage of the homestay in that host families are more likely to act *in loco parentis*, thus keeping a closer watch over them and attending more carefully to their needs than they would with more mature students. We know little about the ways in which American learners of Chinese are received by the communities they join temporarily as sojourners in China.

Drawing on interview data collected over a period of seven years, and based on the first author's decade – long experience as Director of a well – regarded summer study abroad program for high school students in China, this paper explores the potential of high school home-stay experiences as contexts for local engagement and negotiation of difference. The term "local engagement" refers to students taking advantage of opportunities to observe and participate in the routine communicative practices of their host communities. The potential for local engagement is the main rationale for sending learners of language and culture abroad. Yet, for contemporary college aged students, this engagement is at risk due to a variety of circumstances, such as easy access to home-based social networks, sheltered program design (Ogden 2007), and ideologies of study abroad as a leisure pursuit (Gore 2005) (Kinginger 2009a; 2009b).

We borrow the term "negotiation of difference" from Block's (2007) article on second language identities. For Block, contemporary views of identity as a process and as a site of struggle seem particularly well suited to describe immersion in new sociocultural environments where identity is contested and destabilized. In such settings, that which is taken for granted may be questioned, but the result is not merely adding the new to the old. Rather,

> … the result is what is now famously known as the THIRD PLACE (Bhabha 1994; Hall 2006), where 'there is what Papastergiadis (2000) called a NEGOTIATION OF DIFFERENCE during which the past and the present 'encounter and transform each other' in the 'presence of fissures, gaps, and contradictions (p. 170) (Block 2007, p. 864)
>
> (Kinginger 2009a, p. 216)

As Kinginger (2009a) argued, the negotiation of meaning in study abroad programs requires a genuine investment in learning along with active participation and engagement in local social environments. It can yield ambivalence or discomfort but it can also generate significant intercultural insight and competence.

To create contexts for local engagement and negotiation of difference, students must be received with the understanding that they are persons of consequence, deserving of access to everyday communicative practices as well as assistance enabling their participation. The students, in turn, must be mindful of their status as "legitimate peripheral participants" (Lave & Wenger 1991) and positively disposed toward opportunities to learn. The data indicate that these high school students overwhelmingly assess their home-stay experiences and the welcome they received from their hosts in a positive light. They report enjoying many opportunities to participate in the routine practices of their host families while also encountering challenges to their values and common-sense understandings and learning to appreciate the perspectives of their hosts. Unlike college age adult study abroad sojourners who consider themselves independent and choose their own activities – and, perhaps, their own interpretations – more than younger students do, the high school students who participated in this study were relatively well situated to become actively engaged participants in dialogue with local people. Since the data include interviews with college-aged former program participants, we are also interested in retrospective representations of the experience and its influence on post-secondary language learning. We discuss implications of the study for the design of programs aiming to enhance students' language ability.

2. Background

One of the important limitations of the literature on language learning in study abroad is the scope of the current knowledge base (Kinginger 2009c). The great majority of studies focus on the experiences of American college-aged students studying languages, such as Spanish, French or German, that have been traditionally viewed in the United States as commonly-taught. Very few scholars have examined the outcomes or processes involved in study abroad by high school students, despite the fact that such programs have existed for many years. The literature on the learning of Chinese in study abroad contexts is also quite sparse, particularly in light of recent surges of enrollment both in Chinese language courses around the world and in academic programs for foreigners based in China (Liu 2010; Yu 2010). Thus far, scholars of Chinese study abroad have discussed program design for the enhancement of proficiency (Liu 2010). They have also investigated the impact of social psychological variables on the adaptation of international students in China (Yu 2010) and on their language acquisition (Yu & Watkins 2008). Qualitative studies examining the lived experience of student sojourners in China are as yet quite rare (cf. Tan 2008). However, the broader knowledge base does offer some insights on the themes of this study; in particular, a number of projects have investigated the qualities and outcomes of homestay experiences, a smaller number have involved student participants at the secondary school level, and one study (Perrefort 2008) has compared the experiences of high school versus college-aged learners. This literature review will consider these three themes in turn.

Because students who live with host families are commonly believed to enjoy an advantage for language learning in comparison with those who choose other living arrangements, some research with college-level participants has been conducted to provide empirical evidence for this claim. For example, after the fall of the Soviet Union, when homestays became an option for American sojourners in Russia, Rivers (1998) compared the proficiency measures of over 2500 dorm-stay versus homestay students in the American Council of Teachers of Russian (ACTR) Student Records Data Base (1976–1996). The results ran counter to expectations: in comparison to students living in dormitories, students in homestay placements were less likely to gain in speaking and listening proficiency and more likely to gain in reading proficiency. For a better understanding of these results, Rivers turned to an ethnographic study of Russian homestays (Frank 1997). Findings of this study indicated that the students' interactions with host family members were often restricted to "quotidian dialogue and television watching" (Rivers 1998, p. 496), and that the students spent much of their time at home alone, doing homework. A subsequent study (Magnan & Back 2007) also attempted to correlate gains in speaking proficiency to living arrangements with or without native speakers of the language under study, French, along with other variables. No correlation related to living situations could be established. The authors interpret this result in light of the fact that most students arrived with only intermediate proficiency, and were not necessarily able to take full advantage of opportunities for language learning through informal interactions.

A fuller appreciation of the homestay as a learning environment may be gleaned from qualitative projects of various design, including ethnographies and studies of language socialization. In Wilkinson's (1998) ethnography of short-term summer study abroad in France, the experiences of two students are compared. Molise, a young woman whose family had emigrated from Cambodia during her childhood, was welcomed into a host family whose members actively fostered her language learning. She volunteered to help with household tasks, such as garden-ing and babysitting, and eventually became a long-term family friend. By the end of her sojourn, Molise had decided to pursue advanced study of French and return to France for extended study. Ashley was orphaned at the train station on her arrival, and accompanied to her hosts' home by a member of the program staff. According to Ashley, her host family made no particular arrangements to accom-modate her language learning, and eventually she decided to spend most of her free time in the company of other American program participants. She left France at the earliest opportunity, claiming she had no further interest in the language.

Pellegrino Aveni's (2005) ethnography of American language learners in Rus-sia includes many vignettes related to the qualities of homestay experiences both positive and negative. The author credits some host families with offering "positive, supportive behavior" (p. 61) giving students the sense of security they required to pursue their language learning goals. However, there were also cases where the students' perceived their host families' actions as alienating or even threaten-ing. Madeline, an African-American student, was subjected to humiliating racist commentary by her host sister, who treated her as an object of curiosity rather than as an intelligent conversationalist. Bob and Marie, a married couple, were initially placed in the home of family whose adolescent son exhibited a penchant for violence. "Vitalik" bullied the couple physically and emotionally, eventually aiming an unloaded handgun at Bob and pulling the trigger in a game of "shoot the American" (p. 48).

In Kinginger's (2008) case studies of American college students during semester-long sojourns in France, the outcomes of homestay experiences were shown to depend not only on the intentions of the host families, but also on the dispositions and stances adopted by the students in relation to their experiences. Beatrice, for example, entered the study with relatively high proficiency and claimed strong motivation for language learning. However, she eventually became alienated from her host family due to a perceived clash in values. When members of her left-leaning Franco-Tunisian host family asked Beatrice to explain her positive appraisal of the Bush administration's foreign policy, Beatrice's reaction was to attribute an anti-American attitude to her hosts. Bill, on the other hand, approached study abroad and his host family with an attitude of relative cultural humility. Bill was received into a family that regularly invited him to elaborate meals during which the focus was almost exclusively on Bill, his activities, his aspirations, his language development, and his appreciation of French cultural practices.

The precise nature of host families' cultural exchanges with student guests is explored in several studies of language socialization (Cook 2006, 2008; DuFon 2006; Iino 2006). In these studies, recorded and transcribed interactions between students and hosts are examined to study how all parties may be socialized to use language as they are simultaneously socialized into local cultural practices through language. Cook (2006) illustrated how the sharing of folk beliefs over Japanese host family dinner tables served as a learning environment for all of the participants, both student guests and hosts. Iino (2006), however, found that whereas some families practiced the two-way exchange of learning opportunities found in Cook's (2006) research, other families interpreted their guests as fundamentally incompetent participants in Japanese society, requiring massive assistance in everyday tasks. In the latter case, the college-age participants in the study expressed considerable frustration that their adult concerns, such as learning Japanese for business purposes, were sidelined by the need to participate in activities organized by their hosts. DuFon (2006) examined host family mealtime interactions through the lens of the socialization of taste, showing how Indonesian host families helped student guests orient to and name foods while they also learned to appreciate Indonesian values associated with food: aesthetic, ritual, economic, and health-related.

In sum, research on the experiences of college-aged students in homestays abroad shows this experience to be quite varied in nature. Some students enjoy and can appreciate host families who extend warm welcome to their homes and who expend considerable effort to further the students' language and culture learning goals (see also Knight & Schmidt-Rinehart 2002). However, efforts to correlate gains in language proficiency to the homestay or to aspects of living arrangements have not succeeded. The difficulties in establishing connections to the homestay may be attributable to various causes: the host families may receive their guests with indifference or even hostility, the host families' efforts to socialize their guest may not be appreciated, or the students may misinterpret their hosts' intentions and withdraw from active engagement with them.

Turning now to the research on the experiences of high school students in study abroad, the findings are somewhat similar: much depends on how the students are received and how they themselves interpret their experiences. Hashimoto (1993), for example, offers a case study of a 16-year-old Australian student living with several host families in Japan. In this instance, the host families provided rich opportunities for learning to use appropriate style in different contexts. The student was expressly counseled in the use of formal style for a planned public address and she was party to the first language socialization of younger host siblings. When she ventured to use highly colloquial language, her hosts engaged her and the siblings in a discussion about proper register. Although she began her year abroad with no functional ability to use Japanese, by the end of her sojourn the student had developed a broad communicative repertoire and considerable knowledge of social norms related to language use.

A study by Churchill (2006) illustrates the significance of institutions in shaping high school student experiences abroad. Churchill followed a group of Japanese high school students who were received into two different American secondary schools. At St. Martin's, a small boarding school, the Japanese guests were received as persons of consequence and were encouraged, in the classroom, to display their competence (e.g. in mathematics, where they outpaced their American peers). At Belleville High, a large, public "labyrinth of concrete halls" (p. 211) no such welcome was prepared, and the Japanese guests were assigned no schedules. In the classroom their presence was barely acknowledged except as a potentially disruptive inconvenience. Churchill concludes that the extent to which the institutions and teachers value presence and contributions of exchange students has much to do with their achievements as learners of language and culture.

Spenader (2011) offers case studies of four pre-collegiate (high school or gap year students) involved in a year-long study sojourn in Sweden. Although none of the participants had prior knowledge of the language, the three female students reached the Superior (3) level on the ACTFL Oral Proficiency Interview within ten months of study. This finding Spenader attributes to support from host families, schools and peer groups as well as integrative motivation and personality traits such as assertiveness and sense of humor. The fourth participant, Max, found himself housed in a rural community with little access to public transportation and a host environment that "was not a good match for his personality or emotional needs" (p. 393). Less assertive than the others, Max developed very few friendships with Swedes, and became progressively disenchanted, to the point where he ceased to attend classes altogether. After the first five months, the development of his language proficiency appears to have ceased, and at the end of the program his correspondence with the researcher included "many negative comments concerning Swedes in general as well as Swedes he knew personally" (p. 392).

Perrefort (2008) uncovered important differences between study abroad in a European high school exchange program versus the ERASMUS experience of university students. Through the lens of ethnomethodology, and in particular, Member Categorization Analysis (Sacks 1992) she examined how these students represented their experiences during interview sessions. The high school students, aged 15 to 17, were participants in an exchange program involving a six month sojourn in France followed by a similar stay in Germany, with a home stay in both locales. In their comments on the experience, language-related experiences were highly salient and reflected their daily interaction with local hosts of all generations and in very diverse communicative situations. In overcoming linguistic insecurity through intense local engagement, these students also developed greater autonomy and motivation as language learners as well as capacity for reflection on their own language and culture. The German ERASMUS students in France, on the contrary, categorized themselves as "spectators" (p. 77), and spent much of their time interacting in German with other ERASMUS participants. Their main point of contact with French students was the university German classroom, where they were received as intimidating interlocutors to be avoided. Frustrated and disappointed at their inability to become engaged in local communicative situations, these students tended to condemn their French counterparts, based on stereotypical representations, as passive, immature, and therefore unworthy as potential friends.

It would appear that the experiences of high school students in study abroad contexts are potentially just as variable as those of college-aged students. The literature reveals that the homestay can be a rich interactive setting for language socialization, and that students who become well integrated into home and school settings can make dramatic gains in language ability and acculturation. However, high school students are also vulnerable to an indifferent reception by local institutions. If they are withdrawn and left to their own devices, like Max, the sojourn abroad may not yield anticipated growth in language proficiency or intercultural competence.

3. The current project

As noted in the introduction, the aim of this chapter is to explore how high school sojourners in China portray their experiences as contexts for local engagement and negotiation of difference. We are also interested in how the students represent the influence of high school study abroad on future participation in university-level language study, including programs abroad.

As described above, "local engagement" refers to students' active involvement in the routine communicative practices of their host community. Research strongly suggests that when students become engaged in this manner, the quality and outcomes of their sojourns abroad increase (Kinginger 2009c). Students who report having participated in family meals and discussions, joined local organizations, or developed local friendships or social networks show greater gains in documented language ability than those who do not (e.g. Isabelli-García 2006; Kinginger 2008). This effect is likely due not only to increased exposure to the language itself but also to the efforts at language socialization of local people, where students are provided assistance in developing competence as participants in particular settings and are thereby socialized to use the language and also through the language to an appreciation of local values and worldviews (Ochs 2002). As demonstrated in Wilkinson's (1998) study reviewed above, the degree of local engagement can also influence students' formation of goals for the future, including motives for language learning.

In contemporary study abroad, the extent to which students become locally engaged has become an interesting question (Coleman, this volume). Numerous forces have combined to reduce the possibility that American students will in fact desire or gain access to contexts for participation taking place in the local language. To name but a few: Educational sojourns abroad are now typically brief, and programs may discourage students from becoming involved with local people (Levin 2001). Students may remain virtually "at home" through social media, and may receive multiple visits from family members. Students may frame their experience in consumerist terms, as a modern-day Grand Tour in which local people are cast primarily as service providers. The rise of English as a *lingua mundi* has meant that American students find their own language in use and in demand in many contexts. Above all, students who encounter challenges to their values and common-sense understanding of the world may reject language and culture learning as they recoil into a sense of national superiority.

It is this latter issue that we wish to investigate through the construct of "negotiation of difference" (Block 2007; Kinginger 2009a). The negotiation of difference is crucial not only for language learning but also for the development of an intercultural stance, since it involves confronting misunderstandings and attempting to elucidate them in dialogue with others. It requires openness to the notion that one's own interpretations may not have the same foundation as those of the other and readiness to view interpersonal difficulties as potential "rich points" (Agar 1994) where profound learning may emerge from dispassionate investigation of apparent incongruities and events or comments initially perceived as incomprehensible or strange.

Active engagement and negotiation of difference are both clearly very important for the success of a homestay arrangement. Research also demonstrates that the host family normally provides the only significant access to social networks and everyday communicative practices that students enjoy (Kinginger 2009c). However, according to a study examining the development of oral proficiency in 830 student participants studying seven languages (Vande Berg, Connor-Linton, & Paige 2009), it is not the presence or absence of a host family that can predict students' success. Rather, "the variable that matters here is whether students take advantage of home stays by engagement with family members" (p. 16). As noted in the above-mentioned case of Beatrice (in Kinginger 2008), a failure to negotiate different interpretations of the same event can lead to students' estrangement from their host families and corresponding missed opportunities to learn.

4. Program

The participants in this study all took part in the Landon-in-China summer program for high school students at various times from 2001 to 2008. The program is built upon long-standing relationships between the Landon School in Bethesda, MD and its sister schools in China. Over the course of its history, the program has evolved and expanded. The program was launched in 2000 as a 12-day tour taking place during the students' spring break. Later on, both participants and program organizers recognized the need for a longer stay and more local involvement to enhance the students' language proficiency and cultural awareness. Therefore, in 2001, the program was rescheduled for the summer and expanded to include a two-week tour plus a four-week language immersion experience during which students are placed individually with Chinese host families. In the immersion program, students take intensive language classes in the morning, participate in afternoon cultural courses or sightseeing, and go on weekend excursions. The travel portion is open to students in Grades 7 and 8, and the entire program is available to students in Grades 9 through 12. In 2005, an optional internship was added to the existing program, allowing students to pursue China-related research under the guidance of a local university professor who also hosts the student at home. No prior knowledge of Chinese is required, although many students do present some proficiency in the language when they enter the program. Since 2001, Landon-in-China has enrolled over 160 participants from throughout the United States, and has offered Chinese language instruction at all levels, up to and including the level of students who obtain college credit for Chinese language learning through the American Advanced Placement examination.

Two features of the Landon-in-China program warrant further attention, as they distinguish this program for high school students from the typical program design for college – age students. Most importantly, the Landon-in-China program functions in *loco parentis* for the students whereas in principle college level sojourners abroad are usually interpreted as legally and otherwise independent young adults. The program director, chaperones and instructors from the United States, the Chinese host parent and siblings as well as instructors hired locally jointly serve as the students' guides. Landon-in-China participants are very rarely alone, and are expected to be with a program representative at all times.

This feature of the program has significant consequences for the nature and qualities of students' experiences. As Coleman noted (1998) most American study abroad programs involve the short-term transfer of cohesive groups to foreign settings, where the students tend to rely upon each other for social and emotional support and to limit their engagement with local people and social networks. In contrast, the Landon-in-China program explicitly discourages students from gathering together after school. Except for four hours of intensive language classes in the morning, the program invites all Chinese host brothers and sisters to join the afternoon cultural classes and excursions as well as weekend trips to surrounding cultural, historical and scenic sites. The program also attempts to match the interests and hobbies of participants with those of Chinese host siblings, whenever possible.

The second distinguishing feature of Landon-in-China is that it is an exchange program, shorter in duration but otherwise like the one described in Perrefort (2008). In addition to sending American students to China, each year the program also hosts Chinese students from sister school for a three-week period at the end of January or early February, depending upon the dates of the Chinese Lunar New Year. In some cases, Landon School students who have hosted Chinese visitors in their homes will then be placed in the homes of these same Chinese students. Thus, when the American participants have already met their host siblings, interaction is much facilitated.

5.   Data

Data for the study come from emailed questionnaires distributed to 60 students shortly after their return from China. Open-ended questions requested reflections and observations about the experience. Participants were asked to comment on the qualities of their homestay, including highlights and challenges. They were also asked to reflect on the specific advantages of study abroad, as opposed to classroom study, for the learning of language and culture. In addition, they were asked to assess what they had learned not only about China and Chinese cultures, but also about their own identities as learners.

In addition to gathering the perspectives of students just after their sojourn in China, the first author also elicited a convenience sample of comments from seven participants who had gone on to attend university study abroad programs in China but had remained in touch with the first author. These students were asked to compare their Landon-in-China experience with college-level study in China after they had returned to the United States. Specifically, they were asked to compare their own experience with that of college peers who had not studied abroad in high school, and to reflect upon the relative value of studying abroad at an earlier age.

6.   Analysis

The current project set out to answer the following three research questions:

1.   How do the students portray their engagement with their local host families?
2.   In retrospect, how do college students represent their local engagement during high school study abroad?
3.   What evidence exists in the data to suggest that students have been involved in the negotiation of difference?

The methodology of the study involved content analysis consisting of close reading of the students' commentary to discern recurring themes relating to the research questions. In orienting applied linguistics researchers to the use of learner narratives, Pavlenko (2007) notes that such data are inherently interesting and potentially transformative, as they may shift power relations away from scholars' control and give voice to those who are researched. Learner narratives have contributed to the study of language learning by providing the insider's (or emic) view of learning processes and pointing to new research directions. However, these data are also potentially dangerous, particularly when researchers lose sight of the fact that narratives do not necessarily reflect reality: they are representations of reality shaped both by the learner's particular history and subjectivity and by the context of the telling. In other words, this context is both a macro phenomenon, involving the historical, political, or cultural circumstances of narrative production, and a micro phenomenon, where the narrator may be influenced by the audience, the modality, the setting and especially, relationships of power and hierarchy.

Clearly, the macro historical and political circumstances of the study are significant. The participants were able and encouraged to study in China in the first place because of changes in Chinese policies regarding international education. Also, the students come from backgrounds of relative privilege where language and culture learning as well as general cosmopolitanism are valued. However, for the current project, the most salient aspect of Pavlenko's critique has to do with the interactional context. It is important to bear in mind that the learners' observations and reflections came into existence at the first author's request. The first author was the director of the Landon-in-China program and a teacher of Chinese at the Landon School who had interacted with the many of the participants in these roles. Issues of power and hierarchy may well have influenced the ways in which the participants crafted their responses, for example to show respect to a former teacher or to avoid mentioning topics they believed she would not want to hear about. With this caveat in mind, the student reflections featured in this chapter nevertheless do offer some insights about how students portray their study abroad experiences in China.

7.   Results

In this chapter, the findings of the study are reported in three sections, each corresponding to a related research question. In the first section, we consider the value that students ascribed to the homestay. In the second, we review the testimonials of Landon-in-China alumni who have gone on to pursue further study of Chinese at the college level; these retrospective accounts add a longitudinal dimension to the study as the students interpret their past experiences in light of their current preoccupations. Finally, we review the data with a view to discover how the students portray the negotiation of difference (Kinginger 2009a) during their sojourns in China.

8.   Local engagement in Chinese homestay settings

Although the students do also refer to challenges and moments of trepidation, in general, and occasionally in almost hyperbolic terms, they portray the homestay as a rich environment for learning. As noted above, to some degree the student participants may have been influenced by the interactive context of data collection. Nevertheless, examination of the data reveals specific themes and accompanying anecdotes that can inform the reader about the potential homestay advantage for high school students abroad. The themes that the students explore include the remarkable hospitality, kindness and care extended to them by their host families, the many opportunities for observation and discussion of Chinese everyday cultural practices, the discovery of shared values and evidence of basic human nature, and, of course, the transformation of language learning from a sanitized classroom exercise to real and consequential communication.

The level of hospitality extended to students whose host families are acting in *loco parentis* is vividly illustrated in the reflections of William (a pseudonym, as are all names of students in this chapter). For this student, the Chinese homestay experience is qualified as 'eye-opening,' and 'terrifying' but ultimately 'invaluable.' As William grappled with the social differences between his American reform Jewish household and his new situation, he noted that the Chinese families were at constant pains to anticipate, interpret, and meet his needs.

> Despite my protestations, my dirty clothes were inevitably washed by my kindly and persistent host mothers, who also diligently plied me with second and third helpings at dinner and forced me to swallow bitter herbal medicine when I was sick.

His host families vacated bedrooms in their homes to accommodate him, and tried to please him by soliciting his culinary preferences. Sometimes this level of hospitality had accidental consequences, as in the case where, by expressing his love of Peking duck, he inadvertently forced each family to pay for a quite expensive dinner. William notes that he never quite grew completely accustomed to the host families' "unswerving" efforts to make him feel at home, and that occasionally these efforts made him feel guilty, but that eventually he negotiated more comfortable arrangements with his hosts.

The students also explicitly describe the value of the homestay in terms of the opportunities it provided to observe everyday cultural practices, dispel preconceived ideas and learn firsthand about the cultural dialogues and blended identities that characterize modern China in an era of globalization. In writing about his observation of politeness in his Chinese host family, Greg, for example notes that everyday occurrences can become occasions for comparing one's own customs to those of one's hosts, and therefore can also become catalysts for learning:

> I was surprised that my Chinese host family did not immediately open the gifts I gave them but rather set them aside. Initially, I thought it was because they were not interested in them, but as I spent more time familiarizing myself with the culture, I realized this was simply a polite gesture.

Similarly, Larry (who has now been to China over a dozen times) reflects on the relationships between values and communicative practices based on insights initially gained in his high school homestay experience. Larry has come to appreciate the subtlety and indirectness that is valued among expert speakers of Chinese as well as the concept of "face." This knowledge helps him to avoid misunderstandings:

> Frankly, I still have trouble fully accommodating myself to the Chinese method of communication, but at least now I have some understanding of it. So, for example, when I offer a Chinese friend a drink when they visit my home, and they say "No," I understand that this "no" may in fact be a veiled "yes"!

Another student, Jake, offers a particularly sophisticated appreciation of the advantages of the homestay for firsthand observation of contemporary cultural practices. In contrast to textbooks, according to Jake, the homestay provided a "window… into the dynamic crossroads of ancient cultural and modern globalization that is 21st century China." He specifically refers to the stereotypes and preconceived notions he had previous held about China and the Chinese, and how these were challenged in his interactions with Chinese teenagers:

> This experience allowed me to dispel certain preconceptions about Chinese families and children, namely that students were excessively academic-minded and that families adhered to a strict Confucian structure. It also allowed me to observe firsthand the blending and interexchange of traditional Chinese values and external cultural influences, as well as to learn a few interesting (and amusing) things I had never had any idea of beforehand, the popularity of boy bands and karaoke establishments being among them.

In addition to focusing on cultural differences, the student participants in this study also comment at length on the discovery of common preferences and shared values. In moving from Beijing to Chengdu, Jake was concerned that he might have difficulty in communicating with his new host brother. The brother had relatively little proficiency in English, and spoke mostly Sichuanese with his family. Jake was also concerned that Chengdu might be less Westernized than the capital.

> Quite contrary to my expectations, however, we really hit it off. By the end of the two weeks in Chengdu, we had gone hiking, visited museums, played several games of Chinese chess (one of which I actually won), eaten exotic hot-pot meals, tried to out-swim one another – in short, we had shared more fun experiences and inside jokes than I had with some of my American friends, even if we didn't understand each other's language some of the time.

Helen also highlights the similarities in basic values that she shared with her host family. She remarks that real differences do exist in everyday practices, living conditions, and notions of politeness, but that in the end her experience was one in which all parties were striving to please each other:

> What I found was we each had preconceived notions of what was acceptable in the other culture, but basically we were really just trying to please each other. Initially my family was trying so hard to please me in terms of what they thought American students wanted and expected whereas I was trying to be a good guest and was doing what I thought they wanted. Over time we got more comfortable with each other and began to understand each other better.

Finally, the impact of the homestay on students' language ability is also an important theme in these data. Kathy, for example, lists language skill as one of the 'concrete' benefits of her time abroad:

> As for concrete benefits, my language skills improved exponentially due to my small, intense class that helped me reach a new plateau in Mandarin. I consequently became more self-articulate and relational with my new Chinese family and friends as they graciously familiarized me with the contemporary Chinese lifestyle.

However exponentially their language skills increased, it is not just the quantity of proficiency in Chinese that the student writers celebrate, but also the qualities of their language-related experiences in a variety of "real world" communicative settings as well as the insights the students developed about the process of language learning itself. Jonathan set off for China with some trepidation but returned having been "transformed" through the application of his language ability in local communication where his contributions were consequential:

> Every day I spent hours speaking, writing, and learning new phrases and characters. My host mother frequently took me to bargain at some of the local markets. I took what I had learned and applied it in the real world. My education in China was more of a transformation than an education. At home I would simply memorize key phrases and terms. In China, I had to not just learn them, but *know* them. This changed the way I study Chinese as well as studying for other subjects as well.

Although Jonathan does not elaborate on the precise ways in which the homestay experience changed his approach to learning, one way in which this change may have occurred is illustrated in the remarks of another student, Helen. Like some of the other students participating in this research, and indeed as has been documented elsewhere (e.g. Kinginger 2008), for Helen the experience of study abroad embedded language use in the realities of everyday communication. This, in turn, highlighted the need to learn 'natural', or colloquial language that is rarely documented in pedagogical materials for language learners:

> Just to deal with the everyday necessities such as meals, laundry and cab transportation to and from school I have to speak Chinese. In addition the Chinese that is being spoken in the classrooms, although it is supposed to be real life conversation, isn't always the natural way of saying things. Sometimes it even sounds like a classroom drill. […] Speaking in real life situations helps to make the conversation more natural.

Overall, then, the participants in this study evaluated their local engagement in homestay settings in a positive light. Without exception, and despite recollections of some awkward moments, they expressed appreciation for the warm welcome and many kindnesses extended by their host families. They also documented how the homestay experience provided specific opportunities to observe local practices such as politeness and communicative style. While helping them to appreciate these particular cultural practices, they also credited the homestay with the discovery of certain universals of human compassion and mutual respect. In terms of language learning, they portray their experience in China as bringing the language to life, changing their orientation to learning, and highlighting the importance of learning to appreciate and master everyday and colloquial language forms.

9.   Retrospective views of college-aged alumni

As noted above, data for this study includes seven email exchange interviews with college-aged alumni who have gone on to more advanced study of Chinese, including further study abroad, at the university level. The data lend a longitudinal aspect to the study as they show how these students appraise their high school sojourns in China with the wisdom of greater maturity and in light of their current preoccupations as college students. Once again, several themes emerge from a close reading of the data. The participants mention several characteristics of younger learners, such as adaptability or open-mindedness, that tend to enhance the quality of learning in the Chinese homestay. They comment on the ways in which an early immersion experience enhanced their motivation and increased the realism with which they approach Chinese language learning. They also note that early study abroad in a homestay program offered them access to local social networks not necessarily enjoyed by their peers.

Larry, for example, presents several "practical" reasons for choosing to study abroad for the first time while still in high school. He notes that during his first sojourn in China he was relatively better able to adapt to the homestay because he had not yet developed more adult preoccupations with independence or privacy. In comparing himself with his college classmates, he sees himself more easily taking up the challenge of speaking in a "genuine" language environment because of his prior experience. Overall:

> I think it's much easier to adapt when you're younger. The big advantage of doing study abroad in high school is that your mind is just more open – more able to acquire a foreign language, more willing to live in a home-stay, and overall less inhibited to go out and try to use the language.

Another participant, Eugene, studied abroad with Landon-in-China during his freshman and sophomore years in high school and then again during the summer following his second university year. For Eugene, the characteristics of high school students that lead to productive study abroad include open-mindedness and willingness to take risks. In comparing his own approach to those of his college-aged peers, he sees a distinct contrast:

> ...when I studied abroad again [...] in college, I noticed a tendency among the participants who had never been to China before to be less open to new experiences. Weekends became less of an opportunity to explore local culture than a chance to frequent bars only frequented by foreigners. Many students rejected the chance to try new local cuisines in favor of the McDonald's across campus, a pancake dinner in the shopping mall, etc.

Eugene also commented on the ways in which early study abroad provided him with a sense of Chinese as a living language, and thereby enhanced his motivation to continue learning. Eugene considers his own learning experience to be relatively "comprehensive" in comparison with other college students whose tuition in the language began later.

> Compared with my peers who were essentially memorizing what were arbitrary words and phrases, I took learning Chinese in college much more to heart because I better understood when, where, and how what I was learning would be applied in China. I could "visualize" when I could say what I was learning in the classroom, and this fueled my motivation to further learn and embrace Chinese.

Motivation is also a theme brought up by Greg, who claims that the early experience of conversing with Chinese people inspired him to return to China after he had further increased his proficiency. He also claims to have an advantage over his college peers because of his deeper appreciation of his own strengths and weaknesses as well as of the communicative capabilities required in everyday interaction.

> I was encouraged to continue studying Chinese because I had seen the benefits of my study thus far in conversing with native speakers, and I wanted the opportunity to go back after I had learned even more. Also, I gained a better sense of what I needed to practice and learn in order to function in real scenarios that could not be easily replicated by an in-class exercise. In this regard, I was given a significant advantage over my classmates and a head start in improving my weakest areas of language skills.

In addition to these more abstract advantages of early study abroad, some students also commented on the affordances provided to them in college programs through the social networks forged in high school. It is well known that engagement in local social networks can have a highly beneficial effect both on the development of language proficiency and on the furthering of ethnorelative stances (e.g. Isabelli-García 2006). A review of the literature also reveals that American college students face many obstacles when attempting to join these networks. Particularly if their sojourns are short-term, now the default arrangement, without special effort or the assistance of programs or host families, American students rarely develop durable friendships with local peers. However, if the student has already lived in a local home as a high school student, he or she may be connected from the beginning of their stay. Rebecca, for example, kept in touch with her hosts in Beijing and then returned to that city as a college student:

> When I went to a university study in Beijing program, I spent much more time with one of my host sisters and her friends than with the Americans in my program. In fact, I came to China a week early to stay at my friend's college campus, attend classes with her, and go to karaoke with her friends. … One of my host sisters from Beijing still calls me "sis". During my home-stay, her Mom was my Mom.

Overall, and once again, the college-aged alumni whose perspectives are recounted in these data see their high school sojourns in a positive light. They emphasize the difference between older and younger students in terms of their dispositions toward family life, expectations of privacy and independence, openness to new experiences and willingness to take risks. In comparing themselves with peers who have begun to learn Chinese in college, they outline the distinctiveness of their motivation, language awareness, and self-awareness as language learners. They also point out that the importance of relationships forged at an earlier age, and the ways in which these social ties offer opportunities to be included in local social networks.

10.   Negotiating difference

In this final section, we examine how the students portray their own negotiation of difference in encounters with Chinese hosts. That is, how did the experience of high school study abroad enhance their ability to see relationships between different cultures and to interpret each in terms of the other? How did this experience make the students more aware of their own perspective and its specific cultural origins, and how did it challenge their beliefs in the naturalness of the perspectives?

In the data, the participants often refer to the outcomes, rather than the processes of their intercultural experiences. Greg, for example, mentions that he learned through comparison not only about Chinese culture, but also about his own way of life:

> By comparing my values and customs to those of the Chinese, I realized that what I thought was normal wasn't necessarily that way for all people and what I thought was peculiar actually turned out to be quite common.

Similarly, Larry describes a change in perspective through the discovery of other ways of life:

> I think in many aspects of life, it's easy to take your own habits and customs for granted, assuming that these are universal. It's only when you've seen how differently people can live that you realized that your way of life is only one of several alternatives.

While the data for the current project do not include recordings of actual interactions taking place in the Chinese households, the participants do occasionally offer recollections of particular interactive scenes, including some that are reminiscent of the sharing of folk beliefs in Cook's (2006) research. William recalls the curiosity of his host families about the United States and his own attempts, as a 15-year-old, to satisfy it. Some of the questions were quite unexpected:

> For example, my second Beijing host family, gathered together in the living room one Sunday morning, wanted to know about American opinions and attitudes. Through queries like, "Why do the white people in America hate the black people?" or "Why do Americans hate China?" the information gap between our two countries became clearly evident. I continue to be struck by how prevalent such stereotypes are in parts of China, in the absence of dialogue and exchange. I am left wondering what grossly inaccurate characterizations Americans hold about China, acknowledging their inevitable existence.

Having discovered the existence of stereotypes about his own country held by his Chinese hosts, William was led to reflect on the mirror image of these preconceived ideas held by his compatriots. In the end, he writes that while these experiences were quite weighty for a teenager, the experience "imparted invaluable life lessons on understanding cultural differences, adapting to wholly unfamiliar circumstances, exhibiting tact, patience, and curiosity, and bridging cultural divides."

Overall, then, while the participants do not dwell particularly on narratives involving the negotiation of difference, they do clearly value and claim to have developed intercultural perspectives as a result of their high school sojourns in China. Further research into the processes of intercultural development in home-stay arrangements may help to elucidate this issue.

11. Conclusion

In interpreting the results of this study in light of the broader qualitative literature on language and culture learning in homestays abroad, a clear contrast emerges. The homestay experience for American students is usually portrayed as variable in quality, with the potential to transform language and culture learning through rich and varied lived experience, but also the possibility of isolation and even alien-ation. Here, on the other hand, and perhaps in part due to the interactive con-text of data collection, the participants assess their experiences largely in positive, even glowing terms. We have seen that alumni of the Landon-in-China program value their homestays for the warm, if potentially overwhelmingly hospitable wel-come extended by host families. They also praise the opportunities they enjoyed to observe local cultural and communicative practice, to engage in extended dia-logue, and to expand their Chinese language communicative repertoires. The participants also appreciate having been challenged in their preconceived notions about Chinese culture and having had chances to reflect and compare their own perspectives with those of their hosts.

In the retrospective data from college students there emerge some poten-tial reasons for this nearly universal positive appraisal of high school homestay sojourns abroad. These older participants are able to evaluate their own positions as learners in comparison with college-aged peers who did not study abroad in high school. Here we see the alumni discussing the relative merits of study abroad at a younger age, when they were, reportedly, more open-minded, more willing to accept the constraints of host family life, and less risk-averse. We also see them describing the very real social ties forged in high school that continue to support their learning of Chinese and their social integration while in China.

Thus, the findings of this study suggest, if they do not by any means prove, that high school study abroad experiences, at least within carefully designed and moni-tored programs, may in many cases be quite different from parallel experiences in college. College students, both in the US and in China, are defined by the law as adults. In the US they are interpreted (both by institutions and by themselves) as independent persons who are in a process of liberation from the control of fami-lies and of establishment of personal independence (Matthews 1997). Programs for college students do not have moral and legal responsibility to protect their students to the same degree that high school programs do. Taken together, all of this means that high school students are more likely to be accepted into families as temporary adopted "children" and that they are more likely to value and enjoy this acceptance. If all of this is true, then there is a clear advantage to study abroad during the high school years, both immediately and in the longer term, as students move on to further academic achievement. The data suggest that high school study abroad experiences can be successful in many ways, precisely because the students' engagement with host families is both relatively intensive and relatively unproblematic.

The limitations of the study are many. The data were collected by a former teacher and authority figure in the program, which means that they must be interpreted with caution and in light of the possibility that the participants crafted their narratives partly in response to an interactive context overlaid with relations of power and respect. Like many other research projects involving American students abroad, the study sought out the perspectives of students only, and did not include the points of view of other participants, including host family members. Data for the study consist of retrospective accounts only, and there is no explicit triangulation with other data sources, although of course the first author, as Director of the program, enjoys an insider's appreciation of the program goals and design.

Nevertheless, this project does offer some intriguing findings about student evaluations of high school study abroad experiences. Further research, involving multiple data sources and parties to the interactions, may confirm that younger, more impressionable students find their study abroad experiences more significant than do college students, and that they tend to enjoy more social integration, greater access to extended interactions with local hosts and more durable friendships with native and other expert L2 users. Longitudinal research might also show how students navigate different learning environments over time in the process of developing communicative repertoires in additional languages, and how the inspiration developed in high school might help to sustain interest and engagement over the long-term. In the event that these hypotheses are confirmed, implications for language learning policy and for the design of study abroad programs would be very significant indeed.

References

Agar, M. (1994). *Language shock: Understanding the culture of conversation.* New York, NY: William Morrow and Company.

Bhabha, H. (1994). *The location of culture.* London: Routledge.

Block, D. (2007). The rise of identity in SLA research: Post Firth and Wagner (2007). *Modern Language Journal, 91*, 863–876.

Churchill, E. (2006). Variability in the study abroad classroom and learner competence. In M.A. DuFon & E. Churchill, (Eds.), *Language learners in study abroad contexts*, (pp. 203–227). Clevedon, UK: Multilingual Matters.

Coleman, J. (1998). Language learning and study abroad: The European perspective. *Frontiers: The Interdisciplinary Journal of Study Abroad, 4*, 167–203.

Cook, H. (2006). Joint construction of folk beliefs by JFL learners and Japanese host families. In M.A. DuFon & E. Churchill, (Eds.), *Language learners in study abroad contexts*, (pp. 120–150). Clevedon, UK: Multilingual Matters.

Cook, H. (2008). *Socializing identities through speech style: Learners of Japanese as a foreign language*. Clevedon, UK: Multilingual Matters.

DuFon, M.A. (2006). The socialization of taste during study abroad in Indonesia. In M.A. DuFon & E. Churchill, (Eds.), *Language learners in study abroad contexts*, (pp. 91–119). Clevedon, UK: Multilingual Matters.

Frank, V. (1997, March). Potential negative effects of homestay. Paper presented at the Middle Atlantic Conference of the American Association for the Advancement of Slavic Studies, Albany, NY.

Gore, J. (2005). *Dominant beliefs and alternative voices: Discourse, belief, and gender in American study abroad*. New York, NY: Routledge.

Hall, S. (2006). Introduction: Who needs 'identity'? In S. Hall & P. du Gay (Eds.), *Questions of cultural identity* (pp. 1–17). London: Sage.

Hashimoto, H. (1993). Language acquisition of an exchange student within the homestay environment. *Journal of Asian Pacific Communication, 4*, 209–224.

Iino, M. (2006). Norms of interaction in a Japanese homestay setting – Toward two way flow of linguistic and cultural resources. In M.A. DuFon & E. Churchill, (Eds.), *Language learners in study abroad contexts*, (pp. 151–173). Clevedon, UK: Multilingual Matters.

Isabelli-García, C. (2006). Study abroad social networks, motivation, and attitudes: Implications for SLA. In M.A. DuFon & E. Churchill (Eds.), *Language learners in study abroad contexts* (pp. 231–258). Clevedon, UK: Multilingual Matters.

Kinginger, C. (2008). Language learning in study abroad: Case studies of Americans in France. *Modern Language Journal, 92*, Monograph.

Kinginger, C. (2009a). American students abroad: Negotiation of difference? *Language Teaching, 43*, 216–227.

Kinginger, C. (2009b). *Contemporary study abroad and foreign language learning: An activist's guidebook*. University Park, PA: Center for Advanced Language Proficiency Education and Research (CALPER) Publications.

Kinginger, C. (2009c). *Language learning and study abroad: A critical reading of research*. Basingstoke, UK: Palgrave Macmillan.

Knight, S.M., & Schmidt-Rinehart, B.C. (2002). Enhancing the home-stay: Study abroad from the host family's perspective. *Foreign Language Annals, 35*, 190–201.

Lave, J., & Wenger, E. (1991). *Situated learning: Legitimate peripheral participation*. Cambridge: Cambridge University Press.

Levin, D. (2001). *Language learners sociocultural interaction in a study abroad context*. Unpublished doctoral dissertation, Indiana University, Bloomington.

Liu, J. (2010). Assessing students' language proficiency: A new model of study abroad program in China. *Journal of Studies in International Education, 14*, 528–544.

Magnan, S., & Back, M. (2007). Social interaction and linguistic gain during study abroad. *Foreign Language Annals, 40*, 43–61.

Matthews, A. (1997) *Bright college years: Inside the American campus today*. New York, NY: Simon & Schuster.

Ochs, E. 2002. Becoming a speaker of culture. In Kramsch, C. (Ed.) *Language acquisition and language socialization: Ecological perspectives* (pp. 99–120). London: Continuum.

Ogden, A. (2007). The view from the veranda: Understanding today's colonial students. *Frontiers: The Interdisciplinary Journal of Study Abroad, 15*, 2–20.

Papastergiadis, N. (2000). *The turbulence of migration*. Cambridge: Polity Press.

Pavlenko, A. (2007). Autobiographic narratives as data in applied linguistics. *Applied Linguistics, 28*, 163–188.

Pellegrino Aveni, V. (2005). *Study abroad and second language use: Constructing the self*. Cambridge: Cambridge University Press.

Perrefort, M. (2008). Changer en échangeant? Mobilités et experiences langagières [Change through exchange? Mobility and language-related experiences]. In F. Dervin & M. Byram (Eds.), *Echanges et mobilités académiques: Quel bilan?* [Exchanges and academic mobility: What results?] (pp. 65–91). Paris: L'Harmattan.

Rivers, W. (1998). Is being there enough? The effects of homestay placements on language gain during study abroad. *Foreign Language Annals, 31*, 492–500.

Sacks, H. (1992). *Lectures on conversations*. Oxford: Blackwell.

Spenader, A. (2011). Language learning and acculturation: Lessons from high school and gap year students. *Foreign Language Annals, 44*, 381–398.

Tan, D. (2008). Study abroad in China: Transformation of students' perspectives on the world and themselves. In C.K. Lee (Ed.), *Chinese as a Foreign/second language in the study abroad context* (pp. 267–81). Beijing: Peking University Press.

Vande Berg, M., Connor-Linton, J., & Paige, M. (2009). The Georgetown Consortium Project: Interventions for student learning abroad. *Frontiers: The Interdisciplinary Journal of Study Abroad, 18*, 1–75.

Yu, B. (2010). Learning Chinese abroad: The role of language attitudes and motivation in the adaptation of international students in China. *Journal of Multilingual and Multicultural Development, 31*, 301–321.

Yu, B., & Watkins, D. (2008). Motivational and cultural correlates of second language acquisition: An investigation of international students in the universities of the People's Republic of China. *Australian Review of Applied Linguistics, 31*, 17.1–17.22.

Wilkinson, S. (1998). On the nature of immersion during study abroad: Some participants' perspectives. *Frontiers: The Interdisciplinary Journal of Study Abroad, 4*, 121–138.

The transformation of "a frog in the well"*

A path to a more intercultural, global mindset

Jane Jackson
Chinese University of Hong Kong

Have you ever seen a blurred image in a mirror
or a ferry never knowing the right pier?
If you used to think a journey gives a better picture of who you are,
you are wrong because it actually leaves you
with more complexities and complication
when defining the simplest but hardest word 'home'.

Kingston, post-sojourn poem, 28 October 2010

This chapter explores the developmental trajectory of a Hong Kong Chinese university student who participated in a year-long exchange program in Canada. After Kingston (a pseudonym) returned home, he enrolled in *Intercultural Transitions*, an elective course designed to enhance and extend sojourn learning through guided, critical reflection. Kingston's oral and written narratives provided a window into his second language learning, intercultural communication, cross-cultural adjustment, and evolving sense of self. Multiple sociocultural factors (e.g. host receptivity), personality attributes (e.g. ability to overcome psychological barriers, degree of ethnocentricism/reflexivity, willingness to try new things), and depth of investment in language and (inter)cultural enhancement impacted on his "whole person" development. The findings underscore the complexity of learning on stays abroad.

1. Introduction

The above poem was penned by a Hong Kong Chinese university student who had returned home after spending a year in Canada as an exchange student.

---

* In his second reflective essay, Kingston wrote about his limited intercultural understandings prior to going on exchange and described himself as a "frog in the well" at that stage of his life. The "frog in the well" is a Chinese idiom or chengyu (Tsai & Caprio 2008). This old Chinese fable compares a frog who lives in a deep well to a sea turtle living in a vast Eastern ocean. The frog lives blissfully in the well, believing it is the entire world until a sea turtle enlightens him about the vast ocean and wonders that lie beyond.

At the time of the writing, Kingston (a pseudonym) was engaged in the process of guided, critical reflection in a post-sojourn course that was designed to help returnees make sense of their international experience and extend their inter-cultural/second language (L2) learning (Jackson 2011a). As the poem vividly illustrates, crossing borders can raise unsettling questions about one's place in the world.

Living and studying in an unfamiliar linguistic and sociocultural context and then returning to one's home country, where differing social norms may prevail, can entail an "oscillating, dialectal process" of adaptation (Ting- Toomey 1999, p. 258) and lead to disequilibrium in some (Szkudlarek 2010). Sojourners who find it difficult to adjust to anything new may return home with a strength-ened sense of national identity (Block 2007; Byram 2008; Jackson 2010a) and negative stereotypes of the host country further entrenched (Jackson 2008, 2010a; Kinginger 2009). They may then avoid intercultural interaction, curtailing personal expansion and further enhancement of their L2. This need not be the outcome, however. When international, intercultural experience is coupled with guided, critical reflection, it can lead to growth in intercultural (communica-tive) competence and the development of more cosmopolitan, global identities. Kingston's journey of discovery of Self and Other documents the potential for constructive engagement and transformation in L2 sojourners.

This chapter draws upon a larger study which is exploring the "whole person" (Coleman, this volume) development of 105 Hong Kong university students (63 females and 42 males) who took part in a yearlong exchange program in one of 19 countries. The primary aims of this mixed-method investigation are to better understand the L2, intercultural, personal, and academic learning of the student sojourners, as well as their evolving sense of self both at home and abroad. Some of the participants, including Kingston, joined a credit-bearing course for returnees, *Intercultural Transitions: Making sense of international experience,* which was offered at the home institution for the first time in September 2010. This period of intense reflection provided more insight into the social contexts of his international experience and the elements that affected his (re)adjustment and L2/intercultural learning.

This chapter traces this young man's journey over a two-year period, from early January 2009 until late December 2010, including his yearlong sojourn in Canada, which took place from July 2009 to July 2010. The analysis of his story centers on his intercultural/L2 socialization and identity expansion, with special attention paid to his motives for gaining international education, his social net-works, his response to cultural difference, his investment in L2/(inter)cultural growth, and his evolving self-identities both in Hong Kong and Canada.

2. Theoretical framework

Before focusing on Kingston's story, I briefly discuss the conceptual framework for this phase of the study, which has its roots in poststructuralist notions of identity and L2/intercultural socialization, and developmental/transformative learning theories. Intercultural sensitivity is an important element in successful intercultural relations, and, like many study abroad researchers, a model that I have found very useful to track the emergence of intercultural competence is Milton Bennett's (1993) developmental model of intercultural sensitivity (DMIS). Mezirow's (1994, 2000) transformational theory also helps explain the identity reconstruction that sojourners may experience if they are open to the process of personal expansion and critically engaged in deep reflection.

2.1   Situated learning: L2/intercultural socialization and identities

For many decades, L2 researchers have tended to view L2 acquisition as a mental process and, consequently, the social positions, identities, and personal histories of language learners were largely ignored. This conceptualization has been contested by poststructuralists who argue that L2 learning and identity (re)construction should be situated within a particular social, cultural, political, and historical context (e.g. Block 2003, 2007; Firth & Wagner 2007; Lafford 2007). As Swain and Deters (2007) explain, L2 learning is "a highly complex activity in which human cognition and human agency develop and multiple identities are co-constructed through interaction with others, the self, and the cultural artifacts of our environments" (p. 831). These poststructuralists argue that it is incumbent on researchers to incorporate a "social perspective of learners and language learning" (p. 831) into investigations of the L2 learning process (e.g. "by listening to the stories of the learners" (p. 831) and incorporating both emic and etic perspectives in the analysis of first-person oral and written narratives).

Drawing on the work of such visionaries as Bakhtin (1981, 1984, 1986), Vygotsky (1978, 1986) and Wertsch (1998), sociocultural theory provides a useful framework for understanding the socially-situated nature of L2 and (inter) cultural learning (Lantolf 2004; Lantolf & Thorne 2006; Swain, Kinnear & Steinman 2010). Adopting a poststructuralist stance, Pavlenko and Lantolf (2000) characterize L2 learning as: "... a struggle of concrete socially constituted and always situated beings to participate in the symbolically mediated lifeworld of another culture. These individuals have intentions, agency, affect and, above all, histories..." (p. 155). Language and (inter)cultural learning are affected by social, cognitive, and affective dimensions as learners mediate their complex worlds in an L2 and try to make sense of their evolving perceptions of Self and Other.

From a poststructuralist perspective, "identity is generally pluralized as 'identities,' which are seen, not as phenomena fixed for life, but as ongoing lifelong narratives in which individuals constantly attempt to maintain a sense of balance" (Block 2008, p. 142). This sense of balance may be challenged when L2 learners move to an unfamiliar linguistic and sociocultural context and come face to face with different views and practices, which may conflict with what they have been socialized to believe is appropriate. Feeling overwhelmed and under threat, sojourners may limit their social networks to home country nationals (e.g. members of their linguistic/ethnic group) and miss opportunities for L2 enhancement, (inter)cultural learning, and identity expansion.

Other border crossers may follow a different path. Even after they experience difficulties in the host culture, they may exercise their agency and continue to actively seek opportunities for L2/intercultural interaction. If their hosts are open to their participation, the newcomers may then benefit from increased exposure to the host language and local communities of practice (Lave & Wenger 1991; Jackson 2008). As their social networks include host nationals, these border crossers are more apt to become familiar with local norms of interaction in various contexts (e.g. sociopragmatic norms of politeness). By engaging in this process of L2/intercultural socialization, they gradually learn how to participate in local scenes. Those with an open mindset may develop more acceptance of cultural difference and begin to see the world and themselves from a different perspective. Instead of quickly rejecting new behaviors, these individuals experiment with new ways of being (e.g. local discursive practices).

Over time, the newcomers may develop what Menard-Warwick (2008, p. 622) defines as an intercultural identity, that is, "a negotiated investment in seeing the world through multiple cultural lenses." The acquisition of a more cosmopolitan, global mindset need not come at the expense of local selfhood. Individuals may develop an appreciation of *both* local and global identities (Jackson 2010b 2011b) as they engage in the "production of thirdness" – the creation of "new texts, meanings, and identities," which can occur "on the boundaries between the self and the Other" (Kostogriz 2005, p. 198). This notion of identity expansion is in accord with the tenets of the DMIS.

2.2 The developmental model of intercultural sensitivity (DMIS) and identity expansion

The DMIS was devised by Bennett (1993) to explain the process involved in the acquisition of intercultural competence. Based on the observations and reported experiences of people in intercultural encounters, this model centers on the constructs of ethnocentricism and ethnorelativism (Bennett 1993, 1997; Bennett & Bennett 2004; Landis, Bennett & Bennett 2004). According to the DMIS, when one possesses an ethnocentric mindset, "the worldview of one's own culture is central to all reality" (Bennett 1993, p. 30); by contrast, ethnorelativism is linked to "being comfortable with many standards and customs and to having an ability to adapt behavior and judgments to a variety of interpersonal settings" (p. 26). In the DMIS, intercultural sensitivity is believed to entail both personal and cognitive growth, and the gradual acquisition of "a mindset capable of understanding from within and from without both one's own culture and other cultures" (Bennett, Bennett & Allen 2003, p. 252).

In contrast with structuralist depictions of identity as fixed, static, and unitary, this theoretical framework views selfhood as relational, socially constructed, and dynamic. This perspective is aligned with contemporary critical and poststructuralist notions (e.g. Block 2007; Guilherme 2002; Jackson 2008; Norton 2000; Pavlenko & Lantolf 2000) which recognize the fluid, contradictory nature of identity and the potential for identity reconstruction in border crossers who are genuinely open to the process of personal expansion.

At the heart of the DMIS is the notion that ethnorelative worldviews are more effective in nurturing the attitudes, knowledge, and behavior that facilitate successful intercultural communication and adjustment in new cultural environments (Kim 2001, 2005). Intercultural competence is defined by Bennett and Bennett (2004) as "the ability to communicate effectively in cross-cultural situations and to relate appropriately in a variety of cultural contexts" (p. 149). The DMIS posits that individuals move from ethnocentric stages (Denial, Defense, and Minimization), through ethnorelative stages of development (Acceptance, Adaptation, and Integration) as they develop intercultural competence and a more open, global mindset (Bennett 2009). This model is not linear. Individuals do not necessarily advance to the next stage in sequence; due to unpleasant intercultural experiences or acute culture shock, for instance, they may temporarily fall back to a lower level of sensitivity.

In my ethnographic investigations of L2 students from Hong Kong who sojourned in England, the DMIS helped me make sense of variations in developmental trajectories (Jackson 2009, 2010a, 2011b, 2011c). I did not, however, find a "typical fit between language proficiency levels and developmental levels of intercultural sensitivity" as hypothesized by Bennett, Bennett and Allen (2003: 255); that is, students with an advanced level of proficiency in English according to TOEFL or IELTS measures did not necessarily have well-developed intercultural competence. Observations of the participants' intercultural interaction in the host culture, and a content analysis of their oral and written narratives, offered a window into their sociopragmatic development and intercultural sensitivity. Those who displayed a higher level of sociopragmatic awareness in the host language at the end of the sojourn had a more sophisticated understanding of cultural difference, and a higher level of intercultural competence according to the Intercultural Development Inventory (IDI), a 50-item survey instrument that was administered before and after the sojourn. This cross-culturally validated, psychometric instrument, which is linked to the DMIS, is widely used in study abroad research (Hammer 2009a, 2009b; Hammer, Bennett & Wiseman 2003).

2.3   Identity and transformational learning theory

Bennett's (1993) DMIS also resonates with Mezirow's (1994, 2000) transformational learning theory, which maintains that individuals who engage in critical self-analysis may experience transformation in response to significant events in their lives (e.g. moving to an unfamiliar linguistic/cultural environment). In this adult learning theory, intercultural competence is believed to involve a continuous learning process with "new or revised interpretations of the meaning of one's experience" (Mezirow 1994, p. 222). Through intercultural contact, people encounter cultural difference (and similarity) and face challenges that may cause them to question their usual ways of being. Border crossers may experience "disorienting dilemmas" that challenge their long-held beliefs and norms (Mezirow 1996, 2000). Through deep, critical reflection individuals may develop the knowledge and skills that will help them to accommodate radically different ideas and experiences. Mezirow (1996) argues that this process can lead to a life-altering transformation and, ultimately, the restructuring of one's sense of self. As individuals develop more awareness and understanding of cultural difference, they may choose to open themselves up to novel ways of being. Those who acquire an ethnorelative mindset (Bennett & Bennett 2004) may adjust their behaviors to facilitate more effective and appropriate intercultural communication. Similar to the DMIS, this transformational theory allows for the evolution of hybrid, global identities, which is in line with poststructuralist notions of dynamic selfhood and L2/intercultural socialization.

3.   The case study

The remainder of the chapter focuses on Kingston's story, offering insight into the factors that appeared to impact on his L2/intercultural socialization, intercultural communicative competence and evolving sense of self both in Hong Kong and Canada. His journey was selected for closer scrutiny due to the significant growth in his intercultural sensitivity, and the richness of the material that was collected over a two year-period.

Both qualitative and quantitative data were gathered prior to Kingston's exchange experience, immediately after his yearlong sojourn, and through-out the 14-week reentry course that he joined in the semester following his return to Hong Kong. We learn about his journey largely from his perspective, that is, through his oral and written narratives, which are highly personal in nature. When reviewing first-person data it is important to bear in mind that these revelations are *versions* of reality (Pavlenko 2007). Rather than "objective, omniscient accounts," they are "partial representations and evocations of the world" (Ochs & Capps 1996, p. 21) as seen through the eyes of the individual at a particular point in time in a specific location. When reflecting on past events, individuals are also limited by their memory. With these limitations in view, the timing and context of excerpts are provided and, when relevant, I interpose an etic (outsider's) perspective, drawing on my field notes to further contextualize Kingston's story. Objective measures of his intercultural competence at strategic intervals (IDI results) are also provided. To better understand his developmental trajectory, I draw comparisons and contrasts between Kingston's experience and those of the other yearlong sojourners in the larger study, especially those who participated in the reentry course.

Pre-sojourn data consisted of: the application form Kingston completed to join the exchange program (including an essay outlining his aims and expectations for the sojourn), the Pre-International Exchange survey (an in-house instrument), the IDI, and a semi-structured interview. The in-house survey consisted of 93 closed questions and several open-ended questions that focused on pre-sojourn expectations of, preparation for, and perceptions of the impending exchange pro-gram. It also gathered basic demographic information. Before going on exchange, Kingston was also interviewed. On 11 July 2009, he chose to use Cantonese in this session which lasted 68 minutes. He was encouraged to expand on his survey responses and to comment on other issues of relevance to the international exchange experience that interested him.

After his yearlong stay in Canada, in mid-July 2010, Kingston was re-administered the IDI and Post-International Exchange survey in Hong Kong. The latter consisted of 78 closed questions and several that were open-ended. The sur-vey focused on the students' perceptions of and experience in their international exchange program, including their goals and learning outcomes; many items were similar to those in the Pre-International Exchange survey. Data were also gathered about academic performance (e.g. courses undertaken abroad, academic results). To facilitate a deeper understanding of his sojourn and reentry, on 24 July 2010, Kingston was re-interviewed. He again opted to express his views in Cantonese in a semi-structured interview that lasted one hour and thirty-three minutes. This session covered a range of topics related to his sojourn and reentry experiences.

The following semester (September – December 2010), Kingston elected to enroll in my course, *Intercultural Transitions: Making Sense of International Experience,* and kindly gave his consent for his work to be analyzed after it was over. Following a "practice-to-theory-to-practice" pedagogy (Jackson 2011a), I facilitated the students' exploration of their international experience through guided, critical reflection. Moving from description to analysis, they examined their own (and others') intercultural encounters in relation to theories and models of intercultural (communicative) competence and intercultural transitions (Jackson 2011a, 2011d). Kingston and his classmates delved into such topics as language/culture shock, adjustment, reentry, identity expansion, global citizenship and intercultural communicative competence.

Data for this phase of the study were varied and rich. They consisted of informal conversations, in-class discussions, weekly blog entries, online forums (on Moodle, our e-learning course management system), surveys, three reflective essays about his sojourn/reentry experiences, and my field notes. At the end of the semester, Kingston was again administered the IDI to provide a measure of his intercultural sensitivity after this period of intense, critical reflection. He was also interviewed for the third and final time in a session, which lasted an hour. Kingston's oral and written narratives were very detailed, offering a window into his L2/(inter)cultural learning, social networks, and identities.

To make sense of the qualitative data generated in the reentry course (interview transcripts, open-ended survey responses, blog entries, reflective essays, my field notes), I employed an open coding approach (Grbich 2007) and devised codes to reflect what I saw in the material rather than restrict myself to preconceived ideas (Richards 2009). I did not look at the IDI results for individuals until after this analysis was complete.

All Pre- and Post-International Exchange surveys were analyzed by SPSS, while the IDIs were sent to IDI, LLC for processing (http://idiinventory.com/). The analysis of the three administrations of the IDI provided me with an indication of each participant's actual and perceived levels of intercultural sensitivity on entry, immediately post-sojourn, and after the reentry course. Triangulating the quantitative and qualitative data helped me see how Kingston and his peers perceived cultural difference and made sense of intercultural experience while negotiating their identities at home and abroad.

3.1   Kingston's story

I begin Kingston's story by briefly describing his pre-sojourn family life, education, social networks, language proficiency/use, intercultural/international experience and career aspirations. We then learn about his goals, concerns and expectations for the academic yearlong exchange in Toronto. This is followed by an exploration of his sojourn and reentry experiences/reflections, with a focus on his L2/intercultural socialization, identities, and emerging intercultural communicative competence. Throughout, I link Kingston's oral and written narratives and survey results with his IDI scores: on entry, after the yearlong sojourn in Canada, and immediately after the Intercultural transitions course that took place from September to December 2010.

3.2 Profile

At the beginning of this study, Kingston was a twenty-year old, second-year student at a comprehensive university in Hong Kong. As well as majoring in English, he was doing a minor in management in anticipation of a career in the civil service. When I first met him he was a student representative on a committee that I chaired in the English Department. I was immediately struck by his broad smile and apparent eagerness to do a good job representing his fellow students. Soon after our first encounter, I learned of his desire to study abroad and his failed attempt to join an exchange program in the US the previous year. With the support of his family, he aimed to work hard to realize his dream and in the fall of 2008 submitted another application to spend his third-year of university in Canada.

In May 2009, in the pre-sojourn interview and survey, Kingston shared details about his family life. His father was born in Mainland China, while his mother had spent her entire life in Hong Kong. Both of his parents were of Chinese ethnicity; neither had completed secondary school and they had little knowledge of English. Cantonese was the language they used at home and in the community. His older sister was the first one in the family to attend university. In 2006–7, she joined a yearlong exchange program in the US and encouraged him to follow in her footsteps.

3.3 Language ability and usage

Kingston spoke Cantonese as a first language and used it to communicate with his family and closest friends. In his first year of primary school, he began to learn English as an additional language. He did very well in his academic studies and chose to enroll in an English-medium school for his secondary-level education. As the results of his A-level examination in English were very good (B), he applied to study at the Chinese University of Hong Kong and was admitted as an English major in September 2007.

In October 2008, when he applied to join the exchange program in Canada, he did not have any close friends who spoke English as a first language and all of his friends were Cantonese-speaking Hong Kong Chinese. While there were international students on campus, he did not socialize with them. At this stage, his use of English was largely confined to formal classroom settings, similar to most of his peers in the main study. Prior to the sojourn, using a five-point scale ranging from "excellent" to "poor," he rated his listening comprehension and writing skills in the language as "good" and his speaking and reading skills as "very good." In October 2008, he took the TOEFL and received a score of 107/120.

3.4   Self-identity formation

When asked about his identity prior to the sojourn, Kingston preferred to be recognized as a Hong Konger, adding that he believed that his parents would identify themselves as Hong Kong Chinese. He did not feel a strong attachment to his own ethnic group or country and had not given his identity much thought. As more than 95% of the population in Hong Kong is Chinese and he had little intercultural experience, he had rarely found himself in situations compelling him to reflect seriously on his cultural or ethnic identity.

3.5   Intercultural awareness and sensitivity

In May 2009, shortly after he had been selected to join an exchange program in Canada, Kingston completed the IDI for the first time (See Table 1). The results of this survey identify the respondent's Perceived Orientation (PO) and Developmental Orientation (DO). The former indicates where the individual places himself or herself along the intercultural development continuum, which ranges from ethnocentric to ethnorelative stages (Denial, Polarization (Defense/ Reversal), Minimization, Acceptance, or Adaptation) (Hammer 2009a). By contrast, the DO provides an indication of the respondent's "primary orientation toward cultural differences and commonalities along the continuum" (Hammer 2009a: 5). It is this perspective that the individual is most apt to draw on in intercultural encounters. Similar to the Perceived Orientation (PO), the Development Orientation (DO) can be Denial, Polarization (Defense/ Reversal), Minimization, Acceptance, or Adaptation) (Hammer 2009a: 5).

Table 1. Kingston's IDI results at three strategic intervals

	Pre-sojourn	Immediate post-sojourn	Post-reentry course
PO	118.85	119.83	134.60
DO	81.85	93.56	124.27
OG	37.00	26.27	10.33

(PO = Perceived Orientation, DO= Developmental Orientation;
OG = Orientation gap).

As Table 1 shows, pre-sojourn, Kingston's overall *perceived* intercultural sensitivity (PO) was 118.85, in the low end of the Acceptance range (an ethnorelative stage of development). His Developmental Orientation (DO) on entry was 81.85 in the Polarization: Defense/Reversal stage, a very ethnocentric stage of development, in which individuals tend to simplify and/or polarize cultural difference. The Orientation Gap (OG), the difference along the continuum between the Perceived Orientation (PO) and Developmental Orientation (DO), was 37 points. According to Hammer (2009a), a gap score of 7 points or higher indicates a meaningful difference between the Perceived Orientation (PO) and the Developmental Orientation (DO). Hence, at this stage, Kingston greatly overestimated his intercultural competence.

3.6 Pre-departure aims, expectations, and concerns

Prior to departure, in his application letter (see Figure 1), the Pre-International Exchange survey, and pre-sojourn interview, Kingston shared his aims, expectations and concerns about living in Canada for a year.

I want to go on exchange because I hope I can polish up my English. As an English major, I am greatly interested in the subject, especially linguistics. Therefore, I would love to have the chance to go to an English-speaking country. I will mainly study Linguistics and English while abroad. The second reason is that I hope I can have a cultural exchange with native English speakers there and other ethnic groups. Canada is famous for its racial diversity. I am sure if I can go there, I will have a lot of opportunities for cultural exchange. I can introduce the locals to Chinese culture while at the same time know more about different cultures and people from all around the world.

I am confident that the exchange will bring me numerous benefits. I think I will be able to meet people from different backgrounds and have cultural interaction with them. My English will be improved as I am soaked in an English speaking environment. I will also learn to be independent as I should take care of myself when abroad. The most important advantage is that my horizon will be broadened through interacting with people from different backgrounds and living in one of the most globalised, culturally-mixed countries.

The above are all advantages for my future goals. I want to be a governmental officer in the future. English is, thus, prominent. Independency and skills regarding how to deal with people are also essential. Having a broader horizon on the happenings in the world, not just Hong Kong, would also give me an advantage as an administrative officer. All these advantages will equip me better, which in turn raises my competitiveness; a universal scope will be especially important in this changing world.

Figure 1. Kingston's letter of application

In particular, Kingston hoped to enhance his knowledge and skills in his major (especially linguistics), improve his English language proficiency and interpersonal/intercultural communication skills, and experience life in another culture. He was most looking forward to: "(1) meeting friends with a different background/culture and (2) seeing new things in a new place" (pre-sojourn survey). Interestingly, in the Pre-sojourn International Exchange survey, he revealed that he was less interested in increasing his understanding of his "own culture, identity and values." When asked what he hoped to gain abroad that he could not gain if he remained on his home campus for his entire undergraduate degree, he responded: "enhanced English proficiency and an international vision." He expected that managing his finances, making friends, and adapting to the local culture would be the most challenging aspects of life abroad.

3.7   The yearlong sojourn in Canada

In July 2009, Kingston departed Hong Kong for a yearlong adventure in Canada. He spent the first two months visiting close family members in Alberta, before travelling east to Toronto, where he began his exchange program at a large, comprehensive university. The host city, which has a population of 2.5 million, is one of the most multicultural cities in North America. It has a large Asian population, including many immigrants from Hong Kong. In fact, some of Kingston's extended family members lived not far from the host institution.

For both semesters (from September 2009 till April 2010), Kingston opted to live on campus in a single room in a residence housing both local and international students. For his academic program, Kingston selected courses in applied linguistics, human resources management/planning, basic Japanese, and acting for non-majors in drama. His results were uneven and his cumulative GPA declined from 3.43 to 2.8, in part, due to his failure to complete the Japanese course.

From October 2009 to May 2010, Kingston worked on a part-time basis so that he would be able to fund short trips to several Canadian and American cities with "Asian friends" during term breaks and after his final exams. In June 2010, his parents joined him in Toronto and together they spent three weeks travelling around Canada visiting relatives.

3.8   Immediate post-sojourn reflections

In July 2010, shortly after his return to Hong Kong, Kingston completed the IDI for the second time. This time, as indicated in Table 1, his Perceived Orientation (PO) was 119.83, in the Acceptance range, while his Developmental Orientation (DO) was 93.56, in the low end of Minimization. After spending a year abroad, Kingston's actual level of intercultural sensitivity had increased by 11.71 points; he had moved from Denial/Defense or Reversal (an ethnocentric perspective) to the transitional stage of Minimization, in which individuals tend to emphasize cultural commonality and universal issues or values (Hammer 2009b). In this administration of the IDI, the Orientation Gap (OG) was 26.27. Although this was 10.73 points less than the previous administration, it still indicated a significant overestimation of his level of intercultural competence. According to Hammer (2009b), individuals in this stage of development find it difficult to understand and cope with complex cultural difference and tend to view the world in terms of "us and them," whereby "us" is generally superior. Kingston's IDI results also indicated some resistance to the need to change perspective or behavior in different cultural contexts.

In addition to the IDI, Kingston completed the Post-International Exchange survey in mid-July 2010 and then shared his views about his international experience and reentry in a Cantonese-medium interview that lasted 1 hour and 33 minutes. He revisited his aims for the sojourn and disclosed his unmet expectations. In his account, he offered insight into his social networks which impacted on his adjustment, L2 learning, and the development of his intercultural communicative competence.

3.9   Intercultural adjustment and social networks

In the first semester, Kingston attended gatherings organized by the International Student Association and joined a mentorship program that was designed to help newcomers adjust to life in Canada. Katrina, a Russian exchange student, served as his mentor. Early on, Kingston accepted invitations to go to the pub with local and international students but found it difficult to embrace "the pub culture." In his post-sojourn interview, he explained:

> Going to pubs is very common in Canada but not in Hong Kong. Even students who are very quiet and obedient dance and drink. At first, I went there with some people from my residence; however, I just couldn't accept this cultural difference so I decided not to go anymore. If they asked I told them clearly that I didn't want to go…

When describing host nationals, Kingston's discourse was sometimes quite negative and judgmental, and replete with "us versus them" discourse, where "us" (Hong Kong Chinese) was positioned more favorably:

> I think people in North America lead a really dissolute life. They tend to treat sex casually. They also don't have any goals. They just drink, take drugs and have sex all the time. All the students there have the characteristics of a typical North American. They don't know what they are doing in their life. People said foreigners are polite but I don't think so. I think they're rather rebellious and impolite.   (post-sojourn interview, July 2010)

Not all of his comments about host nationals were negative. In his interview, he cited aspects of Canadian society that appealed to him: "People in Canada are more direct. They tell you how they feel. Hong Kongers are more reserved and usually avoid saying how they feel directly from their heart. Being direct is good as you don't have to guess what others think." Even so, he did not feel at ease with host nationals who were not of Asian ethnicity and did not form close ties with any outside of class.

Kingston also found it difficult to accept food that was different from what he was used to; this heightened his desire to spend more time interacting with fellow Chinese:

> Another thing I didn't like was the food choice. There are lots of immigrants in Canada (Greeks, Indians, Italians) but their food is not suitable for Hong Kongers... I missed the Hong Kong style food...Sometimes I just wanted to eat Chinese food. Luckily, it was convenient to get to a Chinese restaurant. Since I had many relatives in Toronto, it was also convenient for me to go to a Chinese teahouse with them and sometimes, I ate at home with them.
>
> (Post-sojourn interview, July 2010)

When not working in his part-time job, he often retreated to his room instead of interacting with other students or talking with his mentor. "I sometimes felt a bit sad as I found it difficult to make friends. I just spent a lot of time watching Japanese cartoons alone. Looking back, I think I wasted a lot of time doing that." By the second semester, he was largely limiting his social contact to Asians, especially people who shared his ethnicity and first language:

> Since there was a cultural difference, it was difficult to find friends who could really share and understand how I felt. In the second semester, probably because I was homesick, I spent most of my time with Asians, especially Hong Kong students who had immigrated to Canada. In fact, the best friend I made there was a Hong Kong student who was an immigrant. I also spent more time with my relatives... It was great to stay in a large city in Canada as there were lots of Chinese. Meeting Chinese people and talking in Cantonese helped me deal with homesickness.   (Post-sojourn interview, July 2010)

In his post-sojourn survey, Kingston indicated that the three greatest challenges he faced on exchange were: coping with culture shock, homesickness, and interacting with people from other cultures. He believed that the mentorship program had "worked well" as Katrina had "helped him overcome culture shock." In his interview, he explained: "Basically, I talked to her about how I felt about North American culture and what I experienced. She was really supportive and advised me to be positive when facing the bad side of Canada." In the second half of his sojourn, however, he spent little time with her and her advice did not appear to have facilitated his interaction with host nationals or international students who were not from Asia.

3.10 L2 learning/intercultural communication skills

When Kingston first arrived in Toronto, he found it very challenging to use English in his daily life. In his post-sojourn interview, he described the steps he took to become more comfortable and confident when using the language:

> Since English is my second language, I couldn't process it in my mind as quickly as Cantonese. I couldn't fully express my feelings spontaneously although it got better when I became accustomed to it. At first, I couldn't understand what locals meant because they used slang but I became more comfortable as I spoke more. I tried to force myself to ask more questions in class so that I could practice speaking English. By the end of my stay, I had become more confident to speak up in class… I'm satisfied with my progress in English. In particular, I improved my informal English language skills and I now know how to communicate with foreigners in English. Though I still couldn't fully express my views and understand all the slang at the end of the sojourn, I think I spoke English more fluently and smoothly. I began to think that I could live there as I had become immersed in the country. I asked some native speakers to rate my English proficiency and they thought that it was just as if I'd lived in Canada for a long time…When I first came back to Hong Kong, I found it weird not to speak in English. It had become a habit rather than an obstacle or a challenge. I'm more willing to talk to foreigners so I now have a competitive edge…

After the yearlong sojourn in an English-speaking country, Kingston rated his overall proficiency in English as "very good."

In Canada Kingston had the opportunity to observe and interact with local and international students both in and outside of class. He believed that this had had a significant impact on him.

> In the past I felt quite scared to meet people from different cultural backgrounds but I no longer have any problem with that. I spent a year in classes in which I had a different skin color from all those next to me. As Canada is a multicultural country, I had lots of chance to communicate with people from different ethnic backgrounds. While abroad, however, I didn't intentionally try to improve my intercultural communication skills. I just wanted to be myself. Anyway, I don't think I had any problem communicating with them. I guess I improved in this aspect but I didn't intentionally try to do so. (Post-sojourn interview, July 2010)

Even though the majority of his free time was spent alone, with relatives, or with other Asian students, he was convinced that he had enhanced his intercultural communication skills. Further, at this stage, he naively assumed that he just needed to be himself in intercultural encounters. He was reluctant to make adjustments to accommodate cultural difference, which was in accord with the IDI results. At this stage, he seemed to believe that being in a culturally diverse environment automatically enhanced one's intercultural competence. In his post-sojourn interview, he explained:

> The most important thing I gained from the sojourn was international experience. I don't really know how to explain it. Just that, as you meet more people with different nationalities, you become more open-minded, and, in turn, you can see things from different angles. In Hong Kong, you just look at things from a single angle... When you go to a Western country, especially Canada, which is a multicultural country, you have the chance to talk to people with different nationalities. You can think in different angles. Now, I've become more open-minded and I embrace other cultures.

In the interview, he added: "At first, I knew nothing about the local society. Everything was fresh and new to me but, by the end of my stay, I was totally immersed in the society. I felt like a Canadian and didn't want to leave. I really felt like I knew this country well and wanted to stay longer." He appeared to inflate his knowledge and understanding of the host culture, as well as his intercultural competence.

3.11   Self-identities and new visions/goals

When feeling out of place, it is not unusual for newcomers to develop a stronger bond with their national or ethnic identity, especially if they are a visible minority for the first time (Block 2007; Byram 2008; Jackson 2008, 2010a). This appears to be what happened to Kingston:

> While on exchange, I became much more clear about my identity. Hong Kongers in general do not have much confidence but I don't think Hong Kongers are inferior to other people in the world. In fact, when I told people where I'm from, I thought I was special as I come from a special place. I'm now proud to be a Hong Kong citizen, especially when I realized how glamorous our city is. After this international experience, I've also become more confident and more clear that I am an Asian in terms of my reserved personality...
> (Post-sojourn interview, July 2010)

Living abroad also impacted on how this young man saw himself and his future. "While in Canada I thought more about what and who I want to be in the future. I thought about my identity and realized that I didn't want to stay in just one place forever. I realized that I can now adjust myself to living in different places." Kingston commented that he had begun to feel more like "a global citizen." In his interview, he added: "I now see the possibility of working and living in a foreign country in the future, which I did not think about before going abroad. And when I get to that place, I will say that I am a citizen of that place." While he had experienced difficulty establishing bonds with host nationals, he had gained in self-confidence and could imagine himself in other international situations.

3.12   The preparation of future exchange students

Prior to going on exchange, Kingston had attended pre-departure sessions organized by the home institution. When asked how the University could better prepare students for international exchange, he paused and then offered the following advice: "I think the University can talk more about identity and cultural adaptation. Students should try their very best to immerse themselves into the other's culture. They should not resist the other's culture and just stick to the mode of living in Hong Kong." (Post-sojourn interview, July 2010) Although he had not really followed this path, it is significant that he offered this advice to others.

3.13   Immediate reentry

While some of the returnees who were interviewed acknowledged that they were experiencing severe reentry culture shock, Kingston appeared to settle into a familiar routine rather quickly. As his social networks abroad had largely consisted of Chinese and other Asian students, he had not been as fully immersed in the host culture as the exchange students whose social networks included host nationals who were not originally from Hong Kong. Further, just before returning home, Kingston had spent three weeks with his parents and this had likely eased his transition.

3.14   The Post-sojourn *intercultural transitions course*

From September to December 2010, in the *Intercultural Transitions* course, Kingston shared his views about his sojourn and reentry experiences. In his first blog entry, he recalled the steps he had taken to cope with culture shock in Canada:

> When the snow came, it was devastating. I felt so lonely and had the sentiment that I didn't really belong to the country. Fortunately, this period of culture shock and depression didn't last long. I found my own ways to tackle it. Looking for people that had similar interests was one. I also met some Asian friends who shared my 'Asianess'. We went to karaoke, my favorite, which North Americans seldom do, and we ate Asian food!!! I was lucky to go to Toronto because a lot of Chinese live there. Whenever I missed Asian culture, I could go to the Chinese community to get a bit of relief.

By spending most of his free time with people who shared his ethnicity, Kingston gained socio-emotional support and more appreciation of his "Asianess;" however, it also limited his exposure to English and other communities of practice.

> I am quite surprised that my identity of being a 'Hong Konger' actually became stronger both during my stay abroad and after I came back. While I like Canada a lot, their open-mindedness, values, people's kindness and tolerance towards

different ethnic groups, I feel that deep down I am 'produced' by Hong Kong. I was born in this little river and got my habits and personality developed here. Therefore, I should never forget this important origin even if I live abroad at certain points in my life…Learning to be a global citizen is important in today's world, but being able to identify our roots wherever we are is equally important.

(essay #1)

Midway through the course, he acknowledged that he had initially "felt over the moon to be back home again." In his second essay he wrote: "The language was so familiar and I had a feeling I took back the lead as one of the majority. I found myself saying 'This is how it should be!'" Then, "reentry culture shock symptoms started to develop" and he began to see himself and Hong Kong through a different lens. In his mind, his values and sense of self had changed. He firmly believed that he had been transformed from a "frog in the well" (someone with limited experiences and a narrow sense of self) to a more worldly individual with an expanded, hybrid identity. In his estimation, he had become more open and willing to embrace positive elements in both the home and host cultures. In his second essay, he wrote:

A year abroad has immensely changed me, especially my values and identity. My value system has become strong and well-defined. I really didn't have a clear sense how I should be before…I now wish to live my life with more flexibility. Quality of life is what I stress. Before I went abroad, I was definitely a frog in the well. I was a Hong Konger for sure and Hong Kong culture was most appealing. After getting a taste of how it is to live abroad, my identity has expanded. The ways of living, like relaxed pace and individual freedom are what I really liked in Canada, also their courtesy towards a stranger and care towards minorities, but at the same time, I don't like being too individualistic. I like their popular culture but find Hong Kong's drama series and music more attractive. I like North American food but Cantonese home food is too good to be compared. Therefore, I feel that my identity is more blurred. I learnt better ways of living my life but also feel the need to cling to some of my home cultural aspects. I am still a Hong Konger but know there is something being added to that.

In his last essay, which was entitled "There's still a long way to go." he displayed much more awareness of the consequences of the choices he had made in the host culture:

The main problems I had in Canada were that I felt reluctant to change and was too lazy to learn local slangs. I learnt some local gestures and verbal ways of greeting others such as "wass'up man" and hitting others' chests as a greeting but I did too little. Many times, my neighbors in the residence invited me to go to their rooms to party but I refused nearly all of their invitations. The topics that they talked about were North American stuff that I rarely knew. At first, I did try to meet more new friends by learning their ways of gesturing and talking. Then, I realized it was not as easy as I thought. I didn't feel comfortable so I stopped trying. Throughout my stay in Canada, I did not watch more North America TV shows, or listen more to their music. I did not even try to search on the web for the expressions they used to see how I could respond better. I just did what I felt comfortable to do. I should have at least tried to learn to blend in more and not given up so easily.

Kingston acknowledged that the development of intercultural communicative competence was "not as easy" as he had first thought. When his "idealized" images of Canada had not matched reality, he had sometimes withdrawn instead of persevering with his intercultural learning.

> This draws me to think more about how competent I actually am as an intercultural communicator. Before I went abroad, I thought that I could adapt to North American culture with ease and accept others' points of view completely. I even thought that as Hong Kong's culture was not very pleasant to me, I should integrate various cultural norms into my behaviors. I perceived myself to be an open-minded person. I also aimed to try all the new things I could right after arrival, learn their slangs and ways of interacting, meet lots of local friends and have fun. I heard from my family and friends how North America was like and I'd long known that liberty and freedom were important values that Canadians treasured. I thought I could just integrate these North American beliefs with my own behaviours for they sounded really great. However, it was not as easy as I thought. When I first arrived, I found everything so alienated from me. The way of ordering food, buying groceries and home supplies and people's ways of expressing themselves were so different and the difference was harder than expected to adjust to. My mind was full of 'in Hong Kong, we do this and it is much more efficient'. It was not my idealized Canada.   (essay #3)

Kingston reassessed the choices he made in the host culture and, in his last interview and essay, acknowledged that he had not taken full advantage of opportunities for intercultural interaction. He had not been very open to cultural difference and this had hampered his communication with host nationals and international students from other parts of the world. In stark contrast with the judgmental discourse that characterized earlier accounts of his sojourn experience, his final essay provided evidence of the cultivation of a more open, ethnorelative mindset. He had developed a more balanced view of Hong Kong and Canada: "I've started to think that both places have good and bad sides. It wasn't fair to say one was better than the other. I've begun to value differences and try to understand them. I realize they can be understood if you view them from the local culture's angle." He had become more realistic about his intercultural communication skills and realized that agency plays a key role in the journey towards intercultural competence:

> Intercultural competence comes from attitude and action. If I am willing and take the initiative to learn more and try to take the good points from other cultures, I believe I will become more interculturally competent eventually... I think I not only have to welcome change, but also have to take the initiative to know more about different cultures and allow myself to change. This was a failure before. During my stay in Canada, I stopped learning about North America after some uncomfortable encounters. Next time I should be braver to take the challenge and let change affect me...Evaluating my own experience in Canada and after returning to Hong Kong, I think there is a huge room for improvement in the future. There is still a long way to go before I really become interculturally competent.   (essay #3)

In the post-course survey, he offered further insight into the profound impact of guided, critical reflection on his intercultural development:

> This course has changed me quite a lot. It guided me to reflect on my international experience and what I could have done better to make it more wonderful and, most importantly, how to keep my learning alive after coming back home. I realize that I could be a better intercultural communicator and adapt more to other cultures. Next time I go abroad I will aim to 'be brave' and try new things. Courage overcomes everything, even cultural differences.

At the end of the reentry course, after considerable critical reflection on his intercultural/international experience, Kingston again completed the IDI. This time, as indicated in Table 1, his Perceived Orientation (PO) was 134.60, in Adaptation, while his Developmental Orientation (DO) was 124.27, in Acceptance (also an ethnorelative stage). This meant that the Orientation Gap (OG) was 10.33, a much smaller overestimation of his level of intercultural competence. While still significant, it was dramatically less than in the earlier administrations of the IDI (37.0, 26.27 points, respectively). The IDI results indicate a significant growth in Kingston's level of intercultural competence. Following a year abroad he gained 11.71 points and after a semester of guided critical reflection on his intercultural/international experience he advanced by 30.71 points, moving from the low end of minimization (93.56) to an ethnorelative stage of development. This period of self-analysis appeared to have had a dramatic impact on his intercultural worldview as he took strides towards a more open, global mindset.

4.   Conclusions

On entry and immediately after the yearlong sojourn, Kingston perceived his intercultural competence to be several IDI band levels above his actual developmental level. Pre-sojourn, he appeared to be overly confident about his ability to interact successfully across cultures, even though he had had very little intercultural experience. In my investigations of short-term and semester-long sojourners from Hong Kong (Jackson 2009, 2010a), the vast majority also significantly overestimated their intercultural sensitivity, especially prior to going abroad. Individuals who lack knowledge and expertise in a particular domain may simply be unaware of their incompetence; their inflated self-perceptions may then limit their motivation to improve (Kruger & Dunning 1999). On a more positive note, metacognitive-awareness training has been found to help individuals recognize gaps in their knowledge and skills, and set realistic targets for improvement (Kruger & Dunning 1999). In Kingston's case, after a semester-long period of structured, critical reflection, he became more aware of gaps in his intercultural communicative competence and began to address ways to improve. His discourse became more ethnorelative as he cultivated a more open, global mindset. Thus, the qualitative findings were generally in accord with the IDI results.

Prior to going to Toronto, Kingston aimed to "meet friends with a different background/culture" and "polish up" his English while "soaked in an English-speaking environment." On arrival, he had high expectations of developing "an international vision" in a country he greatly admired. In the first semester he met many new people from different parts of the world; however, he had difficulty accepting cultural difference and, by the end of his stay, his social networks consisted almost exclusively of Asian students and his Chinese relatives. This raises questions about the wisdom of students going on exchange to environments where they have extended family members; however, with easy access to technology and social media (e.g. Facebook, Skype) the immersion experience has changed dramatically in recent years. Even if students travel to an unfamiliar environment where they know no one, they can chose to remain connected to home on a daily basis.

When he first returned home and reflected on the difficulties he had encountered in the host culture, Kingston sometimes employed very ethnocentric discourse. For example, he stereotyped all local students as "typical North Americans" who live a "dissolute life." While abroad, his negative perceptions and judgmental stance impacted on his willingness to interact with host nationals. This, in turn, limited his exposure to local communities of practice and the opportunity to enhance his L2/intercultural communication skills. It was only after taking the reentry course that he realized the impact of his attitude and behavior on intercultural relations.

Foreign language learners are "people whose history, dispositions toward learning, access to sociocultural worlds, participation, and imagination together shape the qualities of their achievements" (Kinginger 2009, p. 241).

Kingston's self-identities, and language and (inter)cultural learning were affected by a complex intermingling of sociocultural factors (e.g. host receptivity, quality and degree of exposure to the host language and culture, social networks), personality attributes (e.g. ability to overcome psychological barriers, degree of ethnocentricism/reflexivity, willingness to try new things), depth of investment in language and (inter)cultural growth, and degree of self-analysis/reflection.

Although this chapter is limited to a single case study, the findings point to the need for adequate preparation, support, and debriefings for student sojourners. They also draw attention to the importance of the reentry phase, which is often overlooked in study abroad research and practice (Szkudlarek 2010). Finally, this case study challenges the notion that international experience alone will automatically translate into enhanced L2 proficiency, intercultural competence, and a more global mindset for all participants. Clearly, the situated learning of L2 sojourners is far more complicated.

5.   Pedagogical implications

This study points to the benefits of intervention in education abroad programming and, in particular, the value of guided, critical reflection. Ideally, students should engage in the process of critical reflection and self-analysis prior to going on exchange, throughout the sojourn, and after they return home (Jackson 2008, 2010a, 2011a, 2011d; Vande Berg 2007). Pre-sojourn intervention that includes structured reflection and experiential elements (e.g. ethnographic projectwork) can prepare students for study and residence in another culture and help them make sense of intercultural encounters. It can provide the groundwork they need to set realistic goals for the sojourn and become more engaged, systematic language and culture learners in the host environment (Jackson 2006; Roberts, Byram, Barro, Jordan & Street 2001). Well-designed pre-sojourn preparation can help newcomers weather the natural ups and downs of intercultural adjustment and optimize their time in the host culture. In faculty-led programs, ongoing support throughout the sojourn (e.g. regular debriefing sessions) can facilitate student engagement, intercultural development, and a deeper level of learning (Jackson 2008, 2010a). In exchange programs, where large numbers of students study in different parts of the globe, blogging or keeping a private journal of reflection may help them monitor their L2 and intercultural learning, especially if they have developed these skills prior to the sojourn. While perhaps not as effective as guided intervention, the writing process alone has the potential to help individuals make sense of their experiences.

Support during the reentry phase can make a crucial difference in both the short-term and long-term impact of international experience. As this case study attests, in a supportive environment, returnees can be guided to critically evaluate their L2 and (inter)cultural learning and set realistic goals for further enhancement. This period of intense reflection can optimize and extend their learning and open up new possibilities for identity expansion and transformation (Bennett 1997, 2009; Mezirow 2000).

The case study reported here is drawn from a larger-scale study of exchange students from Hong Kong. Much more research is needed in a variety of contexts to better understand the impact of intervention (e.g. pre-sojourn intercultural communication courses, mentorship schemes, sojourn debriefings, post-sojourn courses) on the whole person development of student sojourners. With more awareness of the internal and external factors impacting on sojourner learning, we can determine the best ways to empower L2 sojourners/returnees and optimize the impact of international experience. In my view, guided, critical reflection at all stages is vital to stimulate and sustain the development of intercultural communicative competence, global citizenship, and identity expansion in L2 sojourners. Research-driven programming, which focuses on holistic student learning and development, has the potential to liberate and transform other "frogs in the well."

Acknowledgements

This research has been supported by a General Research Fund (#444709) from the Research Grants Council of Hong Kong and a Teaching Development Grant (#4170338) from the Chinese University of Hong Kong (CUHK). This case study would not have been possible without Kingston's willingness to share his story. I also appreciate the support of the Office of Academic Links (OAL) at CUHK.

References

Bakhtin, M.M. (1981). *The dialogic imagination: Four essays* (C. Emerson & M. Holquist, trans.) Austin, TX: University of Texas Press.
Bakhtin, M.M. (1984). *Problems of Dostoevsky's poetics* (C. Emerson, Ed. & Trans.) Minneapolis, MN: University of Minnesota Press.
Bakhtin, M.M. (1986). *Speech genres and other late essays* (V. McGee, Trans.) Austin, TX: University of Texas Press.
Bennett, M.J. (1993). Towards ethnorelativism: A developmental model of intercultural sensitivity. In R.M. Paige (Ed.). *Education for the intercultural experience* (pp. 21–71). Yarmouth, ME: Intercultural Press.

Bennett, M.J. (1997). How not to be a fluent fool: Understanding the cultural dimensions of language. In A.E. Fantini (Vol. Ed.) & J.C. Richards (Series Ed.), *New ways in teaching culture* (pp. 16–21). Alexandria, VA: TESOL.

Bennett, J.M. (2009). Transformative training: Designing programs for culture learning. In M.A. Moodian (Ed.). *Contemporary leadership and intercultural competence: Exploring the cross-cultural dynamics within organizations* (pp. 95–110). Thousand Oaks, CA: Sage.

Bennett, J.M., & Bennett, M.J. (2004). Developing intercultural sensitivity: An integrative approach to global and domestic diversity. In D. Landis, J.M. Bennett, & M.J. Bennett (Eds.). *Handbook of intercultural training.* (3rd ed.). (pp. 145–167). Thousand Oaks, CA: Sage.

Bennett, J.M., Bennett, M.J., & Allen, W. (2003). Developing intercultural competence in the language classroom. In D. Lange & M. Paige (Eds.). *Culture as the core: Perspectives on culture in second language learning* (pp. 237–270). Greenwich, CT: Information Age Publishing.

Block, D. (2003). *The social turn in second language acquisition.* Edinburgh: Edinburgh University Press.

Block, D. (2007). *Second language identities.* London: Continuum.

Block, D. (2008). EFL narratives and English-mediated identities: Two ships passing in the night? In P. Kalaja, V. Menezes & A.M.F. Barcelos (Eds.). *Narratives of learning and teaching EFL* (pp. 141–154). Basingstoke, UK: Palgrave Macmillan.

Byram, M. (2008). The "value" of student mobility. In M. Byram & F. Dervin (Eds.). *Students' staff and academic mobility in higher education* (pp. 31–45). Newcastle upon Tyne: Cambridge Scholars.

Firth, A., & Wagner, J. (2007). Second/foreign language learning as a social accomplishment: Elaborations on a reconceptualized SLA. *Modern Language Journal, 91,* 798–817.

Grbich, C. (2007). *Qualitative data analysis.* London: Sage.

Guilherme, M. (2002). *Critical citizens for an intercultural world: Foreign language education as cultural politics.* Clevedon, U.K.: Multilingual Matters.

Hammer, M.R. (2009a). Intercultural development inventory v. 3 (IDI). Retrieved from ⟨http://www.idiinventory.com⟩.

Hammer, M.R. (2009b). The Intercultural Development Inventory: An approach for assessing and building intercultural competence. In M.A. Moodian (Ed.). *Contemporary leadership and intercultural competence: Exploring the cross-cultural dynamics within organizations* (pp. 203–217). Thousand Oaks, CA: Sage.

Hammer, M., Bennett, M., & Wiseman, R. (2003). Measuring intercultural sensitivity: The intercultural development inventory. *International Journal of Intercultural Relations, 27,* 421–443.

Jackson, J. (2006). Ethnographic preparation for short-term study and residence in the target culture. *International Journal of Intercultural Relations, 30,* 77–98.

Jackson, J. (2008). *Language, identity, and study abroad: Sociocultural perspectives.* London: Equinox.

Jackson, J. (2009). Intercultural learning on short-term sojourns. *Intercultural Education, 20* (1–2), S59–S71.

Jackson, J. (2010a). *Intercultural journeys: From study to residence abroad.* Basingstoke: Palgrave Macmillan.

Jackson, J. (2010b). Habitus, self-identity, and positioning: The multifarious nature of study abroad. *Cultus: The Journal of Intercultural Mediation and Communication, 3,* 65–78.

Jackson, J. (2011a, November). Making sense of international experience through guided critical reflection. Paper presented at the 7th QS Asia Pacific Professional Leaders in Education conference and Exhibition, Manila, Philippines.

Jackson, J. (2011b). Cultivating cosmopolitan, intercultural citizenship through critical reflection and international, experiential learning. *Language and Intercultural Communication, 11*, 80–96.

Jackson, J. (2011c, Fall). Host language proficiency, intercultural sensitivity and study abroad. *Frontiers: The Interdisciplinary Journal of Study Abroad, 21*, 167–187.

Jackson, J. (2011d, March). Maximizing the impact of international experience through 'practice-to-theory-to-practice' pedagogy, Paper presented at the Asia-Pacific Association for International Education (APAIE) conference in Taipei, Taiwan.

Kim, Y.Y. (2001). *Becoming intercultural: An integrative theory of communication and cross-cultural adaptation.* Thousand Oaks, CA: Sage.

Kim, Y.Y. (2005). Adapting to a new culture: An integrative communication theory. In W. Gudykunst (Ed.). *Theorizing about intercultural communication* (pp. 375–400). Thousand Oaks, CA: Sage.

Kinginger, C. (2009). *Language learning and study abroad: A critical reading of research,* New York: Palgrave Macmillan.

Kostogriz, A. (2005). Dialogical imagination of (inter)cultural spaces: Rethinking the semiotic ecology of second language and literacy learning. In J.K. Hall, G. Vitanova & L. Marchenkova (Eds.), *Dialogue with Bakhtin on second and foreign language learning* (pp. 189–210). Mahwah, NJ: Lawrence Erlbaum.

Kruger, J., & Dunning, D. (1999). Unskilled and unaware of it: How difficulties in recognizing one's own incompetence lead to inflated self-assessments. *Journal of Personality and Social Psychology, 77*, 1121–1134.

Lafford, B.A. (2007). Second language acquisition reconceptualized? The impact of Firth and Wagner (1997). *Modern Language Journal, 7*, 735–756.

Landis, D., Bennett, J.M., & Bennett, M.J. (eds.). (2004). *Handbook of intercultural training.* Thousand Oaks, CA: Sage.

Lantolf, J.P. (2004). Sociocultural theory and second and foreign language learning: An overview of sociocultural theory. In K. van Esch & O. St. John (Eds.). *New insights into foreign language learning and teaching* (pp. 13–34). Frankfurt: Peter Lang.

Lantolf, J., & Thorne, S. (2006). *Sociocultural theory and the genesis of second language development.* Oxford: Oxford University Press.

Lave, J., & Wenger, E. (1991). *Situated learning: Legitimate peripheral participation.* Cambridge: Cambridge University Press.

Menard-Warwick, J. (2008). The cultural and intercultural identities of transnational English teachers: Two case studies from the Americas, *TESOL Quarterly, 42*, 617–640.

Mezirow, J. (1994). *Transformative dimensions of adult learning.* San Francisco, CA: Jossey-Bass.

Mezirow, J. (1996, Spring). Contemporary paradigms of learning. *Adult Education Quarterly, 46*, 158–172.

Mezirow, J. (2000). *Learning as transformation: Critical perspectives on a theory in progress.* San Francisco, CA: Jossey Bass.

Norton, B. (2000). *Identity and language learning: Gender, ethnicity, and educational change.* London: Longman.

Ochs, E., & Capps, L. (1996). Narrating the self. *Annual Review of Anthropology, 25*, 19–43.

Pavlenko, A. (2007). Autobiographic narratives as data in applied linguistics. *Applied Linguistics, 28*, 163–188.

Pavlenko, A., & Lantolf, J. (2000). Second language learning as participation and the (re)construction of selves. In J. Lantolf (Ed.). *Sociocultural theory and second language learning* (pp. 155–177). Oxford: Oxford University Press.

Richards, L. (2009). *Handling qualitative data.* Thousand Oaks, CA: Sage.

Roberts, C., Byram, M., Barro, A., Jordan, S., & Street, B. (2001). *Language learners as ethnographers.* Clevedon: Multilingual Matters.

Swain, M., & Deters, P. (2007). "New" mainstream SLA theory: Expanded and enriched, *The Modern Language Journal, 91*, 820–836.

Swain, M., Kinnear, P., & Steinman, L. (2010). *Sociocultural theory in second language education: An Introduction through Narratives.* Clevedon: Multilingual Matters.

Szkudlarek, B. (2010). Reentry: A review of the literature. *International Journal of Intercultural Relations, 34*, 1–21.

Ting-Toomey, S. (1999). *Communicating across cultures.* New York, NY: Guildford Press.

Tsai, I.Y., & Caprio, P. (2008). *The frog in the well,* Philadelphia, PA: CE Bilingual Books.

Vande Berg, M. (2007). Intervening in the learning of U.S. students abroad. *Journal of Studies in International Education, 11*, Fall/Winter, pp. 392–399.

Vygotsky, L.S. (1978). Interaction between learning and development (M. Lopez-Morillas, trans.) In M. Cole, V. John-Steiner, S. Scribner, & E. Souberman (Eds.), *Mind in society: The development of higher psychological processes* (pp. 79–91). Cambridge, MA: Harvard University Press.

Vygotsky, L.S. (1986). *Thought and language.* Cambridge, MA: The MIT Press.

Wertsch, J.V. (1998). *Mind as action.* New York, NY: Oxford University Press

PART III

Pragmatics and identity

"I joke you don't"

Second language humor and intercultural identity construction

Maria Shardakova
Indiana University

This chapter reports on a cross-sectional experimental study that explored L2 humor as a means of identity construction. The study focused on the relationship between intended identities claimed by American learners of Russian through humor, and their received identities by native speakers and peers alike. To explain observed differences in focal identity traits between the native speaker group and the learner group, the study drew on Schwartz's universal model of human values (1992). The study examined the effects of proficiency and study abroad on learners' identity construction through humor and on the ensuing reception by native speakers as well as learners of Russian.

1. Introduction

For over a decade scholars have explored the connection between humor and individuality, maintaining that humor offers a customary way of displaying and creating one's personal, social, and relational identity (Archakis & Tsakona 2005; Belz 2002; Boxer & Cortés-Conde 1997; Habib 2008; Kotthoff 2000; Lynch 2010; Mullany 2008; Rogerson-Revell 2007; Tannen 1999; Tarone 2000; Terrion & Ashforth 2002). These studies have mostly investigated the jocular behavior of native speakers (e.g. Boxer & Cortés-Conde 1997; Holmes 2006; Holmes & Hay 1997; Jorgensen 1996; Norrick 1993; Schieffelin 1986). The ones addressing second language humor (Bell 2006, 2007a, 2007b; Belz 2002; Broner & Tarone 2001; Cheng 2003; Cook 2000; Davies 2003; Habib 2008; Shardakova 2010) have shown that second language (L2) speakers can successfully participate in these playful practices in a classroom setting (Belz 2002; Broner & Tarone 2001; Cook 2000; Pomerantz & Bell 2007; Sullivan 2000; Tarone 2000) and in spontaneous interactions with native speakers (Cheng 2003; Davies 2003). It remains unclear, however, how L2 speakers actually intend to position themselves, what identity claims they make through humor, and whether their interlocutors understand and uphold these claims.

With language being the primary semiotic tool for constructing one's identity (Davies & Harre 1990; LePage & Tabouret-Keller 1985; Norton 1997), interlocutors rely heavily on linguistic behavior, including humor, to make identity judgments (Giles & Billings 2004). Inevitable limitations in linguistic and sociocultural knowledge present a serious challenge for L2 speakers who are trying to gain membership in various target speech communities.

The present study seeks to explore the relationship between intended identities claimed by American learners of Russian through humor, and their received identities by native speakers as well as learners of Russian. It addresses the effects of study abroad and proficiency on learners' identity construction through humor. It also explores the role of these variables in learners' perception of L2 humor and reconstruction of identities of L2 speakers who use humor.

The study approaches humor from the perspective of pragmatics, examining jocular utterances that accompany four speech acts – apologies, compliments, invitations, and requests. Since most of this humor is formulaic and regularly appears in the company of corresponding speech acts (Shardakova 2010), it can be expected that learners who studied abroad are better prepared to identify and interpret this type of humor (cf. Bardovi-Harlig and Dörnyei's (1998) finding that the study abroad context raises learners' pragmatic awareness).

2.   Study background

2.1   Humor and identity

Studies in sociolinguistics and psychology show that humor is "an essential element of everyday interaction and socialization" (Boxer & Cortés-Conde 1997, p. 275), which serves a variety of functions. While entertaining others and creating a positive self-image is, admittedly, the central role of humor (Hay 2000; Rogerson-Revell 2007; Wanzer, Booth-Butterfield & Booth-Butterfield 1995), most research focuses on interpersonal aspects of humor and its role in constructing and negotiating group identities. The power of humor to heighten the sense of community has been well documented (Archakis & Tsakona 2005; Hay 2000; Holmes 2006; Lynch 2010; Terrion & Ashforth 2002). Some researchers argue that constructing and maintaining group cohesion and identity is the "general function of humor" (Hay 2000, p. 716; Lennox & Ashforth 2002).

Humor is equally instrumental in fusing temporary and enduring groups, including professional organizations (Holmes 2006; Lennox & Ashforth 2002; Lynch 2010; Pogrebin & Poole 1988; Rogerson-Revell 2007). Lynch's year-long study of a hotel kitchen describes the complex processes through which the social organization is (re)produced through its members' everyday humor. Similarly, Pogrebin and Poole (1988) examine humor practices in a suburban police station, and show how jocular aggression helps patrol officers diffuse danger and build group culture. Another study of jocular practices in a police department construes humor as the main device for transmitting organizational culture to new members: "The shift of constables, sergeants, and inspectors gathered together for a chat and a laugh are literally sustaining police work itself" (Holdaway 1988, p. 121).[1]

Bonding humor, which fosters transition from "I" to "we," can take on various forms, from self-mockery (Holmes & Schnurr 2005; Kotthoff 2000; Shardakova 2012) to funny stories about out-group individuals (Bell 2007b; Norrick 1993), or even "inclusionary" putdowns directed at in-group members (Boxer & Cortés-Conde 1997; Lennox & Ashforth 2002; Shardakova in press). Regardless of humor's direction and form, it helps individuals to become part of a group, offering them a shared perspective on reality and a sense of self-worth (Archakis & Tsakona 2005; Hay 2000; Lennox & Ashforth 2002; Lynch 2010; Norrick 1993). The role of humor "as a correction mechanism of in-group behavior" is illustrated by Archakis and Tsakona (2005), who study humor in a group of four young Greek men. In this study, the young men ridicule certain behaviors of targets either outside or inside their group, using humor to censure undesired behavior and construct the model self.

Identity-shaping humor has been shown to rely heavily on context. A number of recent studies focus on humor within local communities of practice (Culpeper 2005; Grainger 2004; Holmes & Schnurr 2005; Mullany 2008), and explore the interplay between pre-communicative social givens and communicative negotiations of relationships and identities (Hay 2001; Holmes 2006; Kotthoff 2000; Norrick 1993), illustrating *in situ* shaping of subjects' identities through humor. Culpeper illustrates the role of local context in construction and interpretation of humor and its role in creating the identity of the host in the television quiz show *The Weakest Link* (Culpeper 2005). The author argues that the show's highly ritualized "activity types" "neutralize" the profuse "game-driven impoliteness," rendering the host's aggressive humor entertaining.

Outside the quiz show, the host's rough putdowns and belittling aphorisms would be interpreted as boorish behavior much to be avoided. The show's participants often fail to pay attention to the context, consequently interpreting

---

1. A more recent study by Lennox and Ashforth (2002) confirms earlier findings: zooming in on a group of police executives assembled for a 6-week residential training program, the authors report that inclusive jocular putdowns help the participants coalesce into a cohesive group.

her "conventional banter" as impolite and insulting. Culpeper's work emphasizes the close connection between humor and identity and problematizes the relationship between the intent and the uptake of conversational humor.

Thus, within the interactional framework the effect of humor has been shown to be context dependent and bilateral, jointly constructed by participants, with potential incongruity between the speaker's intent and the listener's uptake (Culpeper 2005, p. 67; Grainger 2004).

2.2   Cross-cultural humor

The importance of humor for the *North American* culture manifests itself at every societal level, from popular culture to presidential speeches. Researchers studying humor maintain that "[i]n the West, humor is an essential element of everyday interaction and socialization" (Boxer & Cortés-Conde 1997, p. 275), and that "[f]or Americans, joking is a significant manifestation of conversational involvement, because it represents an important way in which rapport is developed and maintained (Davies 2003, p. 1362).[2] Given the overall "conversationalisation" of public discourse (Fairclough 1992), humor has saturated not only private but also public domains, compelling English language educators to argue in favor of teaching humor in schools (Nilsen & Nilsen 1999). Failure to deliver humor has been shown to provoke negative reactions in listeners (Bell 2009a), further corroborating the importance of humor in American culture.

Although humor is a universal phenomenon, it has been suggested that it does not cross cultural boundaries easily, because it is deeply embedded in local contexts (Chiaro 1992; Propp 1999; Sannikov 2002) and requires an extensive knowledge of schemas, associations, and assumptions, besides conventional linguistic mechanisms for creating humorous effects. Some researchers suggest that there exist national, ethnic and cultural variations in humor (Ziv 1988, Holmes & Hay 1997; Mulholland 1997; Trompenaars & Hampden-Turner 1998; Shardakova 2012). Mulholland's (1997) study analyzes humor in international business, and concludes that Australians' preference for teasing makes their Asian colleagues very uncomfortable. Boxer and Cortés-Conde's (1997) study of residents of Philadelphia and Buenos Aires suggests that both speech communities share strategies for using humor to construct their individual and relational identities. American and Argentinean speakers alike avoid "biting" teases when trying to

---

2.   In his seminal work on humor, Norrick states that "joking around is a natural part of friendly conversation, because we talk to enjoy ourselves," and "everyday conversation is the natural showcase – or better, playground – of joking; joking everywhere informs the overall progress and the step-by-step construction of conversation" (1993: 132, 139).

"maximize" their relational identities, however when an individual identity is at stake, the speakers are free to choose any form on "a continuum that ranges from bonding to nipping to biting" (p. 276). In Shardakova's study of humor among young American and Russian speakers both groups are shown to engage in comparable playful practices, but they diverge in their preferred humor styles and corresponding playful identities. American participants are shown to favor friendly banter that endorses the identity of a bully, and Russian participants are reported to indulge in self-flagellation, assuming the corresponding identity of a *durachok-balagur* ("little-fool-chatter-box"). It is also suggested that each culture develops a set of linguistic routines for its preferred entertaining practices and corresponding playful identities.

2.3   Second language humor

Studies in second language acquisition regard humor as both the means and the goal of language learning. As the means, humor creates a positive affective environment, alleviates feelings of anxiety (Chiasson 2002; Wagner & Urios-Aparisi 2008), and promotes noticing and attention to form (Bell 2009b; Belz 2002; Cook 2000; Pomerantz & Bell 2007). As the goal, humor is an important part of linguistic competence (Davies 2003) and identity construction (Boxer & Cortés-Conde 2000; Habib 2008).

Perceiving humor as part of communicative competence, researchers and educators argue for making it a legitimate classroom practice (Bell 2007a, 2009b; Belz 2002; Broner & Tarone 2001; Cook 2000; Davies 2003; Pomerantz & Bell 2007; Tarone 2000; Shardakova 2010). Cook (2000, p. 150) says: "Knowing a language, and being able to function in communities which use that language, entails being able to understand and produce play with it, making this ability a necessary part of advanced proficiency." Despite the complex nature of humor and its considerable demands on an L2 learner – linguistic (e.g. knowledge of various linguistic devices employed to create humorous effect cf. Shardakova 2010), cognitive (e.g. knowledge of competing semantic scripts cf. Raskin 1985; or ability to identify incongruence between text and context cf. Attardo 1994), and socio-cultural (e.g. familiarity with the target culture conventions cf. Davies 2003) – even learners with limited L2 abilities can participate in "joint joking" (Davies's term 2003, p. 1362), particularly when communicating with sympathetic native speakers, and aided by scaffolding (Davies 2003). Although Davies suggests that learning to joke in a second language cannot be done in classrooms with power imbalances between students and teachers, others argue that humor can be learned in a classroom, and is similar to "other types of linguistic behavior [which] can be learned under these conditions" (Bell 2009b, p. 249). Moreover, the classroom offers a safe environment for experimentation with humor and for trying out new voices and personas (Bell 2009b; Belz 2002).

Humor is now seen as indispensable to learners' individual and social identity (Block 2003; Kramsch 2000; Lantolf 2000; Pomerantz & Bell, p. 2007). With L2 learners no longer seen as computer-like devices or one-sided pragmatists who learn a foreign language for transactional purposes (Kramsch 2000, 2006; Lantolf & Pavlenko 2001), L2 humor and play have been approached as ways to contest "institutionally-sanctioned assumptions about what counts as a meaningful or legitimate act of language use" and to redefine linguistic competence and learner identity (Pomerantz and Bell 2007, p. 557; see also Belz 2002; Cook 2000; Lantolf 2000; Tarone 2000). In their analysis of language play in an advanced Spanish conversation course, Pomerantz & Bell (2007) address both sanctioned and unsanctioned L2 play. They conclude that unsanctioned linguistic play typifies learners' maturing agency not only vis-à-vis the material at hand, but also in relation to symbolic resources of the target language, their native language, and any other languages they speak. L2 play and humor have been interpreted as manifestations of learners' multicompetence[3] (Cook 1992; Belz 2002; Hall, Cheng & Carlson 2006; Pomerantz & Bell 2007), and an indication of changes in their self-conceptualizations (Belz 2002).

A number of studies have focused on learners' use of humor in social interactions with native speakers (Bell 2007a, 2007b; Cheng 2003; Habib 2008), concluding that learners use L2 humor to accomplish the same goals native speakers do with L1 humor. Cultural and linguistic boundaries are shown to be conquerable, particularly with increases in learners' linguistic proficiency (Bell 2007a; Shardakova 2010). L2 speakers successfully engage in conversational humor to negotiate their relational identities and establish in-group bonding (Bell 2007a; Cheng 2003; Habib 2008). Humor helps L2 speakers resolve disagreements (Habib 2008) and deal with the marginalization associated with their nonnative speaker status (Bell 2007b, p. 221; Harder 1980). Similarly to L1 humor, L2 humor is situational, often relating to the speakers' role and status in a particular interaction.

Even if the learners' role in an interaction overrides their nonnative speaker status, affording them greater freedom of self-expression, it is unclear whether there is congruence between learners' intended and received meaning and self-positioning. Furthermore, while interactional research focuses on L2 humor in local practices as noted above, there is still a need to account for broader patterns in learners' humor production and reception in relation to identity.

---

3.   The term multicompetence refers to "the compound state of a mind with two grammars" (Cook 1991, p. 112)

Some researchers argue that the status of outsiders allows learners to play with language and create their own ritualistic practices, flouting normative linguistic conventions (Belz 2002; Cook 2000; Kramsch 2000). Others warn that diversion from standard uses may render learners' language incomprehensible (Byrnes 2002). Whenever learners speak, they engage in identity construction and negotiation (Norton 1997, p. 410; LePage & Tabouret-Keller 1985). However, their target audiences may be unable to decipher their intended meaning if they do not share the same linguistic resources. This mismatch may lead to learners' "reduced personalities" (Harder 1980, p. 262), and exclusion from jocular interaction with native speakers (Bell 2006).

Non-native status may preclude learners' full participation in native practices, because native speakers may not appreciate learners' imitation of native-like sociolinguistic norms. Native speakers have been shown to misinterpret learners' target-like linguistic behavior (Hassall 2004) or to take offence at it, considering it a violation of their intrinsic linguistic rights (Chiaro 1992; Hall 1995). Humor as a way of marking in-group membership may be less welcome if delivered by L2 speakers (Chiaro 1992; Bell 2006).

The proposed study examines the ramifications of learners' use of humor, especially, their intended self-positioning and the audience's reception, and considers the effects of proficiency and study abroad on learners' identity construction through humor and on the ensuing reception by native speakers and peers alike.

The study attempts to answer the following research questions:

1. How do learners intend to position themselves through humor? What identity claims do they make?
2. Do native speakers appreciate learners' humor? Do they uphold learners' identity claims?
3. Do learners understand and uphold their peers' identity claims as expressed through humor?
4. Do linguistic proficiency and exposure to the target culture affect learners' self-positioning and peer-reception?

3. Method

3.1 Participants

This is an experimental cross-sectional study with 48 Russian (44 female and 6 male) and 184 American (101 female and 83 male) participants. The Russian sample came from three major Moscow universities, while the American sample included students from an intensive Russian language summer program and three large universities – two on the East Coast and one in the Midwest. The Russian participants' average age was 22.1 years (SD = 1.3), and the American students' average age was 24.2 years (SD = 2.8).

3.2   Data elicitation

Data were collected in two stages. During the first stage, humor samples were collected from discourse completion questionnaires featuring sixteen scenarios with four speech acts – apologies, compliments, invitations, and requests[4] (for more information about this portion of the study see Shardakova 2010). One hundred and fourteen American learners of Russian submitted their responses in writing, pretending to reply in the form of an email. Participants were not specifically instructed to use humor. Speech acts with humorous sequences were independently selected from the collected data by the researcher and a student assistant. Their results agreed on a given selection 93% of the time (kappa = 0.9, p < .0001). Seventy emails with four hundred humorous sequences were selected.[5]

Thirty-two participants who provided humorous responses to the questionnaire scenarios were then asked to complete a separate questionnaire indicating how they wanted to be seen by their addressees. These participants formed the first study group – Self-Projecting Group (SPG). They were asked to write two to four words or phrases describing their intended identities. Additionally, they had to indicate whether the characteristics they wanted their recipients to ascribe to them were positive, negative, neutral, or ambivalent. The descriptive attribute technique was inspired by Simon's 2004 study "Self-Aspect Model of Identity," which suggests that individuals' self-conceptualization consists of beliefs about their own attributes.

Participants' intended self-descriptions produced 159 lexical tokens, distributed as shown in Table 1. In this study only tokens appearing in first and second positions were analyzed, providing 141 lexemes. The first two entries were selected because most participants provided only two responses; additionally, third and fourth entries were usually synonymous with the first two (this distribution was characteristic of both the learner and the native speaker data, yielding 96% of synonyms in third and fourth entries).

---

4.   The questionnaire scenarios included diverse interlocutor relationships, varying from family members to friends, acquaintances to strangers and authority figures, with an equal split between status equals and status unequals.

5.   See appendix for examples of humorous emails.

Table 1. Distribution of lexical tokens across learner groups (intended identity)

	All tokens			First- & second-order tokens		
	Low to Intermediate[6] (20)*	Advanced (12)	Total of all tokens (32)	Low to Intermediate	Advanced	Total of first & second-order tokens
Study abroad experience**	33	69	102	29	62	91
No study abroad experience	11	46	57	9	41	50
Total	44	115	159	38	103	141

*Number of participants in this category.
**Participants who had completed a summer, semester, or academic year study abroad program.

During the second phase two new groups of participants – 48 native speakers and 70 learners – evaluated the humorous emails collected in the first phase, indicating how they perceived the authors of the emails, and whether they found the emails funny. Participants from both groups (NSG – Native Speaker Group and RLG – Receiving Learner Group) were asked to write two to four words or phrases describing the authors, and to mark their responses as positive, negative, neutral, or ambivalent. The two groups used their respective native languages to complete the questionnaire, yielding 1144 lexical tokens, distributed as shown in Table 2.[7]

Table 2. Distribution of lexical tokens across learner groups (received identity)

	All tokens			First- & second-order tokens		
	Low to Intermediate (49)	Advanced (21)	Total of all tokens (70)	Low to Intermediate	Advanced	Total of 1st & 2nd-order tokens
Study abroad	110	90	200	95	81	176
No study abroad	129	102	231	117	74	191
Total	239	192	431	212	155	367

6. The study participants' linguistic proficiency is reported based on their ACTFL oral proficiency interviews at the time of the research.

7. See appendix for participants' reactions to humorous emails.

3.3   Coding

Unlike in most studies dealing with evaluative reactions to speech (e.g. Eisenstein 1983; Lambert. Hodgson, Gardner & Fillenbaum 1960; Llurda 1995; Masterson, Mullins & Mulvihill 1983; Mulac, Hanley & Prigge 1974), participants in this survey were not asked to give ratings based on a series of predetermined individual characteristics; instead they were instructed to provide their own reactions to the humorous emails. Collected lexemes were grouped into twenty-six initial clusters that were further combined into six binary categories through open coding (Strauss & Corbin 1990). The binary categorization was suggested by the data, because participants marked most of their responses as positive (58%) or negative (34%), with only a small fraction of ambivalent entries (8%), and no neutral ones. Further lexical analysis carried out by the researcher and a bilingual assistant confirmed the binary composition. The data were coded accordingly; the researcher and the assistant agreed on 95% of individual lexemes (kappa = 0.94, p < .0001).

The six main binary categories with their respective subcategories are: (1) articulate/inarticulate (further breaks down into "persuasive," "entertaining," "inarticulate," "boring"); (2) sociable/unsociable (with the following five subcategories: "compassionate," "sincere," "gregarious," "genial," "unsociable"); (3) normal/ abnormal; (4) polite/impolite (with six subcategories: "polite," "pushover," "flatterer," "rude," "condescending," "imposing"); (5) composed/discomposed (with five subcategories: "balanced," "positive," "irritable," "vengeful," "unhinged"); (6) responsible/irresponsible (with four subcategories: "dependable," "ethical," "thoughtless," "untrustworthy").

> Example (1) The category articulate/inarticulate – "always finds what to say" (Russian original *vsegda naidet chto skazat*), "knows how to ask humorous questions" (*umeet zadavat umornye voprosy*), "witty" (*ostroumny*), "quick-witted" (*nakhodchivy*), "funny" (*zabavnaya*), "with a sense of humor" (*s chuvstvom umora, umornoy*), "self-humorous" (*otnositsya k sebe s chuvstvom umora*), "ironic," "trivial," "mediocre" (*zauryadny*), "illogical," "boring," "his jokes are incomprehensible" (*on neponyatno shutit*), "terse" (*nemnogoslovny*), "rather dim-witted" (*sovsem tupoy dazhe pozhalui*), "prone to stereotyping" (*podverzhen stereotimpnym mneniam*), "poor choice of words" (*neudachny vybor frazeologicheskoy edinitsy*), "his way of self-expression is incomprehensible" (*ego vyrazhenie mysli neulovimo*), "begins his argument with a wrong theme" (*nachinaet temu ne s togo*).

> Example (2) The sociable/unsociable category – "knows how to support" (*umeet podderzhat*), "sincere," "straightforward" (*pryamoy*), "honest," "good friend," "able to be happy for others" (*umeet poradovatsa za drugikh*), "responsive" (*otzyvchivy*), "sympathetic" (*uchastlivy*), "attentive," "friendly" (*druzhestvenny, druzhelubny*), "nice person" (*priatny chelovek*), "backslapper" (*rubakha-paren*), "knows how to relax/party" (*umeet otdykhat*), "spirit of the party" (*dusha kompanii*), "extravert,"

"open," "spontaneous" (*neposredstvenny*), "easygoing" (*legky v obschenii*), "doesn't like conflicts" (*ne lubiaschy konflikty*), "peace-loving" (*mirolybivy*), "inconsiderate," "egotistical," "veils his requests" (*vualiruet svoi prosby*), "insincere," "hypocrite," "not-straightforward," "vengeful," "rancorous."

Example (3) The normal/abnormal category – "standard," "normal," "acceptable" (*nichego*), "strange," "absurd."

Example (4) The polite/impolite category – "polite," "affable" (*privetlivy*), "complacent" (*pokladisty*), "diligent" (*prilezhny*), "modest", "awkward" (*zakompleksovanny*), "pushover" (*ne umeet skazat net, chuvstvuet prevoskhodstvo drugogo*), "pushover," "flatterer" (*lstets, lizobludstvuet*), "tactless," "unceremonious," "impolite," "rude" (*nagly, naglets, naglovaty, grubiyan, obidchik*), "condescending" (*vysokomerny, chuvstvuet svoe prevoskhodstvo*), "turns everything into transactional relations" (*svoid vse k uslugam*), "someone who believes other people's interests coincide with his own" (*uverenny v tom, chto interesy drugikh ludei sovpadaut s ego sobstvennymi*) "sponger" (*nakhlebnik*), "imposing," "demanding but not from oneself" (*trebovatelny, no ne k sebe*), "egotistical."

Example (5) The composed/discomposed category – "balanced," "calm," "positive," "optimistic," "does not take troubles seriously" (*ne prinimaet vserioz neudachi*), "loves life in all its forms" (*lubiaschy zhizn vo vsekh ee proyavleniakh*), "enthusiast", "short-tempered," "walking catastrophe" (*khodiachaia katastropha*), "capricious," "querulous", "inconsistent," "emotional," "anxious" (*perezhivatelny, perezhivaet zria*), "pessimist," "grumpy," "irritable," "unhappy" (*nedovolny*), "someone prone to depression" (*otnositelno legko vpadauschy v unynie*).

Example (6) The responsible/irresponsible category – "dependable," "serious," "conscientious" (*sovestlivy*), "unfairly delegates responsibility" (*perevodit strelki*), "likes excuses" (*lubitel otgovorok*), "unreliable," "liar" (*vrun*), "not self-critical," "hypocrite," "indirect" (*nepriamolineiny*), lighthearted (*legkomyslenny*).

In addition, collected lexemes were coded as positive, negative or ambiguous:[8]

Example (7) Lexemes denoting positive characteristics – "with a sense of humor," "attentive," "easy going," "straightforward," "sincere," "nice," "affable," "self-critical," "reliable," "norm," "master of formulations."

Example (8) Lexemes denoting negative characteristics – "boring," "banal," "rude," "stupid," "awkward," "unreliable," "insincere," "sponger," "vengeful," "grumpy."

---

8. This additional coding of individual lexemes duplicated the general coding of jocular emails as positive/negative/ambiguous. It seemed necessary because actual lexemes did not always coincide with the spirit of the entire email. For instance, an email could be judged as "positive" (a playful invitation to a birthday party) while a separate lexeme in this email could be unambiguously marked "negative" (e.g. swear words or demands for presents).

Example (9) Ambiguous lexemes – "brisk" and "cunning" (*boiky*), "someone who can defend him/herself" (*sebia v obidu ne dast*), "sounds like what I might say," "he is a foreigner," "you have to get used to it," "American," "running late," "thinks of fashion," "a pick-up line," "just made a mistake," "we don't have 'pensioners' in the US," "argumentative," "simple," "depends on delivery," " busy," "not a very serious person," "flirty," "strange."

Finally, a distinction was made between lexemes describing a person as an individual, as opposed to those characterizing him/her with respect to his/her relations to other people. This coding was carried out by the researcher and a bilingual assistant who agreed in 93% of the cases on a given selection (kappa = 0.92, p < .000).

Example (10) Lexemes denoting personal characteristics – "optimist," "passive," "diligent," "calm," "smart," "witty," "always finds what to say" (*vsegda naidetsa chto skazat*).

Example (11) Lexemes denoting interpersonal characteristics – "polite," "considerate," "intrusive," "condescending," "generous," "reliable," "honest."

A small number of responses was assigned into a separate group and not coded as personal/interpersonal. Most of these commented on the execution of speech acts or expressed the rater's reaction to them.

Example (12) "Out of breath" (*zapykhalsia*), "didn't have to lie to a friend" (*ne dolzhen byl vrat drugu*), "starts with something else" (*nachinaet s drugogo*), "no culture needed," "normal," "American," "unclear," "anything could've happened," "he is a foreigner," "sounds like what I might say," "you have to get used to it," "running late," "thinks of fashion," "just made a mistake," "I understand," "we don't have pensioners in the US," "I like it," "good fabrication," "depends on delivery," "strange," "be flexible!"

4.   Findings

4.1   Intended identity. The self-positioning group

The collective self-portrait American learners of Russian intended to construct through their use of humor was unanimously positive. In their self-descriptions, all learners, regardless of their linguistic proficiency or study abroad experience, emphasized personal qualities (77.3% of the supplied lexical tokens) over interpersonal ones (22.7%), thus, foregrounding their individual identities.

The main criteria underlying the learners' lexical choice were articulateness and sociability; these categories accounted for 54.6% and 24.8% of all collected lexemes respectively. Persuasiveness was the most desired quality. Sense of humor and ability to entertain were rated second, together with sociability. All of the remaining characteristics were significantly less desirable. Table 3 details the qualities identified by the learners as desirable.

Table 3. Intended qualities the learners wanted to project onto their interlocutors

Lexical categories	Number of tokens in category	Total % in category	Lexical subcategories	Number of tokens in subcategory	Total % in subcategory
Polite/Impolite	2	1.4%	polite	2	1.4%
Composed/ Discomposed	20	14.2%	balanced	9	6.4%
			positive	11	7.8%
Sociable/ Unsociable	35	24.8%	compassionate	5	3.5%
			sincere	4	2.8%
			gregarious	8	5.7%
			genial	18	**12.8%**
Articulate/ Inarticulate	77	**54.6%**	persuasive	57	40.4%
			entertaining	20	**14.2%**
Normal/Abnormal	5	3.5%	normal	5	3.5%
Responsible/ Irresponsible	2	1.4%	dependable	2	1.4%
Total				141	100.0%

4.2   Received identity

Participants from two other study groups – the native speaker group (NSG) and the receiving learner group (RLG) – evaluated L2 humorous emails, and constructed imagined identities of the emails' authors. Approximately half of the time, both evaluative groups perceived the emails' authors in a positive light, even though they ranked more than half of the L2 humor as "not funny". The native speaker group correlated positive evaluation with the speakers' perceived ability to entertain; the receiving learner group, on the other hand, did not associate affective evaluation with the speakers' perceived sense of humor.

The two receiving groups diverged in their choice of evaluative principles: while the learners underscored personal characteristics, the native speakers prioritized interpersonal qualities. In this, the receiving learners echoed the self-positioning learners. The difference between the native speakers and the learners was statistically significant (χ^2 (4, $N = 1136$) = 127.43, $p < .000$), suggesting that these differences in evaluative principles reflected deeper cultural patterns. Table 4 and Graph 1 capture the differences in evaluative principles among the study groups.

Table 4. Distribution of evaluative principles among the study groups

		Study groups			
		NSP	RLG	SPG	Total
Evaluative Principles	Interpersonal	331	105	33	469
		52.6%	28.7%	23.4%	41.3%
	Personal	293	224	108	625
		46.6%	61.2%	76.6%	55.0%
	Ambiguous	5	37	0	42
		.8%	10.1%	.0%	3.7%
Total		629	366	141	1136
		100.0%	100.0%	100.0%	100.0%

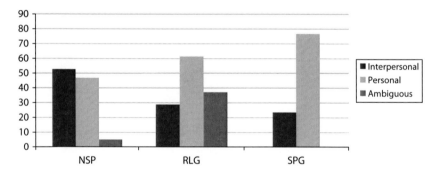

Graph 1. Distribution of evaluative principles among the study groups

All the groups used similar binary criteria to guide the processes of identity construction and interpretation (see categories in Table 3). However, they ascribed different importance to these criteria. While the self-positioning group underscored articulateness and sociability, the receiving learner group chose articulateness, politeness, and normalcy, and the native speaker group prioritized politeness, sociability, and responsibility. Table 5 shows the distribution of guiding criteria among the study groups. The differences in guiding criteria among the groups were statistically significant (χ^2 (10, $N = 1136$) = 220.686, $p < .000$).

Table 5. Distribution of guiding criteria among the study groups

		Study groups			
		NSP	RLG	SPG	Total
Evaluative Criteria	Polite vs. Impolite	177	61	2	240
		28.1%	16.7%	1.4%	21.1%
	Composed vs. Discomposed	82	34	20	136
		13.0%	9.3%	14.2%	12.0%
	Sociable vs. Unsociable	134	63	35	232
		21.3%	17.2%	**24.8%**	20.4%
	Articulate vs. Inarticulate	100	116	77	293
		15.9%	31.7%	**54.6%**	25.8%
	Normal vs. Abnormal	18	60	5	83
		2.9%	16.4%	3.5%	7.3%
	Responsible vs. Irresponsible	118	32	2	152
		18.8%	8.7%	1.4%	13.4%
Total		629	366	141	1136
		100.0%	100.0%	100.0%	100.0%

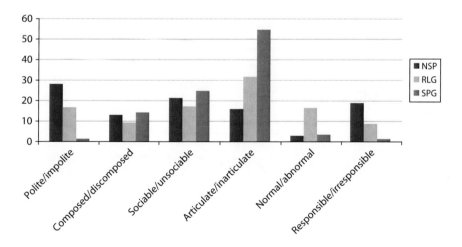

Graph 2. Distribution of guiding criteria among the study groups

At the subcategory level, the two receiving groups expanded the range of lexical tokens they used to describe the authors of humorous emails to 28 subcategories, compared to the initial 11 used by the self-positioning group.

All but one (i.e. "ethical") of these new subcategories were negative counterparts to the positive characteristics listed by the self-positioning group. For instance, the positively viewed characteristic of "being convincing" was countered with the undesirable quality of "lacking in rhetoric." Similarly, the positive evaluation of "being polite" was matched by a list of negative qualities, such as "pushover," "flatterer," "rude," "condescending," "imposing." The difference between the study groups reached statistical significance (χ^2 (54, $N = 1136$) = 407.627, $p < .000$).

4.3   Native speaker data

Despite the self-positioning learners' desire to entertain their interlocutors, the Russian native speakers considered most of the learners' emails humorless (69.2%), marking only 28.1% of intended humor as funny and 2.7% as somewhat funny. The learners' inability to entertain their Russian interlocutors did not, however, result in unequivocally negative evaluations, even though the native speakers tended to associate positive evaluations with the authors' perceived sense of humor (Gamma 4.46, $p < .000$). Apparently, the native speakers did not correlate negative evaluations with failed humor. See Graph 3.

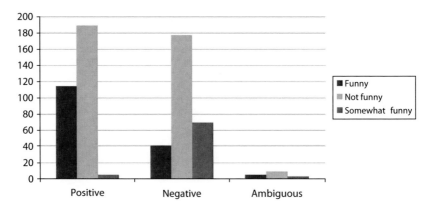

Graph 3. Native speaker group: Correlation between affective evaluation and perceived sense of humor

Nearly half of the time, the native speakers perceived the learners in a positive light, ascribing to them 49% positive, 36.1% negative, and 14.9% ambiguous qualities. In the native speaker group 52.6% of the collected lexemes denoted interpersonal and 46.6% denoted individual characteristics. This difference in focal categories was statistically significant (χ^2 (2, $N = 770$) = 41.85, p < .000).

Another noticeable difference between the learners' intended self-portrayal and the native speakers' reception was that the native speaker group chose different criteria for their evaluation, placing emphasis on politeness (28.1%), sociability (21.3%), and responsibility (18.8%), while the learners underscored articulateness (54.6%) and sociability (24.8%). The difference between the main criteria on which the learner group based its self-positioning and the native speaker group founded its judgment was statistically significant (χ^2 (5, N = 770) = 133.64, p < .000). See Table 5.

Even when the two groups adhered to the same main criterion, they differed in their choice of subcategories. For instance, within the criterion of sociability the learners emphasized geniality (12.8 % in SPG vs. 6.5% in NSG), while the native speakers stressed compassion (6.8% in NSG vs. 3.5% in SPG) and sincerity (6.7% in NSG vs. 2.8% in SPG).

A closer look at the subcategories revealed that the native speakers often perceived the learners as rude. The second highest rated subcategory was the learners' ability to entertain, with compassion and sincerity coming in third, and geniality and thoughtlessness fourth. Table 6 summarizes the native speaker responses.

Table 6. Qualities the native speakers inferred about the learners

Lexical categories	Number of tokens in category	Total % in category	Lexical subcategory	Number of tokens in subcategory	Total % in subcategory
Polite/impolite	177	28.1%	polite	25	4%
			pushover	16	2.5%
			flatterer	11	1.7%
			rude	67	10.7%
			condescending	19	3%
			imposing	39	6.2%
Composed/ discomposed	82	13%	balanced	20	3.2%
			positive	24	3.8%
			irritable	27	4.3%
			vengeful	1	.2%
			unhinged	10	1.6%
Sociable/ unsociable	134	21.3%	compassionate	43	6.8%
			sincere	42	6.7%
			gregarious	5	.8%
			genial	41	6.5%
			unsociable	3	.5%

(*Continued*)

Table 6. (Continued)

Lexical categories	Number of tokens in category	Total % in category	Lexical subcategory	Number of tokens in subcategory	Total % in subcategory
Articulate/ inarticulate	100	15.9%	persuasive	25	4%
			entertaining	45	7.2%
			boring	15	2.4%
			lacking in rhetoric	15	2.4%
Normal/ abnormal	18	2.9%	normal	4	.6%
			abnormal	14	2.2%
Responsible/ irresponsible	118	18.8%	dependable	35	5.6%
			ethical	16	2.5%
			thoughtless	41	6.5%
			untrustworthy	26	4.1%
Total			count	629	100.0%

4.4   Learner data. Receiving Learner Group

Participants from the Receiving Learner Group concurred with the native speakers in their affective evaluation of the L2 authors of humorous emails, regarding them in a positive light almost half of the time: 46.3% of the comments were positive, 32.4% were negative, and 21.3% were ambiguous. However, the Receiving Learner Group did not base its affective evaluation on entertaining qualities of the L2 humorous emails, while the Native Speaker Group did. Receiving learners were more tuned in to L2 humor, dividing it into three categories – "not funny" (59.4%), "funny" (25.6%), and "somewhat funny" (15%); while the native speakers' evaluations bifurcated between "not funny" and "funny" (69.2% vs. 28.1%). The difference between the groups was statistically significant (χ^2 (2, $N = 996$) = 52.3, p < .000). Table 7 captures the distribution of judgments across the native speaker and the receiving learner groups.

Similar to their peers from the self-positioning group, the receiving learners emphasized personal qualities over interpersonal ones, thereby significantly departing from the native speaker practices (χ^2 (2, $N = 996$) = 97.6, $p < .000$).

In their judgment criteria participants from the receiving learner group set themselves apart from both their self-positioning peers and the receiving native speakers. Receiving learners placed articulateness in first place (31.7%), but they considered politeness (16.7%) and normalcy (16.4%) as more important than sociability, which was ranked second and consumed 24.8% of tokens by the self-positioning group. In line with the native speaker priorities,

Table 7. Distribution of humor judgments across NSG and RLG

Humor Judgment	Native Speaker Group	Receiving Learner Group	Total
Funny	177 (28.1%)	94 (25.6%)	271 (27.2%)
Not funny	435 (69.2%)	218 (59.4%)	653 (65.6%)
Somewhat	17 (2.7%)	55 (15.0%)	72 (7.2%)
Total	629 (100.0%)	367 (100.0%)	996 (100.0%)

receiving learners attended to politeness (16.7%). However, they overlooked such rubrics as sociability and responsibility, which the native speakers had in second and third places. The receiving learner group seemed more concerned with normalcy and abnormality than the other two groups (8.7% & 7.4% in RLG vs. 3.5% & 0% in SPG vs. 0.6% & 2.2% in NSG). The differences between the two receiving groups were statistically significant (χ^2 (5, $N = 996$) = 111.373, $p < .000$). See Table 5.

Individual token analysis showed that the receiving learner group was chiefly concerned with the entertaining qualities of humorous emails (13.4%), rather than with persuasiveness (9.8%). This was more in accordance with the native speaker preferences (7.2% of entertaining vs. 4% of persuasiveness). Similarly, the receiving learners also noticed rudeness of their peers' humor (7.1% in RLG vs. 0% in SPG vs. 10.7% in NSG). Table 8 shows the relative importance of the particular qualities observed in the receiving learner group.

Table 8. Qualities the receiving learners inferred about their peers

Lexical categories	Number of tokens in category	Total % in category	Lexical subcategories	Number of tokens in subcategory	Total % in subcategory
Polite/ impolite	62	16.9%	polite	7	1.9%
			pushover	4	1.1%
			flatterer	9	2.5%
			rude	26	7.1%
			condescending	3	.8%
			imposing	13	3.5%

(*Continued*)

Table 8. (Continued)

Lexical categories	Number of tokens in category	Total % in category	Lexical subcategories	Number of tokens in subcategory	Total % in subcategory
Composed/ discomposed	34	9.3%	balanced	8	2.2%
			positive	5	1.4%
			irritable	4	1.1%
			vengeful	7	1.9%
			unhinged	10	2.7%
Sociable/ unsociable	63	17.2%	compassionate	20	5.5%
			sincere	9	2.5%
			gregarious	4	1.1%
			genial	24	6.6%
			unsociable	6	1.6%
Articulate/ inarticulate	116	31.7%	persuasive	36	9.8%
			entertaining	49	13.4%
			boring	18	4.9%
			lacking in rhetoric	13	3.6%
Normal/ abnormal	59	16.1%	normal	32	8.7%
			abnormal	27	7.4%
Responsible/ irresponsible	32	8.7%	dependable	7	1.9%
			ethical	2	.5%
			thoughtless	9	2.5%
			untrustworthy	14	3.8%
Total				366	100.0%

4.5   Effects of proficiency

4.5.1   *Self-positioning learners' proficiency*

Neither of the examined variables – proficiency or study abroad – had a significant impact on learners' self-positioning, with some minor differences observed at the subcategory level.

However both variables affected the reception of L2 humor by native speakers and learners. Increases in proficiency resulted in learners' being perceived by native speakers as less rude (12.3% vs. 7.2%), more polite (5.8% vs. 3.1%), more humorous (8.2% vs. 6.6%), and more normal (2.8% vs. 1%).

Peer reactions showed that those with advanced proficiency were perceived in terms of the self-composure criteria (15.9% vs. 6.4%), while those with intermediate proficiency were judged based on normalcy (20.5 % vs. 8.8%). Examination of subcategories showed that advanced learners were seen as more compassionate (8% vs. 3.8%) and positive (4.5% vs. 0.4%), while their peers with intermediate proficiency were either seen as more normal (10.7% vs. 5.3%) or more deviant (9.8% vs. 3.5%). However, none of these differences were statistically significant.

4.5.2 Receiving learners' proficiency

Increases in proficiency among learners evaluating L2 humor affected their perception significantly (χ^2 (5, $N = 367$) =25.15, $p < .000$) as they began applying the criteria of sociability (23.9% vs. 12.3%) and responsibility (14.3% vs. 4.7%) more frequently than their low proficiency peers, who emphasized normalcy (20.9% vs. 9.7%) and politeness (19% vs. 14.2%). At the subcategory level learners with high proficiency foregrounded qualities such as compassion (7.7% vs. 3.8%), sincerity (8.6% vs. 2.3%), and responsibility (3.9% vs. 1.4%), echoing the native speaker evaluations. These learners were also more tolerant toward rudeness (1.3% vs. 11.3%) and abnormality (3.9% vs. 9.9%).

4.6 Effects of study abroad

4.6.1 Self-positioning learners' cultural exposure

Study abroad experience did not exert any measurable effect on learners' self-positioning, although it affected interlocutors' perception.

Learners without the study abroad experience were positioned as deviating from the native norms of politeness, being either excessively polite (2.1% vs. 1.5%) or condescending (4.9% 1.5%) and imposing (3.8% vs. 1.7%). They were also seen as less normal (3.1% vs. 1.5%) and boring (7% vs. 4.7%). Their peers with the study abroad experience were perceived as more humorous (13.8% vs. 10.4%), more polite (2.2% vs. 0%), more normal (10.3% vs. 6.1%), and slightly more convincing (4.7% vs. 3.1%) and responsible (2.6% vs. 0.9%).

4.6.2 Receiving learners' cultural exposure

The experience of study abroad among the receiving learners reduced their concern with articulateness (28% vs. 35.1%) and self-control or composure (11% vs. 7.4%). At the subcategory level, the receiving learners with in-country experience paid more attention to sounding normal (11.4% vs. 6.8%) and polite (2.8% vs. 1%). Their counterparts without in-country experience underscored knowledge of Russian rhetoric (5.2% vs. 1.7%), and they were also keen on detecting traces of irritability in L2 humor (3.7% vs. 1.7%). The observed differences, however, were not statistically significant.

5.   Discussion

As the study showed, humor invariably brought identity work to the foreground. This was particularly evident through listeners' unsolicited reactions when they engaged in an imaginary argument with the authors of humorous emails, establishing their own position in relation to the speaker with statements such as: "be flexible!" "you have to get used to it," "I understand," "you are being illogical," etc.

Similarly, humor seemed to have marked status in relation to affective sensitivity, as it unfailingly provoked emotional reactions – no neutral comments were found in the data. Even neutral descriptions such as "normal" fell into the category of emotionally charged positive evaluations. Consider the following invitation to a birthday party: *"Kak vsem izvestno, k sozhaleniu, den' rozhdenia – voobsche – tolko raz v godu. Grustno. Tem ne menee prazdunuiu moi den' rozhdenia zavtra i budu ochen' rad, esli ty smozhesh priiti ko mne v gosti,"* which loosely translates to: "As everyone knows, birthdays, in general, come once a year. I'm sad, nevertheless, I'm celebrating my birthday tomorrow and I'll be very happy if you came." The author of this invitation was described by a peer as "normal" and "kind," and evaluated as "positive." In this judgment, the description "kind" had positive overtones, which coincided with the overall positive assessment. Now consider the following apology for being late: *"Ty videla pogodu, da? Ya shla peshkom, ty znaes, eto Rossia – byvaet,"* which roughly translates to: "Did you see the weather? I walked, you know, it's Russia – things happen." A Russian native speaker described the author as "normal," "honest," and "slightly impertinent," but concluded with an overall positive evaluation. In this example, the description "honest" had positive connotations, while the description "slightly impertinent" fell into the category of negative lexemes; however, the overall evaluation overrode the negative overtones.

American L2 speakers of Russian who authored humorous emails uniformly intended to elicit positive reactions from their addressees; a desire which complies with the humor orientation theory correlating individuals' use of humor with their overall communicative adaptability, affective orientation, and concern for eliciting positive impressions (Wanzer et al. 1995).[9] The addressees however, did not uphold the L2 speakers' intentions, responding with nearly an equal number of positive and negative comments and a fraction of ambiguous ones. (e.g. the

---

9.   Numerous studies have shown that humor can serve a host of communicative functions including expression of hostility, aggression, and the like. Current studies move beyond Brown and Levinson's contention that humor serves to uphold positive face (1987). In this study all produced humor was intended as "bonding."

Russian native speakers offered 49% of positive comments and the peer-learners supplied 46.3% of positive responses).

The moderate reception of L2 humor could be attributed to the addressees' desire to separate themselves from the L2 humorists. If submitting to humor manifests a shared worldview (Bell 2009a; Norrick 1993; Tarone 2000), then the receiving study groups were trying to protect their relational identities by positioning L2 humorists as outsiders. The addressees' desire to set themselves apart from the L2 authors of humorous emails was particularly striking in the American learner group, who offered the following comments to their peers' emails: "like an American joke," "she is an American," "you think only Russians can walk the streets in winter?," "a typical American thing to say," "a stereotype about Russia," "very American," "he is a foreigner." The addressees positioned themselves within the Russian culture, and perceived their playful compatriots as outsiders. It was a strong identity gesture on the part of the receiving learner group: members of this group claimed membership in the Russian culture, demarcating themselves from "illegitimate" users. The American addressees did not make any amendments to their affective evaluations (i.e. positive vs. negative) when they found the L2 humor funny or successful. Successful L2 humorists were assigned positive or negative evaluations based on their perceived approximation of the Russian native speaker norms.

Russian native speakers placed greater importance on entertaining qualities of L2 emails than on their compliance with native socio-cultural norms, including politeness; they correlated positive evaluations with perceived L2 humor. A well-told joke absolved even those L2 speakers who were identified as "unceremonious," "insolent," "aggressive," "conceited," "rude," "sponger" (*nakhlebnik*), "lazy," "irresponsible," "attacking" (*prediavliaet*), "doesn't value other people's labor" (*ne tsenyaschy chuzhoy trud*), "walking catastrophe." The native speakers recognized learners' aggressive humor as "ritualized banter," which was a significant communicative accomplishment, given the marginal status of banter in Russian humor practices (Shardakova 2012). They upheld the learners' claims of "articulateness and a good sense of humor," which attests to the good rapport the two groups established (Spencer-Oatey 2005).

Since identities are not simply enacted, but are are co-constructed, negotiated, and contested during interaction, one of the study's primary goals was to uncover whether there existed culture-specific patterns in identity construction and interpretation. The observed differences between how participants positioned themselves by using humor and how their interlocutors perceived them pointed to divergent cultural norms, which underpin the participants' linguistic behavior. While American learners of Russian highlighted personal qualities, their Russian counterparts emphasized interpersonal characteristics. Neither increases in proficiency nor the cultural exposure of study abroad altered learners' behavior, which has important pedagogical implications, because similar divergent principles could govern other linguistic behaviors and cultural practices, and learners need to be aware of them.

The differences between the native speaker group and the learner groups can be explained by Schwartz's universal model of human values (Schwartz 1992). The American learners and the Russian native speakers were driven by divergent motivational principles. While the former prioritized "personal success through demonstrating competence" (Schwartz 1992, p. 8), the latter emphasized group solidarity and traditional "customs and ideas" (p. 10). Since values transcend specific situations and guide the selection of behaviors, it is imperative that learners understand the expectations of their target communities of practice, specifically, which behaviors constitute the norm and which deviate from it, requiring negotiation.

As in related studies (Shardakova 2009, 2010), proficiency and exposure to the target culture worked in tandem, but they produced varying effects across the participant groups. They had almost no impact on the self-positioning group, a minimal one on the native speakers' group, and a significant one on the receiving learner group.

With increases in linguistic proficiency receiving learners perceived their interlocutors, approximating native speaker practices, i.e. they began noticing qualities such as compassion, sincerity, and responsibility. Similarly, exposure to the target culture aligned learners' perception with that of the native speakers in regards to politeness and conformity with social norms. Experience with the target culture had the strongest effect on the low proficiency group (cf. Shardakova 2009, 2010), changing the selection of focal categories, as opposed to reordering of subcategories undertaken by the advanced learners.

Even though increases in linguistic proficiency or exposure to the target culture had no effect on the learners' self-positioning, both variables influenced how these learners were received. The Russian native speakers perceived learners with high linguistic proficiency as more polite, having a greater sense of humor, and being more socially adjusted (i.e. more "normal" and "standard"). Learners with cultural experience were seen by Russian native speakers as more articulate. The American peers perceived their humorous compatriots with high proficiency as more compassionate; while seeing those with study abroad experience as more polite and responsible, more normal, and with a greater sense of humor.

Research into speech act pragmatics in the study abroad context has produced varying, sometimes contradictory results: some studies have reported that learners who study abroad are more likely to acquire native-like pragmatics than their peers who stay at home (Barron 2003; Matsumura 2001; Owen 2001). Others, on the other hand, have argued that study abroad may yield quite modest results (Pellegrino 1998; Rodríguez 2001). A third group of studies determined that study abroad may differently affect learners' pragmalinguistic and sociopragmatic abilities and that understanding of L2 culture, which underlies linguistic uses, may require explicit instruction (Cohen & Shively 2007; Kondo 1997; Shardakova 2010). Finally, it has been shown that learners may resist acquisition of some pragmatic features if they find them incongruent with their concept of self (DuFon 1999). While learners themselves often report cultural differences as a significant challenge (Bell & Attardo 2010), few studies have undertaken the burden of determining exactly what these differences might be, because the task is daunting, perhaps questionably achievable, given that no culture is monolithic. Therefore, any description runs the risk of becoming either too general or haphazard. This study, which sought to unpack the notion of culture and to discern key principles that both native speakers and learners invoke when engaging in humor in various speech acts, revealed that the two groups stress disparate characteristics and that these preferences point toward different value systems. In their production of humor, learners invariably operated under their own cultural values; however, the way they perceived humor has changed. The study abroad environment has been shown to help learners raise their cultural awareness and perceive humor more in line with native speaker expectations about humor in its relation to identity.

6. Conclusion

This project showed that interlanguage humor poses significant challenges for interactants, regardless of whether they share their native culture or belong to different traditions with dissimilar values and behavioral expectations. The multifunctionality and evaluative ambiguity inherent in humor make it a particularly contested form of self-presentation. Speakers' intentions were often misunderstood or disregarded. The intended and received collective identities of L2 learners trying to present themselves through humor were significantly skewed along the continuum of positive and negative evaluations. These identities also differed in the focal traits claimed by the authors of humorous emails versus the ones ascribed to them by their addressees.

The interplay of identity construction, first culture, and second culture differed across the study groups, and was affected by interactive mode and evaluation type. Affective evaluation was independent of cultural affiliation and relied on the interactional mode – i.e. self-construction or reception. Participants' preference for personal or relational characteristics was guided by native cultures and their value systems, which promoted either personal achievement or compliance with tradition. The selection of focal identity traits was shaped by all of the variables – native culture, second culture, and mode of interaction. In the interpretive mode learners began to see their peers through what they perceived as Russian cultural conventions. Increases in proficiency and study abroad experience raised learners' awareness of Russian cultural norms and of the role of language in perception of others. Proficiency was a decisive factor in learners' ability to attend to target culture rules. Study abroad experience was beneficial for learners with low proficiency, but its effect was not statistically significant.

Several issues brought to light by this study merit further exploration, among them, the relationship between identity claims and different second languages studied by American learners, as well as the relationship between various linguistic behaviors and American learners' established preferences for foregrounding personal qualities over interpersonal ones.

References

Archakis, A., & Tsakona, V. (2005). Analyzing conversational data in GTVH terms: A new approach to the issue of identity construction via humor. *Humor, 18*, 41–68.

Attardo, S. (1994). *Linguistic theories of humor*. Berlin: Mouton de Gruyter.

Bardovi-Harlig, K., & Dörnyei, Z. (1998). Do language learners recognize pragmatic violations? Pragmatic versus grammatical awareness in instructed L2 learning. *TESOL Quarterly, 32*, 233–259.

Barron, A. (2003). *Acquisition in interlanguage pragmatics: Learning how to do things with words in a study abroad context*. Amsterdam: John Benjamins.

Bell, N.D. (2006). Interactional adjustments in humorous intercultural communication. *Intercultural Pragmatics, 3*, 1–28.

Bell, N.D. (2007a). Humor comprehension: Lessons learned from cross-cultural communication. *Humor, 20*, 367–387.

Bell, N.D. (2007b). Safe territory? The humorous narratives of bilingual women. *Research on Language and Social Interaction, 40*, 199–225.

Bell, N.D. (2009a). Impolite responses to failed humor. In N.R. Norrick & D. Chiaro (Eds.), *Humor in interaction* (pp. 143–165). Amsterdam: John Benjamins.

Bell, N.D. (2009b). Learning about and through humor in the second language classroom. *Language Teaching Research, 13*, 241–258.

Bell, N., & Attardo, S. (2010). Failed humor: Issues in non-native speakers' appreciation and understanding of humor. *Intercultural Pragmatics, 7*, 423–447.

Belz, J.A. (2002). Second language play as a representation of the multicompetent self in foreign language study. *Journal for Language Identity, and Education, 1*, 13–39.

Block, D. (2003). *The social turn in second language acquisition*. Washington, DC: Georgetown University Press.

Boxer, D., & Cortés-Conde, F. (1997). From bonding to biting: Conversational joking and identity display. *Journal of Pragmatics, 27*, 275–294.

Boxer, D., & Cortés-Conde, F. (2000). Identity and ideology: Culture and pragmatics in content-based ESL. In J.K. Hall & L. Verplaeste (Eds.), *Second and foreign language learning through classroom interaction* (pp. 203–219). Mahwah, NJ: Lawrence Erlbaum.

Broner, M., & Tarone, E. (2001). 'Is it fun?' Language play in a fifth-grade Spanish immersion classroom, *Modern Language Journal, 85*, 363–379.

Brown, P., & Levinson, S.C. (1987). *Politeness: Some universals in language usage*. Cambridge, UK: Cambridge University Press.

Byrnes, H. (2002). Toward academic-level foreign language abilities: Reconsidering foundational assumptions, expanding pedagogical options. In B. Leaver & B. Shekhtman (Eds.), *Developing professional-level language proficiency* (pp. 34–58). Cambridge, UK: Cambridge University Press.

Cheng, W. (2003). Humor in intercultural conversations. *Semiotica, 146*, 287–306.

Chiaro, D. (1992). *The language of jokes: Analysing verbal play*. London: Routledge.

Chiasson, P.-E. (2002, March). Using humour in the second language classroom. *The Internet TESL Journal, 8* (3). Retrieved from ⟨http://iteslj.org/Techniques/Chiasson-Humour.html⟩.

Cohen, A.D., & Shively, R.L. (2007). Acquisition of requests and apologies in Spanish and French: Impact of study abroad and strategy-building intervention. *Modern Language Journal, 91*, 189–212.

Cook, G. (2000). *Language play, language learning*. Oxford: Oxford University Press.

Cook, V. (1991). The poverty of the stimulus argument and multicompetence. *Second Language Research, 7*, 103–117.

Cook, V. (1992). Evidence for multicompetence. *Language Learning, 42*, 557–591.

Culpeper, J. (2005). Impoliteness and entertainment in the television quiz show: *The Weakest Link*. *Journal of Politeness Research, 1*, 35–72.

Davies, B., & Harré, R. (1990). Positioning: The discursive production of selves. *Journal for the Theory of Social Behaviour, 20*, 44–63.

Davies, C.E. (2003). How English-learners joke with native speakers: An interactional sociolinguistic perspective on humor as collaborative discourse across cultures. *Journal of Pragmatics, 35*, 1361–1385.

DuFon, M.A. (1999). *The acquisition of linguistic politeness in Indonesian by sojourners in naturalistic interactions*. Unpublished doctoral dissertation, University of Hawaii, Manoa.

Eisenstein, M. (1983). Native reactions to non-native speech: A review of empirical research. *Studies in Second Language Acquisition, 5*, 160–176.

Fairclough, N. (1992). *Discourse and social change*. Cambridge: Polity Press.

Giles, H., & Billings, A. (2004). Language attitudes. In A. Davies & C. Elder (Eds.), *Handbook of applied linguistics* (pp. 187–209). Oxford: Blackwell.

Grainger, K. (2004). Verbal play on the hospital ward: Solidarity or power? *Multilingua, 23*, 39–59.

Habib, R. (2008). Humor and disagreement: Identity construction and cross-cultural enrichment. *Journal of Pragmatics, 40*, 1117–1145.

Hall, J.K. (1995). (Re)creating our worlds with words: A sociohistorical perspective of face-to-face interaction. *Applied Linguistics, 16*, 206–232.

Hall, J.K., Cheng, A., & Carlson, M.T. (2006). Reconceptualizing multicompetence as a theory of language knowledge. *Applied Linguistics, 27*, 220–240.

Harder, P. (1980). Discourse as self-expression: On the reduced personality of the second language learner. *Applied Linguistics, 1*, 262–270.

Hassall, T. (2004). Through a glass, darkly: When learner pragmatics is misconstrued. *Journal of Pragmatics, 36*, 997–1002.

Hay, J. (2000). Functions of humor in the conversations of men and women. *Journal of Pragmatics, 32*, 709–742.

Hay, J. (2001). The pragmatics of humor support. *International Journal of Humor Studies, 14,* 55–82.

Holdaway, S. (1988). Blue jokes: humor in police work. In C. Powell & G. Paton (Eds.), *Humor in society: Resistance and control* (pp. 106–122).London: Macmillan.

Holmes, J. (2006). Sharing a laugh: Pragmatic aspects of humor and gender in the workplace. *Journal of Pragmatics, 38,* 26–50.

Holmes, J., & Hay, J. (1997). Humor as an ethnic boundary marker in New Zealand interactions. *Journal of Intercultural Studies, 18,* 127–151.

Holmes, J. & Schnurr, S. (2005). Politeness, humor and gender in the workplace: Negotiating norms and identifying contestation. *Journal of Politeness Research, 1,* 121–149.

Jorgensen, J. (1996). The functions of sarcastic irony in speech. *Journal of Pragmatics, 26,* 613–634.

Kondo, S. (1997). The development of pragmatic competence by Japanese learners of English: Longitudinal study on interlanguage apologies. *Sophia Linguistica, 41,* 265–284.

Kotthoff, H. (2000). Gender and joking: On the complexities of women's image politics in humorous narratives. *Journal of Pragmatics, 32,* 55–80.

Kramsch, C. (2000). Second language acquisition, applied linguistics, and the teaching of foreign languages. *Modern Language Journal, 84,* 311–326.

Kramsch, C. (2006). From communicative competence to symbolic competence. *Modern Language Journal, 90,* 249–252.

Lambert, W.E., Hodgson, R.C., Gardner, R.C., & Fillenbaum, S. (1960). Evaluational reactions to spoken languages. *Journal of Abnormal and Social Psychology, 60,* 51–44.

Lantolf, J.P. (2000, March). *Language learning as fun and games: The role of language play in SLA.* Paper presented at the meeting of the American Association for Applied Linguistics, Vancouver, Canada.

Lantolf, J.P., & Pavlenko, A. (2001). Second Language Activity theory: Understanding second language learners as people. In M.P. Breen (Ed.), *Learner contributions to language learning: New directions in research* (pp. 141–158). New York, NY: Longman.

Lennox, J.T. & Ashforth, B.E. (2002). From 'I' to 'We': The role of putdown humor and identity in the development of a temporary group. *Human Relations, 55,* 55–88.

LePage, R.B., & Tabouret-Keller, A. (1985). *Acts of identity: Creole-based approaches to language and ethnicity.* New York, NY: Cambridge University Press.

Llurda, E. (1995). Native-speaker reactions to nonnative speech: A review, *Sintagma, 7,* 43–51.

Lynch, O. (2010). Cooking with humor: In-group humor as social organization. *Humor, 23,* 127–159.

Masterson, J., Mullins, E., & Mulvihill, A. (1983). Components of evaluative reactions to varieties of Irish accents. *Language and Speech, 26,* 215–231.

Matsumura, S. (2001). Learning the rules for offering advice: A quantitative approach to second language socialization. *Language Learning, 51,* 635–679.

Mulac, A., Hanley, T.D., & Prigge, D.Y. (1974). Effects of phonological speech foreignness upon three dimensions of attitude of selected American listeners. *Quarterly Journal of Speech, 60,* 411–420.

Mulholland, J. (1997). The Asian Connection: Business requests and acknowledgements. In F. Bargiela-Chiappini & S. Harris (Eds.), *The languages of business* (pp. 94–117). Edinburgh: Edinburgh University Press.

Mullany, L. (2008). "Stop hassling me!" Impoliteness, power and gender identity in the professional workplace." In D. Bousfield & M.A. Locher (Eds.), *Impoliteness in language: Studies on its interplay with power in theory and practice* (pp. 231–255). Berlin: Mouton de Gruyter.

Nilsen, A.P., & Nilsen, D.L.F. (1999). The Straw Man meets his match: Six arguments for studying humor in English classes. *English Journal, 88,* 34–42.

Norrick, N. (1993). *Conversational joking: Humor in everyday talk.* Bloomington, IN: Indiana University Press.

Norton, B. (1997). Language, identity, and the ownership of English. *TESOL Quarterly, 31,* 409–429.

Owen, J.S. (2001). *Interlanguage pragmatics in Russian: A study of the effects of study abroad and proficiency levels on request strategies.* Unpublished doctoral dissertation, Bryn Mawr College, Bryn Mawr, PA.

Pellegrino, V.A. (1998). Student perspectives on language learning in a study abroad context. *Frontiers: The Interdisciplinary Journal of Study Abroad, 4,* 91–120.

Pomerantz, A., & Bell, N.D. (2007). Learning to play, playing to learn: FL learners as multicompetent language users. *Applied Linguistics, 28,* 556–578.

Pogrebin, M.R., & Poole, E.D. (1988). Humor in the briefing room: A study of the strategic uses of humor among police. *Journal of Contemporary Ethnography, 17,* 183–210.

Propp, V.Y. (1999). *Problemy komisma i smekha. Ritualny smekh v folklore.* Izdatelstvo "Labirint", Moskva. [*Problems of the comical and laughter. Ritualized laughter in folklore*]. The Labirint Publishing House, Moscow.

Raskin, V. (1985). *Semantic mechanisms of humor.* Dordrect: D. Reidel.

Rodríguez, S. (2001). *The perception of requests in Spanish by instructed learners of Spanish in the second- and foreign-language contexts: A longitudinal study of acquisition patterns.* Unpublished doctoral dissertation, Indiana University, Bloomington.

Rogerson-Revell, P. (2007). Humor in business: A double-edged sword: A study of humor and style shifting in intercultural business meetings. *Journal of Pragmatics, 39,* 4–28.

Sannikov, V.Z. (2002). *Russky yazyk v zerkale yazykovoi igry.* Izdanie 2. Yazyki slavyanskoi kultury, Moskva. [*Russian language in the mirror of language play.* 2 Edition. Languages of the Slavic culture, Moscow].

Schieffelin, B. (1986). Teasing and shaming in Kaluli children's interactions. In B. Schieffelin & E. Ochs (Eds.), *Language socialization across cultures* (pp. 165–181). Cambridge: Cambridge University Press.

Schwartz, S.H. (1992). Universals in the content and structure of values: Theory and empirical tests in 20 countries. In M. Zanna (Ed.), *Advances in experimental social psychology,* 25 (pp. 1–65). New York, NY: Academic Press.

Shardakova, M. (2009). *Interlanguage pragmatics of the apology: How Americans acquire sociolinguistic competence in Russian.* Saarbrücken: Verlag VDM Dr. Müller, Germany.

Shardakova, M. (2010). How to be funny in a second language: Pragmatics of L2 humor. In R. D. Brecht, L.A. Verbitskaja, M.D. Lekic, & W. P. Rivers (Eds.), *Mnemosynon. Studies on language and culture in the Russophone world: A collection of papers presented to Dan E. Davidson by his students and colleagues* (pp. 288–310). Moscow: "Azbukovnik," Institut russkogo jazyka, RAN.

Shardakova, M. (2012). Cross-cultural analysis of the use of humor by Russian and American English speakers. In L. de Zarobe & Y. de Zarobe (Eds.) *Speech acts and politeness across languages and cultures.* (pp. 197–241). Bern: Peter Lang.

Simon, B. (2004). *Identity in modern society. A social psychological perspective.* Oxford: Blackwell.

Spencer-Oatey, H. (2005). (Im)politeness, face and perceptions of rapport: Unpackaging their bases and interrelationships. *Journal of Politeness Research, 1,* 95–119.

Strauss, A.C., & Corbin, J.M. (1990). *Basics of qualitative research: Grounded theory procedures and techniques* (2nd edition). Newbury Park, CA: Sage.

Sullivan, P. (2000). Playfulness as mediation in communicative language teaching in a Vietnamese classroom. In J.P. Lantolf (Ed.), *Sociocultural theory and second language learning* (pp. 115–131). Oxford: Oxford University Press.

Tannen, D. (1999). The display of (gendered) identities in talk at work. In M. Bucholtz, A.C. Liang, & L. A. Sutton (Eds.), *Reinventing identities: The gendered self in discourse* (pp. 221–240). Oxford: Oxford University Press.

Tarone, E. (2000). Getting serious about language play: Language play, interlanguage variation and second language acquisition. In B. Swierzbin, F. Morris, M.E. Anderson, C.A. Klee, & E. Tarone (Eds.), *Social and cognitive factors in second language acquisition: Selected proceedings of the 1999. Second Language Research Forum* (pp. 31–54). Somerville, MA: Cascadilla Press.

Terrion, J.L., & Ashforth, B.E. (2002). From 'I' to 'We': The role of putdown humor and identity in the development of a temporary group. *Human Relations, 55*, 55–88.

Trompenaars, F., & Hampden-Turner, C. (1998). *Riding the waves of culture*. London: Nicholas Brealey.

Wagner, M., & Urios-Aparisi, E. (2008). Pragmatics of humor in the foreign language classroom: Learning (with) humor. In M. Pütz, Martin & J. Neff-van Aertselaer (Eds.), *Developing contrastive pragmatics: Interlanguage and cross-cultural perspectives* (pp. 209–231). Berlin: Mouton de Gruyter.

Wanzer, M., Booth-Butterfield, M., & Booth-Butterfield, S. (1995). The funny people: A source-orientation to the communication of humor. *Communication Quarterly, 43*, 142–154.

Ziv, A. (1988). *National styles of humour*. New York, NY: Greenwood Press.

Appendix

Elicited apology

Prompt: You agreed to go shopping with your friend. You decided to meet at 10 a.m. at the mall, but you completely forgot about it and missed your meeting. Email your friend.

Response: Izvini, bylo mnogo snega. *Ia ne planirovala metel.* [Sorry, it was lots of snow. *I didn't plan for the storm.*]

Reactions to this apology:

1. Native speaker reactions: short-tempered (razdrazhitelny), capricious, funny, apologetic (izviniaiushchisia), walking catastrophe (khodiachaia katastrofa)
2. Reactions by learners with advanced proficiency in Russian: straightforward, funny, not-funny, nice, not serious, usual, American, rude
3. Reactions by learners with intermediate proficiency in Russian: rude, stupid, not funny, not interesting, probably best way to dispel tension
4. Reactions by learners with exposure to the target culture: insincere, rude, normal, boring
5. Reactions by learners without exposure to the target culture: he is not a bad person but he didn't think about his friend, it's not a joke, bad joke, stupid, normal

Elicited birthday invitation

Prompt: You are having a birthday party and inviting your friends. Please write an email to one of your friends with your invitation.

Response: Ya znaiu *ty nechego delat' etu piatnitsu ty budesh durak* esli ty ne idesh ko mne na vecherinku [I know *you have nothing to do this Friday you will be a fool* if you don't come to my party]

This invitation was supplied by a nineteen year old female American learner of Russian who was at the intermediate mid proficiency level in Russian at the time of the research. This email contains two humorous sequences that are marked out in cursive: (1) "you have nothing to do this Friday"; (2) "you will be a fool."

Reactions to this invitation:

1. Native speaker reactions: impertinent, rude, extravert, somewhat impudent but with sense of humor (naglovaty, no s chuvstvom iumora), funny, sociable, quick-witted (nakhodchivy)
2. Reactions by learners with advanced proficiency in Russian: egotist, likes to joke, not funny, typical American
3. Reactions by learners with intermediate proficiency in Russian: funny, she's joking, straightforward, they must be good friends, normal
4. Reactions by learners with exposure to the target culture: rude, not funny, tries to joke
5. Reactions by learners without exposure to the target culture: humorous, not funny, funny, stupid, rude

Elicited request

Prompt: You don't have a car but one of your friends does and this person lives a block down from your apartment. Today you are going to stay really late at the university to attend an interesting lecture. It turned out that your friend is also going to the same lecture. Email your friend and ask for a ride.

Response: Ya znaiu ty khochesh videt' menia bolshe. Ty mozhesh esli podvezesh menia domoi. [I know *you want to see me more.* You can if you give me a ride home.]

This request was issued by a twenty year old female American learner of Russian who was at the advance low proficiency level in Russian. This email contains one humorous sequence: "I know you want to see me more."

Reactions to this invitation:

1. Native speaker reactions: egotist, easygoing, self-confident, that's a good boy! (molodets!), with sense of humor, always knows what to say (vsegda naidetsa chto skazat'), humorist (shutnik), amicable (druzhelubny), straightforward
2. Reactions by learners with advanced proficiency in Russian: honest, friendly, sexy, funny, wants to joke
3. Reactions by learners with intermediate proficiency in Russian: funny, flirty, needy
4. Reactions by learners with exposure to the target culture: smart, funny, jokes
5. Reactions by learners without exposure to the target culture: good humored, lighthearted, normal, not kind, strange

Getting over the hedge

Acquisition of mitigating language in L2 Japanese

Noriko Iwasaki

School of Oriental and African Studies (SOAS), University of London

This chapter first discusses an expanded construct of language proficiency, to highlight interpersonal/social dimensions of language, in my work on language learning abroad. I then report on an interpersonally significant but often neglected aspect of learners' language – hedges. It was found that, after study abroad, learners used a wider variety of hedges and did so more frequently. Two participants whose speech segments were highly rated for sociability appeared keen to emulate young L1 Japanese speakers' overuse of some hedges such as *nanka* 'somehow.' Their hedges allow them to socially package their messages (i.e. provide a buffer zone to monitor and accommodate the interlocutor's emotions and feelings) (Maynard 1989). One learner also used sentence-final *mitaina* 'like,' also associated with young speakers.

1. Introduction

In 2002 I asked students about to depart for Japan from a university in the Northeastern U.S. to participate in a study abroad research project. Six students volunteered, and five continued to participate upon their return to the U.S. As I glimpsed the students' lives unfolding and their language developing, I furthered my exploration of these L2 Japanese learners' study abroad experiences while redirecting my research focus along the way.

When initiating this project, I was interested in how the students' language proficiency would develop during their year abroad (Iwasaki 2007). Yet, the construct of language proficiency informing my work was limited to what could be assessed through standardized tests. Unlike other study abroad research which from the outset was informed by sociocultural theories or other theories prioritizing sociocultural and contextual factors, such as Kinginger (2008) and Jackson (2008), my work did not involve ethnographic data. It later became evident that such an approach fell short of understanding the gains and transformations that the students experienced even when the research focuses on language development. Thus, I began to look at socially significant aspects of their language use (e.g. speech styles, fillers), both quantitatively and qualitatively, and complemented this work with a post-study abroad retrospective interview.

This chapter first illustrates how my research was expanded to highlight social and interpersonal dimensions of language. I then proceed to an analysis of hedges, an oft-neglected area in language assessment, yet a socially and interpersonally significant aspect of language. In so doing, I aim to illustrate how a perspective prioritizing such social and interpersonal dimensions of language illuminates L2 learners' pragmatic development and its relevance to their social identities.

2. Previous studies

2.1 Learning Japanese during study abroad programs

Contrary to common belief, L2 learning outcomes from study abroad are not always as dramatic as anticipated (Kinginger 2008). Studies, including those examining L2 Japanese, have shown varied language gains.

When Huebner (1995) compared the learning outcomes of Japanese learners in two 9-week beginner-level summer intensive programs, one in the U.S. and the other in Japan, he found that study abroad learners showed greater gains both in speaking, as measured by the Oral Proficiency Interview (OPI), and in reading comprehension. Huebner concluded that study abroad was beneficial for beginning level students, noting, however, that there was greater individual variation in outcomes among the study abroad group. However, when Dewey (2004, 2007) compared development of L2 Japanese learners' learners in reading and vocabulary in an intensive domestic immersion program and in a study abroad context, he found that gains in reading comprehension (Dewey 2004) and in vocabulary (Dewey 2007) were fairly similar between the two groups on most of the measures.

With regard to sociolinguistic aspects of Japanese, the effects of study abroad experiences are also mixed. Many of these studies focus on learners' speech style choices. In Japanese, the endings of all main predicates indicate one of two speech styles: the plain form, often associated with informality and the *desu/masu* form, often associated with formality or politeness (i.e. addressee honorifics). Marriott (1995) examined six secondary school learners' performances in four aspects of politeness before and after they studied in Japan for 12 months, including the use of *desu/masu* and plain styles in interviews with a Japanese speaker whom they had not met before (where *desu/masu* would be the norm). These learners became very competent in using polite formulaic expressions (e.g. expressions of gratitude) for opening and closing sequences in interviews and role-plays, but all of them overused the plain style, using it more often than they had before studying abroad. Marriott states, "all the students committed a serious deviation by using too many predicates in the plain style" (p. 207).

These outcome-based studies utilized a variety of tests, which were primarily quantitative. Yet, in many of the previous studies, including the above, substantive differences between individuals (both in their experiences and learning outcomes) were noted. Hence, researchers have started to examine individual learners more closely and have also called for more qualitative research to shed light on each individual learner (DeKeyser 1991; Wilkinson 1998, 2000).

2.2   Individual learners and their subjectivities

Ethnographic research conducted with L2 Japanese learners by Siegal (1994, 1995, 1996) and Iino (1999, 2006) has shed light on learners' sociocultural identities, which are increasingly considered to be significant in L2 learning (Block 2003, 2009).

Siegal (1994) revealed that both learners' sociocultural identities and their agency affect their L2 use. Her ethnographic study focused on four Anglo-European women living in Japan. Among them were two college students, Arina from Hungary and Sally from Britain. They were often critical of Japanese women's speech and/or the expectation that women should speak politely. Sally viewed women's demeanor as "silly and shallow" (p. 335) and observed that men were allowed to use the plain form more often. She felt that the plain form was more "friendly" and preferred to use it even in contexts where *desu/masu* might be the norm (p. 338–339). Similarly, Arina could not abide the way a professor's wife spoke; she felt it was too humble. Thus she decided to "stick with *desu/masu*" (p. 340) and thus avoid using humble honorific forms (which are used to be humble about speakers' own actions). But later, when participating in public speech events in which she utilized such honorific language, she realized its importance (Siegal 1995). Siegal (1994) sums up the participants' language choices, stating, "Learners created their own language system based on their perceptions of Japanese women's language and demeanor and their awareness of their position in Japanese society," which sometimes led to inadequate use of pragmatic devices and modality (p. 344).

Siegal (1994) not only illuminated how the individual learners' sociocultural identities affected their language use, but also how target community members' expectations of outsiders' language use are different from those of their own community members. She noted that not only were learners "told that they were 'foreigners' and therefore did not need to be concerned with honorifics or appropriate language usage" but also "there is a subtle dislike of a foreigner who speaks Japanese too well" (p. 401).

Such divergent expectations for outsiders also became evident in Iino's studies (1999, 2006; see also Brown, this volume). He examined L2 learner and host family dinnertime interactions in Kyoto and found that the host family used "unnatural" language (i.e. language that deviated from the L1 norm) when addressing L2 learners. Some L2 Japanese learners felt that they were expected to play a foreigner role and that acting like a foreigner and even pretending not to know much about Japan or the language made their lives easier as Japanese people became more tolerant of their behavior.

Cook (2008), adopting a language socialization perspective (e.g. Ochs 1993), examined dinnertime interactions between nine L2 learners and their host families. She analyzed both the host family and L2 learners' use of the plain and *desu/masu* forms and how each participant used these forms to index their social identities in context. In her analysis, she used her revised construal of the social meanings of *desu/masu* as the presentational mode, from which other social meanings such as politeness emerge in some contexts. She found the predominant speech style at home to be the plain style, but host family members shifted styles to index their social identities: e.g. the host mothers switched from the plain form to *desu/masu* when providing information about dinner and positioning themselves as the "person in charge." By observing these style shifts and participating in interactions with their host families, Cook suggests L2 learners also acquired the social meanings of these forms and learned how to shift styles: e.g. shifting to *desu/masu* to index a stance as a presenter or as the authority (on the English language).

3.   The five participants and earlier work

The five participants in this study abroad research project were all Caucasian males in their early twenties. Table 1 provides their profiles. Two participants, Henry and Peter, majored in Japanese, Sam majored in Linguistics and Japanese, and Alan and Greg majored in computer science but were considering minoring or double-majoring in Japanese at the time of departure.

Table 1. Participants' profiles

Participant[1]	Years of instruction before	Where they studied	Accommodation type	Primary non-academic activities and interactions
Greg	1 year	Hyogo	Homestay	Interacting with host family
Henry	2 years	Aichi	Homestay, then a house share	Interacting with peers in university clubs and home
Alan	2 years	Hyogo	Homestay	Travelling and interacting with friends
Sam	2 years	Tokyo	Homestay	Church choir, glee club, interacting with host family
Peter	2 years	Ibaraki	Dormitory	Kendo club, interacting with other club members

Language proficiency, discussed in my earliest study (Iwasaki 2007) consisted of OPI ratings and sub-section scores of the Japanese-Language Proficiency Test (JLPT). This test is administered by the Japan Foundation and Japan Educational Exchanges and Service, and generally considered to be the most reliable means for evaluating L2 Japanese proficiency. Until 2009, tests had four levels (Level 1 through Level 4, Level 1 being the highest), and the tests for each level consisted of three sections, Writing-Vocabulary, Listening, and Reading-Grammar. Only the Writing-Vocabulary and Reading-Grammar tests were administered to my research participants.

A subsequent study (Iwasaki 2010), however, revealed that such a restricted understanding of language proficiency concealed the more complex and multifaceted nature of the L2 learners' language development. Hence, in later studies (e.g. Iwasaki 2011a), aspects of language development that are not apparent in the test ratings/scores, yet are pertinent to social interaction, were examined. Below, these studies are summarized to illustrate the path this project has taken and to provide fuller descriptions of the participants' language use.

3.1 L2 Learners' priorities and outcomes (Iwasaki 2007)

This study examined whether learners' gains in language proficiency matched the priorities they articulated before studying abroad. Four learners – Greg, Henry,

---

1. Names are all pseudonyms. Peter did not participate in some post-SA assessments in 2003 and thus was not included in Iwasaki's (2007) study. Henry did not participate in the introspective interviews in early 2005 and thus was not included in Iwasaki's (2011b) study.

Alan, and Sam – completed all pre- and post- language proficiency assessments and questionnaires about their pre-study-abroad goals and post-study-abroad achievements (Iwasaki 2007). I refer to assessments before and after study abroad as pre-SA and post-SA henceforth. Two proficiency tests were administered: the OPI and the JLPT. As a certified OPI tester, I conducted both the pre-SA and post-SA OPIs.

Results indicated that their development as measured by the OPI and the JLPT largely matched their own priorities articulated in the pre-SA questionnaires. Alan, who rated the desire to develop his speaking/listening skills higher than his reading/writing skills, greatly advanced his speaking proficiency but did not improve as much in reading and vocabulary. He did not consider classroom learning to be as important as informal learning outside the classroom, and thus, he socialized with Japanese people actively. For him the best aspect of studying abroad was the friendships he established in Japan.

Henry considered using the language more important than acquiring knowledge such as vocabulary and *kanji* (Chinese characters). Upon returning to the U.S., he was relatively satisfied with his progress in speaking/listening but not in other areas such as reading/writing, vocabulary and *kanji*.

Greg and Sam both rated all skills and knowledge equally important at pre-SA. Both demonstrated substantive gains in all areas tested. Sam interacted with a variety of people in Japan by participating in the university glee club and a local church choir in addition to his interactions with his host mother. Greg also enjoyed his interactions with his host mother but was unhappy about not making friends. Consequently, he spent much of his time studying on his own to the extent that he felt his greatest gain was the development of his study skills.

All four participants predominantly spoke in the *desu/masu* style in the pre-SA OPI, but Greg and Henry spoke predominantly in the plain style in post-SA OPIs. Questions arose about how they "overused" plain forms and why.

3.2   L2 Learners' style shifting (Iwasaki 2010)

In order to elucidate the learners' use of speech styles, I examined their pre- and post-SA OPIs (Iwasaki 2010) quantitatively and qualitatively. This included OPI data from the four students above and Peter, who only participated in the OPI upon his return. In particular, I examined how they shifted between the two styles.

Textbooks generally introduce the distinctions between the plain and *desu/masu* forms as if there is a predetermined mapping between form and context/interlocutor (e.g. use the *desu/masu* style when speaking to a teacher). In practice, the choice of speech style is much more complex. In an interaction with the same interlocutor, L1 Japanese speakers shift between two styles to index their social identities and for other purposes such as soliloquy-like utterances, expressing empathy and providing subordinate information in the discourse (e.g. Cook 1999, 2006; Ikuta 1983; Maynard 1993; Okamoto 1999).

Upon returning, all five participants shifted their styles often in ways that align with the social meanings and functions of the style shifts reported in the literature. Table 2 shows the participants' OPI ratings and the proportions of *desu/masu* in the main predicates.

Table 2. Participants' language profiles

	Pre-SA OPI	Post-SA OPI	Pre-SA proportion of *desu/masu*	Post-SA proportion of *desu/masu*
Greg	Intermediate-Low	Intermediate-Mid	79%	10%
Henry	Intermediate-Mid	Intermediate-Mid	72%	20%
Alan	Intermediate-High	Advanced-Low	87%	86%
Sam	Intermediate-High	Advanced-Mid	84%	85%
Peter	Advanced-Low	Advanced-High	80%	70%

Greg and Henry predominantly used the plain forms during the post-SA OPI despite the fact that the speech style norm to address a (former) teacher is *desu/masu*, especially if she is clearly older. However, they used *desu/masu* when asking questions and in role-plays in which they made requests; they were able to use *desu/masu* and other honorific expressions with ease, suggesting their understanding of the social meanings of the forms.

3.3 L2 Learners' personal accounts of *desu/masu* use (Iwasaki 2011b)

To understand learners' own perceptions and experiences of their study abroad year and their learning of language varieties related to politeness, especially *desu/masu* (vs. plain forms), retrospective interviews were conducted in English in early 2005. L2 learners reported discovering that some L1 speakers neither abided by the Japanese norm when interacting with them nor expected them to adhere to the norm. In fact, participants reported that some L1 speakers expected them to be casual and laid back since they were American. Their responses also revealed that language taught in the U.S. diverged from the language used among male college students. For example, Sam observed that words designated as vulgar in the classroom were quite commonly used to express friendliness, intimacy and playfulness.

Moreover, Greg, Alan, and Sam felt some discomfort with the *desu/masu* form, feeling it would distance them from their interlocutors. This may be a result of cultural norms with which they are familiar. Displaying friendliness is important for expressing politeness in American English (Ide, Hill, Carnes, Ogino & Kawasaki 1992). Participants used different strategies to deal with this issue. While Greg opted to use the plain style as his default style, Alan and Sam were mindful of the importance of maintaining the use of *desu/masu* (at least when talking to older people), but tried to be friendly and polite at the same time. These learners' use of *desu/masu* or apparent overuse of plain forms upon their return can be construed as each learner's own creative response to these dilemmas and their struggles to index their social identities through these speech styles.

3.4   Other pragmatic devices: Fillers (Iwasaki 2011a) and hedges

Speech style choice is only one way to express a polite demeanor or index affective stance. The learners' creative ways of expressing politeness and friendliness are likely to involve other pragmatic devices as well. For instance, Greg mentioned, in the retrospective interview for the above study, that to be polite in Japanese is not to say certain impolite things. He says:

(1)   I think a lot of, in my experience, a lot of what's impolite in Japanese is what you don't say. So, for instance, you don't necessarily say, "I don't, I don't want that' or "I don't eat that". You say *"ano, chotto"*…

Both *ano* 'well' and *chotto* (lit. 'little/a bit') which Greg mentions here are quintessential politeness markers in Japanese.[2] *Ano* is a filler or hesitation marker often used for positive politeness by soliciting the listener's cooperation (Cook 1993), and *chotto* is a hedge used to qualify speech acts by "indicating that the degree of intensity of the speech act should be taken as small and that the speaker is assuming an attitude of being deferential, friendly, or less imposing, depending on the speech act" (Matsumoto 2001, p. 2). If we are interested in how L2 learners use language to socialize and to foster interpersonal relationships, we also need to examine these pragmatic devices.

For this reason, I examined learners' use of fillers (Iwasaki 2011a). Maynard (1989) discusses two types of fillers: language-production-based fillers, which speakers produce when "smooth communication is either cognitively or productively hindered" (p. 30) and socially motivated fillers. Speakers use socially motivated fillers to fill potential silence and avoid potential embarrassment, to

---

2.   There are several methods of Romanizing Japanese words. The Japanese word for 'little' is Romanized as *chotto* in the Hepburn method but *tyotto* in other methods. In this chapter I will primarily adopt the Hepburn method that generally follows an English spelling-phonology correspondence, except for the use of double letters for long vowels. Note, however, I use: for non-phonemic vowel lengthening.

show less certainty and hesitancy, or to give a less-imposing impression (p. 30–31). But because the term "motivated" may imply the speaker's conscious motivation for use of each filler, I used the expression "socially useful filler" when discussing L2 fillers that are judged by L1 raters as serving some social functions.

In post-SA OPIs, all learners used a variety of fillers that were socially useful in the given contexts. In example (2) below (Iwasaki 2011a, Example 14, p. 186), Sam is asked about his dorm room, and uses a variety of fillers to mitigate his negative assessment of the dorm.[3] 'I' is the interviewer. All fillers are in bold and those judged to have interpersonal functions are bolded and underlined.

(2)

1 I: *ano, ryoo wa donna tokoro desu ka.* 'Well, what is your dorm like?'
2 S: **<u>e:</u>** *chotto:: urusai desu.*
      F little   noisy   COP.AH.NONPAST
      '<u>uh</u>, it is.. a **bi:t** noisy.'

3 **<u>etto,</u>** *gakusee wa* **n** *gayagaya hanashite, hanashite iru,*
      F   student TOP F noisily   speak.GER speak.GER are
      hanashite iru   node,
      speak.GER are   because
      '<u>um</u>, because students are noisily speaking'

4 **<u>ano:</u>** **<u>nanka</u>** *paati shitari,* **<u>e:to</u>** *sakendari shite   iru node,*
      F   F   party do.such F   yell-such do.GER are because
      '**we:ll**, because they sort of have parties, and, **um** yell and such,'
      chotto benkyoo shinikui toki mo   arimasu.
      little study   do-hard time also exist.AH.NONPAST
      'At times, it is a bit difficult to study.'

In this excerpt, Sam used several fillers including drawls, and *ano,* which help to soften his criticism against his fellow dorm residents. Along with fillers, Sam used hedges, including *chotto.* The current study focuses on learners' hedges.

4. Hedges in L2 language learning

4.1 Hedges

The concept of *hedging* was popularized by Lakoff (1972), who defined hedges as "words whose job is to make things fuzzier or less fuzzy" (p. 195). English

---

3. The following notation is used for glosses: NOM nominative marker, ACC accusative, GEN genitive, DAT dative, LOC locative, TOP topic marker, GER gerund, Q question marker, QT quotative, NEG negative, COND conditional, PASS passive, COP copula, F filler, N nominalizer, SFP sentence final particle, AH addressee honorific, CL classifier.

hedges include *sort of, kind of, loosely speaking, more or less, relatively, somewhat,* and *rather* for the former type, and *technically, strictly speaking, very, especially* for the latter. However, in recent work, the definition of hedges has been limited to Lakoff's first type – words that make things fuzzier (e.g. Kaltenböck, Mihatsch & Scheider 2010).

According to Fraser (2010), the general agreement today is that "hedging is a rhetorical strategy, by which a speaker, using a linguistic device, can signal a lack of commitment to either the full semantic membership of an expression (PROPOSITIONAL HEDGING) ... or the full commitment to the force of the speech act being conveyed (SPEECH ACT HEDGING)" (p. 22). These categories seem to roughly correspond to other terms for classifying the functions of hedges: epistemic vs. affective or socioemotional (e.g. Dixon & Foster 1997; Stubbe & Holmes 1995) and propositional vs. interpersonal (Nittono 2004; Yamakawa 2007). Fraser (2010) underscores the significance of hedging, stating "When non-native speakers fail to hedge appropriately, they may be perceived as impolite, offensive, arrogant, or simply inappropriate" (p. 15).

Maynard (1989) states that Japanese speakers employ multiple rapport-creating linguistic and interactional devices in conversations, socially packaging their messages to protect the recipient's interpersonal emotions, build/maintain good rapport and create a buffer zone between two participants where the two parties' emotions and feelings are carefully monitored (p. 32). Hedges are undoubtedly among those devices that play significant roles in socially packaging messages and may play an important role in L2 learners' language.

Gender-related differences are found with regard to the use of hedges; some researchers reported that women use more hedges (e.g. Holmes 1995). But others found no effect of speaker gender (e.g. Dixon & Foster 1997) or only subtle differences (e.g. Stenström 2003). Stenström (2003) found that 13–17 year-old English-speaking girls in London used more hedges such as *like, just,* and *sort of* than boys. Similarly, as discussed below, Lauwereyns (2002) found that young Japanese females used hedges the most. Yet, pertinent to the current study, young males tended to use more hedges than older speakers.

Below, previous work on L2 speakers' hedges and on Japanese hedges is first summarized, followed by a presentation of the current study on hedges.

4.2   Hedges in L2

Many acknowledge hedges or mitigators to be important pragmatic devices (Skelton 1988) as downgraders in carrying out speech acts such as requests (House & Kasper 1981) and in disagreements and responses that may be dispreferred by the interlocutor (e.g. Pomerantz 1984).

Despite their importance, there is little L2 research focused on hedging (See also Fernandez in this volume about General Extenders in Spanish which can also be used as hedges). Woodfield and Economidou-Kogetsidis (2010) found that on Discourse Completion Tests (DCTs), L2 English learners tend not to use hedges such as "I wondered if I could…" as often as native speakers when making requests. In another study utilizing DCTs, Kreutel (2007) found that L2 English speakers did not use mitigating devices such as hedges (e.g. *I think, I thought, actually, maybe, well*) as often as L1 speakers. Similarly, in a study comparing opinion statements in interviews similar to the OPIs that I conducted (Iwasaki 2009), L2 Japanese learners often used the verb *to omou* '(I) think that' or its *desu/masu* form *to omoimasu* without any further modification, whereas Japanese speakers often used bundles of hedging devices to assert their opinions (e.g. *X n janai kana to omou n desu kedo ne* 'I would think that X might be the case, but, you know').

4.3   Hedges in Japanese

Researchers vary in which elements they consider to be hedges. Nittono (2004) examined a wide range of verbal and non-verbal aspects of communication that served to mitigate speech acts. She found that three quarters of hedges were lexical or phrasal, the majority of which were interactive particles such as *ne*, an agreement seeker. She then classified the functions of hedges as propositional (i.e. intending to convey accurate information) or interpersonal, with 80.4% of hedges being used for interpersonal purposes.

Lauwereyns (2002) defined hedges as "vague expressions whose meaning lexically represents uncertainty, possibility, tentativeness, and approximation" (p. 239). Based on her pilot study, she selected 26 Japanese target expressions. These included "utterance-final" expressions such as *toka* 'or something', *kamoshirenai* 'may; might', *kana* 'I wonder', *soo* 'seem; look like', *mitai; yoo* 'be like; look like' and *to omou* '(I) think that'; adverbial phrases such as *nanka* 'like', *toriaezu* 'for the time being; for now', *ichioo* 'generally, for the time being', *kekkoo* 'quite' and *tabun* 'probably, maybe'; a connective *teyuuka* 'or rather; or what should I say'; and noun suffixes such as *-ppoi* '-ish' and *-kurai/gurai* 'about; around'.

She examined the use of hedges among four groups of L1 speakers (i.e. young men and women aged 17–18, older men and women aged 59–69) and in two settings, informal (i.e. a conversation with a friend) and formal (i.e. an interview with someone they had just met for the first time). She found that younger groups, especially women, used more hedges.

Of interest to the current chapter are the different sets of hedges preferred by different age groups. The younger group used ten hedges significantly more often than older speakers (mean frequency per 1000 words in parentheses): *toka* 'or something' (20.04 vs. 4.96 among older speakers), *nanka* 'like' (11.67 vs. 2.48), *omou* '(I) think' (7.48 vs. 5.42), *kekkoo* 'quite, fairly' (2.92 vs. 1.02), *teyuuka* 'or rather' (2.44 vs. 1.25), *kanji* 'feel like, is like' (2.15 vs. 0.99), *toriaezu/ichioo* 'for now, tentatively' (1.36 vs. 0.41), *tabun/osoraku* 'perhaps' (1.05 vs. 0.04), *soo* 'seem; look like' (0.52 vs.0.01), and *ki ga suru* 'I've got a feeling' (0.43 vs. 0.14).

Lauwereyns' findings corroborate the oft-reported finding that young L1 Japanese speakers prefer vague language (Yonekawa 1995, 1998; Tsuji 1999a, 1999b). In particular, the most often discussed examples of vague language are the frequent use and extended functions of *nanka* and *toka* (Fukuhara 2008, 2009; Tsuji 1999a), and the innovative use of the pre-nominal form of *mitai,* namely, *mitaina,* in sentence-final position (Fujii 2006; Maynard 2004; Suzuki 1995). The following examples illustrate (a) conventional use of pre-nominal *mitaina,* (b) *mitai* in sentence-final position, and (c) innovative use of pre-nominal *mitaina* in the sentence-final position:

(a) *Atatakai! Haru **mitaina** tenki da.* 'It's warm! It's spring-like weather.'

(b) *Atatakai! Haru **mitai**.* 'It's warm! It is like spring.'

(c) *Atatakai! Are, ima nangatsu dakke **mitaina**.* 'It's warm! It's like, which month is it now?'

Young people's general use of vague language or their use of specific markers such as *mitaina* are variably attributed to their preference to avoid imposing on others and being imposed upon in interpersonal relationships (Tsuji 1999a, 1999b), as well as their playfulness and solidarity (Yonekawa 1995, 1998), and expressivity/ emotiveness (Fujii 2006; Maynard 2004; Suzuki 1995). The young speakers' use of these hedges likely reflects linguistic creativity as discussed by Maynard (2007). In addition, several scholars (e.g. Maynard 2007; Suzuki 1995) consider these Japanese young people's use of *mitaina* comparable to young English speakers' use of *like* (Anderson 2000; Tagliamonte & Hudson 1999).

It is important to note that L2 learners also creatively use language. For example, one of Siegal's (1994) participants, Sally, was compensating for her non-use/under-use of *desu/masu* by using *to omoimasu* '(I) think' (p. 335). A similar finding can be found in a study by Ikeda (2009), who, examining advanced L2 Japanese speakers' (albeit older ages of 20s-30s) honorific language, found that L2 speakers compensated for their underuse of honorific language by giving compliments and using hedges such as *ichioo* 'the time being' and *nanka*. Not only are fillers and hedges important in the target language, they may be particularly valued by L2 Japanese learners who may not want to rely on *desu/masu* or other honorifics because of the sense of distance or social hierarchy associated with these forms. This may be especially the case because their L1 Japanese peers favor the use of these hedges.

Interestingly, hedging also appears to be a hallmark of high proficiency. When Yamakawa (2007) examined a corpus of 50 OPIs consisting of 10 L1 speaker interviewees and 10 each of Novice, Intermediate, Advanced, and Superior L2 speakers, she found that only Superior-level L2 speakers used hedges as often as L1 speakers overall, and they were also the only ones who used them for interpersonal purposes just as often as L1 speakers do.

5.   Objectives and method of the study

The current study quantitatively examines the five L2 speakers' use of hedges, in the OPI data, specifically, their frequency of use and repertoire, to discover: (1) whether L2 learners increase their use of hedges and enrich their repertoire post-SA, (2) how often their hedges serve interpersonal functions pre- and post-SA, and (3) whether post-SA they incorporate more hedges which are often used by young L1 speakers. A qualitative analysis on their hedge use was also conducted.

Lauwereyns (2002) found that younger men tend to use more hedges than older men and women and that all groups used more hedges in interviews with the researcher than in chats with friends. This suggests that if they emulate their L1 peers, the young male participants in this study are likely to use many hedges in OPIs.

In addition, considering the importance of socializing with peers of the same age, *sociability* ratings by L1 Japanese college students of the learners' OPI segments were collected. L1 students rated the degree to which they desired to interact with the speaker of each speech segment. The frequency and types of hedges in each selected segment were tallied to see if they conform to each participant's overall use of hedges and to explore the possible relation between the use of hedges and the L1 students' judgments on sociability.

5.1   Participants, instrument and procedures

The participants are Greg, Henry, Alan, Sam and Peter, whose profiles, OPI ratings, and speech style choice are discussed in Section 3 above. The OPIs, excluding the mandatory role play segments, were examined. This is because the types of role-plays given to participants depend on their proficiency levels. With greater proficiency following SA, at their sojourn's end most participants did not perform the same types of role-plays given to them in the pre-test.

Adapting the method used by Freed (1995), two 45-second segments from each of the 5 participants' pre-SA and post-SA OPIs were selected midway through the OPIs for L1 college peer ratings. The segments were selected on the basis of ease of understanding the content without knowledge of the prior discourse and the amount of the L2 participants' utterances (i.e. minimal interviewer speech). A total of 20 selected segments were randomly ordered, and inserted into Power-point slides, one sound file per slide, with the topic under discussion given as the title of each slide (e.g. *daigaku sotsugyoogo* 'After I graduate from the university'). Two randomized orders were prepared. A data sheet with the title of each sound file and two scales of 1–7, including one for sociability, was prepared. Because this rating was used to assess how naïve L1 young speakers feel about L2 learners' utterances, no training was given. This was to avoid artificially leading participants to focus on certain aspects of utterances. Instead, they were instructed to give ratings based on *how* the L2 learners speak rather than *what* they say, because content such as shared interests might have affected the rating otherwise. At a university in Hyogo, 60 students with an average age of 21.3 years old were asked to rate the speaker of each sound file on the scales of sociability in two separate group sessions.

5.2   Analysis

Predicate-ending forms, except for the interactive particle *ne*, whose extensive use in Japanese requires a study in its own right (Watanabe & Iwasaki 2009), noun-ending forms such as *gurai* 'about' and adverbials used by the L2 learners that potentially function as hedges were tallied; two adverbs, *nanka* and *yappari*, which can be classified as either fillers or hedges are included in the current analysis as well as Iwasaki's (2011a) analysis of fillers. Moreover, some formulaic expressions *ki ga suru* 'I have a feeling' and phrases such as *hakkiri ienai n desu kedo* 'though I cannot say with confidence, but' were also tallied. These were all categorized as phrasal/formulaic expressions and thus considered to be the same type. Linguistic elements that were included in Nittono's (2004) and Yamakawa's (2007) studies but not included in this study are: connectives *kedo* and *ga* 'but', the extended predicate *n(o) da* 'it is that', sentence-final particle *ne* (unless part of phrasal hedges), and elements that are typically classified as fillers, *a/aa* 'ah', *ano(o)/ma(a)* 'well'. The total number of tokens and types were tallied, and the number of tokens used per minute was computed to determine the frequency of hedges used by each L2 learner.

Special attention was paid to the L2 learners' use of the hedges used frequently by young Japanese speakers: *toka* 'or something' (used either in noun-ending or sentence-ending positions), *nanka* 'somehow/well/like', *omou* '(I) think', *tari/tari suru* 'do …and such', *soo* 'seem; look like', and *tabun/osoraku* 'perhaps', as well as an innovative use of pre-nominal *mitaina* 'like' as a sentence-final particle. The number of these hedges used by each participant pre- and post-SA were tallied.

Attempts were made to code each hedge by its primary function as propositional, interpersonal, or ambiguous. Note, however, that the coding is rather problematic due to the inherent ambiguity of the meanings of potential hedges whose meanings rely on various factors, as Fraser (2010) puts it:

> The effect of hedging is found in the interpretation of the utterance rather than in the semantic meaning of the sentence uttered, where the interpretation depends on the context of utterance, the semantic meaning of sentence uttered, the particular hedge(s) used, and the belief system of the hearer (p. 25).

Moreover, seemingly distinctive functions are actually not mutually exclusive and both functions can coexist; thus the category "ambiguous/unclear" becomes necessary, as was the case in other studies, e.g. Dixon & Foster 1997. Along with the hedges whose statuses are dual, those that have other functions (e.g. use of *chotto* 'a little' either as a propositional or interpersonal hedge; *nanka* as an interpersonal hedge or production-based filler) are classified as ambiguous/ unclear. The judgment for coding is bound to be somewhat subjective, but the use of an "ambiguous" category offers a way to deal with these problems.

To illustrate the coding, examples are given from the 4th line of Sam's utterance in (1) above, repeated below with all hedges bolded and interpersonal hedges bolded and underlined. Note that the functions of English hedges used in the translation may not exactly correspond to the functions of the Japanese hedges, but the English equivalents are bolded to help non-Japanese-speaking readers understand the examples.

(3)   *ano:* **_nanka_** *paati shitari,   e:to   sakendari siteiru node,*
      F   F   party do.such   F   yell.such do.GER are because
      'we:ll, because they have parties, and, um yell **and such**,'

      chotto *benkyoo   shinikui   **toki mo arimasu.***
      little   study   do.hard   time also exist.AH.NONPAST
      '**At times**, it is **a bit** difficult to study.'

In the above, *nanka* 'somehow' and *chotto* 'a bit' were judged as interpersonal, *-tari, -dari* 'such as' were propositional, and *toki mo arimasu* 'there is also time at which...' were rated as ambiguous. Sam probably meant the noise problem arises occasionally (i.e. propositional), but this expression with *mo* 'also' (rather than *toki ga arimasu* 'there is time at which....') substantially tones down his criticism. Specifically, by using *mo*, Sam implies that there are also times when such problems do not occur.

In the qualitative analysis, how L2 speakers achieve social packaging (Maynard 1989) was examined. Because the constellation of various pragmatic devices together serves social goals, the pragmatic devices that were not tallied in the quantitative analysis are also considered in the qualitative analysis.

6. Findings

6.1 Frequency, repertoire, and interpersonal hedges

It was found that all five L2 Japanese learners increased their use and repertoire of forms potentially used for hedging. Tables 3 and 4 show the number of tokens and types of hedges used by the five L2 learners in the pre-SA OPI and post-SA OPI, respectively. The percentages of interpersonal hedges indicate the proportion of hedges that primarily serve interpersonal functions among all hedges. The learners used twice as many types of hedges post-SA: an average of 8.8 types (ranging from 6 to 13) pre-SA and 17.6 types (ranging from 13 to 21) post-SA.

They also used more than twice as many tokens of hedges post-SA: an average of 37.8 tokens (ranging from 17 to 61) pre-SA and 89.2 tokens (ranging from 62 to 134 tokens) post-SA. Though the much larger number of post-SA tokens was partly due to the amount of speech in the post-SA OPI, the number of tokens per 100 morphemes also increased from an average of 1.44 tokens per 100 morphemes (ranging from 1.22 to 1.63) to 2.67 (ranging from 2.05 to 3.33).[4] The proportions of interpersonal hedges clearly increased among those who used (relatively) small numbers of interpersonal hedges pre-SA (Greg 5.9% to 29.0%, Henry 7.7% to 40%, and Sam 15.2% to 51.6%), but did not increase among those who used many interpersonal hedges to start with (i.e. Alan and Peter) whose percentages of interpersonal hedges were as high as 46.2% and 31.8% pre-SA. Because one needs to use hedges to express propositional meanings (e.g. to express approximation of quantity) as well, it is not surprising that Alan and Peter, who frequently used interpersonal hedges at pre-SA OPI did not increase the proportions of interpersonal hedges at post-SA OPI.

Table 3. Number of tokens and types of hedges pre-SA

	Type	Token	per 100 morphemes	Prop	Interpersonal	Ambiguous	Interpersonal %
Greg	6	17	1.27	7	1	9	5.9%
Henry	6	26	1.33	20	2	4	7.7%
Alan	12	52	1.53	23	24	5	46.2%
Sam	7	33	1.22	16	5	12	15.2%
Peter	13	61	1.63	31	21	14	31.8%
Mean	8.8	37.8	1.44	19.4	10.6	8.8	27.3%

---

4. Morphemes are a more appropriate unit of analysis than words for Japanese since what counts as a word is not very clear. In this computation of hedges per 100 morphemes, only meaningful morphemes are considered. For example, repetitions and repairs were excluded.

Table 4. Number of tokens and types of hedges post-SA

	Type	Token	per 100 morphemes	Prop	Interpersonal	Ambiguous	Interpersonal %
Greg	16	69	3.17	41	20	8	29.0%
Henry	18	65	2.54	26	26	13	40.0%
Alan	20	116	2.37	50	37	29	31.9%
Sam	13	62	2.05	20	32	10	51.6%
Peter	21	134	3.33	63	39	33	28.9%
Mean	17.6	89.2	2.67	40	30.8	18.6	34.5%

6.2 L1 Peers' ratings on sociability

Next, I examined whether and to what extent the participants sounded socially desirable. The frequency of use, types of hedges, and the ways in which they are used are likely to contribute to this, as well as the L2 speakers' overall proficiency. Table 5 shows the total number of hedges used in the two 45-second sound file segments and the mean sociability ratings for each segment. These counts are provided because sound files were not selected to represent each participant's profile of hedge use. The sound segments of Peter, the most frequent user of hedges, contain more hedges than other participants' segments, but the numbers of hedges used by the other participants are not necessarily parallel to each participant's overall use, as displayed in Tables 3 and 4.

Table 5. Hedges in the sound segments and sociability ratings

	Hedges in 45 sec × 2 segments		Sociability ratings		
	Pre-SA	Post-SA	Pre-SA	Post-SA	Increase
Greg	3	2	2.86	3.13	0.27
Henry	2	1	2.81	3.41	0.6
Alan	4	5	3.93	5.41	1.48
Sam	2	5	4	4.67	0.67
Peter	5	13	4.31	5.06	0.75

Alan and Peter, who used many interpersonal hedges pre-SA, were rated high on sociability, and Greg and Henry, who did not use many (interpersonal) hedges pre-SA, were rated low. The gains in the sociability ratings do not necessarily correspond to changes in the numbers of hedges used in the sound segment.

This may underscore the fact that sociability is realized as the constellation of various aspects of speech/interaction in which hedging also plays a part. Thus, the analysis of which hedges L2 learners used and how they used them along with other pragmatic devices is necessary to understand how sociability ratings came about.

In the next section I examine how often the five participants use hedges that are often used by young L1 speakers. Then I focus on two L2 speakers, Alan and Peter, who used hedges frequently (2.37 and 3.33 tokens per 100 morphemes, respectively)[5] and who were rated by L1 Japanese-speaking students as highly desired interlocutors. I examine both the qualitative data and their use of hedges.

6.3   Hedges frequently used by young speakers

Among the hedges that younger speakers were found to use significantly more often than the older age group (Lauwereyns 2002), *teyuuka* 'or rather,' *osoraku* 'perhaps,' *ichioo* 'for now,' and *soo* 'seem' were not used by the participants. In Table 6 the other hedges used often by young people, *toka* 'or something,' *nanka* 'like,' *omou* 'think,' *kekkoo* 'fairly, quite,' *kanji* 'feel like, is like,' *tabun* 'perhaps,' *toriaezu* 'for now,' *ki ga suru* 'I've got a feeling,' and an oft-reported sentence-final hedge, *mitaina* 'like' are listed first, followed by other hedges used by many of the participants – *tari/tari suru* 'do… and such,' *chotto* 'little,' *amari*+negative 'not very,' *gurai* 'about,' *mitai* 'seems like,' *kamo shirenai* 'may/might,' and *kana* 'I wonder.' Table 6 shows how many of these hedges each participant used in the pre- and post-SA OPIs, while the increase in the raw numbers for L1 young speakers' preferred hedges and other hedges, respectively, is in parentheses.

Table 6 reveals drastic differences across individuals. Greg and Sam's increase in the use of hedges preferred by young L1 speakers was minimal (+12 and +9, respectively), while the other three participants substantively increased their "youthful" hedge use. These increases are somewhat compatible with their reports on who they primarily interacted with: Greg with his host mother, Sam with his host family and neighborhood church choir members (but also the university glee club members), Alan and Henry with friends, and Peter with his fellow kendo club members.

---

5.   Alan's use of hedges per 100 morphemes post-SA is lower than Greg's and Henry's, but this is partly due to his very frequent use of the filler *ano* 'well' (a total of 190 or 3.87 tokens per 100 morphemes in the post-SA OPI), which was considered as a meaningful morpheme, and not as hedge, in the current analysis.

Table 6. L2 Participants' use of L1 young speakers preferred hedges

	Pre-SA					Post-SA				
	Greg	Henry	Alan	Sam	Peter	Greg	Henry	Alan	Sam	Peter
toka	0	2	3	0	1	1	8	2	2	19
nanka	0	0	0	0	0	0	8	1	7	25
omou	7	9	6	9	5	7	15	11	9	9
kekkoo	0	0	0	0	0	7	2	0	0	2
kanji	0	0	0	0	0	0	1	3	0	2
tabun	1	1	0	0	5	5	5	23	0	3
toriaezu	0	0	0	0	0	0	0	1	0	0
ki ga suru	0	0	0	0	0	0	0	0	0	2
mitaina	0	0	0	0	0	0	0	1	0	3
tari/tari	2	1	0	9	0	2	2	2	5	13
chotto	1	1	10	8	12	12	3	8	8	11
amari neg	4	6	11	3	11	6	10	19	8	10
gurai	2	5	2	0	2	10	2	10	5	5
mitai	0	0	1	0	1	4	0	3	3	4
kamo shirenai	0	0	2	2	6	0	2	3	1	2
kana	0	0	0	0	0	1	0	6	0	1
Total youth	8	12	9	9	11	20 (+12)	39 (+27)	42 (+33)	18 (+9)	65 (+54)
Total others[6]	9	14	43	24	50	49 (+40)	27 (+13)	75 (+32)	44 (+20)	69 (+19)

6.4 Qualitative analyses: Social packaging

Alan and Peter were the most frequent users of hedges, but obviously using more hedges does not necessarily translate to a more highly developed language competence. Hence, it is imperative to examine how they actually used hedges. The qualitative analysis revealed that both Alan and Peter were generally very cautious when stating their opinions. They provide buffer zones to accommodate their interlocutor (i.e. the interviewer).

---

6. These totals include all other hedges not listed in the table.

When asked about how American and Japanese families differ, Alan states that whereas children in American families are encouraged to be independent as soon as they grow up, those in Japanese families are not. In Line 1 of Excerpt (4), which is part of a post-SA sound segment, he concludes his opinion using *omoimasu* 'I think.' Below, hedges are in bold, and hedges coded as interpersonal are also underlined. Glosses are not provided for the interviewer's utterances.

(4)

1 A: *de,   are   wa,   sono   kodomo   ga   nijuugo-sai   demo   mada*
       and   that   TOP   F   child   NOM   25-years.old COP.even   still

       isshoni   sunde   imasu.
       together   live   is.AH.NONPAST

       'and, that is, even if a child is 25 years old, they still live together with their family'

2   *Sugoku,   ano: kazoku   ga   ano   taisetsu   **tte koto da***
       extremely   F   family   NOM   F   important Q   N   COP

       to   omoimasu.
       COMP   think.AH.NONPAST

       '**I think it means** that families are extremely, uh, important.'

3 I: *sono koto ni tsuite wa,* [ ] 'With regard to that,

4 A: [*un*] 'uh-huh

5 I: *ano nihon no hoo, nihon-tekina kazoku no hoo ga ii to omoimashita ka.*
       'Did you think that Japanese, Japanese style families are better?'

       …

21 I: *Jibun no koto ga chanto dekiru yoo ni naru to iu koto wa nihon no kazoku dewa muzukashii to iu koto desu ka?*
       'Do you mean it is difficult for one to become independent in the Japanese style families?'

22 A: *a: soo desu ka:*
       ah so COP Q 'ah, is that so?'

23   ***tabun***   *sonna* ***koto*** ***mo*** ***nai***   *to*   *omoimasu.*
       perhaps   such   thing   also   NEG   COMP   think.AH.NONPAST
       'I think **perhaps** that is **not really** the case.'

24   ***tabun*** *amerika   no   ii   ten   wa,   ano: n: a: so:*
       perhaps   America   GEN   good   point TOP   F   umm   ah   well

       yoku   wakarimasen   ne: [laughter]
       know.   AH.NEG.   NONPAST   SFP

       '**Perhaps** good aspects of American families are, well, um, ah: **I don't quite know, you know.**'

25 *nani ga   yoku-nai   tte kiitara,*   **tabun**   *nihon dewa,*
    what NOM good-NEG Q ask.COND perhaps Japan LOC.TOP

    ano n:
    F   F

    'If one asks what is not good (about it), **perhaps** in Japan, well:'

26 *ano n: nto mondai   wa   ano amerika dewa   sono*
    F   F F problem TOP F   America LOC.TOP F

    nihon-tekina   kazoku dewa
    Japanese-style family GER.TOP

27 **tabun**   *hatarakenai*   *to*   *omoimasu.*
    perhaps work.potential.NEG COMP think.AH.NONPAST

    [Lines 26–27] 'Well, the problem is, um, in America, um Japanese
    style families **perhaps** would not work, I think.'

28 *Amerika dewa*   **anmari** *yaranai ko,*   **anmari** *nanimo*
    America LOC.TOP very   do.NEG   child very   anything

    yaranai ko   mo   ite
    do.NEG   also exist. GER

    'In America, there are also children who **don't really** do, who **don't
    really** do anything,'

29 *ano: jibun   no,   jibun   no   koto o   shinasai*
    well oneself GEN oneself GEN thing ACC do.IMPERATIVE

    tte   iwarenakattara,
    COMP say.PASS.COND

30 **tabun**   *30-sai   made demo,   ano: uchi ni   suwatte*
    perhaps 30-years.old until COP.even well home LOC sit

31 *nanimo   yaranai ko   mo   iru   to   omoimasu.*
    anything do-NEG   child also exist COMP think AH.NONPAST

    [Lines 29–31] 'I **think** maybe there are also children who would sit
    around at home without doing anything even until they are 30 years
    old, um, unless they are told "do your things yourself".'

In Line 2, Alan makes a statement about the Japanese family based on his
observations. His use of *tte koto da to omoimasu* is very effective here. Because he is
making a statement about a topic related to Japan as an observer while addressing
an interviewer from Japan, a definitive statement without *omoimasu* would sound
too assertive. Moreover, he hedges his opinion further by embedding '(it) means'
(covert 'it' refers to what he observed, i.e. that some people live with their families at
the age of 25), resulting in the sequence "I think it means…". Although he expressed

his somewhat positive views between Lines 6 and 20 (for which hedging is not as important and thus omitted here) when he was asked whether he thinks that the Japanese way is better (Line 5), in Line 21 the interviewer provided a slightly contentious summary of what he suggested prior to Line 1. Alan responded again with a number of hedges including numerous uses of *tabun* and *omoimasu*, and a phrasal mitigator "if one asks what might not be good (with the Japanese way)." He also uses *tabun* to hedge his negative assessment of American youth. His use of *mo* 'also' hedges his statement in Line 31 that there are also children who would not be able to take care of themselves, by suggesting there are also other independent children (who do not need to be told to be independent). The adverb *tabun* is one of the most frequently used hedges among young Japanese speakers, who are said to be "fearful of making assertive statements and who appear to structure their speech so as to avoid saying anything definitively" (Maynard 2007, p. 125, citing Tawara 1999) as well. In the case of Alan, considering the situation at hand (the nature of the topic and the interlocutor), his seemingly excessive use of *tabun* is more desirable than not using *tabun* at all. Regardless of whether L1 speakers use *tabun* in a similar way, his use of *tabun* can be construed as one of the ways he socially packages his messages.

In Excerpt (5), Lines 1 through 7, which were part of the sound segments that L1 peers rated, Peter hedges his negative assessment of his own experience (i.e. the reason why he could not fully take advantage of the kendo club). He often uses *nanka* 'somehow/well/like'.

(5)

1 I: *Kurabu wa yapari ii benkyoo ni narimashita ka?*
'Did you learn a great deal by participating in the club?'

2 P: *N: kurabu wa   soo datta   n desu kedomo,*
F club   TOP so   COP.PAST N COP but
'Yes, that was the case with the club, but,'

3 **Nanka** *[university name] no   kendo-bu   tte iu   to*
well univ.name   GEN kendo-club Q say COND
'**well**, in the case of the X university's kendo club,'

4 *Senpai koohai no   kankei   wa   sugoku kibishikute*
senior junior GEN relationship TOP terribly strict.GER
'the senior-junior relationship was terribly strict and'

5 **Nanka** *itsu joodan, dono, dono kurai ni joodan shi**tari**, ason**dari***
somehow when joke which which extent to joke do.such play.such
shitemo daijoobu ka
do.even ok Q

6   *anmari* wakaranakatta   *n desu*   *kara,*
    really understand-NEG-PAST   N COP.AH.NONPAST   because

7   *nanka* rirakkusu shite minna to asobu koto wa **amari** dekinakatta.
    somehow relax do.GER everyone with play N TOP really can.NEG.PAST

[Lines 5–7] 'Somehow I <u>could not really</u> tell when and to what
extent it was okay to joke **or** play, and so <u>**somehow**</u> I could **not really**
relax and play with everyone.'

8 I: *Sore wa hajime kara saigo made soo deshita ka.*
     'Was it like that from the beginning to the end?'

9 P: *Soo desu*   *ne. Saigo made, n:*
     SO COP.AH.NONPAST SFP   end   UNTIL F
     'Yeah, until the end… hmm,'

10   *nantonaku wa*   *wakaru*   *yoo ni*   *natte kita*   **ki**
    somehow   TOP understand DAT become come feeling NOM

    ga shita *n desu*   *kedo*
    do. PAST N COP.AH.NONPAST but

    'I **felt** that I started to understand it **at least somehow**, but'

11   *Ma sore wa   kaeranakyaikenai tokoro datta   node*
    F   that TOP leave.must   point COP.PAST because

    chotto *osokatta.*
    bit   late.PAST

'well that was the time I had to leave and it was **a bit** too late.'

He describes the difficulty he experienced with multiple uses of the hedge
nanka 'somehow'. He then states in Line 10 that he started to understand the
club culture (i.e. when to joke and be playful) by using a number of pragmatic
devices: *nantonaku wa* wakaru yoo ni natte kita *ki ga shita* n desu kedo. He used
nantonaku with the delimiter *wa* 'at least' and *ki ga suru* 'I got a feeling that…'.
The function of his use of these hedges can be construed as propositional (i.e.
a lack of certainty and confidence that he really understood the club culture),
which conveys a foreign student's struggle to understand Japanese culture. At
the same time, regardless of whether his intended meaning was genuinely lack
of certainty, he likely accommodates a possible expectation and value of L1
Japanese speakers (e.g. Japanese speakers generally describe their achievements modestly, without bragging and by not confidently declaring them). It is
quite plausible that he emulated the language use of Japanese speakers' around
him. His use of *nanka* may be considered by some as overuse, but such is the
case with many young speakers' use of *nanka* from the point of view of older
speakers.

Peter also used the sentence-final *mitaina* 'like', which Maynard (2007, p.124) considers as similar to the English quotative *like* (Anderson 2000). It was primarily associated with young speakers' language in the early 1990s, but has spread to older adults in recent years. Maynard notes that young people use this expression to enhance a sense of group solidarity.

Prior to Excerpt (6), Peter talked about a part-time job that he was about to start but he did not like – calling alumni and soliciting donations from them. He mentioned that it would be all right if he did not worry about the reactions of the alumni. He describes how he would try not to be bothered, using *mitaina*.

(6)

1   I: *Ja, aite no taido toka wa anmari ki ni shinai [koto ni...*
      'Then you would just not to worry...'

2   P: *[Ki ni shinai tte   iu to,*
      mind DAT   do.NEG Q say
      'By saying not minding,'

3   *nanka aite   ga   okottara,   nanka   jibun toshite*
      well partner NOM get.angry.COND somehow self   as

      okotte iru   n janakute
      get.angry-GER N COP.NEG.GER

      '**well**, if the other party gets angry, **uh**, they are not angry towards me and'

4   *Tada taimingu ga   warui toka*
      merely timing   NOM bad   something.like
      'it is just that the timing is bad **or something like that**'

5   *De, **betsu-ni**   henji   shinakute   ii,   **mitaina**.*
      So particularly respond do-NEG-GER alright like
      'So **it is like**, it is okay **not really** to respond,'

6   I: *A: soo desu ka.* 'I see.'

7   P: *Kedo, aite   okotte   mo,*
      but   partner get.angry.GER even.if
      'But even if the other party gets angry,'

8   *be, **betsu-ni**   jibun-ni wa   kamawanai n desu yo,   **mitaina**.*
      Par particularly self-DAT TOP care-NEG   N COP SFP like
      '**it's like,** I **don't really** care myself.'

Citing Tawara (1999), Maynard (2007: 125) explains that the use of *mitaina* effectively distances the speaker from the content of the speech and that the speaker offers information in a tentative way while observing how their partner responds. Such attitudes as "I don't need to bother to respond to the other party (if he is angry)" or "I don't care", effective in dealing with annoyed call receivers, are not desirable for one to declare unless the speaker displays it through distancing himself from them, as attitudes he would temporarily adopt.

7. Discussion and conclusion

The quantitative analysis revealed that all learners drastically increased the repertoire and frequency of hedges after they had studied abroad. This increase in hedge use can be attributed to many factors. While the inventory of hedges introduced in textbooks is limited, the learners had undoubtedly been exposed to an abundant use of hedges among L1 speakers with whom they interacted. Some of the learners may have found hedges as (alternative) devices for being polite, especially if they did not feel comfortable with *desu/masu*.

The qualitative analyses of the most frequent hedge users, Alan and Peter, showed that they use hedges effectively to socially package their messages. Hedges appear to play a significant role in their capacities to interact with an interlocutor socially and interpersonally, although we cannot attribute such capacities solely to (the number of) hedges. This is because how they use hedges also matters for desired social packaging: i.e. which hedge to use, when to use them, and what other devices to use along with hedges. Alan and Peter used hedges that are often used by young speakers, such as *nanka, tabun* and *mitaina*, reflecting their peers' use of hedges. By doing so, they may also project their identities as young adult speakers, which their peers might appreciate.

The current data only involve one interlocutor in an OPI setting; thus, we do not know whether these learners' uses of hedges (e.g. their choice of hedges and frequency) are context sensitive. To further our knowledge of L2 acquisition of hedging, a question worth investigating in future research is how L2 learners use hedges in different contexts (formal interviews versus informal chats) and with different types of interlocutors (teachers versus age peers). Lauwereyns (2002), for example, found that five hedges such as *omou* 'think,' *tari/tari suru* 'do … and such' were more often used in interviews. There were only two hedges that were more often used in chats, namely *ka nanka* 'or something' and *so* 'seems', but these were used rather infrequently even in chats, with the rate of 0.50 and 0.52 out of 1000 words, respectively.

On the surface, hedges may seem meaningless, but in fact they are valuable resources in socially oriented communication. L2 Japanese learners, who find themselves uncomfortable with honorific language and somewhat resistant to it, may find hedges useful resources for creating polite language without the connotation of distance and social hierarchy associated with the honorific language system.

References

Anderson, G. (2000). *Pragmatic markers and sociolinguistic variation*. Amsterdam: John Benjamins.

Block, D. (2003). *The social turn in second language acquisition*. Washington, DC: Georgetown University Press.

Block, D. (2009). *Second language identities*. London: Continuum.

Cook, H.M. (1993). Functions of the filler *ano* in Japanese. In S. Choi (Ed.), *Japanese/Korean Linguistics* (pp. 19–38). Stanford, CA: CSLI.

Cook, H.M. (1999). Situational meanings of Japanese social deixis: The mixed use of the 'masu' and plain forms. *Journal of Linguistic Anthropology, 8*, 87–110.

Cook, H.M. (2006). Japanese politeness as an interactional achievement: Academic consultation sessions in Japanese universities. *Multilingua, 25*, 269–292.

Cook, H.M. (2008). *Socializing identities through speech style: Learners of Japanese as a foreign language*. Bristol, U.K.: Multilingual Matters.

DeKeyser, R. (1991). The semester overseas: What difference does it make? *Association of Departments of Foreign Languages (ADFL) Bulletin, 22*(2), 42–48.

Dewey, D.P. (2004). A comparison of reading development by learners of Japanese in intensive domestic immersion and study abroad contexts. *Studies in Second Language Acquisition, 26*, 303–327.

Dewey, D.P. (2007). Japanese vocabulary acquisition by learners in three contexts. *Frontiers: The Interdisciplinary Journal of Study Abroad, 15*, 127–148.

Dixon, J.A., & Foster, D.H. (1997). Gender and hedging: From sex differences to situated practice. *Journal of Psycholinguistic Research, 26*, 89–107.

Fraser, B. (2010). Pragmatic competence: the case of hedging. In G. Kaltenböck, W. Mihatsch, & S. Scheider (Eds.), *New approaches to hedging* (pp. 15–34). Bingley, UK: Emerald.

Freed, B. (1995). What makes us think that students who study abroad become fluent? In B. Freed (Ed.), *Second language acquisition in a study abroad context* (pp. 123–148). Amsterdam: Johns Benjamins.

Fujii, S. (2006). Quoted thought and speech using the *mitai-na* 'be like' noun-modifying construction. In S. Suzuki (Ed.) *Emotive communication in Japanese* (pp. 53–95). Amsterdam: Johns Benjamins.

Fukuhara, Y. (2008). *Wakamono kotoba no feisu waaku: feisu hoji ni kakawaru disukoosu maakaa no koosatsu* [Young people's face work: Discourse markers related to face maintenance]. Unpublished doctoral dissertation, Tohoku University, Sendai, Japan.

Fukuhara, Y. (2009). Kaiwa ni mirareru 'nanka' no kino kakutyoo: feisu waaku no kanten kara [Expansion of the functions of 'nanka' in conversation: From the perspective of facework]. *Kokusaibunka Kenkyuu [International Culture Studies], 15*, 131–195.

Holmes, J. (1995). *Women, men and politeness*. London: Longman.

House, J. & Kasper, G. (1981). Politeness markers in English and German. In F. Coulmas (Ed.), *Conversational routine: Explorations in standardized communication situations and prepatterned speech* (pp. 157–185). The Hague: Mouton.

Huebner, T. (1995). The effects of overseas language programs: Report on a case study of an intensive Japanese course. In B.F. Freed (Ed.), *Second language acquisition in a study abroad context* (pp. 171–193). Amsterdam: John Benjamins.

Ide, S, Hill, B., Carnes, Y.M., Ogino, T., & Kawasaki, A. (1992). The concept of politeness: An empirical study of American English and Japanese. In R.J. Watts, S. Ide, & K. Ehlich (Eds.), *Politeness in language: Studies in its history, theory and practice* (pp. 281–297). Berlin: Mouton de Gruyter.

Iino, M. (1999). Language use and identity: An ethnographic study of dinner table conversations between Japanese host families and American students. In L.F. Bouton (Ed.), *Pragmatics and Language Learning* (Vol. 9) (pp. 129–162). Urbana-Champaign, Ill.: University of Illinois, Urbana- Champaign, Division of English as an International Language.

Iino, M. (2006). Norms of interaction in a Japanese homestay setting: Toward a two-way flow of linguistic and cultural resources. In M.A. DuFon & E. Churchill (Eds.), *Language learners in study abroad contexts,* (pp. 151–173). Clevedon, U.K.: Multilingual Matters.

Ikeda, K. (2009). Advanced learners' honorific styles in emails and telephone calls. In N. Taguchi (Ed.), *Pragmatic competence* (pp. 69–100). Berlin: Mouton de Gruyter.

Ikuta, S. (1983). Speech level shift and conversational strategy in Japanese discourses. *Language Science, 5,* 37–53.

Iwasaki, N. (2007). Assessing progress towards advanced level Japanese after a year abroad: Focus on individual learners. *Japanese Language and Literature,* 41, 271–296.

Iwasaki, N. (2009). Stating opinions in an interview: L1 and L2 Japanese speakers. *Foreign Language Annals, 43,* 541–556.

Iwasaki, N. (2010). Style shifts among Japanese learners before and after study abroad in Japan: Becoming active social agents in Japanese. *Applied Linguistics, 31,* 45–71.

Iwasaki, N. (2011a). Filling social space with fillers: gains in social dimension after studying abroad. *Journal of Japanese Language and Literature, 45,* 169–193.

Iwasaki, N. (2011b). Learning L2 Japanese politeness and 'impoliteness': Young American men's dilemmas during study abroad. *Journal of Japanese Language and Literature, 45,* 67–106.

Jackson, J. (2008). *Language, identity and study abroad: Sociocultural perspectives.* London: Equinox.

Kaltenböck, G., Mihatsch, W., & Scheider, S. (Eds.) (2010). *New approaches to hedging.* Bingley, UK: Emerald.

Kinginger, C. (2008). Language learning in study abroad: Case studies of Americans in France. *Modern Language Journal, 92,* Monograph.

Kreutel, K. (2007). "I'm not agree with you." ESL Learners' expressions of disagreement. *TESL-EJ, 11(3),* 1–35.

Lakoff, G. (1972). Hedges: A study in meaning criteria and the logic of fuzzy concepts. In P. Peranteau, J. Levi, & G. Phares (Eds.), *Papers from the Eighth Regional Meeting of the Chicago Linguistic Society* (pp. 183–228). Chicago IL: CLS.

Lauwereyns, S. (2002). Hedges in Japanese conversation: The influence of age, sex, and formality. *Language Variation and Change, 14,* 239–259.

Marriott, H. (1995). The acquisition of politeness patterns by exchange students in Japan. In B.F. Freed (Ed.), *Second language acquisition in a study abroad context* (pp.197–224). Amsterdam: John Benjamins.

Matsumoto, Y. (2001). Tyotto: Speech act qualification in Japanese revisited. *Japanese Language and Literature, 35,* 1–16.

Maynard, S.K. (1989). *Japanese conversation: Self-contextualization through structure and interactional management.* New York, NY: Ablex.

Maynard, S.K. (1993). *Discourse modality: Subjectivity, emotion, and voice in the Japanese language*. Amsterdam: John Benjamins.

Maynard, S.K. (2004). Another conversation: Expressivity of mitaina and inserted speech in Japanese discourse. *Journal of Pragmatics, 37*, 837–869.

Maynard, S.K. (2007). *Linguistic creativity in Japanese discourse: Exploring the multiplicity of self, perspective and voice*. Amsterdam: John Benjamins.

Nittono, M. (2004). Hedge no katachi to sono kinoo: Yuujin-kan no kaiwa ni miru [The form and function of hedges: Seen in conversations among friends]. In M. Minami & M. Asano (Eds.), *Gengogaku to Nihongo Kyoiku* (Vol. 3) (pp. 287–304). Tokyo: Kurosio.

Ochs, E. (1993). Constructing social identity: A language socialization perspective. *Research on Language and Social Interaction, 26*, 287–306.

Okamoto, S. (1999). Situated politeness: Manipulating honorific and non- honorific expressions in Japanese conversations. *Pragmatics, 9,* 51–74.

Pomerantz, A. (1984). Agreeing and disagreeing with assessments: some features of preferred/ dispreferred turn shapes. In J.M. Atkinson & J. Heritage (Eds.), *Structure of social action: Studies in conversation analysis* (pp. 57–101). Cambridge: Cambridge University Press.

Siegal, M. (1994). *Learning Japanese as a second language in Japan and the interaction of race, gender and social context*. Unpublished doctoral dissertation, University of California, Berkeley.

Siegal, M. (1995). Individual differences and study abroad: Women learning Japanese in Japan. In B.F. Freed (Ed.), *Second language acquisition in a study abroad context* (pp. 197–224). Amsterdam: John Benjamins.

Siegal, M. (1996). The role of learner subjectivity in second language socio-linguistic competency: Western women learning Japanese. *Applied Linguistics, 17,* 356–382.

Skelton, J. (1988). The care and maintenance of hedges. *ELT Journal, 42,* 37–43.

Stenström, A.-B. (2003). It's not that I really care about him personally you know: The construction of gender identity in London teenage talk. In J. K. Androutsopoulos, & A. Georgakopoulou (Eds.), *Discourse constructions of youth identities* (pp. 93–118). Amsterdam: John Benjamins.

Stubbe, M. & Holmes, J. (1995). You know, eh and other 'exasperating expressions': An analysis of social and stylistic variation in the use of pragmatic devices in a sample of New Zealand English. *Language and Communication, 15,* 63–88.

Suzuki, S. (1995). A study of the sentence-final *mitai na. Journal of Association of Teachers of Japanese, 29* (2), 55–78.

Tagliamonte, S. & Hudson, R. (1999). Be like et al. beyond America: The quotative system in British and Canadian youth. *Journal of Sociolinguistics, 3,* 147–172.

Tawara, M. (1999). *Kotoba no mushimegane* [Magnifying glass of language]. Tokyo: Kadokawa Shoten.

Tsuji, D. (1999a). 'toka'-ben no komyunikeeshon shinri [Japanese young people's new speech style and their interpersonal attitudes]. *The proceedings of the* 3rd *conference of Japanese Association of Sociolinguistic Sciences* (pp. 19–24).

Tsuji, D. (1999b). Wakamono-go to taijin kankei: Daigakusei choosa no kekka kara. [Young people's new speech Style and their interpersonal relationship: The results of a preliminary survey on university students]. *Tokyo Daigaku Shakai Joohoo Kenkyuujo Kiyoo, 57,* 17–42. Retrieved from ⟨http://www.d-tsuji.com/paper/p08/index.htm⟩.

Watanabe, S., & Iwasaki, N. (2009). The acquisition of Japanese modality during the study abroad. In B. Pizziconi & M. Kizu (Eds.), *Japanese modality: Exploring its scope and interpretation* (pp. 231–158). Hampshire, UK: Palgrave.

Wilkinson, S. (1998). On the nature of immersion during study abroad: Some participant perspectives. *Frontiers: The Interdisciplinary Journal of Study Abroad, 4*, 121–138.

Wilkinson, S. (2000). Emerging questions about study abroad. *Association of Departments of Foreign Languages (ADFL) Bulletin, 32*(1), 36–41.

Woodfield, H., & Economidou-Kogetsidis, M. (2010). "I just need more time": A study of native and non-native and non-native students' requests to faculty for an extension. *Multilingua: Journal of Cross-Cultural and Interlanguage Communication, 29*, 77–118.

Yamakawa, F. (2007, March). Hedges in Japanese as a second language. Paper presented at the meeting of the Association of Teachers of Japanese, Boston.

Yonekawa, A. (1995). Wakamonogo no sekai [The world of youngsters' language]. *Nihongogaku, 14*, 102–110.

Yonekawa, A. (1998). *Wakamonogo o kagakusuru* [Scientific study of youth language]. Tokyo: Meijishoin.

Identity and honorifics use
in Korean study abroad*

Lucien Brown
University of Oregon

This study examines quantitative (DCT data) and qualitative (recordings of natural conversations, retrospective interviews) to explore the use of Korean honorifics by four advanced male learners on a study abroad program at a university in Seoul. Although the DCT data reveal that all four learners possessed strong underlying pragmatic knowledge regarding when honorific forms (*contaymal*) and non-honorific forms (*panmal*) should normatively be used, their use of these forms in real world interactions frequently departed from native norms. To explain this gap between knowledge and usage, the paper explores questions of these speakers' identities, drawing on a growing body of literature that sees identity as pivotal to explaining second language acquisition, particularly in the study abroad context.

1. Introduction

In recent years, Korean has become an increasingly popular choice as a foreign language not just for students in Asian countries (notably, Japan, China and Vietnam), but increasingly so in Western countries as well. In the USA, for example, the number of universities offering Korean language courses has grown from 10 in 1975 to 130 in the early 2000s (Byon 2008, p. 244). Byon (2008, p. 244) attributes this expansion to the fast economic growth of South Korea, the rapid rise of South Korean emigrants to Western countries and the promotion of the Korean language by various organizations affiliated to the South Korean government, including notably the Korea Foundation. To this list, we can add the increasing popularity of Korean popular culture, notably films, music and TV dramas – a phenomenon known in South Korea as the "Korean wave" (*hanlyu*). This growth

* This research was supported by the Academy of Korean Studies of the Republic of Korea. Selected examples are reproduced from Brown (2011), with kind permission from the publisher John Benjamins.

in interest in the Korean language has inevitably also led to an increasing number of overseas students studying abroad in South Korea. According to 2007 statistics, there were 46,702 overseas students in Korea (Kim 2009). Korean universities increasingly see the establishment of programs for overseas students not just as a source of revenue, but also as a way to create an international image in a time of increased globalization and multiculturalism in South Korea.

Although these overseas students frequently provide data for research papers in Korean journals such as *Hankwuke Kyoyuk* (*Journal of Korean Language Education*) and *Icwungene kyoyuk* (*Bilingual Research*), to date no research has looked at the experience of these students from a study abroad perspective. Although the field of *Hankwuke Kyoyuk* ("Korean Language Education") appears to assume that studying in Korea results in linguistic gains, no research has been produced that supports this supposition. In addition, no research has considered the kind of individual differences or localized aspects of context that have been found to influence language development during study abroad (Kinginger & Farrell 2005, p. 3). Most crucial to arguments in the current paper, there has been a lack of interest in the Korean context regarding the identity issues that develop during study abroad and the extent to which study abroad students are able to negotiate target language (TL)-mediated subject positions. As noted by Block (2007, p. 21), periods of prolonged contact with an L2, such as those encountered during study abroad, inevitably lead to destabilization of the individual's sense of self. From this state, the extent to which learners are able to re-negotiate their self image and construct a "third place" identity (Kramsch 1993, p. 231 ff) that allows for preservation of pre-existing values but also with chances to participate in the local community appears to be crucial to the level and kind of linguistic competence that learners achieve.

To fill this gap in the literature, the current paper deconstructs the issue of identity negotiation in Korean study abroad by focusing on the learning and usage of Korean honorific forms by advanced male learners based in Seoul. By focusing on Korean's intricate honorifics system, we are provided with a particularly interesting and detailed analysis of what it means to negotiate a Korean-speaking identity and the barriers that might obstruct this process. The reasons for this lie in the pervasive nature of the honorifics system itself and also in the strong associations held between this system and "doing" Korean identity. In every single Korean utterance, the speaker is forced into choices between different honorific verb endings and lexical forms. These forms, by indexing the speaker's relationship with the hearer, ultimately play a role in defining the social relations of the speaker and also in creating the speaker's social identity and image. By using honorifics appropriately according to social norms, the speaker can go some way to negotiating Korean patterns of social interaction and a self-image as a competent member of Korean society. On the other hand, being unable or unwilling to use the forms according to social convention may ultimately limit the ability of the speaker to negotiate an identity as a legitimate speaker. The extent to which second language learners adopt the use of these forms thus works as a useful barometer for assessing the degree to which they have negotiated a TL-mediated subject position. In addition, by focusing on male learners, the study provides important data regarding the identity issues faced by males who study abroad. These have sometimes been overlooked in the study abroad literature which, to date, has tended to focus more on the experiences of female learners.

Arguments will be structured as follows. In the next two sections, I introduce the two key categories under analysis: linguistic identity and Korean honorifics. After detailing the methodology in the following section, I discuss the results. I conclude by summarizing the implications of the study for our understanding of study abroad, particularly in the Korean setting.

2.   Linguistic identity in study abroad

The current paper accepts the definition of "linguistic identity" offered by Block (2007, p. 40) as "the assumed and/or attributed relationship between one's sense of self and a means of communication". In keeping with the way that identity has been treated within SLA, I see this relationship as being dynamic rather than fixed. Although people are not free, as it were, to choose their own identities, they may nevertheless negotiate their self-presentation and the way this relates to the language that they speak. Creating a linguistic identity, it should be noted, is ultimately not just limited to communication. Rather, since language is the most important resource available to people in the negotiation of their self-image, the relationship between self and language is crucial to the wider presentation of one's own identity.

According to Leung, Harris and Rampton (1997), this relationship between self and language has three aspects: language expertise, language affiliation and language inheritance. Language expertise refers to proficiency in the means of communication, which it is assumed must reach a certain level in order for a speaker to be accepted by other users as a member of the community of practice. Affiliation describes the extent to which a person claims attachment to a language and feels part of the community using that language. Finally, inheritance is about being born into a community that is associated with a particular language or being born with other attributes besides language that are associated with that community. These three aspects do not necessarily entail each other.

For example, one can inherit a language but have no proficiency in or affiliation to it. Alternatively, one may become proficient in and affiliated to a non-inherited language.

Study abroad research has highlighted that adopting a target language identity for second language learners is no straightforward process. On the most basic level, their lack of language proficiency coupled with their absence of an inherited language identity may lead to non-acceptance from the local community. This may particularly be the case in countries where acculturation of "foreigners" is not necessarily expected or valued, including East Asian societies such as Korea and Japan. Iino's (2006) study of American students in Japanese home-stays found that the Japanese hosts held low expectations as to how well the students could speak Japanese, adopt other Japanese practices such as eating Japanese food, and ultimately become competent members of Japanese society. Linguistically, this was evinced by the host families' adoption of a very simplified register of foreigner talk when addressing the home-stayers, the acceptance of non-native language use (or even the encouragement of it) and the occasional negative evaluation of pragmatically appropriate native-like Japanese. As an example of the last of these, when one student applied a native-like routine utterance on presenting a gift, the use of humble language was viewed negatively by the Japanese interlocutor who felt that the show of humility was insincere and that the student had been forced into speaking in that way (Iino 2006, p. 166–167).

The second factor that works to complicate the negotiation of language identity in SA contexts is that learners may find that the subject positions available for them in the TL community are limited and conflict with their pre-existing self-images. Here, a particular theme that has attracted attention in previous research is gender. American women on study abroad programs frequently complain of sexual harassment, whether they are in Russia, Argentina, France, Spain or Costa Rica (see Kinginger 2009, p. 7 for full references). More generally, female learners may find that the subject positions available to them as women in the study abroad context are limited or clash with their pre-existing gender identity. Polanyi (1995) discovered that American female learners in Russia at times found themselves in heterosexual relationships where the only subject position made available to them was that of sexual partner. This was inconsistent not only with the way that these learners wanted to present themselves, but was also with the propensity for establishing platonic heterosexual relationships that had been available for them back in their native culture. Ultimately, it worked to limit their opportunities to integrate with Russians and to gain experience interacting in the language. Along slightly different lines, Siegal (1994) found that female learners of Japanese in SA rejected subservient Japanese female identities and the language use that went with it to varying degrees. For these western women, the available linguistic identity as a Japanese female and the humble demeanor and squeaky voice that went with it was considered demeaning. They thus flaunted linguistic norms, particularly those associated with the application of honorifics and other politeness features.

As for male learners, what little research there is tends to portray the experience as being unproblematic or even favorable in terms of gender (Celeste Kinginger, personal communication, November 9, 2011). Churchill (2009) found that Hiro, the lone male participant in a group of high school students sojourning in the USA, received advantages from his identity as the minority male in the study abroad context. Largely thanks to his gender identity, he received more opportunities to interact in English and ultimately he experienced greater gains in oral proficiency than his female counterparts. Similarly, Isabelli-Garcia (2006) found that only male participants developed extensive social networks while studying in Argentina. However, in comparison to research on female learners, the experiences of male learners have as yet received relatively little attention, which may lead us to question whether the experiences are universally so positive. Indeed, data in the current study will show that the gender positions available to male learners in Korea are not always so unproblematic.

Language learners may ultimately reject the adoption of a local language identity when this identity is in opposition to their pre-existing self-image or cultural values. This rejection may take as its focus parts of linguistic behavior that are particularly salient and which seem to be directly connected to questions of identity, whether this be feminine ways of talking or the application of linguistic features that are strongly connected with politeness. In the current paper, I assume that Korean honorifics hold particularly strong relationships with Korean language identity. To adopt their usage according to Korean patterns of usage involves, at least to some extent, the speaker's appropriation of a Korean language identity and the hierarchical and non-reciprocal patterns of interaction that come with it.

3. Korean honorifics: *Contaymal* and *panmal*

I pause at this juncture to briefly introduce the Korean honorifics system and, in doing so, add further comment regarding the connection between using honorifics and "doing" Korean identity.

The description I offer differs from more traditional accounts, which tend to begin by breaking the system into its component parts, typically hearer honorifics (or speech styles), subject honorifics and object honorifics (see for example Lee, I. and Ramsey 2000, pp. 224–272). Instead of orienting to these linguistic categories, my description follows the Korean folk notion of dividing speech into two rough categories: *contaymal* ('respect-speech') and *panmal* ('half-speech').[1] Broadly speaking, the former may be used for addressing age-rank superiors, strangers and non-intimates, whereas the latter is used when interacting with intimate age-rank equals or subordinates and with children.[2] Although there are doubtlessly many gradations within *contaymal* and *panmal* (the description of which lies outside the scope of the current paper), the division between these two broad levels represents the distinction of which Korean native speakers are the most consciously aware. Thus, when developing appropriate use of honorifics, it appears reasonable to suggest that distinguishing between these two registers and being able to apply them appropriately, represents the primary task for L2 learners. In the description below, in addition to detailing the honorific features most commonly associated with *contaymal* and *panmal*, I also comment on other linguistic features that may characterize these registers.

3.1   *Contaymal*

Contaymal is characterized by the use of honorific speech styles, the strict application of referent honorifics, name/pronoun avoidance, wordiness and regular prosody.

Considering speech styles first of all, these are verb endings that are applied to the predicate. When speaking *contaymal*, the speaker will customarily use the *-eyo* or *–(su)pnita* verb endings, which are commonly referred to in the literature as the polite and deferential styles respectfully:

(1)   a.   *–eyo* style   ekwulha-eyo
     b.   *–(su)pnita* style ekwulha-pnita
       'it's not fair.'

Whereas the *–(su)pnita* style is associated with formality, the expression of factual and/or new information and additional deference, *-eyo* is tied up with a more casual mode of interaction, the conveyance of "common sense" level information and the freer expression of affect (see Byon 2007 for details).

Secondly, *contaymal* involves the strict application of referent honorifics, including the use of the verb ending *-si-* and a variety of lexical substitutions.

---

1.   In this paper, I apply *panmal* according to the lay definition of the term. This meaning is broader than that commonly applied in formal linguistics, where it is used only to refer to the *-e* style of speech.

2.   These functions represent only the most stereotypical usages of *panmal* and *contaymal*. The alternation between these forms may express a range of other socio-pragmatic meanings, including formality and affective stance.

Compare the inclusion of -*si*- and the honorific lexical items -*kkeyse* (subject particle), *cinci* ('meal') and *capswu*- ('eat') in (2a) when talking about a grandfather with their absence in (2b) when referring to a younger sibling:

(2) a. *halapeci-kkeyse   cinci-lul   capswu-si-ess-eyo*
         grandpa-SUB:HON   meal-OBJ   eat-HON-PAST-POL
         'grandfather ate his meal'

     b. *tonsayng-i   pap-ul   mek-ess-eyo*
         younger-sibling-SUB   meal- OBJ   eat- PAST-POL
         'younger brother/sister ate his/her meal'

In addition to applying these forms when referring to a third person who is a notable superior (such as a parent, grandparent, teacher or senior at work), lexical honorifics are also used when the hearer him/herself appears as a sentence referent. Although they are always applied in this second function when the hearer is a notable superior or adult stranger, they may at times be dropped when the hearer is of a similar age or younger than the speaker and/or with increased intimacy.

Contaymal is also characterized by the use of titles or kinship terms and the restricted appearance of pronouns and personal names. When speaking *contaymal* to superiors in the work place, for example, names or pronouns are not used and a position-based title must be applied instead, such as *hoycang-nim* (president), *sacang-nim* (manager), *chacang-nim* (deputy manager) and *kwajang-nim* (department head). Here, the -*nim* ending is a suffix that should be attached to render the expression honorific. Intimates of marginally superior age are addressed as 'older brother' (*hyeng* when the speaker is male and *oppa* when female) or 'older sister' (*nwuna/enni*). Although a personal name may be applied towards a non-intimate of similar or younger age, it should not appear on its own but be followed by the address form -*ssi*.

Although the description above represents the traditional categorization of *contaymal*, other linguistic and non-linguistic resources may contribute to establishing this register of speech. Winter and Grawunder (2009) found that oral DCT responses given in *contaymal* were 58% longer than those given in *panmal*, this length being accounted for by a 52% increase in wordiness (measured by the number of spoken syllables), a higher number of hesitation markers and also by a slower speech rate. Winter and Grawunder (2009) found that *contaymal* was clearer, quieter and lower in pitch and was characterized by a more regular and monotonous prosody than *panmal*.

The application of *contaymal* is important to establishing a Korean identity due to the strong connections between appropriate use of this register and traditional Korean social values and also layman ideologies of politeness and respect. Previous studies highlight that appropriate *contaymal* use is seen as vital for the upkeep of hierarchical social relationships and the connected mottos of *kyenglosasang* (敬老思想; 'respecting the elderly') (Yoon 2004, p. 199) and *cangyuyuse* (長幼有序 'the old and the young know their place') (Lee, I. & Ramsey 2000, p. 267). In addition, *contaymal* use is viewed as playing a role in preserving traditional family relationships in which younger generations demonstrate filial piety – or *hyo* (孝) – towards their parents or grandparents and not only obey and respect them, but also nurture them as they enter old age. More broadly, the use of *contaymal* has also been demonstrated to be crucial to commonsense layman conceptualizations of politeness. Indicative of this is the fact that use of *contaymal* is almost synonymous with the Korean layman definition of showing respect. Indeed, Brown (2010a, p. 260) points out that the Korean dictionary definition of *contay* 'respect' includes not only "to deal with someone in a respectful manner of talking" but, more explicitly, "to use honorifics such as the respectful verb endings *-pnita*." With use of *contaymal* being so closely tied up with maintaining traditional Korean values and Korea-specific patterns of politeness, it follows that using these forms appropriately is important for establishing an identity as a competent member of Korean society.

3.2   *Panmal*

Panmal is characterized by the use of non-honorific speech styles, less strict application of referent honorifics, use of personal names, vocative forms and pronouns, reduced wordiness and less regular prosody.

Panmal typically features alternation between two different speech styles: the so-called intimate *-e* style and the plain *-ta*:

(3)   a.   *-e* style   paykoph-**a**
     b.   *-ta* style   paykophu-**ta**
        'I'm hungry'

In addition to being perceived as lower than the *-e* style (Lee, I. & Ramsey 2000, p. 255), the *-ta* style in declarative sentences takes on a number of specific discourse functions. Notably, whereas *-e* tends to occur with pre-stored factual knowledge, *-ta* accompanies newly perceived or retrieved information that is particularly noteworthy for the hearer (Lee, H., 1991, pp. 414–419).

According to prescriptive accounts, *panmal* should always feature use of referent honorifics when a notable elder is the third-person referent of the utterance. Although in many situations speakers do actually adhere to this, the application becomes less strict, particularly in close in-group relationships. A good example of this is provided in Lee, J. (2002), where DCT data show that although speakers quite faithfully apply referent honorifics when referring to their parents to "out-groupers", they most frequently omit them when conversing within the family group.

Whereas the use of personal names and pronouns is largely taboo when interacting in *contaymal*, both these patterns of address are permitted in *panmal*. Personal names may appear either on their own, or more commonly suffixed by the vocative marker -*a*/-*ya*. The pronoun *ne* may also be used in *panmal*, although this tends to be limited to addressing younger interlocutors or the closest of intimates.

Finally, besides the application of honorifics and address forms, *panmal* displays the opposite patterns regarding wordiness and prosody to those noted for *contaymal* above. Whereas *contaymal* utterances are longer, wordier and slower, *panmal* utterances are typically shorter and faster, with a lower number of syllables used to perform the same speech acts and a lower rate of hesitation markers (Winter & Grawunder 2009). Furthermore, in terms of prosody, whereas *contaymal* is clear, quiet, lower in pitch and monotonous, *panmal* is characterized by loudness and a higher and more varied pitch. As pointed out by Winter and Grawunder (2009), the impression of loudness associated with *panmal* is increased through pitch variation, according to what is known as the vibrato effect.

Although speaking *panmal* does not hold the same associations with traditional Korean values as is the case with *contaymal*, being proficient in this register is nonetheless important for establishing an identity as a competent speaker of Korean. First of all, as noted by Choo (1999, p. 80), using *panmal* is essential for speakers to gain entry to close Korean groups. Without the application of this intimate register of speech, it may be problematic for speakers to establish intimate relationships with their Korean interlocutors. Moreover, although it is *contaymal* rather than *panmal* that that is imbued with powerful social ideology, both registers are ultimately two sides of the same coin and play complementary roles in the upkeep of appropriate linguistic behavior and the social system underpinning it. The failure to use *panmal* appropriately, although not associated with the same taboos as the failure to use *contaymal*, may still result in discord within the speech community in question, whose members may feel that the expected social order (and the feeling of harmony that goes with it) is being disrupted.

4. Research design

This paper analyzes four case studies selected from a larger database which was collected to chart the acquisition of honorifics by second language learners of Korean (Brown 2011). The original body of data contained material collected from 20 learners in total, only ten of whom were on study abroad programs. The data was collected during fieldwork in Seoul carried out in 2006.

4.1   Participants

The four participants chosen for the case studies were all participating in one-year study abroad programs at a renowned university in Seoul, with data collected during the second semester of the program. The university in question has over 19,000 undergraduate and 9,000 postgraduate students. In 2009, it admitted approximately 450 exchange students and also had 870 foreign students registered in regular programs (242 undergraduates and 628 postgraduates).

As shown in Table 1, although the participants were of different nationalities, they were all permanently based at universities in English-speaking counties, with all but Patrick[3] living in the UK. Japanese participant Hiroki had lived in Europe (Germany and the UK) from the age of 9 and although fluent in Japanese, admitted to incomplete mastery of pragmatic aspects, including the application of honorifics. The one heritage learner – Daniel – had been raised speaking German as a first language and had only a rudimentary knowledge of Korean before taking Korean classes.

The four learners were selected as case studies based on two factors. Firstly, I purposefully selected learners who were male. This decision was made in response to the obvious need for more literature on the study abroad experiences of male students, as noted above. Secondly, the four case studies were selected to display a range of different ethnic backgrounds and learning experiences. As noted above, the group includes one heritage learner, one subject who is ethnically Japanese and two white Europeans. We shall see that the identities available to learners from these three ethnic backgrounds were quite distinct. Although the white students found that they are "foreignized" more than the Asian students, we see in the cases of Richard and Patrick two quite different ways of dealing with this foreigner identity.

Table 1. Background of participants

	Age	Gender	Nationality	Country of residence	Ethnicity	Other languages
Richard	21	M	UK	UK	White-British	English (native)
Hiroki	23	M	Japan	UK	Japanese	Japanese (native) English (fluent)
Patrick	23	M	Austria	Australia	White-Austrian	German (native) English (fluent) Japanese (adv.)
Daniel	25	M	Germany	UK	Korean	German (native) English (fluent) French (adv.)

---

3.   All names of participants and their interlocutors appearing in this paper are pseudonyms.

No data were collected regarding the proficiency level of the learners. However, at the time of data collection, all had been placed in advanced level Korean classes at the university in question. Patrick was in the highest of six levels and the remaining three were placed in the second highest class.

Some notes are in order at this juncture regarding the program of study provided for these students at the Korean university. The students attended Korean languages classes for four hours a day from Monday to Thursday. In general, the participants expressed fairly negative opinions regarding these classes, with typical comments including that the classes were less demanding and less serious than those they had previously taken at their home institutions, and that the teachers were not strict regarding attendance, tardiness, homework and evaluations. "The teachers were like they didn't care at all", commented Daniel, "they were not really concerned to really teach people something." Exchange students were also given the choice of enrolling for other university courses. However, the language ability of exchange students was generally insufficient for taking Korean-taught classes. As a rather ironic result, this resulted in some students taking English-taught courses, including Daniel and Hiroki. Other exchange students took the opportunity to learn different languages, including Richard who took a module in beginners' Chinese.

The university could provide students with on-campus accommodation in a separate foreigner-only dormitory ('*oykwukin kiswuksa*'). The way that overseas students are thus immediately separated from Korean students mirrors the situation reported for Japanese universities in Siegal (1994, p. 19). Siegal claimed that this physical separation played an important role in ultimately sequestering learners from the local native-speaker community. In the case of this Korean university, however, the dormitory was unpopular with students and many chose not to stay there (or moved out during the first term), including all four participants chosen for the case studies in this paper. Fortunately, many other accommodation options were available in the areas surrounding the university, including *haswuk-cip* (boarding houses, normally offering breakfast and dinner), *kosiwen* (privately run student dormitories) and *wen-lwum* ("one room" – studio flats). Unlike the situation frequently reported in studies of Japanese study abroad (for example, Iino 2006; Cook 2008), it is unusual for Korean SA learners to reside in home-stays with local families.

The university made some positive efforts to integrate exchange students into the wider student community. These included the hosting of an international students festival and inviting exchange students to other large university events, including a high-profile day of sports games that this university held with a rival institution. Most notably, the university provided a "buddy system" that matched exchange students with a Korean "buddy". For many exchange students, this represented an important first point of access for making Korean friends. However, these buddies, it should be remembered, often only volunteered for the program as they saw it as a way to practice their English.

4.2   Methods of data collection

Four different types of data were collected from each participant, employing both quantitative and qualitative methods.

Firstly, to assess the learners' underlying competence in honorifics, Discourse Completion Test (DCT) data were collected. The DCT involved manipulating the same Korean sentence (which translated as "Have you seen that movie/news?") across 24 different contexts and according to four age-rank relationships (addressing a professor in his 50s, a *senpay* 'senior' student two years senior than you, a *hupay* 'junior' student the same age as you and a student two years younger than you), three degrees of intimacy (a stranger, a non-intimate acquaintance and an intimate acquaintance) and two degree of formality (informal lunch and departmental meeting). Samples from the DCT can be found in the appendix. The learners' use of *contaymal/panmal* on the DCT was then judged in comparison to baseline data collected from 40 native speakers.

Secondly, I collected recordings of natural conversations from the learners. The original database of natural conversations collected from all 20 participants had a combined duration of over twelve hours and included 70 interactions in total. This included 41 recordings featuring interactions with status superiors and/or new acquaintances (i.e. where *contaymal* would typically be expected) and 29 featuring interactions with intimate status equals and subordinates (i.e. where *panmal* would typically be expected). In order to reduce observer effects, the data were collected remotely by supplying participants with a recording device.

Thirdly, at the end of the data-collection cycle, I carried out retrospective interviews with all of the participants. In the interviews, learners were quizzed regarding their application of honorifics in the recordings and their general use of and attitudes towards these forms. One additional goal of the interviews was to obtain learner stories or anecdotes regarding their use of honorifics, with learners being asked to specifically talk about times they had experienced conflict and discomfort when using honorific forms. The rationale here was to collect examples of disputes or conflicts between the cultural knowledge and identity of language learners and the norms and expectations of the local community. It was expected that these kinds of conflicts would seldom emerge in recordings of natural conversations, given the reluctance of participants to record such interactions (and given their relatively low frequency). The methodology is in some ways similar to that applied by Spencer-Oatey (2002) in collecting what she calls "rapport sensitive incidents" experienced by Chinese students in the UK. The technique proved successful in that I was able to amass as many as 122 narratives.

Fourthly, the learners participated in a role-play activity with a native Korean speaker partner. However, the data collected from the role-play is not included in the analysis for the current paper.

5.   Data analysis: Underlying honorific competence of participants

Before discussing the situated use of honorifics for each of the four case studies, I begin by presenting results from the DCT. These data provide information regarding the underlying knowledge that these learners possessed regarding the contexts in which *contaymal* and *panmal* should normally be applied. They also provide a baseline against which to evaluate the ways that these learners actually used honorifics in day-to-day interactions.

Results from the DCT showed that the four exchange students selected as case studies all possessed strong underlying pragmatic competence regarding when to use *contaymal* and *panmal*. The results displayed in Table 2 were calculated by awarding three points for appropriate use of honorifics for each of the 24 items on the DCT, making a total of 72 points. One point was awarded for use of honorific versus non-honorific speech styles, one point for inclusion or exclusion of referent honorifics and one point for using terms of address normally associated with *contaymal* versus those commonly associated with *panmal*. Whether the response was appropriate or not was judged against the majority responses (75% or above) of the 40 native speakers who also sat the DCT. When the native speaker rate was below 75%, either the *panmal* or the *contaymal* forms were permitted. As can be seen in the table, all four of the learners chosen as case studies for the current paper scored over 90% when the DCT data were analyzed in this way.[4]

---

4.   The method of analysis presented here is much simplified than that applied in the original study. For more detailed analysis, including discussion of ways that the DCT data of some language learners may actually differ in some ways from that of native speakers, consult Brown (2011, pp. 109–148).

Table 2. Scores on honorifics DCT

	Raw score (out of 72)	Percentage
Richard	67	93.1%
Hiroki	66	91.7%
Patrick	69	95.8%
Daniel	68	94.4%

Since data were not collected from the learners prior to study abroad, whether this high underlying competence in honorifics was established through the naturalistic exposure afforded by sojourning in Korea cannot be proven. However, there are two good reasons to think that this was probably the case. Firstly, as pointed out in Brown (2010b), Korean language textbooks (and by extension, Korean second language teaching instruction) frequently represent a simplified model of honorifics akin to a variety of foreigner talk (Ellis 1997, p. 46) and provide scant information about the pragmatics of honorific forms. It therefore appears likely that the learners' knowledge of honorifics had developed outside of the classroom, particularly given the low quality of instruction that they complained about. Secondly, the interview data revealed a general belief amongst the learners that they had greatly improved their awareness of honorifics since coming to Korea and having more regular interaction with Korean native speakers. Patrick, for example, reported that before coming to Korea he had only learned *contaymal* and that most of the instruction he had received had been in the deferential *–(sup)nita* style. Indeed, his teacher in Austria had apparently informed him that this was the style Koreans used the majority of the time, with occasional use of the polite *-eyo*, and that *panmal* was only used "to friends that they've known all their life." Since coming to Korea, he had noticed that this portrayal differed markedly from honorifics use within the university and had thus drawn the conclusion that his teacher in Austria "hadn't lived in Korea for a long time." He had then picked up "what honorifics to use in each situation" principally from "hearing other people talk" and copying the way that Koreans addressed him. The one exception on this point was heritage learner Daniel, who felt that he had acquired most of his knowledge regarding the use of honorifics before coming to Korea through interacting with his extended family.

6.   Data analysis: Case studies

The use of DCT data in the previous section revealed that the four exchange students chosen as case studies for the current paper all had highly developed knowledge regarding the contexts in which *contaymal* and *panmal* should be applied. However, in this section, I shall demonstrate that this high level of performance on the DCT did not always correlate with the patterns of honorifics use found in recordings of natural conversations and narrated during learner interviews, which at times departed markedly from native speaker norms.

To some extent, the fact that the DCT does not detect the same patterns of honorifics use appearing in real world interactions can be considered an artifact of the DCT as a data collection tool. In an important paper comparing DCT responses to natural conversation, Golato (2003) found that DCT responses may differ to naturalistically collected data in several vital ways. Golato (2003, p. 110) concluded that "DCTs are better suited to the study of 'what people *think they would say*' than to the study of '*what people actually do say*'". Applying this finding to the current project, the DCT results could be said to capture how the learners believe honorifics *would* be used (or *should* be used) according to their understandings of Korean social norms, rather than how they *actually* use them.

However, as we shall see, the observation that there is a gap between the learners' knowledge of the prescriptive norms of how honorifics *should* be used and the way that they *actually* used them is still highly informative. It shows us that these prescriptive native-speaker norms do not always apply to the kinds of interactions and kinds of relationships these exchange students actually have in the real world or, more broadly, to the identities available to them. On the one hand, as exchange students and foreigners, the subject positions available to them existed on the boundaries of the community of practice and thus native-like patterns of honorifics were not always applicable. On the other hand, the learners experienced difficulty in aligning native-like patterns of honorifics use with their pre-existing identities and the way that they chose to present themselves. Ultimately, the learners found themselves caught up in a struggle with their native-speaker interlocutors to establish what it meant to use honorifics appropriately in interactions between L1 and L2 speakers.

6.1   Richard

Of all the exchange students participating in the project, Richard was one of the most active and determined when it came to seeking relationships with Koreans. Even before arriving in Korea, Richard had built up a large group of Korean acquaintances through on-line chatting and he went on to meet many of these in-person during his first few months in Korea. He was also successful in striking up friendships with students on campus (including through the buddy system), was active in the university broadcasting club and even befriended people such as workers at the local convenience store. The vast majority of the Koreans whom

Richard befriended were female. At least on the part of Richard, he viewed these friendships as platonic rather than romantic. However, during the first term he maintained a romantic relationship with one girl, but, as he entered the second term, he became increasingly disillusioned with Korean females, complaining that they were "too jealous" and did not understand that he had other platonic female friends. He then formed a long-term relationship with a Singaporean exchange student, who had only elementary proficiency in Korean. From this time on, his opportunities to speak Korean diminished somewhat.

Although Richard had ample opportunities to speak Korean during his study abroad and had access to the "legitimate peripheral participation" (Lave & Wenger 1991) required to develop a decent fluency in Korean, the identity that he was able to negotiate for himself as an L2 speaker came with its limitations, in part, due to the gendered subject position he found himself in. As mentioned above, the vast majority of his daily interactions were casual encounters with Korean females. In these interactions, the female acquaintances generally initiated *panmal* very quickly, frequently even at the first encounter. The following extract shows Richard reciprocating *panmal* with Su-mi, a girl the same age as himself, to whom he had just been introduced under the pretext of helping her with English homework. Although they are the same age, the use of *panmal* is somewhat marked given the fact that they are virtual strangers interacting outside of any formal group and also because of the gender difference. Note in the extract how Su-mi uses *panmal* in all utterance units, even those with higher potential face threat such as imperatives (lines 4 and 5). Also note Richard's one slip into the *contaymal* in line 2, perhaps betraying some discomfort in using *panmal* to a non-intimate:

(4)   Natural Conversation: Richard
      [**coffee shop, just after ordering coffee, only minutes after they have
      first met**]

      1   Su-mi i ke nay ke-**ya**?
                 '*is this one [coffee] mine-{e}?*'

      2   Richard i ke-**yo**?
                   '*this one?-{eyo}*'

      3   molu-keyss-**e**
                   '*I don't know-{e}*'

      4   Su-mi ne meke pw-**a**
                 '*have a taste-{e}*'

      5   ney key tal-myen i ke-n nay ke-**ya**
                '*if yours is sweet, then this one's mine-{e}*'

      6   cokum-man mek-**e**
                '*just try a little-{e}*'

7   Richard mas-iss-**e** ((laughter))
          'it's good-{e}'

8   Su-mi kulay ((laughter)). kulem nay ke-nka po-**ta**
          'alright, then it must be mine-{ta}'

9   [BOTH]   ((laughter))

10   Richard   kunyang na-nun khokhoa-na masil ttay selthang manhi
          neh-umyen [coh-**a**]
          'It's just that when I drink cocoa, I like to add a lot of sugar-{e}'

11   Su-mi   ung ung]
                                                      'yeah'

12   kuntey way ilehkey mall-ass-**e**?
          'so, why are you so thin-{e}?'

Two explanations appear to be available to understand why Korean females were quick to initiate *panmal* in interactions with Richard. Firstly, during the interviews, Richard expressed the opinion that Koreans tended to use *panmal* to him from the start due to his non-Korean identity ("I think it's because I'm a foreigner"). This hints at an apparent belief amongst some Koreans that honorifics are not necessarily required in interactions with non-Koreans, a point I return to in discussions of the case of Patrick below (Section 6.3). Secondly and more importantly, the use of *panmal* appears to be connected to the gender dynamics of these relationships. In some cases, it may have been that the girls were simply romantically interested in Richard and used *panmal* as a strategy to increase the level of intimacy. However, rather than an object of romantic interest as such, more commonly the girls appeared to view Richard as a younger brother or even as a child. One clue to this was Richard's frequent complaint that they would call him *kwiyewe* 'cute' – a term not typically used to describe an adult male:

(5)   Interview Data: Richard
      They are always calling me kwiyewe *and for a while that was very annoying.*
      It stopped for a while and then just yesterday with a friend she said kwiyewe.

This repeated comment seemed to reveal that these females, rather than seeing Richard as a fully-formed adult member of the community, instead viewed him more like a cute child, towards whom the use of *panmal* was most appropriate. In summary, the subject position available to Richard in these interactions was that of a cute, younger foreign friend who was a possible object of romance and who thus did not need to be addressed in *contaymal*. Although Richard found himself addressed in *panmal* by these female acquaintances, he also encountered situations in which Koreans addressed him in *contaymal* according to patterns that differed from typical Korean norms. His Chinese teacher, for example, despite using *panmal* when addressing Korean students individually, always spoke *contaymal* to him ("I think she is not sure how to address me more that than anything else") (see Brown 2011, p. 238). In addition, when Richard joined the university broadcasting club, he found that all of the *senpay* 'seniors' in the club spoke to him in *contaymal*, whereas they would always use *panmal* to other *hwupay* 'juniors'. This situation, however, became complicated when Richard became intimate with the (female) vice president of the club who, according to the previously noted pattern for female acquaintances to initiate *panmal* with Richard, asked him to drop the honorifics:

(6)   Interview Data: Richard
      *On Monday, I went to the OOOO [name of university broadcasting club]
      attendance meeting. The vice president [female; same age] came out and sat
      right next to me. Seeing as she is vice president and I am just a new member,
      I should be using* contaymal *to her. But on Monday, the first thing she asked
      me was if I knew how to speak* panmal. *I said "yeah, of course". What all this
      was working up to was telling me it was ok to speak* panmal *to her. Now, I use*
      contaymal *to everyone in OOOO except the vice president to whom I use*
      panmal. *And everyone else uses* contaymal *to her, except the other managers.
      And all the other seniors use* panmal *to everyone, except to me.*

As shown in this extract, the patterns of honorifics use involving Richard thus contradicted the strict hierarchical use within the group in several ways. This created a subject position for Richard that was quite separate from that available to Korean *hwupay* 'juniors'.

As noted originally noted in Brown (2011, pp. 192–193), although Richard complained that it was "irritating" when Koreans addressed him in *panmal* from the beginning, he nevertheless expressed an overall preference for using this register, which he found more "comfortable" than *contaymal*. Provided that he felt close enough to his Korean interlocutor, he was happy for *panmal* to be used regardless of age-rank dimensions. Indeed, the interview sessions revealed a belief on the part of Richard that, in his identity as foreigner, it may be possible to negotiate the use of *panmal* with those older than him "to almost any age":

(7)   Interview Data: Richard
  1   Richard   *Well, of course I'm not going to invent my own language. But as
                much as I can, I mentioned with my olders, I do generally try to at
                some point during our interactions get to a stage where we would
                use* panmal, *which I am sure is possible to almost any age.*
  2   LB   *So you'll try as much as possible to establish a horizontal
                relationship?*
  3   Richard   *I'll try as much as possible to speak Korean like a Korean, but
                I will also try to get to the point where, in as many situations as*

> *possible I don't need to- [...] I would much rather speak* panmal
> *because I actually feel that there's a lot of situations in which*
> *Koreans would also really want to speak* panmal. *But they feel it*
> *would be inappropriate for them to suggest it.*

4   LB   *So you think that because you are not Korean you can suggest using*
            panmal *in those situations?*

5   Richard   *I feel Koreans would object less to me suggesting it. Yeah, and they*
            actually seem more comfortable afterwards as well in situations
            where its happened. Which I find- which is something that again,
            a little peculiarity of Korea.

Richard's claim that "almost any" age difference can be overcome "at some point" by familiarity represents an obvious break from the Korean L1 reality, where, as previously mentioned, such usage towards notable superiors is taboo. In this extract from the interview sessions, we see a tension between Richard's statement that he aims to "speak Korean like a Korean" and his claims that, due to his non-Korean identity, he may be able to establish a more egalitarian pattern of language usage. His comment that Korean interlocutors "actually feel more comfortable" in situations in which he has negotiated *panmal* usage in the face of status differences is particularly interesting. Although this claim is impossible to verify, it reveals that the foreigner identity may at times be perceived as an advantage rather than a disadvantage when it comes to establishing intimate relationships with Koreans. In this case, being able to suggest the use of *panmal* despite age differences was a strategy available at times to Richard as a foreigner to establish closer relationships with Koreans that fell outside the normal hierarchical roles and responsibilities of Korean society.

Although the recorded interactions and interview data showed no evidence for Richard actually negotiating use of *panmal* with notable superiors (such as teachers and the elderly), there are examples of him initiating *panmal* within more marginal age dimensions. In the following extract from the interview files, Richard relays an incident in which he suggested reciprocal *panmal* use to someone who was actually four years older than himself:

(8)   **Interview Data: Richard**
      There was this one girl who was four years older than me. We were conversing
      and it was obvious that we were getting quite close. So I asked her if it was
      okay to speak panmal. *And she just said "yeah." It would probably be fairly*
      bad manners to do that if I was a Korean. But she didn't have any complaints
      and we both just dropped down.

Of particular interest here is Richard's comment that suggesting *panmal* in this way "would probably be fairly bad manners ... if I was a Korean". Indeed, Richard's proposal in his role as the younger party contrasts with the more typical way that downgrading works in native speaker interaction, where it is customary for the younger speaker to first invite the elder speaker to use *panmal* (and for the younger speaker to retain use of *contaymal*).

Thus, we find in the case of Richard a stark contrast between his underlying competence in honorifics (as noted in the previous section) and his actual usage in real-world interactions. Despite possessing a strong knowledge of the contexts in which *contaymal* and *panmal* should normatively be used, Richard found that his non-Korean identity often positioned him outside of this hierarchical social structure and resulted in patterns of honorifics use that did not always follow native speaker patterns. Particularly interesting here is the way that his gender seemed to have a direct influence on the subject positions available to him and, ultimately, on the patterns of honorifics use that emerged.

6.2   Hiroki

Despite having the apparent advantage of being a native speaker of a language with a developed honorifics system, the recordings of natural interactions found Japan-born Hiroki's use of honorifics to differ in one vital way to that of native speakers. Namely, when speaking *contaymal*, Hiroki reserved the use of referent honorifics only for the highest of age-rank superiors (see Brown 2010a, pp. 255–258, Brown 2011, pp. 196–198). When interacting with new acquaintances and/or those who had a more marginal age advantage, he dropped these forms, (mistakenly) perceiving the repeated use of these forms as feeling too "high". This omission of referent honorifics can be seen in lines 1 and 3 of the following extract from a conversation between Hiroki and Min-su, a Korean student two years his senior whom he was meeting for the first time. The lack of referent honorifics here could be particularly face threatening given the sensitive nature of Hiroki's questions as to whether Min-su has fulfilled his military service. In South Korea, around two years of military service is obligatory for males, with this obligation typically being served after completing one or two years of university study. However, Hiroki discovers that even though Min-su has almost completed his undergraduate studies and plans to go straight to graduate school, he has yet to serve in the military.

   (9)   Natural Conversation: Hiroki

     1   Hiroki   kulemyen ku kwuntay ka-ss-**eyo**?
                    *'so, you haven't been to the army yet-{**eyo**}?'*

     2   Min-su acik an ka-ss-**eyo**
                    *'I haven't been yet-{**eyo**}'*

     3   Hiroki   acik an ka-ko tayhakwen ka-lyeko-**yo**?
                    'you are planning to go to graduate school without having been
                    *[to the army]-{**eyo**}?'*

4   Min-su   hakpwu machi-ko ku taum-ey tayhakwen ka-se kongpwuha-ko
            ku taum-ey ettehkey kwuntay mwuncey haykyel ha-lyeko
            sayngkakha-ko iss-ketun-**yo**
            *'I'm thinking that I'll finish my undergraduate degree and after that
            go to graduate school and then after that take care of the military
            service problem-{**eyo**}'*

When interviewed regarding the way that his honorifics differed from the Korean norm, Hiroki was keen to blame this on the limitations of the exchange student identity. As an exchange student, he reported first of all that he mostly interacted only with "other foreigners". And even when he did encounter Koreans, they were normally peers of similar age and thus, in his own words, "I don't have so much opportunities to use these kinds of words [referent honorifics]". He further claimed that it was "difficult" for exchange students to "integrate into Korean society very much", blaming this on the temporal and sequestered identity of exchange students. As an exchange student, Hiroki realized that he occupied a subject position outside of the relational and hierarchical structure of the university. Crucially, he was aware that he lacked one crucial component of a Korean student identity: he had no *haknyen* ('university year', as in first year, second year, etc). Without this, there was no clear indication of where he fitted into the university's hierarchical structure:

(10)   Interview Data: Hiroki
       *It's different, you know, as an exchange student [...] Things would
       be much more clear if I'm il-haknyen [a first year] or i-haknyen [a second
       year] here, then people would just- because it's- I think it's one of the
       ways which you can- it's like one measurement- like, "oh, you- which year
       are you in?", "I'm the second". Okay, I should use* contaymal *[honorific
       language] to you.*

Hiroki also saw this lack of place in the university hierarchy as being crucial to the fact that he sometimes received what he considered to be inappropriate use of *panmal*. Interestingly, the two episodes narrated below both involve female interlocutors, perhaps hinting at similar gender dynamics to those that Richard was caught up in. Unlike in the case of Richard, Hiroki reported that this at times caused him a degree of discomfort:

(11)   Interview Data: Hiroki
       *I met a girl who was friends with OOOO [name of another exchange student]
       and she just spoke to me in* panmal *from the beginning even though I'm one
       year older than her. We had lunch together and right from the start she spoke*
       panmal. *I was surprised. Maybe it was because I was a foreigner, or maybe
       some Koreans are just like that – they want to be friendly.*

(12)   Interview Data: Hiroki

A girl who was four or five years younger than me spoke to me in panmal.
*I guess it's kind of her character because she was doing it to other people
as well. I would prefer* contaymal, *actually. It made me feel uncomfortable
because I didn't understand why she was doing it. The people around us were
saying to her that she should speak in* contaymal, *but she just kind of said
"I want to speak in* panmal."

Similar to the observations of Richard, Hiroki concluded that this inappropriate
use of *panmal* was related to his identity as a foreigner:

(13)   Interview Data: Hiroki

*I think even Korean people, they- when they speak to foreigners, sometimes
they don't use the polite form because they are foreigners. Because they think
in foreign culture, they don't have this* contaymal-panmal *culture, so they
think its okay to just use* panmal *to people.*

To sum up, the case of Hiroki illustrates that the identities of exchange student
and foreigner position learners on the peripheries of Korean society. From this
position, the opportunities to use Korean are limited and may be insufficient for
developing full competence in honorifics. In addition to lacking the opportunities
to acquire native-like patterns of *contaymal*, learners may also be exposed to patterns of *panmal* use different from those that typify native speaker talk.

6.3   Patrick

Unlike the three other case studies, Patrick had extensive experience of using
Korean outside of the confines of the exchange student setting. One of his initial
experiences using Korean had occurred back in his native Austria, where he had
worked as a translator on the set of the Korean TV drama *Spring Waltz* (*Pom-uy
walchu*). He kept in touch with the some of the crew from *Spring Waltz*, including one *hyeng* ('older brother') in his 30s (In-ho). The recordings show Patrick
addressing In-ho in *contaymal* but receiving *panmal* in a pattern quite natural in
the Korean context given the age difference:

(14)   **Natural Conversation: Patrick**

1   In-ho   Patrick-un kule-myen hocwu-ey ka-se cip-ul kwuha-nun ke-<u>ya</u>
          'are you, Patrick, going to find a house when you go back to
          Australia?-{e}'

2   ani-myen cip-ul mili kwu-hay noh-ass-e?
          'or have you found a house in advance?-{e}'

3   Patrick   yey kwuha-y noh-ass-eyo
          'yes, I've already found one-{eyo}'

4   In-ho   a kwuha-y [noh-ass-e?]
          'oh, you've already found one?-{e}'

5	Patrick	[kiswuksa]

                        'dormitory'

6   In-ho   a kiswuksa
               'oh, a dormitory'

7   Patrick   kiswuksa-ey tul-e ka-kilo ha-yss-eyo
               'I've decided to go into the dormitory-{eyo}'

During his year in Korea, Patrick had also undertaken work experience in a Korean company. Coupled with these experiences, he had improved his fluency in Korean through interacting with his Korean girlfriend. In sum, Patrick had achieved the highest level of fluency from the four case studies discussed in this paper and had a highly perceptive knowledge regarding the appropriate application of *contaymal* and *panmal*.

With his high level of attainment in Korean and the efforts he had made to integrate into Korean society, Patrick reacted extremely negatively to any attempts by Korean interlocutors to treat him differently because of his non-Korean identity. This included a high sensitivity when he was not addressed in appropriately deferential language (as in 15) and annoyance at the suggestion that Korean honorific categories and the use of kinship terms did not apply to him as a foreigner (16 and 17). In keeping with the pattern noted for Richard and Hiroki, episodes (15) and (17) both feature female interlocutors (Patrick does not specify the gender of the interlocutors in (16)).

(15)   Interview Data: Patrick
     I mean if somebody doesn't use the appropriate like- appropriate- you know- honorifics to me, if they are younger than me then I actually sometimes do get upset. Maybe I don't really show the person that [...]. There was a situation when a girl who was three years younger than me, she always kept talking to me using panmal, *almost from the start. But if the person thinks they don't need to use honorifics to me because I'm a foreigner, then that's rude.*

(16)   Interview Data: Patrick
     There was a conversation going on about whether people should use honorifics to foreigners between myself and three Koreans, two older and one younger than me. And one of them said that he thought you wouldn't need to use honorifics to a foreigner. At that time, I felt a bit offended.

(17)   Interview Data: Patrick
     There were a couple of Korean girls younger than me amongst the OOOO [name of buddy system] people and most of them who I was close with call me oppa *[a kinship term meaning 'older brother']. But then there is one girl who like implied that she found it funny for those other girls to call me that. At that time, I felt that was really a rude thing to say. She was laughing about it.*

From these experiences, Patrick had developed a strong belief that it was rude, offensive and discriminatory for Korean native speakers apply anything less than native-like patterns of honorifics use towards him. He also reported that he was "offended" by suggestions that, "because I'm a foreigner I can't use Korean the same way as Koreans". He thus made every attempt to adhere to native speaker norms of language use, including honorifics, and by doing so claim for himself an identity of equal status to Korean native speakers.

6.4   Daniel

With their inherited Korean identity, we may expect heritage learner exchange students to be at an advantage when it comes to integrating into the Korean community and negotiating self-image through their use of honorific forms. This is particularly the case given the linguistic advantages that such learners have been noted to enjoy, not just in terms of phonology and syntax, but also sociopragmatics (O'Grady, Lee & Choo 2001). In addition, in the process of negotiating a local identity, heritage learners benefit from the close connections in Korean ideology between race, nation and language (Coulmas 1999, p. 408). In the Korean national consciousness, anyone who is ethnically Korean is attributed an inherited Korean identity and is expected to be able to speak the Korean language. The result is that overseas Koreans, or *kyopho*, are generally expected to speak Korean fluently, almost as if the ability can be genetically inherited.

On the face of it, Daniel accepted the expectation that as an ethnic Korean he should speak the language and saw appropriate use of the language as an important tool for claiming this Korean identity. Central to this was the ability to use honorifics appropriately, which he saw as essential for establishing himself as "a real Korean, so no one is thinking he's a *kyopho* and he doesn't know about that." The recordings of natural conversations showed Daniel to be highly proficient in the use of honorifics and to slip comfortably and appropriately between *panmal* and *contaymal*. In the following recording, Daniel is interacting with a Korean student (Sang-u) he is meeting for the first time. On discovering earlier in the conversation that he is the same age and, in this extract, then that they live in the same *haswukcip* 'boarding house,' his language gradually becomes more casual and the speakers both start to switch between *panmal* and *contaymal*, a move that often precedes a complete drop to *panmal*.

(18)   **Natural Conversation: Daniel**
  1   Sang-u   na-to OOsa aph-ey sa-nuntey
              '*I also live in front of OO temple-{e}*'
  2   Daniel   etise [sal-ayo?]
              '*where do you live-{eyo}*'

3   Sang-u [kulayse-] kulayse pw-ass-na po-nta
             'so I think I've seen you before-{ta}'

4   na-n wungcin hawusu-lako
             'I, it's called wungcin house-{e}'

5   Daniel na-to wungcin hawusu-ey sa-nuntey
             'I also live in wungcin house-{e}'

6   Sang-u a::: [in loud amazement]
             'ah'

7   Daniel a:::
             'ah'

[…]

14   Sang-u a kulay
             'oh yes-{e}'

15   pon ke kath-a
             'I think I've seen you-{e}'

16   wuli cip-ey iss-ess-kwuna
             'you were staying at our house-{e}'

17   Daniel [hits hands together] a mac-ta::
             'oh, that's right-{ta}'

18   han pen thosuthu hay mek-ko ama elkwul po-n ke kath-ayo
             'once when I made toast I think I saw your face-{eyo}'

[…]

27   Sang-u il-chung-i-lase sikkulewu-n ke eps-eyo?
             'because you're on the first floor, isn't it noisy-{eyo}'

In the above extract, Daniel applies the -*eyo contaymal* style ending in declarative statements (line 17) and also questions (line 2) addressed directly at Sang-u, but leaves other sentence-final endings such as -*nuntey* (an ending signaling incompleteness, or that the speaker has more to say on the topic, line 5) as bare *panmal* forms. In addition, he utters exclamations regarding newly perceived information in the -*ta panmal* style (line 17). Under the circumstances, this pattern of switching can be considered native-like. This observation is confirmed by the same patterns of *contaymal* (line 27) and *panmal* (lines 1, 3, 14 and 15) in the speech of Sang-u.

Despite Daniel's proficient control of *panmal* and his expressed desire to speak like a "real Korean", this aim was at times tempered by the difficulties he found integrating with Korean native speakers and the treatment he received from them. Although he experienced "little hardship or difficulty" in terms of linguistic proficiency when interacting with Koreans, he reported a failure to "connect" with

Korean acquaintances, the company of whom he described as "boring." Instead, he preferred to socialize with "German guys and American guys" and spent more time out of class speaking German and English rather than Korean.

More specific to the use of honorifics, Daniel reported experiencing "culture problems" in adapting to a social structure in which there was no "equal basis." Although he accepted the obligation to use *contaymal* towards his superiors, he did not see the need for his subordinates to use *contaymal* towards him. Indeed, he would "always tell them to use *panmal*" regardless of their age: "as long as I know them, that's ok." Brown (2011, p. 192) found this practice of quickly asking younger intimates to downgrade to *panmal* was a common pattern in non-native speaker Korean, particularly in the case of *kyopho*. In the words of one heritage learner, "I'm not going to sit there and say you have to respect me by the rules of your society that I'm not actually really – I think that's kind of stupid." Elsewhere in the study, Brown (2011, p. 242) claimed that heritage learners, despite their Korean cultural backgrounds, may actually experience more acute conflict between their identities of Westerners and the normative use of Korean honorifics. The reason for this is the social pressure placed on these heritage learners to "be Korean" and unquestionably adopt native-like patterns of language use, while non-heritage learners are generally permitted more freedom to stray from native-speaker norms.

The lack of leeway allowed to heritage learners in their use of honorifics was underlined in the case of Daniel by his reports of the overzealous way that native Koreans would correct his use of these forms. At times, he felt that native speakers would make an "issue" out his use of honorifics that would not occur if he was not a *"kyopho"* ('overseas Korean'). In the following extract from the interview files, Daniel recounts a time when his intentional flouting of honorific conventions (he jokingly uses *panmal* to an acquaintance of marginally older age) coupled with an isolated pragmatic slip-of-the-tongue (he slips into *contaymal* when addressing someone of younger age) result in him being cast in the role of someone "not familiar" with the norms of honorifics use.

(19)   Interview Data: Daniel
I was with a friend who was younger than me and this hyeng *['older brother'; acquaintance of marginally higher age] who was actually three years older than me. I was kind of joking with the* hyeng *that I didn't believe he was older than me so I was speaking* panmal *to him. Then, when I was speaking to the younger friend in* panmal, *accidentally I slipped into* contaymal. *The* hyeng *said to me jokingly "why do you speak* panmal *to me and* contaymal *to him?" But then, he was like "no, no, no, I totally understand that you are not familiar with these issues." I felt that if I had been Korean it wouldn't have been an issue, but he treated me differently because I was not.*

This incident is interesting in the way that it positions Daniel in the role of non-Korean and in the way that a lack of knowledge regarding the use of *panmal* and *contaymal* is central to this process. Despite the close ideological connections between Korean ethnicity and Korean language, we see that *kyopho* learners may be cast in the role of foreigner if their honorific use appears to fall short of local norms. Furthermore, the incident shows that even heritage learners with advanced competence in honorifics may find that any intentional deviation from native speaker norms is judged as pragmatic failure rather than as humor. As such, this incident is reminiscent of the remark made by Thomas (1983, p. 96) that language learners "are rarely permitted the luxury of a flout" (see also Shardakova this volume).

7. Discussion and conclusion

Discussions in the current paper have shown that possessing strong underlying pragmatic competence and a general desire to speak Korean like a Korean may not be sufficient for learners on study abroad to use honorifics according to "native-like" patterns. On one side of the coin, it was shown that native-like patterns of interaction might not be available to these learners in the subject positions they are able to negotiate as exchange students and foreigners – outsiders who are just passing through. On the other side of the coin, it was shown that these learners were not always willing to adopt native-like patterns of use when these clashed with their identities as Westerners and the more egalitarian use of language that this entailed.

The data show that learners were engaged in a struggle to establish the extent to which categories of honorifics usage applied to them as foreigners. For the non-heritage learners, their lack of an inherited Korean identity resulted in an active belief on the part of some Korean interlocutors that *contaymal* was not needed in interactions with them. Interestingly, the data examined here suggest that this may be influenced by an interesting gender dynamic, whereby these learners are positioned as "cute younger brothers" by female interlocutors. Alternatively, other interlocutors did not drop into *panmal* according to native-like patterns when interacting with these language learners. Although this belief that the *contaymal/panmal* distinction did not apply to foreigners did not extend to the case of heritage learners, overseas Koreans such as Daniel also found themselves placed in the subject position of novice and struggling against a preconception that they would not understand the fineries of honorifics use.

The resolution of this struggle was ultimately found to be dependent on individual factors relevant to the learner in question. For some learners such as Richard, the foreigner identity was seen as an advantage of sorts. Although being treated differently was a frustration, Richard was also happy to exploit the less strict way that honorifics applied to him as a non-Korean. He saw it as allowing him to use *panmal* in a more liberal way than native Koreans and to establish intimate relationships outside of the normal bounds of native Korean relationships. This finding that an outsider identity and being treated different to the native norm may sometimes be viewed as an advantage is worth underlining, given the general preconception in previous literature that these factors are necessarily negative (cf. Norton 2000, p. 8 and the claim that speakers who are not viewed as potential members of the community may not be deemed "worthy to speak").

For other learners, the suggestion that native categories of honorifics use did not apply to them resulted in a determination to disprove such preconceptions. This was particularly the case with Patrick, who was determined to show that, despite being a non-native speaker, he could use the language correctly and appropriately according to native speaker norms. The data suggest that, ultimately, his ability to do this allowed him to negotiate Korean modes of interaction and gain the appropriate degrees of respect and intimacy in the way that his Korean acquaintances addressed him. As a note of caution, however, Patrick was perhaps only able do this through establishing relationships outside of the university setting, where he was no longer restricted by the identity of exchange student.

References

Block, D. (2007). *Second language identities*. London: Continuum.

Brown, L. (2010a). Politeness and second language learning: The case of Korean speech Styles. *Journal of Politeness Research, 6*, 243–270.

Brown, L. (2010b). Questions of appropriateness and authenticity in the representation of Korean honorifics in textbooks for second language learners. *Language, Culture and Curriculum, 23*, 35–50.

Brown, L. (2011). *Korean honorifics and politeness in second language learning* [*Pragmatics and Beyond* 206]. Amsterdam: John Benjamins.

Byon, A. (2007). Teaching the polite and deferential speech levels, using media materials: The advanced KFL classroom settings. In D. Yoshimi & H. Wang (Eds.), *Selected papers from pragmatics in Chinese, Japanese, and Korean classroom: The state of the art* (pp. 21–64). Honolulu, HI: NFLRC, University of Hawaii at Manoa. Retrieved from ⟨http://nflrc.hawaii .edu/CJKProceedings/⟩.

Byon, A. (2008). Korean as a foreign language in the USA: The instructional settings. *Language, Culture and Curriculum, 21*, 244–255.

Choo, M. (1999). Teaching language styles of Korean. *Korean Language in America, 3*, 77–95.

Churchill, E. (2009). Gender and language learning at home and abroad. *JALT Journal, 32*, 141–158.

Cook, H. (2008). *Socializing identities through speech style*. Clevedon, UK: Multilingual Matters.

Coulmas, F. (1999). The Far East. In J. Fisherman (Ed.), *Handbook of language and ethnic identity* (pp. 399–413). Oxford: Oxford University Press.

Ellis, R. (1997). *Second language acquisition*. Oxford: Oxford University Press.

Golato, A. 2003. Studying compliment responses: A comparison of DCTs and recordings of naturally occurring talk. *Applied Linguistics, 24*, 90–121.

Iino, M. (2006). Norms of interaction in a Japanese homestay setting: Toward a two-way flow of linguistic and cultural resources. In M. DuFon & E. Churchill, *Language learners in study abroad contexts* (pp. 151–176). Clevedon, UK: Multilingual Matters.

Isabelli-Garcia, C.L. (2006). Study abroad social networks, motivation, and attitudes: Implications for SLA. In M. DuFon & E. Churchill, *Language learners in study abroad contexts* (pp. 231–258). Clevedon, UK: Multilingual Matters.

Kim, S. (2009, May). Multicultural education in South Korea: Current state, focus and problems. Paper presented at the School of Oriental and African Studies, University of London.

Kinginger, C. (2009). American students abroad: Negotiation of difference? *Language Teaching, 43*, 1–12.

Kinginger, C., & Farrell, K. (2005). Gender and emotional investment in language learning during study abroad. (CALPER Working Paper Series, No. 2.) The Pennsylvania State University: Center for Advanced Language Proficiency Education and Research.

Kramsch, C. 1993. *Context and culture in language teaching*. Oxford: Oxford University Press.

Lave, J., & Wenger, E.. (1991). *Situated learning: Legitimate peripheral participation*. Cambridge: Cambridge University Press.

Lee, H. (1991). *Tense, aspect and modality: A discourse pragmatic analysis of verbal affixes in Korean from a typological perspective*. Unpublished doctoral dissertation, University of California, Los Angeles.

Lee, I., & Ramsey, S. R. (2000). *The Korean language*. Albany, NY: SUNY.

Lee, J. (2002). *Kwuke kyengepep-kwa sahoyenehak* [*Korean honorifics and sociolinguistics*]. Seoul: Welin.

Leung, C., Harris, R., & Rampton, B. (1997). The idealized native speaker, reified ethics and classroom realities. *TESOL Quarterly, 31*, 543–560.

Norton, B. (2000). *Identity and language learning*. London: Longman.

O'Grady, W., Lee, M., & Choo, M. (2001). The acquisition of relative clauses by heritage and non-heritage learners of Korean as a second language: A comparative study. *Hankwuke kyoyuk* [*Journal of Korean Language Education*] 12(2), 283–294.

Polanyi, L. (1995). Language learning and living abroad: Stories from the field. In B.F. Freed (Ed.), *Second language acquisition in a study abroad context* (pp. 271–291). Amsterdam: John Benjamins.

Siegal, M. (1994). *Looking East: Learning Japanese as a second language in Japan and the interaction of race, gender and social context*. Unpublished Ph.D. dissertation, University of California-Berkeley.

Spencer-Oatey, H. (2002). Managing rapport in talk: Using rapport sensitive incidents to explore the motivational concerns underlying the management of relations. *Journal of Pragmatics, 34*, 529–545.

Thomas, J. (1983). Cross-cultural pragmatic failure. *Applied Linguistics, 4*, 91–112.

Winter, B., & Grawunder, S. (2009, June). The physics of politeness: Approaching Korean politeness from a phonetic perspective. Paper presented at the meeting of the Association for Korean Studies in Europe, Leiden, The Netherlands.

Yoon, K. (2004). Not just words: Korean social modes and the use of honorifics. *Intercultural Pragmatics, 1*, 189–210.

Appendix

The following shows the instructions given to the participants for items 1–12 on the DCT. The Korean sentence translates as "have you seen that movie?" and is presented in *panmal*. For items 13–24, the formality of the situation was increased and the sentence content changed slightly to "have you seen that news?".

> You are having lunch with some students and professors (all native Korean speaker) from the Korean university at which you are studying. You are having a one-on-one chat with the person next to you, who is male. You are talking about a movie you have seen. You want to ask the person you are talking to if they have also seen this movie:
>
> **너는 그 영화를 봤어?**
>
> How would you say this sentence if you were talking to the different people listed in the tables below?

Within each set of twelve questions, three subsets were created to reflect three degrees of intimacy ("meeting the person for the first time", "you have met the person three times before but are not close" and "you are close with the person"). Each subset then contained four questions reflecting four degrees of age-rank, as shown in the following example:

Identity	Your answer
1 professor (age = 50)	_____은/는 그 영화를 _____?
2 *senpay* 2 years older	_____은/는 그 영화를 _____?
3 classmate same age	_____은/는 그 영화를 _____?
4 *hwupay* 2 years younger	_____은/는 그 영화를 _____?

A corpus-based study of vague language use by learners of Spanish in a study abroad context

Julieta Fernandez
Northern Arizona University

This chapter seeks to demonstrate some of the potential contributions of a corpus-based approach to study abroad research. Drawing on the Spanish Learner Language Oral Corpora, the present analysis examines a set of vague expressions known as general extenders (GEs) (Overstreet 1999) utilized by undergraduate English L1 learners after a year abroad. Specifically, the analysis focuses on patterns emergent from the concordancing analysis of learner language production alongside four exploratory case studies of learners' motives and dispositions towards their study abroad experience. The discussion draws parallels between the corpus-derived types, frequencies and pragmatic functions of GEs, and individual learner access to everyday language use in various study abroad situations.

1. Introduction

The proliferation of corpus linguistic studies in additional language learning contexts has inspired increasingly multidisciplinary research. The profession has witnessed growing interaction between corpus linguistics and areas that range from contrastive linguistics to second language acquisition. Within pragmatics, the use of corpora and corpus linguistic analysis has come to represent an ecologically valid alternative to reliance on native speaker intuition (e.g. Romero-Trillo 2008; Jucker, Schreier & Hundt 2009). Within study abroad research, however, while some researchers have called for the use of corpus linguistic analyses (e.g. Collentine 2004), "corpus-based descriptions of language use and assessment tools (McCarthy 2006), for example, have yet to be employed (…) in any serious way" (Kinginger 2009, p. 214).

Corpus linguistic applications offer numerous benefits. Corpus tools, such as *Antconc*, allow for the efficient examination of large databases and offer an increasingly automatized alternative to manual analysis. With the help of corpus linguistic software, large amounts of written and/or spoken data (together with accompanying multimedia) can be analyzed both quantitatively and qualitatively for various language features. Corpus tools can reveal patterns that would otherwise go unnoticed while also allowing for rich linguistic description of naturally-occurring and elicited language production. Often, concordancing software is employed to obtain frequency counts, and to identify co-occurrences of words and phrases. Corpus access software is also increasingly used to obtain various indices of lexical and syntactic complexity (e.g. Lu 2011). Going beyond a word's frequency, corpora can also be used to uncover more qualitative patterns of use by tracing words or phrases across the corpus. In sum, corpus linguistic methods afford the automatic quantitative and/or qualitative empirical examination of a collection of authentic texts compiled with a guiding principle, sampled, and thus representative of a target domain (Gray & Biber 2011, p. 140).

Analyses of spoken corpora have revealed that large portions of discourse consist of recurrent chunks of language, including vague multiword expressions, such as *(or) something like that* (McCarthy 2004). The term *vague language* refers to a range of language phenomena that very frequently occur in everyday speech, such as approximations (e.g. *about, sort of*) and vague words (e.g. *something, thingy*) or a variety of multiword expressions (e.g. *and stuff, and what not*). While vague expressions are very common, people rarely notice them and, in fact, studies of vagueness have found that, when noticed, they tend to be stigmatized as imprecise (Channell 1994; Overstreet 1999). Vagueness has also traditionally been attributed to a lack of familiarity with more complex forms of expression, or treated as a marker of inarticulateness and/or unfocused thinking (Thornbury & Slade 2006, p. 54). Vague language suffers from a similar reputation among speakers of peninsular Spanish (Cortés 2006b, p. 83). As a result, it continues to receive little empirical attention and tends to be ignored both in the language classroom and within language research.

As demonstrated in studies on vagueness (particularly corpus-based research on general extenders), however, vague expressions have essential discursive and pragmatic functions in interaction, carrying substantial pragmatic force. The choice to use vague language, the frequency with which it is used, and the vague forms preferred also index macrosociological factors such as age (Cheshire 2007; Murphy 2010), social class (Dines 1980; Stenström, Andersen & Hasund 2002; Dubois 1992), dialectal group (Youssef 1993) and level of education (Stenström et al. 2002). In the context of language learning in study abroad, all these factors play a crucial role in the acquisition of such pragmatically salient phenomena as vague expressions-an important motivating force behind choosing general extenders to illustrate corpus linguistic analysis in this chapter.

The study reported in this chapter seeks to extend our understanding of vague language use by means of a corpus-based exploration of the vague multiword expressions utilized by L2 Spanish learners after a sojourn abroad while performing a series of elicitation tasks. It draws upon a selected portion of the Spanish Learner Language Oral Corpora (SPLLOC) (University of Southampton, 2006–2010).[1] SPLLOC is a cross-sectional corpus collected through different tasks performed by British students learning L2 Spanish at three proficiency levels and L1 Spanish expert speakers (control group) over a period of two years (Mitchell, Dominguez, Arche, Myles & Marsden 2008). The focus of this study is on the type, frequency and functions of a particular type of vague multiword expressions, labeled *general extenders* (henceforth, GEs) (Overstreet 1999), utilized by a group of learners in SPLLOC who have spent a year-long sojourn abroad.

In this chapter, I make a case for the use of corpus linguistic affordances in study abroad research by presenting quantitative results to illustrate the frequency of use of GEs and a more detailed analysis of the language production of 40 study abroad learners. The patterns of vague language use emergent from the data are discussed in the context of their significance for Spanish sociopragmatics and the contributions of corpus linguistic analysis to the study of language production.

2. General extenders in Spanish and in study abroad

GEs are routinized chunks of language frequently utilized for shared pragmatic functions in interactions among language users with different levels of shared sociocultural experience. GEs in Spanish often result from the combination of a conjunction and either a (1) (vague) noun phrase (such as *cosas* 'things'), (2) a pronoun (such as *eso* 'that') or an adverb (phrase) (such as *tal* 'such'). A conjunction does not always lexically surface in collocation with a GE in actual language use, in which case they are referred to as "reduced" GEs (Aijmer 2002, p. 212). Based on their initial conjunction, GEs are generally of two types – adjunctive and disjunctive. When they are adjunctive, Spanish GEs can be either affirmative or negative (Cortés 2006b, p. 89–92). Affirmative GEs add elements to those already expressed and can be headed by adjunctive coordinator *y* 'and,' such as *y eso* 'and

---

1. Publicly available for online use and download at http://www.splloc.soton.ac.uk/

that,' or they can be "reduced", such as *todas esas cosas* 'all those things.' Negative GEs, on the other hand, cancel any other further possibilities (other than the ones already listed). These GEs generally start with the conjunction *ni* 'neither/nor.' Disjunctive GEs are preceded by the conjunction *o* 'or' or are reduced, such as *algo así* 'something like that.' They are often used to imply that the speaker is unsure about the antecedent (Cortés 2006b).

GEs are highly recurrent in naturally-occurring Spanish discourse (e.g. Alvarado 2006). They are also fairly recurrent in elicited data. The types and raw frequencies of Spanish GEs in elicited data are illustrated in Appendix 1. These figures are based on the SPLLOC (i.e. SPLLOC 1 & 2, both learners and expert speakers). Expert speakers in SPLLOC showed a preference for three adjunctive GEs – *y eso* 'and that,' *y nada* 'and nothing,' and *y tal* 'and stuff/so on.' Learners, on the other hand, showed a preference for *(y) todo (eso)* 'and all and *(o) algo (así)* '(or) something (like that).' Interestingly, in these data there are several adjunctive GEs only found in the language production of learners in the SPLLOC. With the exception of two (*y cosas como eso* 'and things (feminine/ plural) like that (masculine/singular)' and *y otros cosas* 'and other (plural/ masculine) things (feminine/plural)),' the other GEs are grammatical, perhaps less idiomatic, chunks with functions similar to the rest of the adjunctive GEs found in SPLLOC.

The use of GEs by speakers of Spanish remains an under-researched area (Gille & Haggkvist 2006, p. 67). In one of the few studies profiling the *interactional functions* of GEs in Spanish spoken discourse, Cortés (2006a) categorizes them based on (1) the type and closeness of the relationship that the speaker wants to establish with the interlocutor(s) and (2) the speaker's attitude towards the truth of her utterance (epistemic stance) (e.g. doubt, certainty), which, as Cortés notes, has indirect repercussions on the first function (p. 110). In the first case, the use of a GE foregrounds the relationship with the interlocutor(s) over the topic of the conversation, showing closeness or complicity with them or facilitating their engagement and response by allowing them to choose among many alternatives. For epistemic uses, Cortés lists the following three major functions. GEs can reinforce information when used to show how categorical the truth of a statement is, especially when this has not become evident in the previous elements in the enumeration. GEs can also be utilized with a hedging function when the speaker has doubts about the truth of her statements and wants to qualify them, for example, through the use of *o algo así* 'or something like that.' A third use of GEs is showing indifference or rejection when reinforcing a contemptuous, derogatory or indifferent attitude towards the previous elements in an enumeration. It is argued in this paper, however, that the discourse and pragmatic functions of GEs should be seen as a continuum with overlapping functions. Although researchers disagree with regard to whether their "core" function involves categorization or intersubjectivity (Overstreet 1999), GEs typically involve the construction or assumption of common ground among interlocutors.

In a rare study of vague language use by L2 Spanish speakers, Barkelius (2009) compared the use of GEs in the speech of L1 Chilean speakers of Spanish versus Swedish L1 speakers who had been living in Chile for a relatively long period of time and had advanced proficiency in L2 Spanish. The corpus resulted from the transcription of 145 minutes of interviews conducted by four different speakers with 7 non-expert speakers (3 males, 4 females, ages ranging 25–64) and 7 expert speakers (3 males, 4 females, ages raging 22–71). Barkelius contrasted these two groups in terms of the types of GEs utilized, the frequency of use and the contexts in which they were used during semi-structured interviews. He hypothesized that because the participants had been living in Chile, where they had had ample access to input in Spanish and had been in close contact with expert speakers, the types of GEs they would use would not differ greatly from those used by expert speakers. The results of this study suggest that, in spite of wide individual differences, both groups used GEs with similar frequency. In terms of types, non-expert speakers used more types of GEs. While non-expert speakers used a modest number of disjunctive GEs (a total of 4), expert speakers did not use any at all. The most recurrent GE in Barkelius' data was (*y*) *todo eso* '(and) all that,' with a total of 12 uses out of a total of 35 GEs. In terms of their functions, Barkelius assigns GEs the function of mitigating "what has previously been said, placing it under a broader category, which indicates that the formulation was somewhat deficient" (p. 5, my translation).

While it has been found that language learners use more GEs after a period abroad (Overstreet & Yule 1999, p. 4; Grieve 2011, p. 254), how study abroad students come to use vague language is an area still in need of further exploration. Grieve (2011) examined how German students on a 5 to 10 month sojourn in Australia used interpersonal markers in semi-structured informal interviews and in retelling stories based on selected clips from the movie *Mr. Bean*. In this study, Grieve considered general extenders such as *and stuff, or something* and *and what not* as a subcategory (i.e. "approximation") of interpersonal markers. Interpreting her results, Grieve argued that while the students acquired many interpersonal markers associated with adolescent language, their use did not align with expert speaker performance, even after 10 month-long exchanges. With respect to the acquisition of GEs in particular,

Grieve found that at 5 months, students used many more GEs than they did at 0 months, moving from less frequent forms in oral speech (such as *and so on*), to GEs with *stuff* and *thing*, which have been found to be the most frequent ones among expert speakers of Australian English. Students on a 10-month exchange used more GEs than the students on a 5-month exchange. Grieve attributed these differences to the fact that those staying for a shorter period of time showed less personal investment and social integration into the Australian imagined adolescent community (p. 229). Interview data with the participants revealed that different levels of integration were often tied to the types of relations they were able to establish with their respective host families. Grieve found that lower interpersonal marker use was linked to lower levels of integration (especially investment in the relationship with the host family of the 5-month cohort).

The present study extends this line of research by investigating the use of vague expressions by Spanish language learners who have spent a year studying abroad as evidenced in a learner corpus collected via different elicitation tasks. Specifically, the corpus-based exploration describes the types, frequency and functions of the GEs utilized by individual learners. A general account of the learners in the entire SPLLOC and all the tasks that they performed follows. For the individual learner data analysis, only the subset of the data from Year 4 learners (i.e. undergraduate students with one year of study abroad) was utilized.

3. Research design

3.1 The Spanish Learner Language Oral Corpora (SPLLOC 1 & 2)

The Spanish Learner Language Oral Corpora (SPLLOC) consist of cross-sectional data collected through different tasks performed by L2 Spanish learners at three proficiency levels (Mitchell et al. 2008) (see Table 1). A smaller, control group of L1 Spanish expert speakers (of similar age) was also recorded performing the same tasks. The data were collected for two years at schools and colleges in three locations in the United Kingdom. The main difference between SPLLOC 1 (collected April 2006–March 2008) and SPLLOC 2 (collected August 2008–January 2010) is their research foci, which directly influenced the type and structure of tasks used to collect the data (described under "Tasks" below). All tasks in SPLLOC involved one (or two) Spanish L2 learner(s) and an expert speaker of Spanish. All interactions were audio-recorded, transcribed and originally rendered into the Computerized Language Analysis (CHAT) transcription system developed by the Child Language Data Exchange System (CHILDES) project (MacWhinney 2000). For the purposes of this study, however, both sub-corpora (i.e. SPLLOC1 and SPLLOC2) were downloaded and converted into text files (from their original CHA format). The data were rearranged into four subcorpora by (1) language learner group (Year 9, 13 and 4), (2) expert speaker, (3) task and (4) individual speaker.

Table 1. Learners in each SPLLOC cohort[2]

Corpus	L2 Spanish level	Typical age	Approx. hours of Spanish instruction	Educational level (English system)
SPLLOC 1	Beginners N = 20	13–14	c 180 hours	Lower secondary school (Year 9)
	Intermediate N = 20	17–18	c 750 hours	Sixth form college (Year 13)
	Advanced N = 20	21–22	c 895 hours + year abroad	University (Year 4)
SPLLOC 2	Low intermediate N = 20	14–15	c 240 hours	Lower secondary school (Year 10)
	Intermediate N = 20	17–18	c 750 hours	Sixth form college (Year 13)
	Advanced N = 20	21–22	c 895 hours + year abroad	University (Year 4)

For the data analysis, the freeware concordance program *AntConc* 3.2.1 was employed. To obtain the raw frequency of token use when it was necessary to normalize the data, a Python script was run to "clean up" the data (eliminating, for example, researcher annotations). Concordances were produced for each of the Spanish GEs identified by Cortés (2008) and Barkelius (2009) in the subcorpus selected for this study. The selected data were also queried for key words, such as *cosa* 'thing' or *algo* 'something' to identify potential GEs not listed by these authors. Finally, given the relatively small size of the corpus, a bottom-up approach was utilized to locate further possible GEs utilized by learners not reported in previous studies.

All expressions identified were manually checked and disambiguated resorting to the interactional context and/or the available recordings when necessary in order to verify whether they extended an otherwise complete utterance via unspecified reference (Overstreet 2005, p. 1847). Those which were not utilized

---

2. Note. From http://www.splloc.soton.ac.uk/splloc1/index.html

with this function were excluded from the analysis. Finally, since the corpus is of dialogic nature (with two, sometimes three speakers in one interaction) care was also taken to attribute the GE to the right speaker. All GEs utilized by the interviewers were excluded from the analysis.

3.2 The participants

The SPLLOC 1 and SPLLOC 2 each consist of the transcription of the oral production of learners at three proficiency levels (n = 120). The learners' L1 is English. They acquired Spanish in different educational contexts within the UK. No proficiency measures are reported for either of the groups. Although the corpus is not controlled for gender or age, the individual transcriptions for each task are coded for gender (for example, S70||female |Undergraduate||) and a "typical age" for each proficiency level is provided (for example, the age of Year 4 learners ranges from 21 to 22 years). According to the corpus compilers, both corpora exclude data from learners who had either a bilingual English /Spanish background or who reported having contacted Spanish speakers on multiple occasions. However, advanced learners (Year 4) had had one year of study abroad, which was a requirement for all learners pursuing a university degree in the UK (Coleman 1996). Learners in the SPLLOC sojourned in different Spanish-speaking countries, mostly Spain. Learners who were studying more than one additional language distributed their year abroad in more than one country (such as Austria, Brazil, or France).

Language learners in the UK often embark on study abroad with extensive previous travel experience (under different circumstances) within the European Union and elsewhere (Coleman 1998). The learners in SPLLOC are not an exception, having often visited many countries before the study abroad experience. As part of the interview tasks, the learners reflected on their year abroad, often relating their evaluation of their experiences to issues of local attitudes towards Erasmus students, gender roles in the workplace, interracial and intercultural (in) tolerance, and language divides and attitudes.

Given that the language learning experiences of the solely at-home groups (i.e. beginners and intermediate) and those who also had a study abroad experience (i.e. advanced) are qualitatively different, my purpose is not to make comparisons of linguistic features across all the groups of learners represented in the SPLLOC. I focus on individual variations in the use of GEs among Year 4 learners (n = 40), who have had approximately 895 hours of Spanish instruction and have spent a year abroad. As it becomes evident in Year 4 learners' own narratives, they also had qualitatively different experiences while sojourning abroad and a broad range of individual differences is displayed in their use of vagueness. The approach taken in this study provides a corpus-based description of learner language use. While I cannot and do not intend to establish causality, parallels are made, where appropriate, between each learner's experiences and his/her patterns of vague language use. The issues addressed in the discussion are whether certain linguistic patterns obtained via corpus linguistic tools can be explicated by the analysis of individual learner history and what role corpus linguistic approach may play in such research.

3.3   The tasks

Year 4 learners in SPLLOC 1 and SPLLOC 2 performed a series of different tasks (very briefly summarized in Appendix 2 and 3).[3] Learners in the SPLLOC 1 performed five different types of tasks, originally designed to elicit the production of morphosyntactic properties of Spanish, such as word order and clitics. Year 4 learners in the SPLLOC 2 were also asked to perform a series of tasks orally, this time in order to show their ability to describe events in the past. They also performed an interpretation task to show their ability to discern the meaning of the Spanish imperfect and preterit past tenses. These tasks are briefly described in Appendix 3.

Although the tasks in SPLLOC were designed to collect data with these specific aims in mind, this learner corpus has also been used to study other aspects of L2 acquisition such as lexical diversity and formulaic sequence use in L2 Spanish classroom discourse (Marsden & David 2008). Marsden and David (2008), for example, used the SPLLOC and its French equivalent to compare the lexical diversity of Year 9 and 13 learners. They only used the Photos + Individual Interview task on the grounds that it has a "higher measure of lexical diversity" (p. 184) when compared to other tasks. Also, the language produced in this task allowed them to place the learners in different proficiency groups in terms of their lexical variation. The present study draws on the portion of the learner discourse generated by Year 4 learners in all of the tasks in SPLLOC 1 and 2 and discusses the possible effects of the level of interactivity of the tasks on the discursive and pragmatic functions of GEs.

---

3.   These were the tasks available for download at the time of writing this paper. For information about all the tasks learners performed (including more detailed information about those described here) and to access sample directions, pictures and answers, see http://www.splloc. soton.ac.uk/index.html. All learners in the corpus performed the tasks described. However, in this study I only report on Year 4 learners, who have had a study abroad experience in Spanish-speaking countries.

4.   Results

Table 2 shows the frequency of GE use by Year 4 learners of Spanish in the SPLLOC:

Table 2. Frequencies of GE use

	SPLLOC 1	SPLLOC 2	TOTAL
ADJUNCTIVE GEs	53	44	97
DISJUNCTIVE GEs	22	9	31
REDUCED GEs	22	11	33
TOTAL OF GEs	97	64	161

As can be seen, adjunctive GEs were more frequently used than any other type of GEs in the corpus, reflecting a tendency also observed in the use of GEs by expert speakers of Spanish in corpora of naturally occurring speech (Cortés 2006 a, p. 88). The most frequently used GE in the corpus, however, was *(o) algo (así)* '(or) something (like that)' with a combined total of 50 instances, closely followed by *(y) todo (eso)* '(and) all (that)' with a total of 48 instances – in combination accounting for almost two thirds of all the GEs used. Although I am not concerned with L1 transfer here, prior studies of GE use in British English found the English equivalents of these two GEs at the top of their frequency list. For example, in a corpus of London teenage vernacular, Stenström et al. (2002) found or *something (like that)* and *and all* to be the most frequent.

4.1   Frequency of GE use by task in SPLLOC 1 & SPLLOC 2

This portion of the analysis describes the types and frequency of GE by task with a view to drawing parallels between task and GE use. The first figure in this section shows that in the SPLLOC 1 adjunctive, disjunctive and reduced GEs were most frequently used in the Photos & Interview task (24 adjunctive, 13 disjunctive and 17 reduced GEs), followed by the Pair Discussion Task (20 adjunctive, 5 disjunctive, and 4 reduced GEs). No GEs at all were used in the Clitics Production task (understandably, given the purpose and nature of the task) and very few were used in the two other, narrative tasks (5 adjunctive GEs in the Loch Ness task, and 4 adjunctive, 5 disjunctive and 1 reduced GEs in the Modern Times task, respectively). Besides the higher interactivity, the Photos & Interview and Pair Discussion tasks generated more talk from the learners.

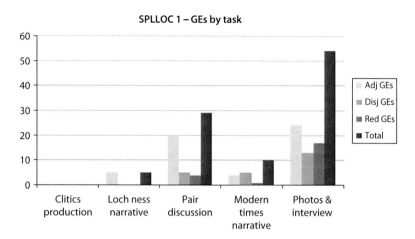

Figure 1. Raw frequency of General Extenders by Task in SPLLOC 1

In SPLLOC 2, no GEs were used in the Nati y Pancho narrative and simultaneous actions description tasks. A few GEs were used in the hermanas narrative task (6 adjunctive and 1 reduced) with the great majority being used in the interview guided task (37 adjunctive, 9 disjunctive and 11 reduced GEs).

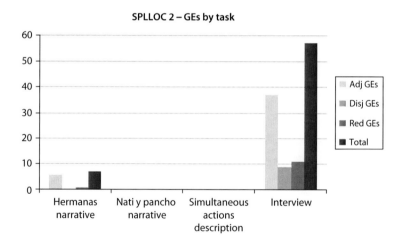

Figure 2. Raw frequency of General Extenders by Task in SPLLOC 2

In terms of frequency (that is, without considering the different types and functions), the normalization of GE use by total number of words produced in the task to 10,000 words reveals that in SPLLOC 1 and SPLLOC 2 GEs were largely more frequent in the Pair Discussion task and the Interview task, respectively, than in other tasks.

4.2   Functions of GE used in SPLLOC 1 & SPLLOC 2

In this section, the discursive and pragmatic functions of the most recurrent GEs in SPLLOC are described. Adjunctive GEs were often used as part of enumerations, especially in the tasks where learners were asked to describe pictures or to retell a story based on a cartoon (e.g. Loch Ness narrative task). In most cases the GE closed the series after (often two) elements had been listed. In (1), for example, the GE *y tal* "and so on" closes the series after the nouns *turistas* "tourists" and *periodistas* "journalists":

(1)

> 1 *L73:   *y mira la cara de ella que está muy choqueada @n de ver esta [///] esa cosa que parece como el [/]*
> and look at her face who is very shocked at seeing this [///] that thing that looks like the [/]
> 2 *L73:   *el monstruo del lago Ness.*
> the Loch Ness monster.
> 3 *L73:   *eh un poco después llega muchos <u>turistas</u> y <u>periodistas</u> y tal.*
> uh and a bit later many <u>tourists</u>, <u>journalists</u> **and so on** arrive (sing).
> 4 *L73:   *están sacando fotos y mirando esa cosa que parece como el monstruo del lago Ness y.*
> they are taking pictures and looking at that thing that looks like the Loch Ness monster and.

Overstreet and Yule (1999, p. 6) state that learners can strategically resort to a GE when they do not know or cannot remember a superordinate level word. In contrast, a few SPLLOC learners provided a general or superordinate expression or term, followed by one instance or example of that superordinate and a GE that engulfs the rest of the elements in that category. This is illustrated in (2). Following the general expression *haciendo deporte en el mar* 'doing sports in the sea,' the speaker continues the description with *nadando* 'swimming' and *y tal* 'and so on'):

(2)

> 1 *P73:   *ehm # están # +/.*
> uh # they are # +/.
> 2 *P73:   *no sé.*
> I don't know.
> 3 *P73:   *+, <u>haciendo deporte en el mar</u> eh <u>nadando</u> y tal.*
> +, <u>doing sports in the sea</u> uh <u>swimming</u> **and so on.**

Learners also occasionally resorted to a GE in enumerations when avoiding something unpleasant or when listing the other elements in a series would reflect negatively on them (Cortés 2006a, p. 114). In (3), for example, learner 85 avoids listing
all the gory details that make the television commercial she is describing "very
graphic," especially because her interlocutor, learner 77, is aware of the commercial she is referring to (line 3) and agrees with her that the commercial is *fuerte*
"disturbing" or "violent" (lines 5–7):

(3)

1 *D85:	*y también er ehm el um anuncio en la tele eh sobre la gente que*	
	and also er uhm the um commercial on tv uh about people who	
2	*bebe y después conduce +/.*	
	drink and drive +/.	
3*D77:	*sí.*	
	yes.	
4 *D85:	*es muy gráfica <u>la sangre</u> y todo eso y es bastante +…*	
	it is very graphic <u>the blood</u> **and all that** and it's pretty +…	
5 *D77:	*fuerte.*	
	disturbing.	
6 *D85:	*es muy fuerte sí.*	
	it is very disturbing yes.	
7 *D77:	*sí.*	
	yes.	

Learners used GEs when unsure of the appropriate or relevant expression. In (4),
learner 88 does not know the word *imbatibilidad* "invincibility" in Spanish (evidenced by her "I don't know how to say it" in line 3), and therefore first coins the
word invincibilidad (line 4) and then explains what she means by explaining "like
you can do anything *and that.*"

(4)

1 *D88:	*pero hay más peligros que [/] que eso porque como por ejemplo el*
	but there are more dangers than [/] than that because like for example
2	*alcohol ehm te da como un [/] un sentido de no sé cómo se dice*
	alcohol uhm gives you like a [/] a sense of I don't know how to say it
3	*invincibilidad@n como <u>se puede hacer cualquier cosa</u> y eso y.*
	invincibility @n like <u>you can do anything</u> **and that** and.
4 *D88:	*también cuando [/] cuando se bebe como pierde toda [///] todos sus no*
	also when [/] when you drink it's like you lose all [///] all your I don't
5	*sé pensamientos ⟨ya no⟩ [/] ya no puede pensar claramente y.*
	know thoughts ⟨you no longer⟩ [/] you can no longer think clearly and.

GEs were also used to show closeness with the interlocutor(s). This use has been
referred to as intersubjectivity or "being similar" and described as operating under

the "assumption of shared knowledge and similarity of experience" (Overstreet & Yule 1999, p. 5). The type of intersubjectivity built by the learners appears to mostly appeal to either the knowledge about what is involved in learning a second language (that both learners and interviewers seem to share) or issues directly related to British or Spanish lifestyles, customs and identity (again presumably shared with the interviewers). In (5) learner 90 appeals to her interlocutor with another *y tal* 'and so on' and what it means to be British (line 2):

(5)

   1 *P90:   *yo soy británica y.*
                i'm British and.
   2 *P90:   *me encanta <u>ser británica</u> **y tal**.*
                i love <u>being British</u> **and so on**.
   3 *P90:   *pero si alguien hubiera llegado a Inglaterra y.*
                but if someone had arrived in England and.
   4 *P90:   *yo no le llevaría a cualquier rincón pero.*
                i wouldn't take them to just any corner but.

Both adjunctive and disjunctive GEs were used when learners seemed unsure of the appropriate expression and wanted to paraphrase or search for a particular word. When unsure of a word, learners also used disjunctive GEs in questions to the interviewer to either clarify a point or offer her alternatives (to either obtain more information or corroborate their interpretation of a particular task). In (6) learner 90 is describing a clip (while performing the Modern Times Narrative) and she is unsure of how to describe Chaplin beating the policeman with his baton. She offers the word *palo* "stick" and then with rising intonation she uses *o algo así* "or something like that" (line 2) showing that she is unsure of the best word to describe it and attempting to get a better alternative from the interviewer, which she does in line 3:

(6)

   1*M90:   *Charlie le dio un [/] o sea un xxx con el +/.*
             Charlie gave him a [/] that is a xxx with the +/.
   2*M90:   *qué es un <u>palo</u> **o algo así** ?*
             what is it a <u>stick</u> **or something like that** ?
   3*MPS: *un golpe ?*
             a beating?
   4 *M90:   *+, un@g golpe@g gracias.*
             +, a beating @g thanks.
   5 *M90:   ⟨*le da*⟩ *[///] le dio un golpe con el [/] el palo*
             <gives him> [///] gave him a beating with the [/] with the stick

In the vague language literature, the use of disjunctive GEs to offer alternatives has been argued to be a common marker of politeness, utilized mainly when requesting something of the interlocutor(s) (that is, when showing a desire not to impose). The learners in the SPLLOC, however, seem to have mostly used disjunctive GEs to represent actual alternatives – mainly to obtain information about the tasks from their interviewers. Most instances of *o algo así* 'or something like that' were used during the interview tasks, when the learners had the opportunity to ask interviewers different questions about their pictures. In this task, learners asked questions about photographs leading to a conversation with the researcher. In (7), after the interviewer says that the people depicted are students (line 1), in the next turn learner 90 asks about whether they are college students *o algo así* 'or something like that,' which the interviewer corroborates (line 3):

(7)
    1 *MPS: *son un grupo de estudiantes.*
              they are a group of students.
    2 *P90: *de dónde <u>de una universidad</u> **o algo así** ?*
              from where from <u>a university</u> **or something like that?**
    3 *MPS: *sí creo que es de una universidad.*
              yes I think that it is from a university

In SPLLOC, GEs were also used with a hedging function when learners wanted to qualify the truth of their statements, such as when unsure of a historical fact related to one of the people depicted in a picture or when simply hypothesizing characteristics of the people or places on the picture. For example, in (8), it appears that the learner utilizes the GE *o algo* 'or something' because she cannot discern from the picture she has been given whether she should be referring to the mass of water as *un mar* 'a sea' or *un lago* 'a lake' (line 2). When she realizes that they are standing on the beach (line 3), she goes back and self-repairs (introduced by *bueno* 'well') by explaining that *es el mar* 'it is the sea' (line 4) and repeating that there is a beach:

(8)
    1 *P76: *aquí son [///] ehm hay muchos jóvenes con un barco ehm al lado del*
              here they are [///] uhm there are many teenagers in a ship uhm by the
    2   *[/] del mar un [/] un [/] <u>un lago</u> **o algo** y.*
              [/] the sea a [/] a [/] <u>a lake</u> **or something** and.
    3 *P76: *están en [/] en la playa.*
              they are at [/] at the beach.
    4 *P76: *bueno es el mar y una playa y.*
              well it is the sea and there is a beach and.

In sum, learners used GEs to list elements in an enumeration, to search for words, paraphrase or fill lexical gaps, to categorize, to avoid going into detail, to offer alternatives to interviewers in order to either seek information or confirm a candidate answer, to show closeness with their interlocutors (i.e. the interviewer and/or another learner), and to show uncertainty or hedge.

4.3   GE use by individual learners in SPLLOC 1 & SPLLOC 2

In consonance with previous studies of language development during a residence abroad, the analysis of GE use by individual learner uncovers wide individual variations, in terms of both total numbers of GEs used, the types GEs preferred and their pragmatic and discourse functions. While reading these results, it is important to bear in mind that these are raw numbers – when comparing the frequency of GE use by learner not all of them produced the same amount of language in response to the same tasks.

As illustrated in Table 3, the use of adjunctive GEs among Year 4 learners in SPLLOC 1 is evenly distributed among individual learners – only two learners did not use any adjunctive GEs at all. However, while most learners used between 1–9 GEs, learner 90 (henceforth, "Ana") stands out as she used a total of 26. In the SPLLOC2 (Table 4), the picture is slightly different, with the use of GEs less distributed among the learners:

4.4   Focal learners

In line with poststructuralist theories of language learning with a focus on the identity of the learners and their different access to and opportunities for language learning (Kinginger 2004; Kinginger & Blattner 2008), it is assumed that SPLLOC learners had different types and levels of engagement and language learning experiences. Learners' narratives of their own experience while studying in Spain were thus briefly explored in an effort to illuminate "why some students prevail whereas others display only modest gains in documented language ability" (Kinginger 2009, p. 31).

Four focal individual learners were chosen based on their (lack of) use of GEs (as evidenced in the corpus) in order to illustrate the nature and quality of the wide variety of experiences from SPLLOC learners abroad. Though exploratory, these case studies are included to argue for the "significance of understanding not only what students do while abroad but also how they interpret their experience and how this process as a whole influences engagement in language learning while abroad and desire for enhanced language competence in the future" (Kinginger 2008, p. 33). Relying on the information provided by the learners mostly during the interview tasks, I now provide a closer look at the study abroad experiences of four learners – one learner who used many GEs (SPLLOC 1 learner 90, "Ana"), one learner who used a few GEs (SPLLOC 1 learner 71, "María"), and two learners who did not use any GEs at all (SPLLOC 1 Learner 72, "Isabel"; SPLLOC 1 Learner 83, "José").[4]

---

4.   Pseudonyms were assigned to learners otherwise referred to by number in the corpus and the quantitative portion of the analysis.

Table 3. Year 4 GEs in the SPLLOC1

ADJ. GES	Year 4 Learners – SPLLOC1																			
	70	71	72	73	75	76	77	78	79	80	81	82	83	84	85	86	87	88	89	90
y cosas																			1	
y cosas así														1						2
y de todo																				1
y eso												1						1		2
(y) etcétera (etcétera)		1									1									
y muchas cosas				1																
y nada																				2
y nada más				1	1	2										1				
y otras cosas	1																			
y tal	1			3																9
y tales cosas																				1
y todo	1	4					1		1	1	1	1				2	1			
y todo eso					1									1	3			1		
TOTAL	3	5	0	5	2	2	1	0	1	1	2	2	0	2	3	3	1	2	1	17

(Continued)

Table 3. Year 4 GEs in the SPLLOC1 (Continued)

ADJ. GES	Year 4 Learners – SPLLOC1																			
	70	71	72	73	75	76	77	78	79	80	81	82	83	84	85	86	87	88	89	90
DISJ. GES																				
o algo		4			0	2										1			1	1
o algo así								2	1	2					1	1			1	4
u otras cosas									1											
TOTAL	0	4	0	0	0	2	0	2	2	2	0	0	0	0	1	2	0	0	2	5
RED. GES																				
algo así	1			4	1		1	2		1	2				1					2
cosas así									2					1						2
todo eso																		1		
un poco de todo											1									
TOTAL	1	0	0	4	1	0	1	2	2	1	3	0	0	1	1	0	0	1	0	4
TOTAL GE X PARTICIPANT	4	9	0	9	3	4	2	4	5	4	5	2	0	3	5	5	1	3	3	26

Table 4. Year 4 GEs in SPLLOC2

ADJ. GES	Year 4 Learners – SPLLOC1																			
	70	72	73	74	75	76	77	78	79	81	82	83	84	85	87	88	89	90	96	98
y cosas	1													1						
y cosas así			1								1									
y eso									1		1									
y muchas cosas			1											1						
y nada						3														
y otras cosas										1										
y tal	2					1														
y todas esas cosas											1									
y todo												1	2			11	8	1		
y todo eso																				5
TOTAL	3	0	2	0	0	4	0	0	1	1	3	1	2	2	0	11	8	1	0	5
DISJ. GES																				
o algo			2															2		
o algo así	1	1				1					1									1
o cosas como así																1				
TOTAL	1	1	2	0	0	1	0	0	0	0	1	0	0	0	0	1	0	2	0	1

(Continued)

Table 4. Year 4 GEs in SPLLOC2 (Continued)

ADJ. GES	Year 4 Learners – SPLLOC1																			
	70	72	73	74	75	76	77	78	79	81	82	83	84	85	87	88	89	90	96	98
RED. GES																				
algo así	2	2											2							
cosas así									1								1			
cosas como así				1																
de todo																			1	
por ahí														1						
todas esas cosas	1																			
TOTAL	3	2	0	1	0	0	0	0	1	0	0	0	2	1	0	0	1	0	1	0
TOTAL GE X PARTICIPANT	7	3	4	1	0	5	0	0	2	1	4	1	4	3	0	12	9	3	0	6

It is important to stress that this portion of the analysis is exploratory given that SPLLOC was collected with a different research purpose (see description of the corpus in the research design section) utilizing semi-structured interviews and not available with the same detail for all the participants. With a few variations, the interviewers asked the learners several specific questions about the place(s) where they spent the year abroad; whether they went abroad alone or with friends from their school in the UK; what occupations they had; the nationalities, occupations and time spent with roommates and/or (other) locals; what they liked best from the host country and their opinion about their overall study abroad experience.

4.5 Ana (Learner 90; SPLLOC 1)

Ana, who used GEs more frequently than all other learners in both corpora, spent time in Spain as well as in the north of Brazil,[5] which she had previously visited during a sabbatical year she took before starting her university studies. Ana appears to be an independent traveler – going abroad on her own and staying with host families. She explained how, during her time abroad, she had to make an effort to overcome her "laziness" and spend more time with expert speakers of either Portuguese or Spanish. She described this as strenuous due to her terrible command of her additional languages (and, as a counterpart, locals' often excellent command of English), but she also recounted spending much time with her friends going to night clubs or engaging in other activities. She retold how she first decided to travel to Pamplona, Spain, where she lived with a Spanish family while working as a nanny. In her narrative, it seems that Ana had developed a close bond with her family of stay (*ya casi tengo una familia allí* "I already almost have a family there"). She expressed a desire to go back, even if for only a year, to work on her Spanish. While she described herself as both British and English, loving her nationality, she fantasized about going back to Pamplona on her own and "almost having a Spanish life" (*casi tener una vida española*). When asked whether she would like to live there with her English friends, she explained that this would not allow her to improve her command of Spanish, which seems to represent one of her major goals.

With a total of 26 GEs, Ana was found to make the most frequent use of vague expressions in the corpus. While other learners rely on one or two GEs, and these tend to be different from the ones most frequently used by expert speakers, Ana

---

5. This experience could have potentially helped her use of Spanish GEs given the proximity between Portuguese and Spanish, and the fact that GEs are very frequent in Portuguese as well (Roth-Gordon 2007).

makes the most extensive use of those GEs preferred by the expert speakers in SPLLOC (such as *y tal* and *o algo así*) while performing the same tasks. She uses 6 different types of GEs (Table 3) spread out across 4 different tasks. She uses those GEs for a variety of discursive and pragmatic functions, such as providing a candidate answer (Example 6, Section 4.2), offering alternatives (Example 7, Section 4.2) or building intersubjectivity (Example 5, Section 4.2 and 9), insinuating or shortening (Example 9). In (9), Ana could have said more about what she needed to learn but did not consider it necessary:

(9)

> 1 *MPS: *y qué hiciste en estos cinco meses ?*
> and what did you do during these five months ?
> 2 *P90:   *pues la verdad es que no mucho.*
> well, honestly not much.
> 3 *P90:   *tenía [///] pues tuve que <u>aprender más portugués</u> y tal pero.*
> I had [///] well I had to <u>learn more Portuguese</u> **and so on** but
> 4 *P90:   ⟨*trabajé*⟩ *[///] trabajaba en una escuela de idiomas y.*
> ⟨I worked⟩ [///] I worked in a language school and.

Together with her ample use of GEs, she displays expert-like use of many other pragmatic markers, such as *pues* 'cos/well' (line 2). She does, still, struggle with some of the grammar, such as past tenses (lines 3 and 4). Anna notes that her ample experience telling stories as a nanny helped her perform better in the narrative tasks, and this is also evident when she retells her activities during her year abroad.

4.6   María (Learner 71; SPLLOC 1)

María both studied at the Complutense University of Madrid and worked at the soccer Club Atlético Madrid while living in Spain for a year. María continued to use English on a regular basis, since her work at Club Atlético involved designing the English version of their website and working in the communication and image department managing their public relations with the international press (e.g. from Britain, the US and Japan). However, this position also allowed her to travel around the country to watch different soccer matches, sometimes with friends and often with her Spanish co-workers. She seemed attuned to language variation as she commented that the many interactions she had with different speakers during these trips helped her understand different, sometimes strong accents. From this experience working for Club Atlético she has a lasting fascination with the way of living and working in Spain – according to her, Spaniards are more relaxed and more flexible while maintaining the same level of productivity.

During her stay, María also did some English tutoring on the side. She tutored a privileged group of women, namely the wives of rich executives from the soccer club who, according to her, did nothing but stay at home, chat with their friends, and wait until it was time to pick up their kids from school and welcome their husbands back home at night. In this job she came to resent gender roles in Spain, although she admits that she was exposed to a very peculiar population.

María lived with several students from the university, some Spanish speakers (i.e. Mexico, Salvador), some Americans, and some Europeans (i.e. French and Italian). While spending time with them, she was shocked to experience racial discrimination towards her roommates and friends (especially Latinos and Africans), being delayed by security guards at stores or not being allowed into night clubs. Although she had no personal problems and seemed to get along with locals, she expresses her disappointment at experiencing this type of behavior in a multicultural city such as Madrid, which constantly sees a great influx of tourists from Europe and all over the world.

In contrast with Ana, María only used one type of adjunctive (i.e. *y todo* 'and all/everything') and one type of disjunctive (i.e. *o algo* 'or something') GE in the context of two tasks, the Photos + Interview task and Modern Times narrative. It should be noted, however, that there were no data available for her Pair-Discussion Task, which also reduces her overall language production. All 8 of the GEs she uses extend a noun, as in (10),

(10)

    1 *P71:   *es la oportunidad a ehm ir a otros partes del país para que*
               it's the opportunity to uhm go to other parts of the country in order to
    2   *ver familia extendida y ehm.*
               see the extended family and uhm
    3 %err: *lejo = lejos*
               %err: fa = far
    4 *P71:   *sí ⟨es un⟩ [/] es un festival donde la familia y amigos para*
               yes ⟨it's a⟩ [/] it's a festival where the family and friends to
    5.   *mí son más importantes que <u>regalos</u> **y todo** y +...*
               to me they are more important than <u>presents</u> **and all** and + ...
    6 *P71:   *no sé.*
               I don't know.

She uses those GEs for two major functions: (1) listing elements in an enumeration and (2) showing approximation, uncertainty, or hedging (3 of the 4 disjunctive GEs co-occurring with *supongo* 'I guess', *no sé* 'I don't know', *puede ser que* '(it) could be that', respectively).

4.7 Isabel (Learner 72; SPLLOC 1)

Isabel spent ten months in Barcelona, although during her stay she traveled around Spain (for example, Madrid and Malaga) visiting with friends she made while in Spain. Her favorite pastime during those trips was visiting museums and art galleries. Although these activities might not seem to require a lot of social interaction, Isabel stressed the fact that she particularly enjoyed taking these trips because they gave her the opportunity to use Spanish. In Barcelona, on the other hand, this was often not the case even though she lived with locals. To her frustration, her two roommates from Barcelona spoke Catalan with each other most of the time and even watched television in Catalan. They only used Spanish when talking to her. Isabel singled out the "very strong feelings" that people in Barcelona have against the rest of Spain (expressed in their reluctance to use Spanish) as the worst part of her stay. She complained that this atmosphere interfered with her learning of Spanish. Outside of the home, Isabel spent most of her time with four English girls she had met in Spain. Though she expressed that she might like to go back to Spain in the future, she would not go back to Barcelona – instead she lists Madrid (which is "a beautiful city with nice people") and Mallorca and Menorca (because she'd like to live by the sea) as possible destinations. Isabel did not use any GEs while performing the SPLLOC tasks.

4.8 José (Learner 83; SPLLOC 1)

José is another student who did not use any GEs in SPLLOC. He spent his year abroad in *Aguas Calientes*, Mexico. During the first two-weeks of his stay, he stayed with one of his teachers but was unsatisfied with this living arrangement. Instead, he decided to move to an apartment that he shared with two French students. However, he explained that he did not enjoy spending time with them either because they did not like to drink as much as he did. He then turned to his friends from his university, with whom he would go out often. He also liked to play soccer frequently (although he does not elaborate on whether he played with locals or other study abroad students). José mentions that while several students from his home university went abroad, only he and one other male student lived in this area of Mexico. While he spent some of his time with this other student because "he lived nearby", José displays a certain detachment that indicates they were not very close. In his responses about his study abroad experience, José displays fairly limited vocabulary and grammar (e.g. mixing up gender and past tense), keeping his answers brief. Although he does use other frequent pragmatic markers such as *bueno* 'well' and *pues* 'cos/well', he does not use GEs. Throughout the interview task, there is much negotiation with the interlocutor, showing that José was having some trouble understanding the interviewer's questions and formulating his answers.

In these four cases, we see that the learners who sought out and were given access to routine everyday language use in a variety of circumstances did indeed begin to employ GEs in an appropriate way. As a case in point, Ana, the learner who used GEs most frequently and for different functions in the SPLLOC, worked in a somewhat informal context (as a nanny) and had had frequent informal interactions with peers her own age. In contrast with other learners, such as Isabel or José, who did not bond with their respective roommates, Ana was able to forge a close relationship with her host family and develop a sense of belonging. It would seem reasonable that Ana would be more exposed to the use of GEs since they have been found to be most recurrent in intimate, informal interactions among people who know each other well (Overstreet 1999).

5. Limitations of the study

Winter and Norrby (2000) argue that their participants used GEs to construct distance between the (adolescent) interviewee and (the slightly older) interviewer, showing a tension between positive and negative politeness, mainly due to different levels of shared meanings between the interlocutors. In the SPLLOC, this does not seem to always be the case. One of the potential limitations of this study is that while some learners seemed to construe the interview as an informal interaction, others did not automatically do so (or did not at all). These differences in interpretation, for example, become evident through the use of informal and formal address terms (i.e. *tú* and *usted*) with the interviewer, especially in the first portion of the Photos + Individual interview task, where learners had to ask the interviewers direct information questions about a set of pictures. Some students used *tú* (i.e. informal 'you') to address the interviewers, as illustrated in this portion of Ana's response: *no sé qué ejemplo te puedo dar* 'I don't know which example I can give you' (informal). Other learners, on the other hand, opted for the formal "usted" (*P81: *ah y um ah de # eh **sabe usted** ⟨de dónde es⟩ [///] de dónde son la gente que hacen ciclismo?* 'uh and um of # uh do you (formal) know ⟨where they are from⟩ [///] where are the people who are cycling from?'), or decided to negotiate the choice with the interviewer:

(11)
    *P78:   *ehm y ya hago preguntas ?*
                uhm and (I) ask questions ?
    *MJA: mmhm.
                mmhm.

*P78:	*vale eh bueno ehm # ⟨somos tú o usted⟩ [//] la forma tú o usted cuando hago preguntas ?*
	okay uh well uhm # ⟨are we you (informal) or you (formal)⟩ [//] the form you (informal) or you (formal) when I ask questions?
*MJA:	*ah para mí ?*
	uh with me?
*P78:	*sí.*
	yes
*MJA:	*tú está bien.*
	you (informal) is okay.
*P78:	*tú vale.*
	you (informal) okay
*MJA:	*sí [/] sí.*
	yes [/] yes.
%com:	Subject Laughing.
*P78:	*no estaba segura ⟨eh⟩ [<].*
	(i) wasn't sure ⟨uh⟩ [<].

It would appear that those learners who construed the interview as a more informal interaction used GEs for more varied functions (especially involving intersubjectivity, which was more frequent in this task given its nature). This study is therefore limited by the nature of the language use emerging in response to the SPLLOC tasks – while adequate for the purposes of this chapter (i.e. showing some of the potential contributions of corpus linguistics to the description of learner performance in a study abroad context), a richer picture of learners' use of GEs would necessarily involve the analysis of language use in different discourse genres and with different interlocutors.

While Year 4 learners are grouped at the advanced language proficiency level (as determined by hours of instruction), no other proficiency measures were made available. As discussed in the focal learners section, analysis of language use by different learners in SPLLOC reveals various levels of overall linguistic ability. Together with other variables that have been identified as having an impact on language development in study abroad (for example, learner motivation and cultural sensitivity), learners' acquisition of GEs and subsequent use in SPLLOC could undoubtedly be related to their overall language ability.

In addition, because the SPLLOC is cross-sectional, this study provides only a snapshot of the vague language use of a group of learners at a given moment. To capture the dynamics offered by accompanying data (e.g. participants' histories, motivations and choices of communicative activities out of class), it would be vital to look at learners' language use over time. A longitudinal approach to compiling learner language would provide a more complete picture of learners' language choices, an insight acknowledged in the corpus linguistic literature. However, as Granger (2012, p. 11) notes, while longitudinal corpora allow tracking language use over time, the logistical difficulties involved in its compilation mean such corpora are scarce. Finally, while corpus linguistics methodology is instrumental in describing language performance (particularly, by yielding rich descriptions of what learners *can do*; Barker 2010, p. 635), in the future its uses could be extended to units of a larger scale, e.g. the tracking of themes in learners' narratives and reflections about their study abroad experience.

6. Conclusion

This chapter has demonstrated the potential contribution of a corpus-based approach in blending the patterns emergent from study abroad participants' documented language performance (in the form of frequency and types of GEs) with an exploration of their motives and dispositions towards their experience (based on their narratives). The analysis focused on the use of vague language by English L1 learners (Year 4) with exposure to Spanish L1 through a sojourn abroad, as evidenced in a cross-sectional learner corpus collected through nine different tasks. The results show that these learners resorted to a total of 161 GEs in a range of 6 tasks (with different frequencies) and for a variety of discursive and pragmatic functions. Individual learner analysis revealed wide individual differences in the frequency, types and functions of GEs. It was also found that GEs were more frequently used in the more "interactive" tasks, such as the interviews and pair discussions. Four exploratory case studies of learners with varying frequencies of GEs were then presented as resources for potential interpretation of the corpus-based results. While no claims about causality can be made, these brief case studies suggest that in-depth qualitative research of learners' study abroad experience might illuminate the findings of corpus-based investigation on vague language use by such learners.

Research on the impact of study abroad experiences on language learning has primarily focused on oral proficiency development and, in particular, gains in oral fluency, from a perspective of its surface properties such as lengths of speech runs (e.g. Segalowitz & Freed 2004) and cognitive factors that appear to impact individuals' fluency, such as speed of processing (e.g. Segalowitz, Freed, Collentine, Lafford, Lazar & Díaz-Campos 2004). One of the benefits of using corpus linguistics to describe learner language is that it allows for the rich description of oral language performance (as demonstrated in the corpus being used) based on the detailed tracking of pragmatically salient lexical features, such as the use of vague vocabulary, which are quintessential in unplanned or naturally-occurring spoken discourse (Cutting 2011). In addition, corpus linguistic software allows for the exploration of recurrent language features that emerge without prior researcher nomination and thus of pragmatic acts that might otherwise go unnoticed.

The study of vague language use in study abroad is particularly appealing given that language learners very rarely get exposed to it in the classroom. Not only neglected in textbooks, vague expressions are a type of language that instructors often advise learners to stay away from regardless of genre or mode of interaction. The language used in classroom activities is usually confined to that which is deemed appropriate and/or acceptable for language learners, or limited by its perceived pedagogical use (Kinginger & Blattner 2008, p. 224). Classroom language learning may thus constrain learners' linguistic choices for self-representation in the additional language. While studying abroad, on the other hand, learners often have access to much more linguistic variety, including forms that are not always considered appropriate for the language classroom. Given the higher consequentiality of the language choices a learner has to make when immersed in the L2 social setting, as compared to at-home, formal instruction contexts (including immersion programs), it would seem that study abroad is still a context conducive to the development of pragmatic awareness. This may be especially true of controversial functions such as the expression of vagueness. Indeed, Overstreet and Yule (1999, p. 4) observe that while English GEs are "extremely rare in the speech of instructed ESL learners" during classroom interactions, they are "noticeably present" in the discourse of teenagers who had been living in an English-speaking environment and "had developed spoken English skills, but with relatively little formal ESL classroom instruction".

Reflecting a larger paradigm shift in second language studies, recent study abroad research has tried to provide a richer description of learners' experiences while abroad in an effort to provide clues as to why language gains are not evenly distributed among study abroad participants (Kinginger 2009, p. 31). This has been achieved by taking into account "students' dynamic motivations, perceptions, and choices of activity as well as the diverse ways in which they are received within host communities" (Kinginger 2008, p. 3). The interpretation of patterns of use resulting from corpus-based analysis of (large quantities of) learner language can be productively complemented and enriched by the exploration of emic data illuminating the types of activities learners were involved in while abroad, how they construed their own experiences, and the opportunities they actually had to speak or listen to speakers of host community. A combination of the two sources of data would undoubtedly allow for a more sophisticated and richly textured analysis of language development in a study abroad context.

References

Aijmer, K. (2002). *English discourse particles. Evidence from a corpus*. Amsterdam: John Benjamins.

Alvarado Ortega, M.B. (2006). ¿Son las fórmulas rutinarias enunciados independientes? [Are conversational routines independent utterances?] In T.L. Face & A. Klee (Eds.), *Selected proceedings of the* 8th *Hispanic linguistics symposium* (pp. 214–220). Somerville, MA: Cascadilla Proceedings Project.

Barkelius, J. (2009). *El uso de apéndices conversacionales en hablantes nativos y no nativos de español chileno* [The use of conversational appendices in native and non-native speakers of Chilean Spanish]. Unpublished Masters Thesis, Stockholm University.

Barker, F. (2010). How can corpora be used in language testing? In A. O'Keeffe & M. McCarthy (Eds.), *The Routledge handbook of corpus linguistics* (pp. 633–645). New York, NY: Routledge.

Channell, J. (1994). *Vague language*. Oxford: Oxford University Press.

Cheshire, J. (2007). Discourse variation, grammaticalization and stuff like that. *Journal of Sociolinguistics, 11*, 155–193.

Coleman, J.A. (1996). *Studying languages: A survey of British and European students. The proficiency, background, attitudes and motivations of students of foreign languages in the United Kingdom and Europe*. London: Centre for Information on Language Teaching and Research.

Coleman, J.A. (1998). Language learning and study abroad: The European perspective. *Frontiers: The Interdisciplinary Journal of Study Abroad, 4*, 167–2003.

Collentine, J. (2004). The effects of learning contexts on morpho-syntactic and lexical development. *Studies in Second Language Acquisition, 26*, 227–48.

Cortés, L. (2006a). Los elementos de final de serie enumerativa del tipo *y todo eso, o cosas así, y tal*, etc. Perspectiva interactiva [Closing markers in enumerative listing sequences of the type *and all that, or things like that, and so on*, etc. Interactional perspective]. *Boletín de Lingüística* XVIII/ 26.

Cortés, L. (2006b). Los elementos de final de serie enumerativa del tipo y todo eso, o cosas así, y tal, etcétera en el discurso oral en español: Perspectiva textual [Closing markers in enumerative listing sequences of the type *and all that, or things like that, and so on*, etcetera in Spanish spoken discourse: Textual perspective]. *BISAL, 1*, 82–106.

Cortés, L. (2008). *La serie enumerativa en el discurso oral español* [*Enumerative listing sequences in Spanish spoken discourse*]. Madrid: Arco Libros.

Cutting, J. (2011). Chapter 10. Spoken discourse. In K. Hyland & B. Paltridge (Eds.), *The Continuum companion to discourse analysis* (pp. 155–170) London: Continuum.

Dines, E.R. (1980). Variation in discourse and stuff like that. *Language in Society, 9*, 13–33.

Dubois, S. (1992). Extension particles etc. *Language Variation and Change, 4*, 179–204.

Gille, J., & Häggkvist, C. (2006). Los niveles del diálogo y los apéndices conversacionales [The levels of dialogue and conversational appendices]. In J. Falk, J. Gille & F. Wachtmeister Bermudez (Eds.), *Discurso, interacción e identidad* [Discourse, interaction, and identity] (pp. 65–80). Stockholm: Stockholm University.

Granger, S. (2012). How to use foreign and second language learner corpora. In A. Mackey & S. M. Gass (Eds.), *Research methods in second language acquisition. A practical guide* (pp. 7–29). London: Basil Blackwell.

Gray, B., & Biber, D. (2011). Corpus approaches to the study of discourse. In K. Hyland & B. Paltridge (Eds.), *The Continuum companion to discourse analysis* (pp. 138–152). London: Continuum.

Grieve, A. (2011). *Adolescent identity and pragmatic marker acquisition in a study abroad context*. Unpublished doctoral dissertation, The University of Melbourne.

Jucker, A., Schreier, D., & Hundt, M. (Eds.). (2009). *Corpora: Pragmatics and discourse*. Amsterdam: Rodopi.

Kinginger, C. (2004). Alice doesn't live here anymore: Foreign language learning and identity reconstruction. In A. Pavlenko & A. Blackledge (Eds.), *Negotiation of identities in multilingual contexts* (pp. 219–242). Clevedon, UK: Multilingual Matters.

Kinginger, C. (2008). Language learning in study abroad: Case studies of Americans in France. *Modern Language Journal, 92*, Monograph.

Kinginger, C. (2009). *Language learning and study abroad: A critical reading of research*. Houndsmills, Basingstoke, UK: Palgrave/Macmillan.

Kinginger, C., & Blattner, G. (2008). Histories of engagement and sociolinguistic awareness in study abroad: Colloquial French. In L. Ortega & H. Byrnes (Eds.), *The longitudinal study of advanced L2 capacities* (pp. 223–246). Mahwah, NJ: Lawrence Erlbaum Associates.

Lu, X. (2011). A corpus-based evaluation of syntactic complexity measures as indices of college-level ESL writers' language development. *TESOL Quarterly, 45*, 36–62.

Marsden, E., & David, A. (2008). Vocabulary use during conversation: a cross-sectional study of development from year 9 to year 13 among learners of Spanish and French. *Language Learning Journal, 36*, 181–198.

MacWhinney, B. (2000). *The CHILDES project: Tools for analyzing talk*. 3rd Edition. Mahwah, NJ: Lawrence Erlbaum Associates.

McCarthy, M. (2004). Lessons from the analysis of chunks. *The Language Teacher, 28* (7), 9–12.

McCarthy, M. (2006). *Explorations in corpus linguistics*. New York, NY: Cambridge University Press.

Mitchell, R., Dominguez, L., Arche, M.J., Myles, F., & Marsden, E. (2008). SPLLOC: A new database for Spanish second language acquisition research. *EUROSLA Yearbook, 8*, 287–304.

Murphy, B. (2010). *Corpus and sociolinguistics. Investigating age and gender in female talk*. Amsterdam: John Benjamins.

Overstreet, M. (1999). *Whales, candlelight and stuff like that. General extenders in English discourse*. Oxford: Oxford University Press.

Overstreet, M. (2005). And stuff und so: Investigating pragmatic expressions in English and German. *Journal of Pragmatics, 37*, 1845–1864.

Overstreet, M., & Yule, G. (1999). Fostering pragmatic awareness. *Applied Language Learning, 10*, 1–13.

Romero-Trillo, J. (2008). Introduction. Pragmatics and corpus linguistics – A mutualistic entente. In J. Romero-Trillo (Ed.), *Pragmatics and corpus linguistics. A mutualistic entente* (pp. 1–10). Berlin: Mouton de Gruyter.

Roth-Gordon, J. (2007). Youth, slang, and pragmatic expressions: Examples from Brazilian Portuguese. *Journal of Sociolinguistics, 11*, 322–345.

Segalowitz, N., & Freed, B.F. (2004). Context, contact, and cognition in oral fluency acquisition: Learning Spanish in at home and study abroad contexts. *Studies in Second Language Acquisition, 26*, 173–199.

Segalowitz, N., Freed, B., Collentine, J., Lafford, B., Lazar, N., & Díaz-Campos, M. (2004). A comparison of Spanish second language acquisition in two different contexts: Study abroad and the domestic classroom. *Frontiers: The Interdisciplinary Journal of Study Abroad, 10*, 1–18.

University of Southampton (2006–2010). SPLLOC, Spanish Learner Language Oral Corpora. Retrieved from ⟨http://www.splloc.soton.ac.uk/index.html⟩.

Stenström, A.B., Andersen, G., & Hasund, I.K. (2002). *Trends in teenage talk: Corpus compilation, analysis and findings*. Amsterdam: John Benjamins.

Thornbury, S., & Slade, D. (2006). *Conversation: From description to pedagogy*. Cambridge: Cambridge University Press.

Winter, J., & Norrby, C. (2000). Set marking tags – "and stuff". In J. Henderson (Ed.), *Proceedings of the 1999 Conference of the Australian Linguistics Society* (pp. 1–8).

Youssef, V. (1993). Marking solidarity across the Trinidad speech community: The use of *an ting* in medical counseling to break down power differentials. *Discourse and Society, 4*, 291–306.

Appendix 1

GEs in SPLLOC

ADJUNCTIVE GES	TRANSLATION	LEARNERS (N = 120)		EXPERT USERS (N = 30)		TOTAL
		SPLLOC 1	SPLLOC 2	SPLLOC 1	SPLLOC 2	
y algo	and something	1	0	0	0	1
y cosas	and things	1	2	0	0	3
y cosas así	and things like that	3	5	0	0	8
y cosas como eso	and things (pl) like that (sing)	1	0	0	0	1
y cosas de ésas	and things of that sort/ like that	0	0	1	0	1
y de todo	and of/about everything	1	0	0	0	1
y esas cosas	and those things	0	0	4	3	7
y eso	and that	5	2	27	8	42
y estas cosas	and these things	0	0	1	0	1
(y) etcétera (etcétera)	(and) etcetera (etcetera)	6	5	0	2	13
y en fin	and that's that	0	1	0	0	1
y las cosas	and the things	0	0	1	0	1
y muchas cosas	and many things	1	2	0	0	3
y nada	and nothing	2	3	7	33	45
y nada más	and nothing else	5	0	0	0	5
y no sé qué	and i don't know what	0	0	0	1	1
y otras cosas	and other things	2	1	0	0	3
y otros cosas	and other (masc) things (fem)	1	0	0	0	1

(Continued)

Appendix 1 (Continued)

ADJUNCTIVE GES	TRANSLATION	LEARNERS (N = 120)		EXPERT USERS (N = 30)		TOTAL
		SPLLOC 1	SPLLOC 2	SPLLOC 1	SPLLOC 2	
y poco más	and (a) bit more	0	0	1	0	1
y tal	and so on/ and stuff	13	3	19	27	62
y tales cosas	and such things	1	0	0	0	1
y todas esas/ estas cosas	and all these/those things	0	1	0	0	1
y todas las cosas	and all the things	0	0	1	1	2
y todo	and all	14	22	15	9	60
y todo eso	and all that	11	6	10	6	33
TOTAL ADJ. GES		68	53	87	90	298
DISJUNCTIVE GES						
o algo	or something	11	5	6	3	25
o algo así	or something like that	12	4	10	4	30
o cosas así	or things like that	0	0	1	1	2
o cosas como así	or things like that	0	1	0	0	1
o cualquier cosa	or whatever	0	0	1	0	1
o qué	or what	0	0	2	0	2
o por ahí	or around that/or something	0	0	1	0	1
o una cosa así	or a thing like that	0	0	1	0	1
u otras cosas	or other things	1	0	0	0	1
TOTAL DISJ. GES		24	10	22	8	64
REDUCED GES						
algo así	something like that	16	6	2	2	26
cosas como así	things like that	0	1	0	0	1
cosas así	things like that	6	3	0	1	10
de todo	everything	1	1	2	0	4
muchas cosas	many things	0	0	0	1	1
por ahí	around that/ something	0	1	2	0	3
todas esas cosas	all those things	0	1	0	0	1
todo eso	all that	2	0	1	0	3
un poco de todo	a bit of everything	1	0	2	0	3
TOTAL RED. GES		26	13	9	4	52
TOTAL GES		118	76	118	102	414

Appendix 2

Summary of tasks performed by learners in SPLLOC 1

	SPLLOC 1
TASKS	**BRIEF DESCRIPTION**
Clitic production	Learners were presented with a sequence of two pictures on the screen and asked questions about the activities depicted.
Loch Ness narrative	The investigator presented the "Monster of Loch Ness" cartoon story to the learners, which they followed as the investigator narrated the scripted Spanish version (adapted for beginner and intermediate learners). Learners were then asked to re-tell the story using the same cartoon.
Modern Times narrative	Learners were asked to watch a short excerpt from Charlie Chaplin's "Modern Times". Then, the investigator provided a list of words and a number of stills from the movie, which the learners used as prompts to retell the story in their own words.
Pair discussion	Two learners were offered 4 cards with arguments about various "current topics" and asked to choose one or more arguments. Through discussion, the learners had to rank the arguments in order of importance.
Photos + Individual Interview	Learners were asked to describe pictures of people vacationing overseas or doing leisure activities. They then asked the investigator information questions about the people depicted in the pictures. Finally, the investigator asked the learners questions involving their past present and future activities, interests, and plans.

Appendix 3

Summary of tasks performed by learners in SPLLOC 2

	SPLLOC 2
TASKS	**BRIEF DESCRIPTION**
Guided interview	First, learners picked 4 pictures of famous world figures (such as Adolf Hitler or John Lennon) and told the investigator what they knew about these particular people. Then, the learners were asked to fill in a personal timeline of major events in their lives and to narrate them. The investigator then asked follow-up questions.
Las Hermanas Narrative	Learners were given illustrations, instructed to take a few minutes to look at the story and then retell it to one of the investigators using the keywords and expressions also provided. The story involves two sisters taking a trip from Madrid to Barcelona and their reminiscing of different people or experiences from their childhood until an unexpected event occurs.
Nati y Pancho Narrative	Learners were given a booklet with pictures of a girl named Nati and her cat Pancho, together with a list of vocabulary (mostly verbs). After a few minutes to prepare their story, learners retold it to one of the investigators.
Simultaneous Actions Description	Learners were asked to describe two activities that had taken place at the same time the day before. The learners were given 12 pictures of two cousins (6 pairs of simultaneous actions) doing different activities together with a set of verbs. Then they were asked to retell the simultaneous actions in each pair of pictures.

Afterword

Celeste Kinginger
Pennsylvania State University

As noted in the introductory chapter, the overarching aim of this volume was to showcase the diversity of contemporary, socially-oriented research on language learning in study abroad, both in terms of theoretical frameworks and in terms of the populations and languages involved. The case studies in Part Two do in fact offer in-depth and varied consideration of a range of learning contexts, helping to illuminate sources of individual differences and thereby addressing a perennial concern of language educators. The studies in Part Three address pragmatic competence, or what Benson, Barkhuizen, Bodycott and Brown (2012) have recently labeled *identity related proficiency*. These chapters demonstrate that identity does in fact have much to do with the development of pragmatic abilities, both in terms of the ways in which students are received and in terms of the way they position themselves. In line with the larger research base, the chapters in this book indicate that study abroad can be a significant context for development not only of language proficiency *per se*, but also of related capacities, such as self-regulatory strategies, intercultural competence, and multilingual subjectivity (Kramsch 2009). However, study abroad is not a cure-all for linguistic incompetence. Some students perform demonstrably better than do others, and mastery of some aspects of second language use, such as the display of one's sense of humor (Shardakova, this volume), may require investment of time and effort beyond the customary range.

It follows that both teachers and researchers should be aware that language learning is a complex, human endeavor, involving unique people, "not just communicators and problem solvers, but whole persons with hearts, bodies, and minds, with memories, fantasies, loyalties, identities" (Kramsch 2006, p. 251). As Klapper and Rees (2012) have recently pointed out, this endeavor is rendered particularly unpredictable in study abroad contexts, where much depends on students' emotional response to the arbitrary hand they are dealt in terms of opportunities for engagement in communicative settings and development of social networks.

Although the knowledge base has certainly grown and become more inclusive since Freed's (1995) volume, Coleman's argument, in Chapter 2, is well taken: the field still has a long way to go in portraying the experiences of "whole persons." Certain aspects of learner identity, such as religion, sexuality, or social class, may exert significant influence on the qualities of sojourns abroad, yet these topics are rigorously avoided, as if taboo. Religious identities only enter the research picture in the case of missionary work and language learning abroad (Hansen 2012). Coleman's findings about the extent to which adult sojourners abroad find new intimate partners lends credence to his argument that "if seen less as an indexical characteristic and more as a language learning strategy, sex perhaps deserves more attention in study abroad research." Block (2012) has recently put forth the view that social class may be *the* key variable influencing language learning, yet it is nowhere to be seen in applied linguistics research. Study abroad is clearly a class-inflected activity, involving class-related desires and aspirations (Kinginger 2004) and a population overwhelmingly of middle class origin. Study abroad is also a commodity marketed in response to these desires and aspirations, and should be critically examined in this light.

The people whose experiences are portrayed in this book are of diverse origin and interests, yet we are well aware that the scope of study abroad research requires further expansion not only in topical focus but also in term of the populations studied. This is true in and of itself, as a matter of social justice, but it is also true that interesting comparisons can emerge when examining the same phenomenon from multiple perspectives. To give just one example, Block (2007) devotes one chapter of his book on second language identities to study abroad and, at the time, found this literature dominated by stories of Americans who, when confronted with difference, recoiled into various discourses of national superiority. Among these were discourses related to gender equity which then generated complaints about sexual harassment on the part of local men throughout the world. A contrasting view appears in the work of Patron (2007) on the astonishment of female French students encountering "politically correct" gender relations in Australia. In brief, the absence of gallantry or flirtation, practices that could be construed by Americans as harassment, deeply wounded these students' sense of self. Clearly, study abroad research would be much enhanced and would yield truer insight if it became collaborative across contexts, involving the voices of students but also of their hosts.

We trust that the chapters in this volume will lend further substance to research-derived knowledge about language learning in study abroad. Perhaps they will also inspire innovation in future research. Above all, however, our hope is that this work will contribute to language educators' realistic awareness of the affordances and constraints involved in language learning abroad, and that it will also offer insights for the design of programs and for advocacy on behalf of all learners who sincerely desire and envision a multilingual future.

References

Benson, P., Barkhuizen, G. Bodycott, P., & Brown, J. (2012). Study abroad and the development of second language identities. *Applied Linguistics Review, 3*, 173–193.

Block, D. (2007). *Second language identities*. London: Continuum.

Block, D. (2012). Class and SLA: Making connections. *Language Teaching Research, 16*, 188–205.

Freed, B. (Ed.) (1995). *Second language acquisition in a study abroad context*. Amsterdam: John Benjamins.

Hansen, L. (2012). *Second language acquisition abroad: The LDS missionary experience*. Amsterdam: John Benjamins.

Kinginger, C. (2004). Alice doesn't live here anymore: Foreign language learning as identity (re) construction. In A. Pavlenko & A. Blackledge (Eds.), *Negotiation of identities in multilingual contexts* (pp. 219–242). Clevedon, UK: Multilingual Matters.

Klapper, J., & Rees, J. (2012). University residence abroad for foreign language students: Analysing the linguistic benefits. *The Language Learning Journal, 40*, 335 – 358.

Kramsch, C. (2006). From communicative competence to symbolic competence. *Modern Language Journal, 90*, 249–252.

Kramsch, C. (2009). *The multilingual subject*. Oxford: Oxford University Press.

Patron, M.-C. (2007). *Culture and identity in study abroad contexts: After Australia, French without France*. Bern: Peter Lang.

Name index

Subject index